THE
MEDAL
YEARBOOK

2024

Edited by
Philip Mussell & Carol Hartman
and
the Editorial Team of MEDAL NEWS

ISBN: 978-1-908828-66-8
Deluxe edition ISBN: 978-1-908828-67-5

A Token TITLE

Published by

TOKEN PUBLISHING LIMITED
8 Oaktree Place, Manaton Close,

Matford Business Park,

Exeter EX2 8WA

Telephone: 01404 46972
email: info@tokenpublishing.com   Website: www.tokenpublishing.com

Front cover illustration: The new portrait of His Majesty the King by Jack McDermott

Printed in Great Britain by Short Run Press, Exeter

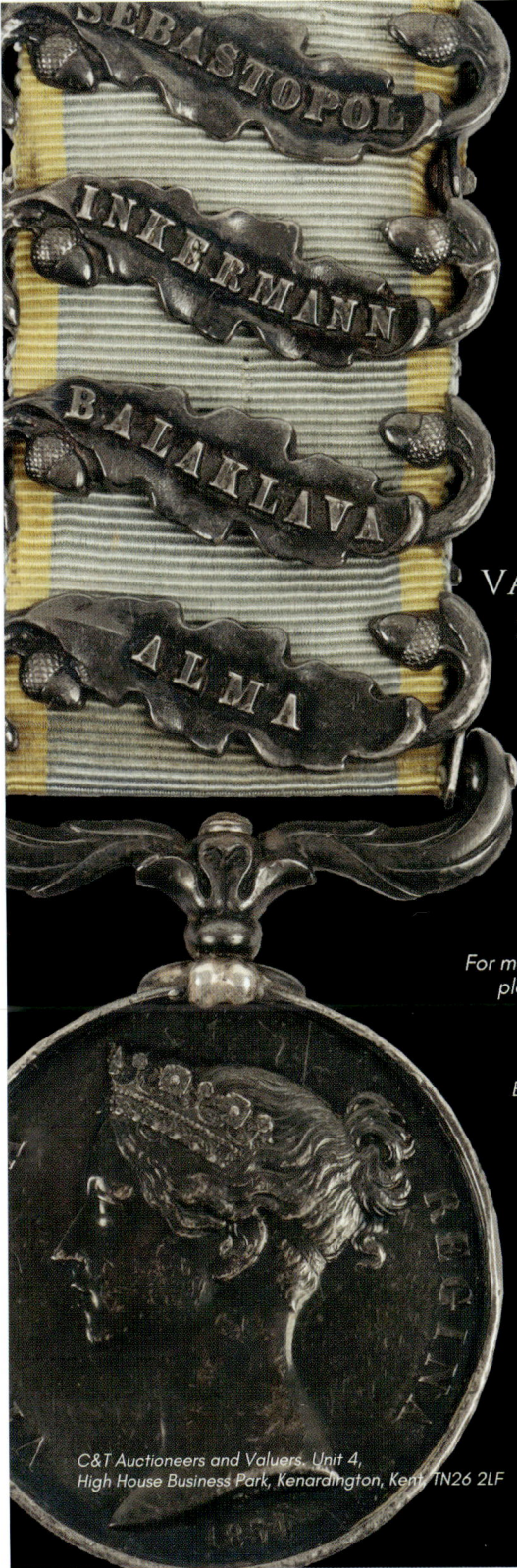

CONTENTS

Index to advertisers

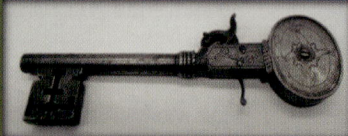

FOREWORD

THIS year's MEDAL YEARBOOK, the 30th we have published here at Token Publishing Ltd, is a little different. First and foremost it is the first since the passing of Token's Group Managing Editor John Mussell, the man behind the decision to start publishing a YEARBOOK in the first place. His death, at 81, following a short illness, was well documented in MEDAL NEWS magazine and little needs be said here apart from a nod to the fact that without John this book simply would not exist.

Secondly, you may have noticed, depending on which version you're holding, that the emphasis has changed a little. The softback now concentrates exclusively on official British Medals, whilst the deluxe hardback holds everything—that includes the index, absent from the standard version but available separately online at www.tokenpublishing.com. The reasons for this change are twofold—first is, inevitably, cost. The price of paper, of postage, of everything has skyrocketed and it was a straightforward choice: we keep the book as it is and charge even more for it or we make changes. The second is that in the past few years many readers have expressed their desire for a basic price guide and handbook for British Medals without all the "add-ons" that they are neither interested in nor have in their collections. Now, of course to completely discard those medals, the unofficial ones that appear in groups these days (even if they shouldn't) the Life Saving awards, etc., would be unfair to those people who do want to know about them and so the decision has been made to include them but only in the deluxe edition—that way we make the book lighter and easier to use for some whilst still producing a full, comprehensive guide to medals for others! We hope you'll approve of us going "back to basics" but if you don't then please do let us know as only through feedback can we get it right. This is the decision for this year, but that doesn't mean it's set in stone. This time next year we may have changed our minds but for now we think this is the way forward.

Lastly, there have, of course, been a number of medallic changes this year because of the accession to the throne of His Majesty King Charles III; in addition to the inevitable new portrait(s) there have been a number of brand-new medals not to mention name changes for many others. Where new medals have been introduced they will have their own entry, however, where a name has changed (Queen's Police Medal to King's Police Medal for example) the entry will remain as was with an acknowledgment of any changes. At this stage we don't have any values for the new raft of medals as of course, some, like the Humanitarian Service Medal, have yet to be issued and others, like the Nuclear Test Medal or King's Volunteer Reserves Medal, will still be in the hands of the recipients who are unlikely to part with them just yet. We anticipate that the Coronation Medal of the new King is likely to be the first that appears on the open market but they haven't done so to date. We'll be keeping an eye on the auctions and dealers' lists and will introduce values when a reasonable number have appeared for sale—the first ones to be offered always attract a premium and a true representation of value will only come in time.

In addition to the new medals (Coronation Medal, Nuclear Test Medal and Humanitarian Service Medal) the big news this year has to be the new obverses, of which there are actually six (seven if you include the Martin Jennings designed conjoined busts on the Coronation Medal). Admittedly the left-facing bust in uniform (Admiral of the Fleet, Field Marshal, Marshal of the Royal Air Force) only appears on the Long Service & Good Conduct Medals of the respective service and the right-facing crowned bust with coronation robes only features on the oval medals, the Volunteer Reserves Service Medal and Efficiency Medal, but they are still official obverses and, alongside the right-facing crowned effigy that appears on 32 medals and the uncrowned portrait that appears on a further 12, they represent the largest obverse issue we have seen to date. Every one of the new portraits, apart from that on the aforementioned Coronation Medal, has been designed by Jack McDermott (his middle name is Stanley and JSM appears on the designs) and the level of detail that has gone into the uniformed busts in particular is quite astonishing, they are reminiscent of the best obverses of George V and before. Where possible we have made a note of which bust is being used for which medal but as new medals are issued this will not be exhaustive. One thing we did discover, both on His Majesty's coins and his medals, is that he did not opt for the Latin version of his name as his grandfather, great grandfather and great-great grandfather had done. Charles stayed Charles and did not become Carolvs as some had suspected he might. There had also been comment that he didn't "change direction" on his medals like he did on the coins. On our new coinage he is facing left, the opposite way to his mother, and when the Coronation Medal was released, there was speculation that he was to face left on his medals too but, with the exception of the LS&GC medals, he is most decidedly facing right, the same as Queen Elizabeth II did. In fact there is no hard and fast rule with medals, and even in coinage it is only tradition not a rule as such. If you look at the effigies of Victoria, Edward (with one exception) and both King Georges they all face left, it was actually Her Majesty Queen Elizabeth II that broke with that tradition. King Charles is simply following his mother. The reason for the left-facing bust on the LS&GCs is, apparently, to be able to better show the details of the uniform and medals being worn, something it does well.

Of course, whilst we may not have values for the King's medals yet the medal market itself continues to grow and prices are, in the main, holding steady, with some increasing quite considerably. As ever we are indebted to everyone who has helped us check the pricing in particular Richard Black, Charles Brooks, Chris Dixon, Colin Hole, Michael Kaplan, John Millensted, Michael O'Brien, Charles Riley, Allan Stanistreet, John Wilson, and, of course, many members of the online British Medal Forum. We are also especially indebted to Phil McDermott and his team at Worcestershire Medal Services for their invaluable help with the new issue of medals following the King Charles' accession.

Happy reading!

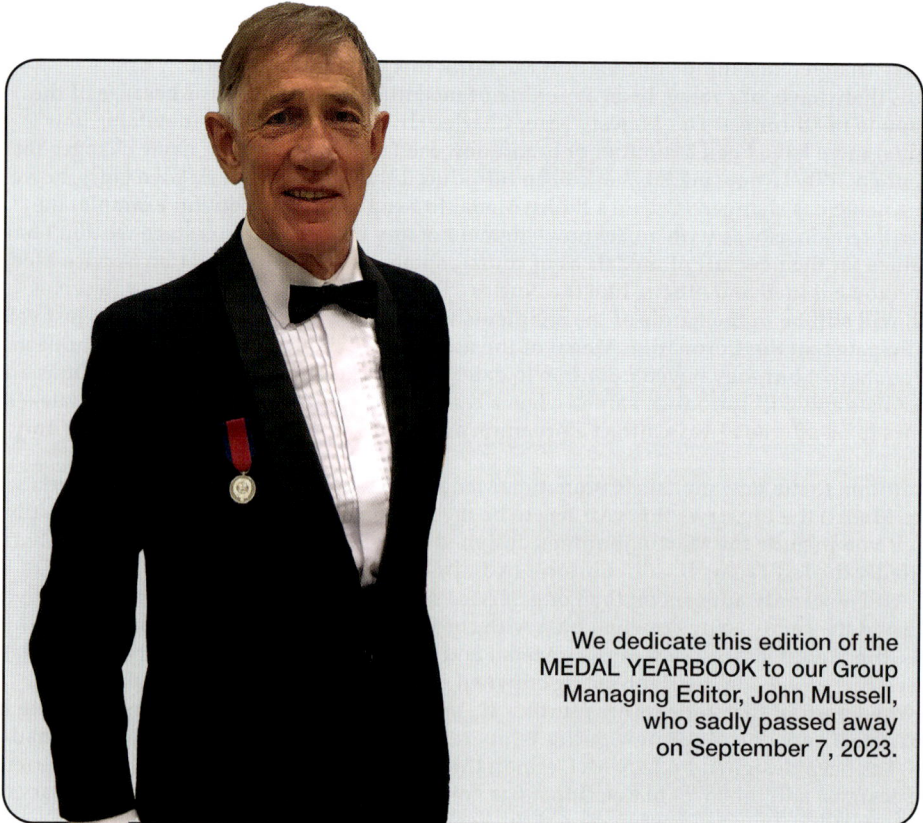

We dedicate this edition of the MEDAL YEARBOOK to our Group Managing Editor, John Mussell, who sadly passed away on September 7, 2023.

With the passing of Queen Elizabeth II and the accession of King Charles III on September 8, 2022 there was, as one might expect, much that needed changing. Everything that bore the late Queen's image or cypher will, in time, be updated as necessary—every time a post box is replaced, for example, it will now bear CIIIR rather than EIIR. The coinage and notes will all change (the coins are being released now, the notes sometime next year) and any organisation that uses the Royal Cypher or name of the current monarch will need to update too—this was especially evident with British Army regiments, with some cap badges changing radically. In the medal world a number of medals have changed name (our cover star this year has gone from Queen's to King's Volunteer Reserves Medal for example) and there have been a raft of new obverses. Seven in total to date. The conjoined busts on the Coronation Medal were designed by Martin Jennings (the sculptor who designed the new coinage effigy of His Majesty) but the other six obverses, which will be used on medals as laid out below, have all been designed by Jack Stanley McDermott and the initials JSM appear below the busts. We were particularly taken by the level of detail on the LS&GC Medals with His Majesty facing left on these in order for his full regalia and medals to be on display.

Conjoined busts of King Charles III
and Queen Camilla.

*King Charles III
Coronation Medal (MYB 318D)*

Crowned with
Coronation robes.

*Volunteer Reserves Service
Medal (MYB 242A)
Efficiency Medals (MYB 237)*

In Admiral of the Fleet uniform.

*Royal Naval Long Service
& Good Conduct Medal
(MYB 218)*

In Field Marshal uniform.

*Army Long Service &
Good Conduct Medal
(MYB 229)*

In Air Chief Marshal uniform.

*Royal Air Force Long Service
& Good Conduct Medal
(MYB 268)*

Uncrowned head to be used on:

Associate Royal Red Cross (MYB 31)
Coastguard Long Service Medal (MYB 227)
Jersey Honorary Police Long Service Medal (MYB 281)
King's Merchant Navy Medal for Meritorious Service (MYB 242K)
Meritorious Service Medal (MYB 208–210)
Overseas Territories Special Constabulary Long Service Medal (MYB 275)
Polar Medal (MYB 322)
Royal Household Long & Faithful Service Medal (MYB 217)
Royal Red Cross (MYB 31)
Royal Victorian Medal (MYB 13)
Sea Gallantry Medal (MYB 67)
Special Constabulary Long Service Medal (MYB 272)

Crowned head (Tudor crown) to be used on:

Accumulated Campaign Service Medal (MYB 198B and 198C)
Ambulance Long Service Medal (MYB 264A)
Badge of Honour (MYB 328)
Cadet Forces Medal (MYB 262)
Civil Defence Long Service Medal (MYB 264)
Fire and Rescue Service Long Service & Good Conduct Medal (MYB 286)
General Service Medal 2008 (MYB 198D)
George Medal (MYB 45)
Humanitarian Medal (MYB 397)
Imperial Service Medal (MYB 29)
King's Gallantry Medal (MYB 63)
King's Ambulance Medal (MYB 48B)
King's Fire Service Medal (MYB 48)
King's Medal for Champion Shots in the Military (MYB 334)
King's Medal for Champion Shots in the Royal Air Force (MYB 336)
King's Medal for Champion Shots in the Royal Navy
    and Royal Marines (MYB 335)
King's Police Medal (MYB 46)
King's Volunteer Reserve Medal (MYB 48A)
National Crime Agency Long Service Medal (MYB 291CC)
Northern Ireland Home Service Medal (MYB 261B)
Northern Ireland Prison Service Medal (MYB 288A)
Nuclear Test Medal (MYB 396)
Operational Service Medal (MYB 198A)
Overseas Territories Fire Brigade Long Service Medal (MYB 287)
Overseas Territories Police Medal (MYB 61)
Overseas Territories Police Long Service Medal (MYB 274)
Overseas Territories Prison Service Medal (MYB 289)
Police Long Service & Good Conduct Medal (MYB 271)
Police Service of Northern Ireland Service Medal (MYB 273A)
Prison Services Long Service & Good Conduct Medal (MYB 288B)
Realms—Governor General's Medal of Honour (MYB 329A)
Royal Fleet Auxiliary Service Medal (MYB 264C)

(Pictures courtesy of www.gov.uk)

Guide To
PRICES PAID
When buying at auction

Buying at auction can be confusing to those not used to it—it isn't like buying from a dealer's list nor, crucially, like buying from an Internet auction. With a dealer the price you see is the price you pay (unless you can do some haggling that is) and with eBay and the like you bid up to the price you want and the price the auction ends at is how much the item will cost. "Real" auctions are a little different and you have to remember that when the hammer falls the final price might not be what you think.

Auctioneers make their money through buyers' premiums (and sellers' premiums' but that's another matter), i.e. a "fee" on top of the hammer price that goes directly to them, not the vendor. On top of that premium is VAT—which currently stands at 20% in the UK. VAT is only really relevant to those in the EU—buyers from outside are exempt although they may be liable for their own import duties and other taxes so it's always worth checking.

These "extras", often referred to by seasoned auction goers as the "bits", can add a significant sum to your purchase. For example, if you bid on an item up to £100 and that's where the hammer falls, it isn't £100 you pay—you will have to find that £100 plus the premium (this varies from auction house to auction house) plus VAT on that premium (not on the £100, just the premium)—that can add up to £24 to the original hammer price—not something to be ignored! It can all get rather confusing and can come as a shock to those new to the game or only used to buying at on-line auctions (it's worth noting that even if you bid on-line at a "real" auction you are still liable for the "bits": there have been those who believe that on-line bidding exempts them from the fees as they treat it like eBay!). Some buyers ignore the "bits" and concentrate on the hammer price, worrying about the extras only when they've secured their purchase. But as premiums rise most of us have to factor them in at the start—so remember, if you have a strict budget you may well have to stop bidding quite a bit before that figure is reached in order to come in on target. Of course, when you just have to have something, what do budgets matter…?

Below is an indication of what you will have to pay on certain hammer prices depending on the Premium (we've given you 10%, 15% 20% and 22.5% options—the actual premium varies so check with the auctioneer before bidding). These figures assume VAT at 20%. Happy bidding!

10%		
Hammer	Plus premium	Plus premium and VAT
£75	£82.5	£84
£175	£192.50	£196
£500	£550	£560
£1500	£1650	£1680
£2500	£2750	£2800

15%		
Hammer	Plus premium	Plus premium and VAT
£75	£86.25	£88
£175	201.25	£206.50
£500	£575	£590
£1500	£1725	£1770
£2500	£2875	£2950

20%		
Hammer	Plus premium	Plus premium and VAT
£75	£90	£93
£175	£210	£217
£500	£600	£620
£1500	£1800	£1860
£2500	£3000	£3100

24%		
Hammer	Plus premium	Plus premium and VAT
£75	£93	£96.60
£175	£217	£225.40
£500	£620	£644
£1500	£1860	£1932
£2500	£3100	£3220

WEARING

Awards

The wearing of Orders, Decorations and Medals is a complex subject too complicated to cover in a publication such as this. However, there are a number of questions that collectors frequently ask, so we have attempted to deal with these as fully as possible.

Full-size Awards Mounted for Wear

Orders, decorations and medals are worn on the left breast in a line suspended from a single brooch mount or a rectangular frame (court mounted), the latter gives a firmer grip which occasions less damage than medals hanging more loosely from a brooch. The brooch/frame is covered by the medal ribbons. The most senior medal (see the following Order of Precedence) is furthest from the left shoulder. The obverse of the medals should show (this will usually be the sovereign's head, coat of arms, cypher, etc.).

If more than five medals are worn (three for the Navy), they should not be suspended side by side, but overlapped, the senior medal and ribbon is the one to be positioned so it can be seen completely. Medals should be lined up straight by the bottom rim/point, the length of ribbon should be one and a quarter inches (33mm) from the top of the mount to the first clasp or the suspension, which ever is appropriate (one and three quarters (45mm) for the Navy). Where the awards differ in size then a ribbon adjustment will be necessary to ensure a straight line.

Emblems for Mentions-in-Despatches or King's and Queen's Commendations for personnel and civilians should be worn on the relevant campaign medal, for example on the Victory Medal for the First World War and the War Medal 1939–45 for the Second World War. Where a recipient has no relevant campaign medal, the MID or commendation emblem is worn directly on the coat after any medal ribbons, or, if no ribbons then in the position of a single ribbon.,

There are a number of awards for which the sovereign has granted permission that they be worn on the right breast, including:

Royal Humane Society Medals
Stanhope Gold Medal
Royal National Lifeboat Institution Medals
Order of St John of Jerusalem Life Saving Medal.

Foreign Orders, Decorations and Medals

The British sovereign's subjects are not permitted to accept and wear the orders, decorations and medals of a foreign country of which the sovereign is not head of state. Application can be made for wear and permission is of two types: (a) restricted, that is instructions are given as to the exact occasions on which the award(s) may be worn; (b) unrestricted which allows the item(s) to be worn on all occasions according to the Order of Precedence, that is, generally speaking, arranged after British awards by date—first orders, then decorations, followed by medals (there are exceptions for the members of the armed services serving in an overseas force and receive that country's awards).

Awards are worn on a variety of State, evening or other occasions and the rules governing the wearing of orders according to dress are quite detailed. The subject is covered fully in *Medals Will Be Worn* by Lieutenant Colonel Ashley R. Tinson (Token Publishing Ltd., 1999) and in Spink's *Guide to the Wearing of Orders, Decorations and Medals* (Spink, 1990). The wearing of awards in civilian clothes is also fully detailed in *Wearing Your Medals in Civilian Clothes* by Lieutenant Colonel Ashley R. Tinson (Token Publishing Ltd., 2003).

THE ORDER
of Wear

The following list shows the order in which Orders, Decorations and Medals should be worn in the United Kingdom, certain countries of the Commonwealth and in Overseas Territories, as announced by the Central Chancery of the Orders of Knighthood (*London Gazette* Supplement No. 1, January 10, 2019). However, since the passing of Her Majesty Queen Elizabeth II there will inevitably be changes to the name of some medals, which will be recorded in the next edition of the Yearbook.

Victoria Cross
George Cross
Most Noble Order of the Garter
Most Ancient and Most Noble Order of the Thistle
Most Illustrious Order of St Patrick (obsolete since the death of the Duke of Gloucester, the last holder)
Knights Grand Cross, The Most Honourable Order of the Bath
Order of Merit
Baronet's Badge
Knight Grand Commander, The Most Exalted Order of the Star of India
Knights Grand Cross, The Most Distinguished Order of St Michael and St. George
Knight Grand Commander, The Most Eminent Order of the Indian Empire
The Order of the Crown of India
Knights Grand Cross, The Royal Victorian Order
Knights Grand Cross, The Most Excellent Order of the British Empire
Order of the Companions of Honour
Knight Commander, The Most Honourable Order of the Bath
Knight Commander, The Most Exalted Order of the Star of India
Knight Commander, The Most Distinguished Order of St Michael and St. George
Knight Commander, The Most Eminent Order of the Indian Empire
Knight Commander, The Royal Victorian Order
Knight Commander, The Most Excellent Order of the British Empire
Knight Bachelor's Badge
Companion, The Most Honourable Order of the Bath
Companion, The Most Exalted Order of the Star of India
Companion, The Most Distinguished Order of St Michael and St George
Companion, The Most Eminent Order of the Indian Empire
Commander, The Royal Victorian Order
Commander, The Most Excellent Order of the British Empire
Distinguished Service Order
Lieutenant, The Royal Victorian Order
Officer, The Most Excellent Order of the British Empire
Imperial Service Order
Member, The Royal Victorian Order
Member, The Most Excellent Order of the British Empire
Indian Order of Merit—Military

DECORATIONS, MEDALS FOR GALLANTRY AND DISTINGUISHED CONDUCT

Conspicuous Gallantry Cross
Distinguished Conduct Medal
Conspicuous Gallantry Medal
Conspicuous Gallantry Medal (Flying)
George Medal
Royal West African Field Force Distinguished Conduct Medal
Queen's Police Medal for Gallantry
Queen's Fire Service Medal for Gallantry
Royal Red Cross, Class 1
Distinguished Service Cross
Military Cross
Distinguished Flying Cross
Air Force Cross
Royal Red Cross, Class II
Order of British India
Kaisar-I-Hind Medal
Order of St John
Union of South Africa Queen's Medal for Bravery in gold
King's African Rifles Distinguished Conduct Medal
Indian Distinguished Service Medal
Union of South Africa Queen's Medal for Bravery in silver
Distinguished Service Medal
Military Medal
Distinguished Flying Medal
Air Force Medal
Constabulary Medal (Ireland)
Medal for Saving Life at Sea
Indian Order of Merit (Civil)
Indian Police Medal for Gallantry
Ceylon Police Medal for Gallantry
Sierra Leone Police Medal for Gallantry
Sierra Leone Fire Brigades Medal for Gallantry
Colonial Police Medal for Gallantry
Overseas Territories Police Medal for Gallantry
Queen's Gallantry Medal
Royal Victorian Medal (gold, silver and bronze)
British Empire Medal
Queen's Police Medal for Distinguished Service
Queen's Fire Service Medal for Distinguished Service
Queen's Ambulance Service Medal
Queen's Volunteer Reserves Medal
Queen's Medal for Chiefs

BADGE OF HONOUR

CAMPAIGN MEDALS AND STARS

Campaign Medals and Stars, including authorised UN, EU, EC and NATO medals in order of date of participation in the campaign for which awarded, as well as GSMs and OSMs.

POLAR MEDALS—in order of date of award

MEDALS FOR VALUABLE SERVICE

Imperial Service Medal
Indian Police Medal for Meritorious Service
Ceylon Police Medal for Merit
Sierra Leone Police Medal for Meritorious Service
Sierra Leone Fire Brigades Medal for Meritorious Service
Colonial Police Medal for Meritorious Service
Oversea Territories Police Medal for Meritorious Service

JUBILEE, CORONATION, DURBAR MEDALS

Queen Victoria's Jubilee Medal 1887 (gold, silver and bronze)
Queen Victoria's Police Jubilee Medal 1887
Queen Victoria's Jubilee Medal 1897 (gold, silver and bronze)
Queen Victoria's Police Jubilee Medal 1897
Queen Victoria's Commemoration Medal 1900 (Ireland)
King Edward VII's Coronation 1902
King Edward VII's Police Coronation 1902
King Edward VII's Durbar 1903 (gold, silver and bronze)
King Edward VII's Police Medal 1903 (Scotland)
King's Visit Commemoration Medal 1903 (Ireland)
King George V's Coronation Medal 1911
King George V's Police Coronation Medal 1911
King George V's Visit Police Commemoration Medal 1911 (Ireland)
King George V's Durbar Medal 1911 (gold, silver and bronze)
King George V's Silver Jubilee Medal 1935
King George VI's Coronation Medal 1937
Queen Elizabeth II's Coronation Medal 1953
Queen Elizabeth II's Silver Jubilee Medal 1977
Queen Elizabeth II's Golden Jubilee Medal 2002
Queen Elizabeth II's Diamond Jubilee Medal 2012
Queen Elizabeth II's Platinum Jubilee Medal 2022
Royal Household Long and Faithful Service Medal

EFFICIENCY AND LONG SERVICE DECORATIONS AND MEDALS

Meritorious Service Medal
Accumulated Campaign Service Medal
Accumulated Campaign Service Medal 2011
Army Long Service and Good Conduct Medal
Naval Long Service and Good Conduct Medal
Medal for Meritorious Service (Royal Navy 1918–28)
Indian Long Service and Good Conduct Medal (for Europeans of Indian Army)
Indian Meritorious Service Medal (for Europeans of Indian Army)
Royal Marines Meritorious Service Medal (1849–1947
Royal Air Force Meritorious Service Medal 1918–28
Royal Air Force Long Service and Good Conduct Medal
Ulster Defence Regiment Long Service and Good Conduct Medal

Indian Long Service and Good Conduct Medal (Indian Army)
Royal West African Frontier Force Long Service and Good Conduct Medal
Royal Sierra Leone Military Forces Long Service and Good Conduct Medal
King's African Rifles Long Service and Good Conduct Medal
Indian Meritorious Service Medal (for Indian Army)
Police Long Service and Good Conduct Medal
Fire Brigade Long Service and Good Conduct Medal
African Police Medal for Meritorious Service
Royal Canadian Mounted Police Long Service Medal
Ceylon Police Long Service Medal
Ceylon Fire Services Long Service Medal
Sierra Leone Police Long Service Medal
Sierra Leone Fire Brigade Long Service Medal
Colonial Police Long Service Medal
Overseas Territories Police Long Service Medal
Mauritius Police Long Service and Good Conduct Medal
Mauritius Fire Service Long Service and Good Conduct Medal
Mauritius Prisons Service Long Service and Good Conduct Medal
Colonial Fire Brigades Long Service Medal
Overseas Territories Fire Brigades Long Service Medal
Colonial Prison Service Medal
Overseas Territories Prison Service Medal
Hong Kong Disciplined Services Medal
Army Emergency Reserve Decoration
Volunteer Officers' Decoration
Volunteer Long Service Medal
Volunteer Officers' Decoration (for India and the Colonies)
Volunteer Long Service Medal (for India and the Colonies)
Colonial Auxiliary Forces Officers' Decoration
Colonial Auxiliary Forces Long Service Medal
Medal for Good Shooting (Naval)
Militia Long Service Medal
Imperial Yeomanry Long Service Medal
Territorial Decoration
Ceylon Armed Service Long Service Medal
Efficiency Decoration
Territorial Efficiency Medal
Efficiency Medal
Special Reserve Long Service and Good Conduct Medal
Decoration for Officers of the Royal Naval Reserve
Decoration for Officers of the Royal Naval Volunteer Reserve
Royal Naval Reserve Long Service Medal
Royal Naval Volunteer Reserve Long Service Medal
Royal Naval Auxiliary Sick Berth Reserve Long Service Medal
Royal Fleet Reserve Long Service and Good Conduct Medal
Royal Naval Wireless Auxiliary Reserve Long Service Medal
Royal Naval Auxiliary Service Medal
Air Efficiency Award
Volunteer Reserves Service Medal
Ulster Defence Regiment Medal
Northern Ireland Home Service Medal
Queen's Medal (for Champion Shots of the Royal Navy and Royal Marines)
Queen's Medal (for Champion Shots of the New Zealand Naval Forces)

Queen's Medal (for Champion Shots in the Military Forces)
Queen's Medal (for Champion Shots of the Air Forces)
Cadet Forces Medal
Coastguard Auxiliary Service Long Service Medal
Special Constabulary Long Service Medal
Canadian Forces Decoration
Royal Observer Corps Medal
Civil Defence Long Service Medal
Ambulance Service (Emergency Dutioes) Long Service
and Good Conduct Medal
Royal Fleet Auxiliary Service Medal
Prison Service (Operational Service) Long Service and
Good Conduct Medal
Jersey Honorary Police Long Service and Good
Conduct Medal
Merchant Navy Medal for Meritorious Service
Ebola Medal for Service in West Africa
National Crime Agency Long Service and Good
Conduct Medal
Rhodesia Medal 1980
Royal Ulster Constabulary Service Medal
Northern Ireland Prison Service Medal
Union of South Africa Commemoration Medal
Indian Independence Medal
Pakistan Independence Medal

Ceylon Armed Services Inauguration Medal
Ceylon Police Independence Medal (1948)
Sierra Leone Independence Medal
Jamaica Independence Medal
Uganda Independence Medal
Malawi Independence Medal
Guyana Independence Medal.....
Fiji Independence Medal
Papua New Guinea Independence Medal
Solomon Islands Independence Medal
Service Medal of the Order of St. John
Badge of the Order of the League of Mercy
Voluntary Medical Service Medal
Women's Voluntary Service Medal
South African Medal for War Services
Colonial Special Constabulary Medal
Honorary Membership of Commonwealth Orders
(instituted by the Sovereign, in order of date of award)
Other Commonwealth Members, Orders, Decorations
and Medals (instituted since 1949 otherwise
than by the Sovereign, and awards by States of
Malaysia and Brunei in order of date of award)
Foreign Orders in order of date of award
Foreign Decorations in order of date of award
Foreign Medals in order of date of award

THE ORDER IN WHICH CAMPAIGN STARS AND MEDALS AWARDED FOR SERVICE DURING WORLD WAR I AND II AND KOREA WAR ARE WORN

1914 Star with dated "Mons" clasp "
15th AUGUST–22nd NOVEMBER 1914"
1914 Star
1914/15 Star
British War Medal
Mercantile Marine War Medal
Victory Medal
Territorial Force War Medal
1939/45 Star
Atlantic Star
Arctic Star
Air Crew Europe Star
Africa Star

Pacific Star
Burma Star
Italy Star
France and Germany Star
Defence Medal
Canadian/Newfoundland Volunteer Service Medal
1939/45 War Medal
1939/45 Africa Service Medal of the Union of South Africa
India Service Medal
New Zealand War Service Medal
Southern Rhodesia Service Medal
Australian Service Medal
Korea Medal
United Nations Service Medal with bar KOREA

POST-NOMINAL LETTERS (as published in the London Gazette)
Recipients of some awards are entitled to use post-nominal letters including the following:

AE	Air Efficiency Award (officers)
AFC	Air Force Cross
AFM	Air Force Medal
AM	Albert Medal
ARRC	Royal Red Cross, Second Class
BEM	British Empire Medal
BGM	Burma Gallantry Medal
Bt or Bart	Baronet
CBE	Commander, The Most Excellent Order of the British Empire
CB	Companion, The Most Honourable Order of the Bath
CD	Canadian (Forces) Decoration
CGC	Conspicuous Gallantry Cross
CGM	Conspicuous Gallantry Medal
CH	Order of the Companion of Honour
CIE	Companion, The Most Eminent Order of the Indian Empire
CI	The Order of the Crown of India (women only)
CM/MduC	Canada Medal
CMG	Companion, The Most Distinguished Order of St Michael and St George
CPM	Overseas Territories Police Medal
CSI	Companion, The Most Exalted Order of the Star of India
CVO	Commander, The Royal Victorian Order
DBE	Dame Commander, The Most Excellent Order of the British Empire
DCB	Dame Commander, The Most Honourable Order of the Bath
DCMG	Dame Commander, The Most Distinguished Order of St Michael and St George
DCM	Distinguished Conduct Medal (King's African Rifles)
DCM	Distinguished Conduct Medal (West Africa Frontier Force)
DCM	Distinguished Conduct Medal
DCVO	Dame Commander, The Royal Victorian Order
DFC	Distinguished Flying Cross

DFM	Distinguished Flying Medal		KG	Knight, Most Noble Order of the Garter
DSC	Distinguished Service Cross		KP	Knight, Most Illustrious Order of St Patrick
DSM	Distinguished Service Medal			
DSO	Distinguished Service Order		KPFSM	King's Police and Fire Service Medal
ED	Efficiency Decoration		KPM	King's Police Medal
EGM	Empire Gallantry Medal		KT	Knight, Most Ancient and Most Noble Order of the Thistle
EM	Edward Medal			
ERD	Army Emergency Reserve Decoration		LVO	Lieutenant, The Royal Victorian Order
GBE	Knight Grand Cross, The Most Excellent Order of the British Empire		MBE	Member, The Most Excellent Order of the British Empire
GCB	Knight Grand Cross, The Most Honourable Order of the Bath		MC	Military Cross
			MM	Military Medal
GCIE	Knight Grand Commander. The Most Eminent Order of the Indian Empire		MSM	Meritorious Service Medal (Navy, awards up to 20.7.28)
GCMG	Knight Grand Cross—The Most Distinguished Order of St Michael and St George		MVO	Member, The Royal Victorian Order
			OBE	Officer, The Most Excellent Order of the British Empire
GCSI	Knight Grand Commander, The Most Exalted Order of the Star of India		OBI	Order of British India
			OB	Order of Burma (distinguished service)
GCVO	Knight Grand Cross, The Royal Victorian Order		OB	Order of Burma (gallantry)
			QASM	Queens Ambulance Service Medal
GC	George Cross		OM	Order of Merit
GM	George Medal		QAM	Queen's Ambulance Medal
IDSM	Indian Distinguished Service Medal		QFSM	Queen's Fire Service Medal
IOM	Indian Order of Merit (civil)		QGM	Queen's Gallantry Medal
IOM	Indian Order of Merit (military)		QPM	Queen's Police Medal
ISO	Imperial Service Order		QVRM	Queen's Volunteer Reserves Medal
KBE	Knight Commander, The Most Excellent Order of the British Empire		RD	Royal Naval Reserve Decoration
			RRC	Royal Red Cross First Class
KCB	Knight Commander, The Most Honourable Order of the Bath		RVM	Royal Victorian Medal
			SGM	Sea Gallantry Medals
KCIE	Knight Commander, The Most Eminent Order of the Indian Empire		TD	Territorial Decoration
			UD	Ulster Defence Regiment Medal (officers)
KCMG	Knight Commander, The Most Distinguished Order of St Michael and St George		VC	Victoria Cross
			VD	Volunteer Officers' Decoration
			VR	Volunteer Reserve
KCSI	Knight Commander, The Most Exalted Order of the Star of India		VRD	Royal Naval Volunteer Reserve Decoration
KCVO	Knight Commander, The Royal Victorian Order			

Only honours, decorations and medals which an individual has been authorised to wear by the Sovereign may be worn in uniform. As a general rule this also applies when wearing civilian clothes. Medals should not be worn on the right hand side, with the following exceptions: Royal Humane Society Medals, Stanhope Gold Medal, RNLI Medals, Order of St John of Jerusalem Life Saving Medal. Occasionally one may witness medals worn on the right hand side at church parades, Remembrance Day, etc. In this case the medals will be have been awarded to the wearer's next of kin, and the wearer will not be the recipient.

NB By Royal Warrant dated June 14, 2012, medals titled "Colonial . . ." are to be renamed "Overseas Territories . . .".

BRITANNIA MEDAL FAIR 2024

Europe's Largest Independent Medal Bourse

·

SUNDAY 12 MAY & SUNDAY 17 NOVEMBER
9:30 AM–2 PM

CARISBROOKE HALL, THE VICTORY SERVICES CLUB
63/79 SEYMOUR STREET, LONDON W2 2HF

FREE ENTRY

·

We are pleased to announce that there continues
to be no charge for visitors or trade stands

Specialist Collectors, Dealers and Auctioneers
from across the UK and beyond will be in attendance.

The event is hosted by Noonans on a not-for-profit basis
as a service to the medal collecting community.

The popular Britannia curry will be available from the canteen!

NOONANS MAYFAIR

NOONANS MAYFAIR
ALL ENQUIRIES PLEASE CALL 020 7016 1700 OR EMAIL EVENTS@NOONANS.CO.UK
WWW.NOONANS.CO.UK

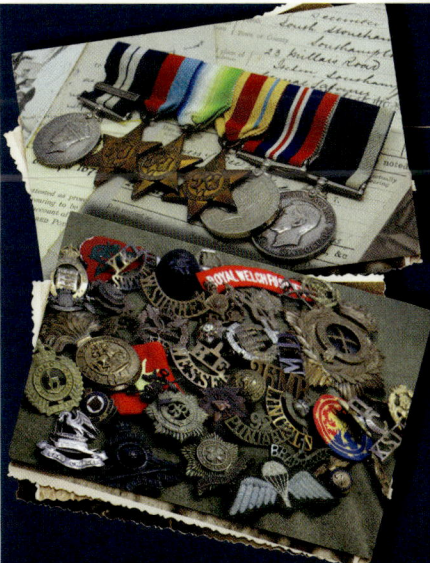

COLLECTING
Medal Ribbons

There is nothing new or old about collecting medal ribbons, in fact the founders of the present Orders and Medals Research Society originally set out as medal ribbon collectors. The ribbon has, ever since the early 18th century, been an important complement to the medal or badge of an order and its importance has grown over the years. Since those early orders of chivalry when it was deemed necessary to identify the various religious or secular orders one belonged to by the colour of its ribbon, the emphasis has been on the ribbon to identify the order or medal. This practice has continued down through the centuries, even to today when the avid enthusiast can recognise a warrior's medals simply by identifying his ribbons.

However, times are changing. The practice of wearing medals is on the decline, reserved only for ceremonial occasions, whilst the wearing of ribbon bars and the awarding of a single campaign or service medal with different ribbons to denote specific operations is on the increase. Our very own Operational Service Medal (OSM), the NATO medal and of course the plethora of United Nations medals are all classic examples of today's expansion of the medal ribbon. There is of course the growing cost of collecting medals and decorations compared to that of medal ribbons. There is also the down side to all of this—the opportunity to acquire medal ribbons has become a challenge to many, as sources such as tailors' shops, small ribbon manufacturers and numerous regimental or quartermasters stores have all gone into decline, if not altogether vanished.

Before one can collect ribbons properly one must first be able to identify them. It is therefore important to have a reasonable reference library—nothing elaborate or expansive is needed. It is probably wise to start collecting ribbons of the United Kingdom before branching out into those of other countries. There are several good books on the subject and most ribbons can be obtained quite easily.

The more one handles ribbons the quicker one starts to get a feel for the subject and gets to know which colours are used by certain countries or organisations; whether they always use silk or fine cottons; prefer moiré (watered) or corded ribbons; whether they use wide or narrow ribbons—all are skills one picks up along the way. However, today this can sometimes prove difficult as the quality of many modern manufactured ribbons is really quite poor compared to the silk watered ribbons of bygone days.

Once over the initial teething problems of deciding how to store ribbons and ultimately mount or display them, the desire to expand and even specialise creeps in. Do you collect ribbons from just one country, state or organisation such as the Red Cross or the United Nations? Campaign medals and their numerous emblems? Famous chests? Regimental battle streamers? Religious or chivalric orders past and present? British or foreign orders and their various rosettes? The choice can be endless. Whatever the path you choose, you will almost certainly have to do a little research to obtain the reason for the award and the colours adopted for the ribbon. In reality, a true ribbon collector will know just as much about the medal or decoration as they will about the ribbon. Depending on the amount of time you have, research can lead you to museums, reading rooms or even portrait galleries, as well as societies such as the Ribbon Branch of the Orders and Medals Research Society (see their advertisement opposite). But whatever path is chosen you will be in awe of the sacrifices made by mankind down the centuries.

The Orders and Medals Research Society

MINIATURE MEDALS BRANCH

If you have an interest in miniature medals, you should join the only organisation dedicated to their collection and study – the Miniature Medals Branch of the OMRS.

This friendly group was founded in 1986 and now boasts an enthusiastic world-wide membership. The quarterly branch journal – *Miniature Medals World* – is illustrated in colour and remains the only publication specifically about this absorbing subject.

Whatever your interest – single medals or groups, from Victorian to current – there will be something to attract, delight and inform you.

There are five meetings a year in central London, with a mix of speakers, members' displays, auctions and members' own sessions.

Contact the Branch Secretary or visit the Branch table at the OMRS Convention to learn how you can tap into the broad experience and unrivalled expertise that has been accumulated.

Mark Furniss-Roe, Branch Secretary,
The Miniature Medals Branch, OMRS
miniaturemedalsbranch@gmail.com

MINIATURE
Medals & Decorations

There was a time when you had to ask a dealer if they had any miniature medals. A box was normally produced from under the counter and you were told to get stuck in, picking up pieces for pennies. Those days are long gone with this side of the hobby now being taken more seriously. When someone does start to collect miniature medals they are guaranteed one thing and that's variety.

Collecting miniatures can provide the same amount of excitement that full-size medals bring, only they take up less space and can be a fraction of the price. Most people start collecting full-size medals only to reach a point where the mind says buy it but the bank says no. Wanting to continue with the hobby, miniature medals are the next best thing, but what to collect? Orders, decorations, campaign medals, long service, military, civilian . . .? The list is endless. Most collectors keep to a theme while others will buy absolutely everything they see.

The next question is where can you find them? The answer is at auctions, medal fairs, medal dealerships, online catalogues or online auction sites. The first three would be preferable, with the all-important opportunity to handle the piece before parting with your hard earned cash. Occasionally miniature medals are sold with their full-size counterpart. A polite conversation can sometimes convince the vendor to let them go their separate ways, but make sure you get the details of the recipient from the full-size, as this will save a lot of time later.

There are other avenues to take in your quest and they can sometimes prove to be very productive if prepared to get up early and maybe drive a few miles. These are antique, flea and collectors' fairs, markets, bric-a-brac shops, emporiums and car boot sales.

Deciding what to do with your new find has always raised eyebrows. Should it be cleaned or left like it is? New ribbon or keep the old one on? Pin on, pin off? Only you the collector can make this decision. Taking a group to pieces for the sake of gaining one medal should certainly be discouraged as once this is done it is a little bit of history lost.

There are many ways of storing miniatures. Many collectors use albums, but be careful as some plastic envelopes can degrade a medal. Occasionally taking them out and giving them a wipe over is recommended. Mounting in frames is a nice way to show off your collection, but just make sure they are out of sight from windows and prying eyes. Display cases with the medals laid out in trays is another way to keep them, but ensure you don't use a cheap felt lining as this can also degrade the metal over a long period of time.

There are plenty of books on miniatures available and it is useful to start building up your own library. You can't have enough books on the subject. A good start has already been made in buying this Yearbook. The same publishers also produce the magazine MEDAL NEWS which has a regular feature, "Talking Miniatures", where particular topics are covered. The internet obviously has made researching medals so much easier in recent years with many of the auction houses having an archive section available to all on-line.

If you're happy to continue collecting on your own that is fine but sometimes help, advice and guidance is crucial if you don't want to end up with an album full of worthless items. Societies and clubs exist throughout the country (such as the Miniature Medals Branch of the Orders and Medals Research Society) and are certainly worth joining, as are social media groups. They will contain many learned individuals who will steer you in the right direction when it comes to identifying and researching miniature medals.

Note that the prices given in this publication are for contemporary medals unless otherwise stated.

ORDERS
of Knighthood

The most colourful and romantic of all awards are those connected with the orders of chivalry. Many of them have their origins in the Middle Ages, when knights in armour formed the elite fighting force in every European country. From the idea of a select band of knights, pledged to the support of a king or an ideal (usually religious), sprang the orders of chivalry.

Many of the orders of chivalry existed in the Middle Ages but most of them died out as feudalism went into decline. In some cases they survived; in others they disappeared for centuries, only to be resurrected at a later date. Still others were devised and instituted in relatively modern times, and indeed, continue to evolve. For example, Canada instituted the Order of Canada in 1967 and both Australia and New Zealand introduced their own orders in 1975.

In their original form membership of the orders of chivalry were just as highly coveted as they are today, but the insignia was usually simple or even non-existent. The complicated system of insignia which now surrounds these orders is fairly modern, dating from the 16th century or later. Nowadays most orders also exist in several classes, with the insignia becoming increasingly elaborate with each higher class.

Britain's senior order is the Garter, and although it consists of one class only it provides a good example of the pomp and ceremony which often surrounds these awards. It was founded by King Edward III and is said to derive its name from the fact that the King was attending a dance one day, when a lady's garter slipped from her leg and fell to the floor. To save her the embarrassment of retrieving her garter—and thus letting everyone know it was hers—the King himself picked it up and tied it round his own leg. Lest anyone should doubt that it was his garter he said, in court French, "Let evil be to him who evil thinks". From this curious incident came the idea of a very exclusive order of knighthood, consisting of the sovereign and 26 knights.

The insignia of this order consists of a Garter, a mantle of blue velvet lined with taffeta with the star of the Order embroidered on the left breast, a hood of crimson velvet, a surcoat of crimson velvet lined with white taffeta, a hat of black velvet lined with white taffeta, with a plume of white ostrich and black heron feathers fastened by a band of diamonds, a collar of gold composed of buckled garters and lovers' knots with red roses, the George (an enamelled figure of St George slaying the dragon) suspended from the collar, the Lesser George or badge, worn from a broad blue sash passing over the left shoulder to the right hip,

and the star, a silver eight-pointed decoration bearing the red cross of St George surrounded by the garter and motto.

The insignia is exceptionally elaborate, the other orders of chivalry varying considerably in their complexity according to the class of the order. The full insignia is only worn on special occasions. In the case of the Garter usually the Lesser George and the breast star are worn on their own.

On the death of a Knight of the Garter the insignia should be returned to the Central Chancery of Orders of Knighthood, and therefore few examples of the Garter ever come on to the market. Those that do are usually examples from the 17th and 18th centuries when regulations regarding the return of insignia were not so strict. In the case of the lesser orders, insignia is returnable on promotion to a higher class. All collar chains are returnable, although that of the Order of St Michael and St George could be retained prior to 1948.

British orders are manufactured by firms holding contracts from the Central Chancery of Orders of Knighthood, and the values quoted in this Yearbook are for the official issues. It should be noted, however, that holders of orders frequently have replicas of breast stars made for use on different uniforms and it is sometimes difficult to tell these replicas from the originals as in many cases the replicas were made by the court jewellers responsible for making the originals. In addition, many jewellers in such European capitals as Vienna, Berlin and Paris have a long tradition of manufacturing the insignia of orders for sale to collectors.

The badges and breast stars of orders of chivalry are very seldom named to the recipient and therefore often lack the personal interest of campaign medals and many gallantry awards. For this reason they do not command the same interest or respect of collectors. Nevertheless, in cases where the insignia of orders can be definitely proved to have belonged to some famous person, the interest and value are enhanced. In any case, these orders are invariably very attractive examples of the jeweller's art, and they often possess titles and stories as colourful and romantic as their appearance.

1. THE MOST NOBLE ORDER OF THE GARTER

KG Star
(a Victorian example)

Lesser George
(this early example has the garter enamelled in blue)

Instituted: 1348.

Ribbon: 102mm plain dark blue. Not worn in undress uniform.

Garter: Dark blue velvet. Two versions may be encountered, with embroidered lettering and other details, or with gold lettering, buckle and tab. Worn on the left leg by gentlemen and on the left forearm by ladies.

Collar Chain: Gold composed of alternate buckled garters, each encircling a red enamelled rose, and lovers' knots in gold although sometimes enamelled white.

Collar badge: An enamelled figure of St George fighting the dragon.

Star: Originally always embroidered in metal thread, a style which continues in the mantle to this day. Prior to 1858 knights often purchased metal stars in addition and since that date metal stars have been officially issued. These consist of a silver eight-pointed radiate star bearing in its centre and red cross of St George on a white ground, surrounded by the garter and motto HONI SOIT QUI MAL Y PENSE (Evil be to he who evil thinks).

Sash Badge: The Lesser George, similar to the collar badge but encircled by an oval garter bearing the motto.

Comments: *Membership of the Order of the Garter is confined to the reigning sovereign, the Prince of Wales and 25 other Knights, and is the personal gift of the monarch. In addition to the 25 Knights there have, from time to time, been extra Knights, occasionally non-Christians such as the Sultans of Turkey or the Emperor of Japan. The Emperor Hirohito, incidentally had the dubious distinction of being the only person awarded the Garter twice: in 1922 and again in 1971, having forfeited the original award as a result of the Japanese entry into the Second World War in 1941. Sir Winston Churchill was invested with the insignia originally presented in 1702 to his illustrious ancestor, the Duke of Marlborough. All official insignia should be returned to the Central Chancery of Knighthood on the death of the holder. Ladies (other than royalty) are now eligible for the Order.*

VALUE:

Collar chain	Rare
Collar badge (the George)	From £50,000*
Star (in metal)	From £6500
Star (embroidered)	£1000–2000
Mantle star	£1000–2000
Sash badge (Lesser George)	From £20,000
Garter (embroidered)	£800–1000
Garter (gold lettering and buckle)	£4000–8000
Miniature	
Star (metal)	£500–650
Collar badge	£875–1000
Sash badge	£450–550

*This price is for privately made examples, many of which are jewelled and enamelled.

2. THE MOST ANCIENT AND MOST NOBLE ORDER OF THE THISTLE

KT Star

Instituted: 1687.

Ribbon: 102mm plain dark green. Not worn in undress uniform.

Collar Chain: Gold of alternate thistles and sprigs of rue enamelled in proper colours.

Collar Badge: The jewel is a gold and enamelled figure of St Andrew in a green gown and purple surcoat, bearing before him a white saltire cross, the whole surrounded by rays of gold.

Star: Silver, consisting of a St Andrew's cross, with other rays issuing between the points of the cross and, in the centre, on a gold background, a thistle enamelled in proper colours surrounded by a green circle bearing the Latin motto NEMO ME IMPUNE LACESSIT (No-one assails me with impunity).

Sash Badge: The medal of the Order is a gold figure of St Andrew bearing before him a saltire cross, surrounded by an oval collar bearing the motto, surmounted by a gold cord fitted with a ring for suspension. Examples are found in plain gold, or with enamelling and/or set with jewels.

Comments: *This order is said to have been founded in AD 787, alluding to barefoot enemy soldiers who cried out when they trod on thistles and thus alerted the Scots of an imminent attack. The order had long been defunct when it was revived by King James VII and II and re-established in December 1703 by Queen Anne. It now consists of the sovereign and 16 Knights, making it the most exclusive of the orders of chivalry. At death, the official insignia is returned to the Central Chancery. Ladies (other than royalty) are now eligible for the Order.*

VALUE:

Collar chain	Rare
Collar badge	Rare
Star (metal)	From £6000
Star (embroidered)	From £1000
Mantle star	From £850
Sash badge	From £10,000
Miniature	
Star (metal)	£500–550
Collar badge	£550–600
Sash badge	From £450

Examples of Sash Badges

3. THE MOST ILLUSTRIOUS ORDER OF ST PATRICK

KP Star

Sash badge

Instituted: February 5, 1783.

Ribbon: 100mm sky-blue. Not worn in undress uniform.

Collar Chain: Gold, composed of five roses and six harps alternating, each tied together with a gold knot. The roses are enamelled alternately white petals within red and red within white.

Collar Badge: An imperial crown enamelled in proper colours from which is suspended by two rings a gold harp and from this a circular badge with a white enamelled centre embellished with the red saltire cross on which is surmounted a green three-petalled shamrock its leaves decorated with gold crowns, the whole surrounded by a gold collar bearing the Latin motto QUIS SEPARABIT (Who shall separate us?) with the date of foundation in roman numerals round the foot MDCCLXXXIII.

Star: A silver eight-pointed star, having in its centre, on a white field, the saltire cross of St Patrick in red enamel charged with a green trefoil bearing a gold crown on each leaf.

Sash Badge: The saltire cross in red enamel surmounted by a green shamrock with gold crowns as above, surrounded by an oval collar of pale blue with the Latin motto round the top and the date of foundation round the foot, the whole enclosed by a gold and white enamel surround charged with 32 shamrocks.

Comments: *Founded by King George III to reward the loyalty of Irish peers during the American War of Independence, it originally comprised the monarch and 15 Knights. In 1833 it was extended to include the Lord-Lieutenant of Ireland and 22 Knights, with certain extra and honorary knights. Appointments of non-royal Knights to the Order ceased with the partition of Ireland in 1922, although three of the sons of King George V were appointed after that date—the Prince of Wales (1927), the Duke of York (1936) and the Duke of Gloucester (1934). It became obsolete in 1974 with the death of the last holder. All items of official insignia were returned at death. Unlike the other two great orders, the sash for this Order is worn in the manner of the lesser orders, over the right shoulder.*

VALUE:

Collar chain	Rare
Collar badge	From £15,000
Star (metal)	From £5500
Star (embroidered)	£850–1000
Mantle star	£850–1200
Sash badge	From £5000
Miniature	
Star (metal)	£400–500
Collar/Sash badge	£650–750

4. THE MOST HONOURABLE ORDER OF THE BATH

GCB Star (Military)

Instituted: 1725.

Ribbon: GCB 102mm (58mm for ladies); KCB/DCB 44mm; CB 38mm, deep red.

Collar Chain: Gold composed of nine crowns and eight devices, each consisting of a rose, a thistle and a shamrock issuing from a sceptre all enamelled in their proper colours. The crowns and devices are joined by gold, white-enamelled knots.

Collar Badge: A skeletal gold badge with an oval collar inscribed TRIA JUNCTA IN UNO (Three joined in one) in white enamelled letters, enclosing a thistle, rose and shamrock issuing from a sceptre, with a crown above the sceptre and two crowns below, at the sides.

Star: A silver flaming star surmounted by a circular gold band enamelled red bearing the motto round the top and having a laurel spray round the foot, enclosing three gold crowns enamelled in red.

Sash Badge: As the Collar Badge but smaller and without white enamelling.

Comments: *Established by King George I, this was a single-class Order comprising the monarch, a prince of the blood royal, a Great Master and 35 Knights of Companions. It was re-organised at the conclusion of the Napoleonic Wars (see below). Ladies (other than royalty) are now eligible for the Order. Promotion to a different division permits the wearing of both types of insignia.*

VALUE:

Collar chain	Rare
Collar badge	£3000–4000
Star (metal)	From £5500
Star (embroidered)	£500–1000
Sash badge	£2000–3000

KNIGHTS/DAMES GRAND CROSS (GCB)

The Order was re-organised in 1815 in two divisions, Military and Civil. The Military Division had three classes: Knight Grand Cross (GCB), Knight Commander (KCB) and Companion (CB), while the Civil Division continued with the single class of Knight Grand Cross. In 1847 the Civil Division came into line with the Military, and divided into three classes.

Metal: Gold (1815–87), silver-gilt (1887–1901), silver gilt with gold centre (1902 on).

Collar Badge: The Military Badge is a gold Maltese cross of eight points, each point tipped with a small gold ball, and in each angle between the arms of the cross is a gold lion. In the centre of the cross is a device comprising a rose, thistle and shamrock issuing from a sceptre, and three imperial crowns . This device is surrounded by a red enamelled circle on which appears the Latin motto TRIA JUNCTA IN UNO (three joined in one) in gold lettering. The circle is surrounded by two branches of laurel, enamelled green, and below is a blue enamelled scroll with the German motto ICH DIEN (I serve) in gold.

The Civil Badge is of gold filigree work, and oval in shape. It consists of a bandlet bearing the motto, and in the centre is the usual device of the rose, thistle and shamrock issuing from a sceptre, together with the three crowns.

Star: A gold Maltese cross of the same pattern as the Military Badge, mounted on a silver flaming star (Military); or a silver eight-pointed star with a central device of three crowns on a silver ground, encircled by the motto on a red enamelled ribbon (Civil).

Sash Badges: Similar to the Collar Badges, they were originally made in gold but since 1887 silver-gilt has been substituted. They may now be worn at the neck when sashes are not worn.

VALUE:	Military	Civil
Collar chain (gold)	Rare	Rare
Collar chain (silver-gilt)	£8000–10,000	£8000–10,000
Collar badge (gold)	£4500–5500	£1250–1750
Star (metal)	£3500–4000	£1250–1750
Star (embroidered)	£350–500	£250–350
Mantle star	£750–1000	£650–850
Sash badge (gold)	£5500–7500	£2500–3500
Sash badge (silver-gilt)	£1500–2000	£800–1200

4. THE MOST HONOURABLE ORDER OF THE BATH *continued*

KCB Star (Civil)

GCB Sash badge (Civil)

Emblem worn in civilian dress

KCB Neck badge (Military)

KNIGHTS/DAMES COMMANDERS (KCB/DCB); COMPANIONS (CB)

Holders of the KCB (DCB) wear a neck badge suspended by a ribbon as well as a breast star. Prior to 1917 Companions wore a breast badge, the same way as a medal: but in that year it was converted into a neck badge.

Star (KCB/DCB): (Military) a star with the gold Maltese cross omitted, and in the shape of a cross pattée, the three crowns and motto in the centre surrounded by a green enamelled laurel wreath. (Civil) similar but omitting the laurel wreath.

Breast Badge (CB): Similar to the Star but smaller.

Neck Badge (KCB/DCB): Similar to the Collar badges of the GCB but smaller, in Military and Civil versions as above.

Neck Badge (CB): Similar to the above, but smaller.

VALUE:	Military	Miniature	Civil	Miniature
Knight Commander				
Star (metal)	£1250–1500		£750–850	
Star (embroidered)	£550–650		£450–550	
Neck badge (gold)	£4500–5500		£1200–1500	
Neck badge (gilt)	£1200–1500		£650–750	
Companion				
Breast badge (gold)	£3500–4500	£175–250	£850–1000	£150–200
Breast badge (gilt)	£1000–1200	£75–100	£350–450	£75–100
Neck badge (gilt)	£800–950		£300–375	

5. THE ROYAL GUELPHIC ORDER

Instituted: 1815.
Ribbon: 44mm light blue watered silk.

KNIGHTS GRAND CROSS (GCH)

KCH Star (Military)

Collar Chain: Gold, with lions and crowns alternating, linked by scrolled royal cyphers.

Collar Badge: An eight-pointed Maltese cross with balls on each point and a lion passant gardant in each angle. (Obverse) in the centre, on a ground of red enamel, is a white horse of Hanover surrounded by a circle of light blue enamel with the motto in gold lettering NEC ASPERA TERRENT (Difficulties do not terrify). Surrounding this circle is a green enamelled laurel wreath. (Reverse) the monogram GR in gold letters on a red ground, surmounted by the British crown and surrounded by a gold circle with the date of the institution MDCCCXV. In the Military version two crossed swords are mounted above the cross and below a Hanoverian crown. In the Civil version the swords are omitted, and the wreath is of oak-leaves instead of laurel.

Star: A radiate star with rays grouped into eight points, the centre being similar to the Collar Badge. Behind the laurel wreathed centre are two crossed swords (Military); in the Civil version the swords are omitted and the wreath is of oak leaves.

Sash Badge: Similar to the Collar Badge but smaller.

Comments: *Founded by HRH the Prince Regent (later King George IV), it took its name from the family surname of the British sovereigns from George I onwards and was awarded by the crown of Hanover to both British and Hanoverian subjects for distinguished services to Hanover. Under Salic Law, a woman could not succeed to the Hanoverian throne, so on the death of King William IV in 1837 Hanover passed to Prince Augustus, Duke of Cumberland, and thereafter the Guelphic Order became a purely Hanoverian award.*

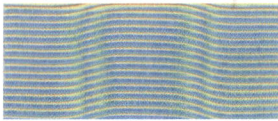

VALUE:

	Military	Civil
Collar chain (gold)	From £25,000	From £20,000
Collar chain (silver gilt)	£10,000–12,000	£8000–10,000
Collar Chain (copper gilt)	£5000–6000	£3500–4500
Collar badge	£6000–8000	£2500–3500
Star	£5000–7000	£3000–4000
Sash badge	£8000–10,000	£6000–8000

KNIGHTS COMMANDERS (KCH) AND KNIGHTS (KH)

Knights Commanders wore a neck badge suspended by a ribbon, and a breast star, while Knights wore a breast badge only.

Star: As above, but smaller.
Neck Badge: Similar to the Collar Badge but smaller.
Breast Badge: Two versions, in gold and enamel or silver and enamel.

VALUE:

	Military	Miniature	Civil	Miniature
Star	£2500–3000		£1500–2000	
Neck badge	£3500–4000		£2000–2500	
Breast badge (gold)	£2500–3000	£450–550	£1200–1500	£500–600
Breast badge (silver)	£1000–1200			

KH Breast Badge (Military)

6. THE MOST DISTINGUISHED ORDER OF ST MICHAEL AND ST GEORGE

Instituted: 1818.
Ribbon: 102mm, 58mm for ladies (GCMG), 50mm (KCMG), 44mm (DCMG), 38mm (CMG) three equal bands of Saxon blue, scarlet and Saxon blue.

GCMG Star

KNIGHTS GRAND CROSS (GCMG)

Knights Grand Cross wear a mantle of Saxon blue lined with scarlet silk tied with cords of blue and scarlet silk and gold, and having on the left side the star of the Order. The chapeau or hat is of blue satin, lined with scarlet and surmounted by black and white ostrich feathers. The collar, mantle and chapeau are only worn on special occasions or when commanded by the sovereign, but in ordinary full dress the badge is worn on the left hip from a broad ribbon passing over the right shoulder and the star on the left breast.

Collar Chain: Silver gilt formed alternately of lions of England, Maltese crosses enamelled in white, and the cyphers SM and SG with, in the centre, two winged lions of St Mark each holding a book and seven arrows.

Star: A silver star of seven groups of rays, with a gold ray between each group, surmounted overall by the cross of St George in red enamel. In the centre is a representation of St Michael encountering Satan within a blue circular riband bearing the motto AUSPICIUM MELIORIS AEVI (A token of a better age).

Sash Badge: A gold seven-pointed star with V-shaped extremities, enamelled white and edged with gold, surmounted by an imperial crown. In the centre on one side is a representation in enamel of St Michael encountering Satan and on the other St George on horseback fighting the dragon. This device is surrounded by a circle of blue enamel bearing the Latin motto in gold lettering. Silver-gilt was substituted for gold in 1887.

Comments: *Founded by HRH the Prince Regent and awarded originally to citizens of Malta and the Ionian Islands in the Adriatic Sea, both of which had been ceded to Britain during the Napoleonic Wars. The Ionian Islands were transferred to Greece in 1859. Towards the end of the 19th century, however, the Order was awarded to those who had performed distinguished service in the colonies and protectorates of the British Empire and in more recent times it has been widely used as an award to ambassadors and senior diplomats as well as colonial governors. Ladies are now eligible for this Order. In recent operations a number of awards have been made to military officers, presumably for "diplomatic" work.*

VALUE:

Collar chain	£5000–6500
Star	£2500–3000
Sash badge (gold)	£5000–6000
Sash badge (gilt)	£2000–3000

6. THE MOST DISTINGUISHED ORDER OF ST MICHAEL AND ST GEORGE *continued*

KCMG Star

CMG Neck badge

KNIGHTS COMMANDERS (KCMG) AND COMPANIONS (CMG)

Knights Commanders wear the badge suspended round the neck from a narrower ribbon of the same colours, and a breast star; Companions wear a neck badge. In undress uniform Knights Grand Cross and Knights Commanders wear the ribbon of Companions of the Order. Prior to 1917 Companions wore a breast badge, worn the same way as a medal, but this was then changed to a neck badge.

Star: A silver eight-pointed star charged with the red St George's cross and having the same central device as the GCMG Star. This was introduced in 1859.

Neck Badge: Similar to the sash badge of the GCMG but smaller. Those worn by Knight Commanders were of gold and enamel until 1887 but silver-gilt and enamel thereafter. The CMG neck badges are invariably of enamel and silver-gilt.

Breast Badge: Similar to the star of the KCMG but smaller and made of gold and enamel till 1887, and silver gilt and enamel from then till 1917.

VALUE:		Miniature
Knight Commander		
Star	£1200–1500	
Neck badge (gold)	£2500–3500	
Neck badge (gilt)	£1000–1500	
Companion		
Breast badge (gold)	£2000–2500	£150–200
Breast badge (gilt)	£800–1000	£85–125
Neck badge (gilt)	£550–600	

A NOTE ON IMAGERY

In the wake of the Black Lives Matter protests in the summer of 2020, there were calls in some quarters for a redesign of the breast star of the Order of St Michael and St George as, it was claimed, the central image of St Michael with his foot on Satan's neck had racist undertones as Lucifer is depicted with a much darker skin tone than the saint. Whilst few believed that the image was originally designed with any racist intent, it seems that the issue has arisen before and the Cabinet Office were quick to point out that the image was actually redrawn in 2011. Now the two figures have a similar skin tone. They went on to say that anyone wishing to change their insignia for the newer version was welcome to do so.

7. THE MOST EXALTED ORDER OF THE STAR OF INDIA

Instituted: 1861.
Ribbon: Light blue with white edges (50mm GCSI, KCSI; 38mm CSI).

KNIGHTS GRAND COMMANDERS (GCSI)

KCSI Neck badge

The insignia consisted of a gold collar and badge, a mantle of light blue satin with a representation of the star on the left side and tied with a white silk cord with blue and silver tassels. The collar and mantle were only worn on special occasions and in ordinary full dress uniform a GCSI wore the star on the left breast and the badge on the left hip from a broad sash of light blue edged in white.

Collar Chain: Gold formed of lotus flowers, palm branches and united red and white roses. Later chains are silver-gilt.

Badge: An onyx cameo bearing the left-facing bust of Queen Victoria wearing an imperial crown, set in a gold ornamental oval containing the motto of the Order HEAVEN'S LIGHT OUR GUIDE in diamonds, on a pale blue ground surmounted by a five-pointed star in chased silver.

Star: A five-pointed star in diamonds resting on a circular riband of light blue enamel bearing the motto in diamonds, the whole set on a circular star of golden rays.

Comments: *Founded by Queen Victoria a few years after the British Crown took over the administration of India from the Honourable East India Company, it was intended primarily as an award to loyal Indian princes. The highest class was designated Knight Grand Commander, rather than Cross, because the majority of recipients were not Christians (either Hindus or Muslims). The Order at first consisted of the sovereign, a Grand Master (the Viceroy of India), 36 Knights Grand Commanders (18 British and 18 Indian), 85 Knights Commanders and 170 Companions. The GCSI was the most lavish of all British orders. It lapsed in 1947 when the sub-continent attained independence. Until then all insignia of this Order was returnable on the death of recipients. After 1947, however, recipients or their heirs were allowed in certain cases to purchase the star and badges of any of the three applicable classes, but not the collar chain of the Knight Grand Commander.*

VALUE:

Collar chain	—
Star and badge	From £40,000

KNIGHTS COMMANDERS (KCSI) AND COMPANIONS (CSI)

Knights Commanders wore a badge round the neck and a star on the left breast, while Companions originally had a breast badge which was transmuted into a neck badge from 1917 onwards.

Star: Similar to that of the GCSI but in silver.

Neck Badge: Similar to the collar badge of the GCSI but smaller and less ornate.

Breast Badge: Similar to the above but smaller and less ornate and fitted with a straight bar suspender. Subtle differences in the ornament at the foot of the blue border and the external ornament at the sides and foot of the oval.

Comments: *The second and third classes of the Order were awarded to Indian and British subjects of the armed forces and Indian Civil Service for distinguished service of not less than 30 years' duration.*

VALUE:

		Miniature
Star and Neck badge (KCSI)	From £15,000	
Breast badge (CSI)	£6500–7500	£350–500 (gold), £200–250 (silver gilt)
Neck badge (CSI)	£6000–9000	

8. THE MOST EMINENT ORDER OF THE INDIAN EMPIRE

Instituted: 1878.
Ribbon: Deep indigo blue.

KNIGHTS GRAND COMMANDERS (GCIE)

The insignia consisted of a collar, badge and mantle of imperial purple or dark blue satin lined with white silk and fastened with a white silk cord with gold tassels, and having on the left side a representation of the Star of the Order. On ordinary full-dress occasions, however, Knights Grand Commanders wore the badge on the left hip from a broad sash, and a star on the left breast.

Collar Chain: Silver-gilt, composed of elephants, lotus flowers, peacocks in their pride and Indian roses with, in the centre, the imperial crown, the whole linked together by chains.

Badge: A gold five-petalled rose, enamelled crimson and with a green barb between each petal. In the centre is an effigy of Queen Victoria on a gold ground, surrounded by a purple riband originally inscribed VICTORIA IMPERATRIX but from 1901 onwards inscribed IMPERATRICIS AUSPICIIS (Under the auspices of the Empress). The letters I N D I A are inscribed on the petals in the first version, but omitted in the second.

Star: Composed of fine silver rays with smaller gold rays between them, the whole alternately plain and scaled. In the centre, within a purple circle bearing the motto and surmounted by the imperial crown in gold, is the effigy of Queen Victoria on a gold ground.

Comments: *Founded by Queen Victoria after assuming the title of Empress of India, it was originally confined to Companions only, together with the Sovereign and Grand Master. Members of the Council of the Governor-General were admitted* ex officio *as Companions. It was intended for award in respect of meritorious services in India but from the outset it was regarded as a junior alternative to the Star of India. In 1886 the Order was expanded to two classes by the addition of Knights Commanders up to a maximum of 50 in number. In 1887, however, it was again re-organised into three classes: up to 25 Knights Grand Commanders (GCIE), up to 50 Knights Commanders (KCIE) and an unlimited number of Companions (CIE). The Order has been in abeyance since 1947.*

KCIE Neck badge

VALUE:

Collar chain	From £20,000
Star and badge	£7000–9000

KNIGHTS COMMANDERS (KCIE) AND COMPANIONS (CIE)

The insignia of Knights Commanders consisted of a neck badge and a breast star, while that of Companions was originally a breast badge, converted to a neck badge in 1917.

Star: Similar to that of the GCIE but fashioned entirely in silver.

Neck badge: Similar to the collar or sash badge of the GCIE but in correspondingly smaller sizes and differing in minor details.

Breast badge: Similar to the sash badge of the GCIE but differing in minor details, notably the spacing ornament at the foot of the blue circle. Two versions exist, with or without INDIA on the petals of the lotus flower.

VALUE:		*Miniature*
Knights Commanders		
Star and Neck badge	£5000–7000	
Companions		
Breast badge (INDIA)	£2000–3000	£450–500 (gold)
Breast badge (smaller, without INDIA)	£1000–1250	£300–400 (gold)
Neck badge	£900–1000	£175–250 (gilt)

9. THE ROYAL FAMILY ORDER

QEII (reduced)

Edward VII

George V

George VI

Elizabeth II

Instituted: 1820.

Ribbon: 50mm sky blue moiré (1820); 38mm dark blue bordered by narrow stripes of yellow and broader stripes of crimson with narrow black edges (1902); 50mm pale blue moire (1911); 50mm pink moire (1937); 50mm pale yellow silk moire (1953). These ribbons are tied in a bow and worn on the left shoulder.

Descriptions: An upright oval heavily bordered by diamonds and surmounted by a crown, also embellished in diamonds. The oval contains a miniature portrait of the sovereign in enamels.

Comments: *Awarded to female relatives of the reigning monarch. It was instituted by King George IV who conferred such orders on his sister, Princess Charlotte Augusta, wife of Frederick William, King of Wurttemberg, and his niece Princess Augusta Caroline, who married the Grand Duke of Mecklenburg-Strelitz. Queen Victoria instituted a separate Order (see next entry), but this Order was revived by King Edward VII in 1902 and continued by successive sovereigns ever since. The insignia of these Family Orders very seldom appear on the market and on account of their immense rarity they are unpriced here. Special badges are given to ladies-in-waiting.*

VALUE:

George IV	—
Edward VII	—
George V	—
George VI	—
Elizabeth II	—
Ladies-in-waiting badges	**From £1000**

10. THE ROYAL ORDER OF VICTORIA AND ALBERT

Instituted: 1862.

Ribbon: 38mm white moiré, in the form of a bow worn on the left shoulder.

Description: An upright oval onyx cameo bearing conjoined profiles of HRH Prince Albert, the Prince Consort and Queen Victoria. The badges of the First and Second Classes are set in diamonds and surmounted by an imperial crown similarly embellished, the badge of the Second Class being rather smaller. The badge of the Third Class is set in pearls, while that of the Fourth Class takes the form of a monogram "V & A" set with pearls and surmounted by an imperial crown.

Comments: *Personally awarded to female members of the Royal Family by Queen Victoria. This order became obsolete in 1981 with the death of Princess Alice, Countess of Athlone, the last surviving grandchild of Queen Victoria.*

VALUE:

First Class	From £35,000
Second Class	£25,000–30,000
Third Class	£15,000–18,000
Fourth Class	£8000–10,000

11. THE IMPERIAL ORDER OF THE CROWN OF INDIA

Instituted: January 1, 1878.

Ribbon: 38mm light blue watered silk with narrow white stripes towards the edges, formed in a bow worn on the left shoulder.

Description: A badge consisting of the royal and imperial monogram VRI in diamonds, turquoises and pearls, surrounded by an oval frame and surmounted by a jewelled imperial crown.

Comments: *Awarded by Queen Victoria to the princesses of the royal and imperial house, the wives or other female relatives of Indian princes and other Indian ladies, and of the wives or other female relatives of any of the persons who had held or were holding the offices of Viceroy and Governor-General of India, Governors of Madras or Bombay, or of Principal Secretary of State for India, as the sovereign might think fit to appoint. Her late Majesty Queen Elizabeth II was the last surviving member of the Order.*

VALUE:

From £15,000   *Miniature*   £500–600

12. THE ROYAL VICTORIAN ORDER

Instituted: April 1896.

Ribbon: Dark blue with borders of narrow red, white and red stripes on either side, 95mm (GCVO), 44mm (KCVO, DCVO and CVO), or 32mm (LVO, MVO and RVM, also all classes on uniform when insignia not worn).

KNIGHTS GRAND CROSS/DAMES GRAND CROSS (GCVO)

The insignia consists of a mantle of dark blue silk, edged with red satin, lined with white silk, and fastened by a cordon of dark blue silk and gold; a gold collar and a badge, worn only on special occasions. Knights wear the badge on the left hip from a broad ribbon worn over the right shoulder, with a star on the left breast, while Dames wear a somewhat narrower ribbon over the right shoulder with the badge, and a star similar to that of the Knights. Dames' insignia are smaller than those of the Knights.

Collar: Silver gilt composed of octagonal pieces and oblong perforated and ornamental frames alternately linked together with gold. The pieces are edged and ornamented with gold, and each contains on a blue-enamelled ground a gold rose jewelled with a carbuncle. The frames are gold and each contains a portion of inscription VICTORIA BRITT. FID. DEF. IND. IMP. in letters of white enamel. In the centre of the collar, within a perforated and ornamental frame of gold, is an octagonal piece enamelled blue, edged with red, and charged with a white saltire, superimposed by a gold medallion of Queen Victoria's effigy from which is suspended the badge.

Badge: A white-enamelled Maltese cross of eight points, in the centre of which is an oval of crimson enamel bearing the cypher VRI in gold letters. Encircling this is a blue enamel riband with the name VICTORIA in gold letters, and above this is the imperial crown enamelled in proper colours.

Star: Of chipped silver of eight points on which is mounted a white-enamelled Maltese cross with VRI in an oval at the centre.

Comments: *Awarded for extraordinary, important or personal services to the Sovereign or the Royal Family. Ladies became eligible for the Order in 1936. Most of the badges of the Royal Victorian Order are numbered on the reverse and are returnable on promotion. The early (QV) awards are unnumbered.*

GCVO star

VALUE: Knights	Dames	*Miniature*
Collar		
gold	From £15,000	From £15,000
silver gilt	From £6000	From £8000
Star and Badge (GCVO)	From £3000	From £3000	£300–400

KNIGHTS COMMANDERS (KCVO), DAMES COMMANDERS (DCVO), COMMANDERS (CVO), LIEUTENANTS (LVO) AND MEMBERS (MVO)

The insignia of the Second, Third, Fourth and Fifth Classes follows the usual pattern. Knights wear a neck badge and a breast star, Dames a breast star and a badge on the left shoulder from a ribbon tied in a bow, Commanders the same neck badge (men) or shoulder badge (women), Lieutenants a somewhat smaller breast badge worn in line with other medals and decorations (men) or a shoulder badge (women) and Members breast or shoulder badges in frosted silver instead of white enamel. The two lowest classes of the Order were originally designated member Fourth Class or member Fifth Class (MVO), but in 1984 the Fourth Class was renamed Lieutenant (LVO) and the Fifth Class simply Member (MVO).

VALUE:	Gentlemen	*Miniature*	Ladies
Neck badge and breast star (KCVO)	£2000–3500	£200–250	£1400–1800
Neck badge (CVO)	£500–600	£40–60	£450–500
Breast or shoulder badge (LVO)	£400–500	£40–60	£370–400
Breast or shoulder badge (MVO)	£350–450	£35–50	£300–350

13. ROYAL VICTORIAN MEDAL

Instituted: April 1896.
Ribbon: As for the Royal Victorian Order (above); foreign Associates, however, wear a ribbon with a central white stripe added.
Metal: Silver-gilt, silver or bronze.
Size: 30mm.
Description: (Obverse) the effigy of the reigning sovereign; (reverse) the royal cypher on an ornamental shield within a laurel wreath with ROYAL VICTORIAN MEDAL below.
Comments: *Awarded to those below the rank of officers who perform personal services to the sovereign or to members of the Royal Family. Originally awarded in silver or bronze, a higher class, in silver-gilt, was instituted by King George V. Only two medals (both silver) were issued in the brief reign of King Edward VIII (1936) and only four bronze medals were issued in the reign of King George VI. Any person in possession of the bronze medal to whom a silver medal is awarded, can wear both, and the silver-gilt medal in addition if such be conferred upon him or her. Clasps are awarded for further services to each class of the medal, while the medals may be worn in addition to the insignia of the Order if the latter is subsequently conferred. To distinguish between British and foreign recipients, King George VI decreed in 1951 that the ribbon worn by the latter should have an additional stripe, these recipients to be designated Associates. In 1983 the order for wearing this medal was altered and it was no longer to be worn after campaign medals but took precedence over them. The medal is issued unnamed. A lapel badge or emblem for members of the Order to wear on everyday clothing was introduced in 2011.*

Ribbon for foreign Associates.

Emblem worn by members when in civilian dress.

VALUE:

	Silver-gilt	Miniature	Silver	Miniature	Bronze	Miniature
Victoria	—	£85–120	£350–400	£100–150	£200–250	£85–100
Edward VII	—	—	£325–375	£85–100	£200–250	£55–80
George V	£400–450	—	£275–350	£50–85	£250–300	£25–50
Edward VIII	—	—	Rare	—	—	—
George VI	£450–500	—	£275–350	£35–50	Rare	£20–30
Elizabeth II	£400–450	—	£275–350	£35–50	£400–450	£20–30

14. THE ROYAL VICTORIAN CHAIN

Instituted: 1902.
Ribbon: None.
Metal: Silver gilt
Description: A chain consisting of three Tudor roses, two thistles, two shamrocks and two lotus flowers (the heraldic flowers of England, Scotland, Ireland and India respectively), connected by a slender double trace of gold chain. At the bottom of the front loop is a centre piece consisting of the royal cypher in enamel surrounded by a wreath and surmounted by a crown. From this centrepiece hangs a replica of the badge of a Knight Grand Cross of the Royal Victorian Order. Ladies wear the insignia in the form of a shoulder badge suspended from a miniature chain with links leading to a rose, thistle, shamrock and lotus. An even more elaborate collar, with diamonds encrusting the crown and cypher, was adopted in 1921 and there is a ladies' version of this as well.
Comments: *Sometimes regarded as the highest grade of the Royal Victorian Order, it is actually a quite separate Order and was introduced by King Edward VII for conferment as a special mark of the sovereign's favour, and then only very rarely, upon Royalty, or other especially distinguished personages, both foreign and British.*

VALUE

	Gentlemen	Ladies
Chain	From £20,000	From £20,000
Chain with diamonds	Rare	Rare

15. ORDER OF MERIT

*Order of Merit
obverse*

Instituted: 1902.
Ribbon: 50mm half blue, half crimson.
Metal: Gold.
Size: Height 80mm overall; max. width 53mm.
Description: A pattée convexed cross, enamelled red, edged blue. (Obverse) FOR MERIT in the centre surrounded by a white band and a laurel wreath enamelled in proper colours. (Reverse) the royal cypher in gold on a blue ground with a white surround and a laurel wreath as above. The cross is surmounted by a crown (changed from a Tudor crown to St Edward crown in 1990) to which is attached a ring for suspension. Naval and military recipients have crossed swords in the angles of the cross.

Comments: *This highly prestigious Order consists of the sovereign and a maximum of 24 members in one class only. There is, however, no limit on the number of foreign honorary members, although only 11 have so far been admitted to the Order. It is intended to honour exceptionally meritorious service in the Crown Services or towards the advancement of the Arts, Learning, Literature and Science or other exceptional service. To date 185 awards have been made, including only nine ladies, from Florence Nightingale (1907) to Baroness Boothroyd (2005). The insignia of those appointed since 1991 have to be returned on the death of the recipient. The insignia of members appointed prior to that date is retained, but understandably few items have come on to the market.*

*Order of Merit
reverse*

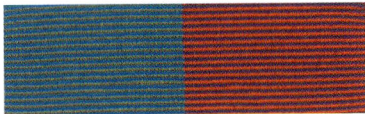

VALUE:

	Military	Civil
Edward VII	From £25,000	From £15,000
George V	From £25,000	From £15,000
George VI	Very Rare	From £15,000
Elizabeth II	Rare	From £10,000
Miniature	£250–300	

16. THE MOST EXCELLENT ORDER OF THE BRITISH EMPIRE

GBE Star (2nd type)

Instituted: June 1917.

Ribbon: Originally purple, with a narrow central scarlet stripe for the Military Division; since 1936 rose-pink edged with pearl grey, with a narrow central stripe of pearl-grey for the Military Division. A silver crossed oakleaf emblem for gallantry was instituted in 1957. 100mm with 6mm edge stripes (57mm with 4mm edge stripes for ladies) (GBE); 44mm with 2.5mm edge stripes (KBE/DBE/CBE); 38mm with 2.5mm edge stripes (OBE/MBE); 32mm with 1.6mm edge stripes (BEM).

Comments: *Founded by King George V during the First World War for services to the Empire at home, in India and in the overseas dominions and colonies, other than those rendered by the Navy and Army, although it could be conferred upon officers of the armed forces for services of a non-combatant character. A Military Division was created in December 1918 and awards made to commissioned officers and warrant officers in respect of distinguished service in action. The insignia of the Civil and Military Divisions is identical, distinguished only by the respective ribbons. A promotion in a different division permits the wear of both types of insignia and in the case of gallantry awards a third type may be worn. A lapel emblem for wear on ordinary clothing was introduced in December 2006.*

KNIGHTS/DAMES GRAND CROSS (GBE)

The insignia includes a mantle of rose-pink satin lined with pearl-grey silk, tied by a cord of pearl-grey silk, with two rose-pink and silver tassels attached. On the left side of the mantle is a representation of the star of the First Class of the Order. The mantle, collar and collar badge are only worn on special occasions. In dress uniform, however, the badge is worn over the left hip from a broad (96mm) riband passing over the right shoulder, while Dames wear the badge from a narrower (57mm) ribbon in a bow on the left shoulder; both with the breast star of the Order.

Collar: Silver-gilt with medallions of the royal arms and of the royal and imperial cypher of King George V alternately linked together with cables. In the centre is the imperial crown between two sea lions. The collar for Dames is somewhat narrower than that for Knights.

Star: An eight-pointed star of silver chips on which is superimposed the enamelled medallion as for the badge (Britannia or George V and Queen Mary). The star worn by Dames is smaller.

Badge: A cross patonce in silver-gilt, the arms enamelled pearl-grey. In the centre, within a circle enamelled crimson, the figure of Britannia, replaced since 1936 by the conjoined left-facing crowned busts of King George V and Queen Mary, surrounded by a circle inscribed FOR GOD AND THE EMPIRE.

Emblem worn by Members of the Order in civilian dress.

CBE Badge (2nd type)

VALUE:	1st type Britannia	2nd type King & Queen
Knights Grand Cross		
Collar	Rare	Rare
Badge and star	£3000–4000	£3000–4000
Dames Grand Cross		
Collar	From £6000	From £6000
Badge and star	£3000–4000	£3000–4000
Miniature stars	£300–350	£300–350

16. THE MOST EXCELLENT ORDER OF THE BRITISH EMPIRE continued

KBE Star

KNIGHTS COMMANDERS (KBE), DAMES COMMANDERS (DBE), COMMANDERS (CBE), OFFICERS (OBE) AND MEMBERS (MBE)

The insignia of these five Classes follows the same pattern as other Orders. Both Britannia and King and Queen medallion types have been issued.

Star: A star of four large points and four minor points in chipped silver, with the enamelled medallion superimposed. The star worn by Dames is smaller.

Neck Badge: Similar to the badge of the GBE but smaller and worn from a 44mm ribbon round the neck (men) or from a shoulder bow (ladies). Worn by KBE, DBE and CBE.

Breast Badge: As above, but in silver-gilt (OBE) or frosted silver (MBE), with shoulder versions for ladies, worn with a 38mm ribbon.

Gallantry Award: An emblem of silver crossed oak leaves was added to the ribbon of the CBE, OBE and MBE (1957–74).

Oak leaf emblem for gallantry (smaller when ribbon only worn).

VALUE:	1st type Britannia	Miniature	2nd type King&Queen	Miniature
Badge and Star (KBE)	£1500–2000	£250–300	£1200–1500	£285–345
Badge and Star (DBE)	£1500–2000		£1200–1500	
Neck badge (CBE)	£350–400	£35–50	£350–400	£40–55
Shoulder badge (CBE)	£350–400		£350–400	
Breast badge (OBE)	£200–250	£15–25	£180–200	£20–40
Shoulder badge (OBE)	£200–250		£180–200	
Breast badge (MBE)	£200–250	£15–25	£180–200	£20–40
Shoulder badge (MBE)	£200–250		£180–200	

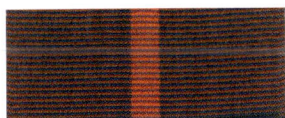

Ribbons: (top to bottom) OBE (Military) 1st type, OBE (Military) 2nd type, OBE (Civil) 1st type, OBE (Civil) 2nd type.

OBE badge (silver-gilt) and reverse of the MBE badge (frosted silver).

17. MEDAL OF THE ORDER OF THE BRITISH EMPIRE

Civil ribbon

Military ribbon

Instituted: June 1917.
Ribbon: 32mm plain purple (Civil), with a narrow scarlet central stripe (Military).
Medal: Silver.
Size: 30mm.
Description: (Obverse) a seated figure of Britannia facing right, her left arm extended and her right holding a trident, with the inscription FOR GOD AND THE EMPIRE round the upper part of the circumference; (reverse) the royal and imperial cypher GRI surmounted by a Tudor crown, the whole enclosed in a cable circle. Fitted with a plain ring for suspension.
Comments: *Instituted as a lower award connected with the Order, it consisted originally of a Civil Division, but a Military Division, distinguishable solely by the ribbon, was added in December 1918. This medal was issued unnamed but many were subsequently engraved or impressed on the rim privately. Fewer than 2000 medals were awarded before they were discontinued in 1922.*

VALUE:

		Miniature
Medal unnamed as issued	£375–450	£85–125
Attributable medal	£550–850	

18. EMPIRE GALLANTRY MEDAL

1st type rev.

Instituted: December 29, 1922.
Ribbon: Originally plain purple (Civil), with a thin scarlet central stripe (Military); from July 1937 rose-pink with pearl-grey edges (Civil) and a central pearl-grey stripe (Military). A silver laurel branch was added to the ribbon (1933), with a smaller version for wear on the ribbon alone.
Metal: Silver.
Size: 36mm.
Description: (Obverse) the seated figure of Britannia, her left hand resting on a shield and her right holding a trident, with a blazing sun upper right. The words FOR GOD AND THE EMPIRE inscribed round the upper part of the circumference, with FOR in the wave lower left above the exergue which bears the word GALLANTRY. (Reverse) 1st type has six lions passant gardant, with the Royal cypher in the centre surmounted by an imperial crown. The George VI issue has four lions, two either side and round the foot, in two concentric arcs, the words INSTITUTED BY KING GEORGE V. It is suspended from a straight bar ornamented with laurel leaves. Named in seriffed capitals engraved round the rim.
Comments: *This medal, officially known as the Medal of the Order of the British Empire for Gallantry, replaced the Medal of the Order of the British Empire and was awarded for specific acts of gallantry. It was abolished on the institution of the George Cross in September 1940, while it was announced in the London Gazette of April 22, 1941 that a recipient still living on September 24, 1940 but including posthumous awards after September 3, 1939 should return it to the Central Chancery of the Orders of Knighthood and become a holder of the George Cross instead. Not all EGMs, however, were exchanged or returned. Only 130 medals were issued, 64 being civil, 62 military and four honorary.*

VALUE:

		Miniature
George V	£5000–7000	£170–230
George VI	£5000–7000	£170–230

Civil 1922

Military 1922

Civil 1937
(emblem smaller when ribbon only worn).

Military 1937

19. BRITISH EMPIRE MEDAL

Instituted: December 1922.
Ribbon: As MYB 18, but without the silver laurel branch.
Metal: Silver.
Size: 36mm. Specimens are known up to 37.5mm.
Description: As MYB 18 above, but with the words MERITORIOUS
SERVICE in the exergue. Suspended from a straight bar
ornamented with oak leaves. A silver bar decorated with oak
leaves was introduced in March 1941 for further acts, and is
denoted by a silver rosette on the ribbon worn on its own. An
emblem of crossed silver oak leaves was introduced in December
1957 to denote a gallantry award, a smaller version being worn
on the ribbon alone. Named in engraved capitals round the rim.

Comments: *Formally entitled the Medal of the Order of the British Empire
for Meritorious Service, it is generally known simply as the British
Empire Medal. It is awarded for meritorious service by both civil and
military personnel although for some years it was issued as a third grade
bravery award, particularly for air raid deeds not considered to be of
the level of the GC or GM. The medal may be worn even if the recipient
is promoted to a higher grade of the Order. The gallantry awards,
instituted in December 1957, ceased in 1974 on the introduction of the
Queen's Gallantry Medal. No British awards were made for the BEM
between 1995 and 2012 although Commonwealth awards were still
being made, however, the medal was resurrected for Her Majesty the
late Queen's Diamond Jubilee Honours List for civilians only with over
250 awards announced. The Order of the British Empire emblem for
gallantry instituted in December 2006 (qv) may also be worn by holders
of the BEM.*

Civil 1922

Military 1922

Civil 1937

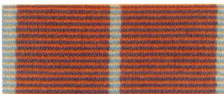

Military 1937

BEM Gallantry Emblem

VALUE:

	Military	Civil	Miniature
George V	£450–550	£300–400	£25–40
George VI GRI cypher	£350–450	£150–200	£20–35
George VI GVIR cypher	£350–450	£150–200	£20–35
Elizabeth II	£350–450	£150–200	£20–35
Elizabeth II with gallantry emblem	£850–1000	£750–850	—

20.   THE ORDER OF THE COMPANIONS OF HONOUR

Instituted: June 1917.
Ribbon: 38mm carmine with borders of gold thread.
Metal: Silver gilt.
Size: Height 48mm; max. width 29mm.
Description: An oval badge consisting of a medallion with an oak tree, a shield bearing the royal arms hanging from one branch, and on the left a knight armed and in armour, mounted on a horse. The badge has a blue border with the motto IN ACTION FAITHFUL AND IN HONOUR CLEAR in gold letters. The oval is surmounted by an imperial crown. Gentlemen wear the badge round their necks, while ladies wear it from a bow at the left shoulder.
Comments: *Instituted at the same time as the Order of the British Empire, it carries no title or precedence although the post-nominal letters CH are used. The Order consists of the sovereign and one class of members. Not more than 50 men or women who have rendered conspicuous service of national importance were admitted, but in 1943 this was increased to 65. The Order is awarded in Britain and the Commonwealth on a quota basis: UK (45), Australia (7), New Zealand (2), other countries (11). It is awarded for outstanding achievements in the arts, literature, music, science, politics, industry and religion.*

VALUE

Gentlemen	£3000–3500	
Ladies	£3000–3500	
Miniature	Uniface £200–250	Monogrammed reverse £300–400

21. THE BARONET'S BADGE

Instituted: 1629.
Ribbon: 30mm orange watered silk (Nova Scotia); 44mm orange bordered with narrow blue edges (other Baronets).
Metal: Gold or silver-gilt.
Size: Height 55mm; max. width 41mm(Nova Scotia) or 44mm (later badges).
Description: An upright oval badge with a plain ring suspension. The badge of the Baronets of Nova Scotia was originally skeletal, with a shield bearing the lion rampant of Scotland, decorated with pearls and enamels, surmounted by a Scottish crown and surrounded by a blue border inscribed in gold FAX MENTIS HONESTAE GLORIA. The remaining badges (authorised in 1929) have a solid ground and a central shield with the red hand of Ulster surmounted by a crown and a border of gold and blue enamel decorated with roses (England), shamrocks (Ireland), roses and thistles combined (Great Britain) or roses, thistles and shamrocks combined (United Kingdom). Often engraved on the reverse with the recipient's title and date of creation.
Comments: *By Letter Patent of 1611 James I created Baronets whose knighthood became hereditary. In 1624, to raise money independently of Parliament, James I sold grants of land in Nova Scotia (New Scotland) to Scotsmen. In 1625 Charles I conferred on the holders of this land the title and dignity of Baronets of Nova Scotia with the title of Sir, and decreed that they should wear round their necks "an orange tawny ribbon whereon shall be pendent an escutcheon". After the Union with England (1707) English and Scottish baronetcies ceased to be created, being replaced by baronetcies of Great Britain. Irish baronetcies continued to be created until 1801 after which all new creations were of the United Kingdom.*

Baronet's badge—United Kingdom

(Nova Scotia)

(other Baronets)

VALUE:	Gold	Silver-gilt
Nova Scotia, 18th–early 19th centuries	£3500–4500	£850–1000
Nova Scotia, late 19th and 20th centuries	£2000–2500	£850–1000
England (rose surround)	£1000–1500	£800–1000
Ireland (shamrock surround)	£1000–1500	£800–1000
Great Britain (roses and thistles)	£1000–1500	£800–1000
United Kingdom (roses, thistles and shamrocks)	£1000–1500	£800–1000

22. THE KNIGHT BACHELOR'S BADGE

Instituted: April 21, 1926.
Ribbon: 38mm scarlet with broad yellow borders.
Metal: Silver-gilt and enamels. Some pre-war breast badges are in base metal.
Size: Height 76.50mm; max. width 56.50mm. Reduced in 1933 to 63.25mm and in 1973 to 54mm.
Description: An upright oval medallion enclosed by a scroll, bearing a cross-hilted sword, belted and sheathed, pommel upwards, between two spurs, rowels upwards, the whole set about with the sword-belt.
Comments: *The title Knight Bachelor (KB) was introduced by King Henry III to signify a battelier (one who fought in battle). The badge was authorised by King George V in response to a request from the Imperial Society of Knights Bachelors who wished to have a distinctive badge denoting their rank. The original badge was of the dimensions given above and affixed to the breast by means of a pin on the reverse. This badge was reduced in size in 1933 and again in 1973 when it was fitted with a ring for suspension by a ribbon round the neck. On 4 December 1998 Her late Majesty Queen Elizabeth II signed an amending warrant permitting recipients of this honour to wear both a neck badge and breast badge.*

Emblem worn in civilian dress.

VALUE:

		Miniature
First type breast badge (1926–32)	£550–650	£55–75
Smaller type breast badge (1933–72)	£450–550	(Skeletal type
Neck badge (1973–)	£450–550	£40–55)

23. THE ORDER OF ST JOHN

Neck badge

Emblem worn in civilian dress

Shoulder badge

Instituted: May 14, 1888 and at various dates in other countries.

Ribbon: Plain black watered silk. Sash ribbons for Bailiffs, 102mm; Dames Grand Cross, 57mm. Ribbons for Knights, 51mm; Ribbons for Dames were formerly in a 32mm bow and ribbons for Commanders, officers and Serving Brothers 38mm and 32mm for ladies, but under new regulations (October 2001) all ribbons below Grand Cross are now standardised at 38mm. In 1947, for all grades of the Order, when the ribbon only is worn, a small Maltese Cross in silver is carried on the ribbon to distinguish it against a dark background.

Metal: Gold, silver-gilt and silver, or base metal.

Sash badge: An eight-pointed gold Maltese cross in white enamel with two lions and two unicorns in the angles (*other countries have different beasts in the angles*). Confined to Bailiffs and Dames Grand Cross.

Neck badge: Hitherto in the grades Knight/Dame, Commander and Officer badges worn by women were smaller than those worn by men, but in 2001 this distinction was abolished. The badges worn by Knights of Justice and Chaplains are in gold, while those worn by Knights of Grace and Commanders are in silver.

Star: The eight-pointed Maltese cross in white enamel without the lions and unicorns (Grand Cross and Justice) or with lions and unicorns (Grace and Sub-Prelate). A sub-Prelate is an Order Chaplain (so his badge is included above) who held high rank in the Church as distinct from the Order. The order ceased appointing Sub-Prelates in 1999, and as a result the Sub-Prelate's star (gilt with beasts) is now obsolescent.

Shoulder badge: Worn by Dames of Justice in gold and Dames of Grace, Commanders, Serving Sisters and Officers (Sisters) in silver. It is now mounted on a ribbon with "tails" as in other British orders.

Breast badges: (Officers) The Order badge with beasts (UK lion and unicorn) in angles, from 1926 until 1936 in silver, from 1936 to date the arms of the cross have been enamelled in white.

(Serving Brothers/Sisters, from 2012 known as Members) originally in silver and enamel, in white metal or rhodium subsequently. Those worn by Serving Brothers/Members have undergone six main phases:

  1892–1939: a circular badge with white enamel cross and silver beasts raised above the surface of the black enamel medal in a silver rim (two types of suspender) (type 1 & 2).

  1939–1949: circular skeletal badge with ring suspension and the cross set in a silver rim, no black background (type 3).

  1949–1974: the first badge resumed but with different ring suspender (type 4).

  1974–1984: a badge of the same design but with the cross and beasts flush with their background (type 5).

  1984–1991: the cross and beasts in white metal alone with no background or rim, slightly smaller than the Officer (Brother) cross and the whole convex on the obverse (type 6).

  Since 1991: cross and beasts thicker, with each arm raised and shaped on both sides of a central channel, the whole in rhodium (type 7).

A woman Officer or Serving Sister (from 2012 known as a Member) in uniform was originally invested with her breast badge on a bow but since 1999 a straight ribbon has been used.

Donats' badges: Gold, silver or bronze, consisting of the badge of the Order with the upper arm of the cross replaced by an ornamental piece of metal for suspension.

Comments: *The Most Venerable Order of the Hospital of St John of Jerusalem was incorporated by Royal Charter of Queen Victoria and granted the epithet Venerable in 1926 and Most in 1955; despite its title, it has no connection*

Serving Brothers/Sisters breast badge.

1st type (1892–early 1930s). *2nd type (late 1930s).* *3rd type (Wartime issue up to 1947).* *4th type (1948– c. 1973).*

5th type (1974–84). *6th type (1984–91).* *7th type (1991–).*

with the Knights Hospitallers of Jerusalem, who were subsequently based at Rhodes and Malta and now have their headquarters in Rome. In 1926 the Order was reorganised into five Classes like certain other Orders. A sixth class was added later. Both men and women are eligible for membership. His Majesty the King is the Sovereign Head of the Order. Next in authority is the Grand Prior, followed by Bailiffs and Dames Grand Cross, Chaplains, Knights and Dames of Justice, Knights and Dames of Grace, Commanders, Officers, Serving Brothers and Sisters and Esquires. Associates were people who were not citizens of the United Kingdom, the British Commonwealth or the Republic of Ireland, or are non-Christians, who have rendered conspicuous service to the Order and may be attached to any grade of the Order. They wear the insignia of that grade, at one time distinguished only by a central narrow white stripe on the ribbon, but now all ribbons are identical. Donats are people who have made generous contributions to the funds of the Order. They are not enrolled as members of the Order but receive badges in gold, silver or bronze. The Statutes and Regulations were revised in 2004. The grade of Chaplain (gold badge) was abolished, but existing Chaplains could retain their insignia or be regarded as Commanders. Before 1999 a Chaplain could be appointed a Sub-Prelate if he held high office in the Church. A sub-Prelate wore the badge of a Chaplain and also a star with gilt lions and unicorns. Those few remaining have now been renamed Honorary Sub-Prelates, a term revived to designate the senior ecclesiastical officer of a Priory. This appointment carries no distinctive insignia.

VALUE:	Gold	Silver/Gilt	Bronze	*Miniature*
Bailiff badge and star	£2500–3000	£800–1000	—	
Dame Grand Cross	£2500–3000	£600–750	—	
Knight of Justice neck badge and star	£1000–1500	£500–650	£200–300	
Dame of Justice shoulder badge and star	£1000–1500	£500–650	£200–300	
Knight of Grace neck badge and star	—	£350–450	£175–275	
Dame of Grace shoulder badge and star	—	£350–450	£175–275	£25–40
Sub-Prelate neck badge		£200–250	£75–100	
Commander (Brother) neck badge	—	£200–250	£75–100	
Commander (Sister) shoulder badge	—	£50–75	£35–50	
Officer				
1926–36 Silver	—	£85–100	—	
From 1936 Silver with white enamelling	—	£100–150	—	
Serving Brother/Sister (since 2012, this grade was replaced by "Member") breast badge				
1st or 2nd type	—	£65–85	—	£50–70
3rd type	—	£50–75	—	£50–70
4th or 5th type	—	£50–75	—	£30–40
6th or 7th type	—	£50–75	—	£20–30
Donat's badge	£250–300	£55–85	£45–55	£35–50

DECORATIONS

The award of decorations for distinguished military service is an ancient institution. In his Antiquities of the Jews, the historian Josephus relates that, in the second century BC, King Alexander was so pleased with Jonathan the High Priest that he sent him a gold button as a mark of favour for his skill in leading the Jews in battle. Subsequently Jonathan was presented with a second gold button for his gallant conduct in the field, making these incidents among the earliest recorded for which specific military awards were granted. The award of jewels, gold buttons and badges for valour was carried on in most European countries on a sporadic basis but the present system of decorations is essentially a modern one dating back no farther than the middle of the seventeenth century. Earlier medals were quasi-commemorative and include the famous Armada Medal of 1588. A few medals in silver or gold were awarded to officers for distinguished service during the English Civil War, although the first "official" rewards in Britain were probably those issued by Parliament to naval officers following their victories over the Dutch fleet in 1653.

Decorations may be divided into those awarded for individual acts of heroism and those conferred in recognition of distinguished military, political or social service. In general terms collectors prefer a decoration awarded for bravery in the field rather than a political honour given automatically to a civil servant, just because he happens to have been in a particular grade for a certain number of years. The debasement of civil awards, such as the OBE and MBE, is reflected in the relative lack of interest shown by collectors.

It is generally true to say that military decorations are more desirable, but it is important to note that one decoration may be more highly prized than another, while the same decoration may well be more valuable to collectors when issued in one period rather than in another. At one extreme is the greatly coveted Victoria Cross, few of which (including three bars) have been awarded since its inception. VCs won during the Crimean War (111 awarded) are usually less highly regarded than Crosses awarded during the First World War, where, although numerically greater (633) they were far more dearly won. Second World War Crosses are correspondingly more expensive as only 182 were awarded and even now comparatively few of them have ever come on to the market. Today, while pre-1914 Crosses would rate at least £100,000 and those from the First World War slightly more, Second World War Crosses start around £150,000 but have been known to fetch several times as much, depending on the precise circumstances and the branch of the services.

At the other extreme is the Military Medal, of which no fewer than 115,589 were awarded during the First World War alone. For this reason a MM from this period can still be picked up for under £600, whereas one from the Second World War would usually fetch about four times as much, and awards made during the minor campaigns of the 1930s or the Korean War often rate at least ten times as much.

The value of a decoration, where its provenance can be unquestionably established, depends largely on the decoration itself, whether awarded to an officer or an enlisted man, the individual circumstances of the award, the campaign or action concerned, the regiment, unit or ship involved, and the often very personal details of the act or acts of bravery. These factors are extraordinarily difficult to quantify, hence the frequent large discrepancies in the prices fetched by decorations at auction.

The addition of even relatively common decorations, such as the Military Cross or the Military Medal to the average First World War campaign medal group, invariably enhances its value very considerably while the addition of bars for subsequent awards likewise rates a good premium. Decorations awarded to officers tend to fetch more than those awarded to other ranks, mainly because they are proportionately rarer but also because it is usually easier to trace the career details of an officer.

Sometimes the rank of the recipient may have a bearing on the demand for a particular decoration: e.g. Military Crosses awarded to warrant officers are scarcer than those awarded to subalterns and captains. The branch of the armed services may also have some bearing. Thus a Military Medal awarded to a member of the RAF rates far higher than one awarded to a soldier, while a medal awarded to a seaman in one of the naval battalions which fought on the Western Front is also equally desirable.

Initially the Distinguished Service Order could be won by commissioned officers of any rank but after 1914, when the Military Cross was instituted, it was usually restricted to officers of field rank. DSOs awarded to lieutenants and captains in the Army in both World Wars are therefore comparatively rare and invariably expensive, usually as they were awarded for acts of heroism which in earlier campaigns might have merited the VC. As part of the 1993 review of awards, the Conspicuous Gallantry Coss (CGC) replaced the DCM and CGM to remove the distinction between officers and other ranks.

The opportunity for individual acts of bravery varied from service to service, and in different conflicts. Thus sailors in the Second World War generally had less scope than air crew. Consequently specifically naval awards, such as the Conspicuous Gallantry Medal and the Distinguished Service Cross, are much more scarce than the corresponding RAF awards for Conspicuous Gallantry and the Distinguished Flying Cross.

The addition of bars to gallantry decorations greatly enhances the scarcity and value of such medals. The VC, for example, has been won by only three men on two occasions; none of these VC and bar combinations has ever come on the market, but should one come up for sale, it is certain that the price would be spectacular. The average First World War MM is today worth around £500, but with a bar for second award its value immediately jumps to about three times as much, while MMs with two or more bars are very much more expensive.

It is important to note that in some cases (the DSO for example) decorations were issued unnamed; for this reason the citation or any other supporting documents relevant to the award should be kept with the decoration wherever possible to confirm its attribution.

Engraving of Gallantry Decorations

After the special investiture for the South Atlantic campaign held on February 8, 1983, the question as to why certain awards were engraved with the date only was raised within the Ministry of Defence. A joint service working party considered the matter and recommended that procedures for all decorations and medals for gallantry in the face of the enemy and for the Air Force Cross when awarded for a specific act of gallantry should be brought into line. A submission was accordingly made to the late Queen by the Committee on the Grant of Honours, Decorations and Medals and in April 1984 Her Majesty approved the following:

(i)   That the Distinguished Service Cross, Military Cross, Distinguished Flying Cross and Air Force Cross when awarded for gallantry should be engraved with the personal details of the recipient with effect from January 1, 1984.

(ii) That there should be no retrospection;

(iii) That the badge of a Companion of the Distinguished Service Order should not be engraved (in common with the badges of other orders); and

(iv) That the Royal Red Cross (RRC and ARRC) and the Air Force Cross when awarded for meritorious service should not be engraved.

Condition

The same terms are applied to describe the condition of medals and decorations as apply to coins, although the wear to which they are put is caused by other factors. In modern times, when the number of occasions on which medals are worn are relatively few and far between, the condition of most items will be found to be Very Fine (VF) to Extremely Fine (EF). Indeed, in many cases, the medals may never have been worn at all. A good proportion of Second World War medals and decorations are found in almost mint condition as they were not issued till long after the war, by which time their recipients had been demobilised. In some cases they even turn up still in the original cardboard box in which they were posted to the recipients or their next-of-kin.

Before the First World War, however, the wearing of medals was customary on all but the most informal occasions and when actually serving on active duty. Thus medals could be, and often were, subject to a great deal of wear. Medals worn by cavalrymen are often found in poor condition, with scratches and edge knocks occasioned by the constant jangling of one medal against another while on horseback. Often the medals in a group have an abrasive effect on each other. For this reason the Queen's Medal for Egypt (1882) for example, is comparatively rare in excellent condition, as it was usually worn in juxtaposition to the bronze Khedive's Star whose points were capable of doing considerable damage to its silver companion.

Apart from these factors it should also be remembered that part of the ritual of "spit and polish" involved cleaning one's medals and they were therefore submitted to vigorous cleaning with metal polish over long periods of service.

For these reasons medals are often sold by dealers "as worn"—a euphemism which conceals a lifetime of hardy service on the chest of some grizzled veteran. Because of the strong personal element involved in medal-collecting, however, genuine wear does not affect the value of a medal to the same degree that it would in other branches of numismatics. There is a school of thought which considers that such signs enhance the interest and value of a medal or group.

This line of thinking also explains the controversy over medal ribbons. Some military outfitters still carry extensive stocks of medal ribbons covering every campaign from Waterloo onwards, so that it is a very easy matter to obtain a fresh length of ribbon for any medal requiring it, and there is no doubt that the appearance of a piece is greatly improved by a clean, bright new ribbon. On the other hand, that ribbon was not the one actually worn by Corporal Bloggs on parade and, to the purist, it would spoil the total effect of the medal. Some collectors therefore retain the original ribbon, even though it may be faded and frayed. As ribbons are things which one cannot authenticate, however, there seems to be little material benefit to be gained from clinging rigidly to a tattered strip of silk when an identical piece can be obtained relatively cheaply. In reality, most collectors compromise by obtaining new ribbons while preserving the old lengths out of sentiment.

The prices quoted in this publication are average figures for medals and decorations as individual items. Combinations with other decorations and campaign medals will produce a value usually well in excess of the aggregate of the individual items. Value will depend to a large extent on the personal factors and circumstances of the award, but where general factors are involved (e.g. the design of the medal, the period of issue or the campaign concerned, or in some cases the branch of the services) these are itemised separately. "—" indicates that either no examples have come onto the market or no examples have been issued. The figure in brackets (where available) is the approximate number awarded. In the lists which follow, it should be assumed that decorations were instituted by Royal Warrant, unless otherwise stated.

SELLING YOUR MEDALS?

Warwick and Warwick have an expanding requirement for medal collections, medal groups and related documentation and individual medals of value. Our customer base is increasing dramatically and we need an ever larger supply of quality material to keep pace with demand. The market has never been stronger and if you are considering the sale of your medals, now is the time to act.

FREE VALUATIONS
We will provide a free, professional and without obligation valuation of your collection. Either we will make you a fair, binding private treaty offer, or we will recommend inclusion of your property in our next specialist public auction.

FREE TRANSPORTATION
We can arrange insured transportation of your collection to our Warwick offices completely free of charge. If you decline our offer, we ask you to cover the return carriage costs only.

FREE VISITS
Visits by our valuers are possible anywhere in the country, usually within 48 hours, in order to value larger collections. Please telephone for details.

EXCELLENT PRICES
Because of the strength of our customer base we are in a position to offer prices that we feel sure will exceed your expectations.

ACT NOW
Telephone or email Richard Beale today with details of your property.

ONLINE BIDDING
Available via www.easyliveauction.com.

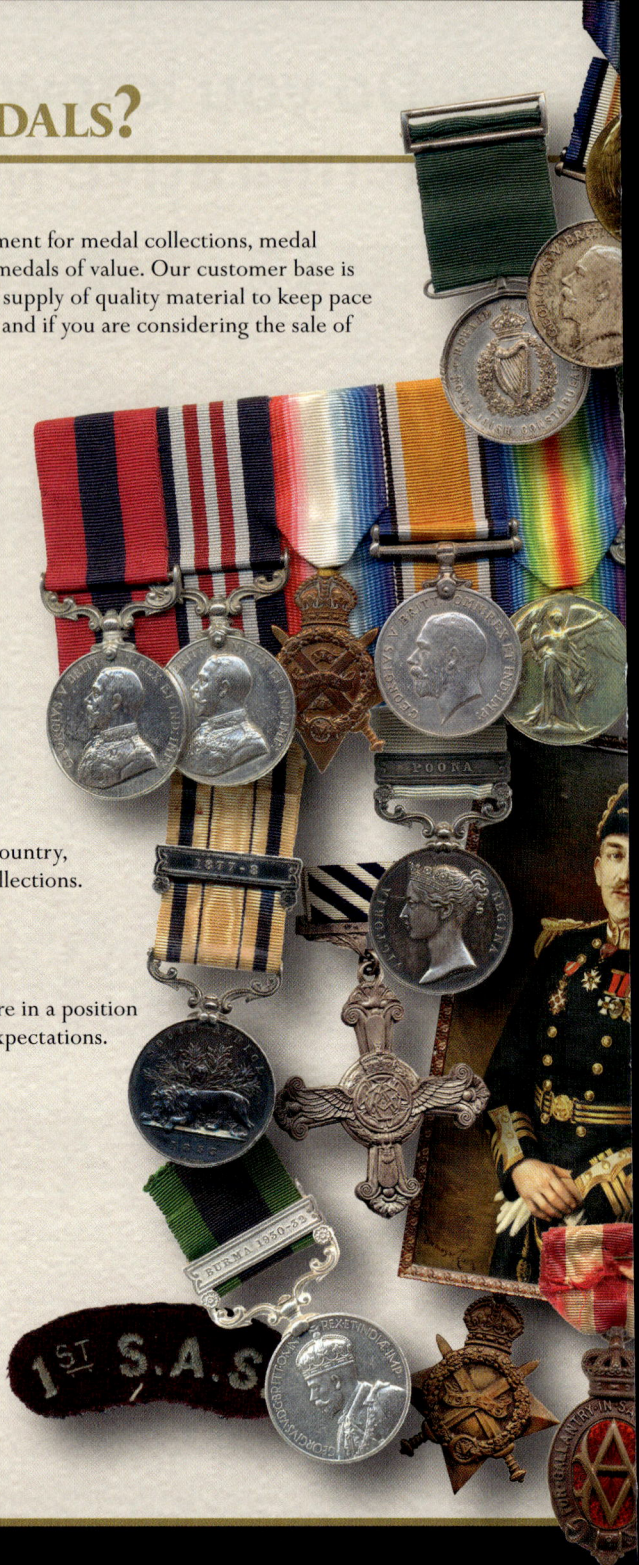

24. THE VICTORIA CROSS

Naval ribbon pre-1918.   *Naval, Army and RAF ribbon since 1918.*

Instituted: January 1856.

Ribbon: Crimson. Originally naval crosses used a dark blue ribbon, but since 1918 the crimson (Army) ribbon has been used for all awards. A miniature cross emblem is worn on the ribbon alone in undress uniform.

Metal: Bronze, originally from Russian guns captured in the Crimea. Modern research, however, reveals that guns captured in other conflicts, e.g. China, have also been used at various periods.

Size: Height 41mm; max. width 36mm.

Description: A cross pattée. (Obverse) a lion statant gardant on the royal crown, with the words FOR VALOUR on a semi-circular scroll. (Reverse) a circular panel on which is engraved the date of the act for which the decoration was awarded. The Cross is suspended by a ring from a seriffed "V" attached to a suspension bar decorated with laurel leaves. The reverse of the suspension bar is engraved with the name, rank and ship, regiment or squadron of the recipient.

Comments: *Introduced as the premier award for gallantry, available for all ranks, to cover all actions since the outbreak of the Crimean War in 1854, it was allegedly created on the suggestion of Prince Albert, the Prince Consort. Of the 1,358 awards since 1856, 836 have gone to the Army, 107 to the Navy, 31 to the RAF, ten to the Royal Marines and four to civilians. Second award bars have been awarded three times. The facility for posthumous awards, made retrospective to 1856, began in 1902 and was confirmed in 1907, while the early practice of forfeitures (eight between 1863 and 1908) was discontinued after the First World War. Two posthumous awards were made in the Falklands War, 1982. In 2005 Private Johnson Beharry was awarded the VC for valour in Iraq, and since then two posthumous awards have been made for Afghanistan: Corporal Bryan Budd in 2006 and Lance Corporal James Ashworth in 2012. The latest award is to L/Cpl Joshua Leakey of the Parachute Regiment (LG February 26, 2015) also for Afghanistan. In 2015 the Government increased the annuity paid to £10,000, tax free.*

VALUE:

	Royal Navy/Army	RFC/RAF	Miniature
1856–1914 (522)	From £150,000	—	£50–80
1914–18 (633)	From £175,000	From £200,000	£20–35
1920–45 (187)	From £200,000	From £250,000	£20–35
post-1945 (15)	From £250,000	—	£10–20

NB: These prices can only be construed as a general guide. Quite a few awards would exceed these price ranges, particularly Commonwealth examples or those appertaining to well known actions. A new world-record price for a VC sold at auction was achieved by Noonans auctioneers in September 2022 when a "civilian" VC awarded to Thomas Kavanagh secured £750,000 (£930,000 total).

25. NEW ZEALAND CROSS

Instituted: 10 March 1869 (by an Order in Council, Wellington).

Ribbon: 38mm crimson. A silver miniature cross emblem is worn on the ribbon alone.

Metal: Silver with gold appliqué.

Size: Height 52mm; max. width 38mm.

Description: A silver cross pattée with a six-pointed gold star on each limb. In the centre are the words NEW ZEALAND within a gold laurel wreath. The cross is surmounted by a gold Tudor crown which is attached by a ring and a seriffed "V" to a silver bar ornamented with gold laurel leaves, through which the ribbon passes. The recipient's name and details are engraved on the reverse.

Comments: *The rarest of all gallantry awards, it was conferred for bravery during the second series of Maori Wars (1860-72). Only 23 Crosses were awarded, the last being authorised in 1910. This medal was called into being solely because local volunteer forces were not eligible for the VC. Today the Cross, with slight amendments to the design, is New Zealand's premier civilian award for bravery (see NZ2).*

VALUE:

	From £75,000	
	Official Specimen	£3000–4000
	Modern copy	£650–750
	Miniature	
	Contemporary	£750–1000
	Modern copy	£20–25

26. GEORGE CROSS

Instituted: 24 September 1940.

Ribbon: 38mm dark blue (originally 32mm). A silver miniature cross emblem is worn on the ribbon alone.

Metal: Silver.

Size: Height 49.75mm; max. width 45.85mm.

Description: A plain bordered cross with a circular medallion in the centre depicting the effigy of St George and the Dragon after Benedetto Pistrucci, surrounded by the words FOR GALLANTRY. In the angle of each limb is the Royal cypher GVI. The plain reverse bears in the centre the name of the recipient and date of the award. In the case of exchange awards, the date of the deed is given. The Cross hangs by a ring from a bar adorned with laurel leaves.

Comments: *The highest gallantry award for civilians, as well as for members of the armed forces in actions for which purely military honours would not normally be granted. It superseded the Empire Gallantry Medal whose holders were then required to return it and receive the GC in exchange. By Warrant of December 1971 surviving recipients of the Albert and Edward Medals were also invited to exchange their awards for the GC. Perhaps the most famous Cross was that conferred on the island of Malta in recognition of its gallantry during the Second World War. To date no second award bars have been awarded. Since its inception in 1940 the George Cross has been awarded 165 times, including four women (85 of these have been posthumous). In addition, 112 Empire Gallantry medallists, 69 Albert medallists and 70 Edward medallists who were eligible to exchange their awards for the GC have increased the total to 416. This also includes the collective award to the Royal Ulster Constabulary, presented by Her late Majesty Queen Elizabeth II at Hillsborough Castle on April 12, 2000. On July 5, 2021, the 73rd anniversary of its founding, the National Health Service was awarded a collective GC in recognition of its service to the country, particularly during the Covid pandemic. Arthur Bywater (who died in April 2005) was the only civilian to win both the GC and the GM but seven servicemen have won both. In 2015 the Government increased the annuity to £10,000.*

VALUE:

Service awards 1940 to date	From £30,000	
Civilian awards 1940 to date	From £25,000	
Service exchange pre-1940	From £12,000	
Civilian exchange pre-1940	From £12,000	

Miniature **£15–20** (*in silver add £10*)

27. DISTINGUISHED SERVICE ORDER

Instituted: 1886.
Ribbon: 29mm crimson with dark blue edges.
Metal: Originally gold; silver-gilt with 18 carat gold centre since 1889.
Size: Height 44mm; max. width 41.5mm.
Description: A cross with curved ends, overlaid with white enamel. (Obverse) a green enamel laurel wreath enclosing an imperial crown on a red enamel background; (reverse) the royal monogram within a similar wreath. The ribbon is hung from a top laureated bar and the cross is suspended from the ribbon by a swivel ring and another straight laureated bar. Additional awards are denoted by bars ornamented by a crown. Silver rosettes on the ribbon alone are worn in undress uniform. Since its inception, the DSO has been issued unnamed, but since 1938 the year of award has been engraved on the reverse of the lower suspension bar as well as the reverse of the bars for second or subsequent awards.
Comments: *Intended to reward commissioned officers below field rank for distinguished service in time of war, and for which the VC would not be appropriate. Previously the CB had sometimes been awarded to junior officers, although intended mainly for those of field rank. It was also available to officers in both the other armed services. In September 1942 the regulations were amended to permit award of the DSO to officers of the Merchant Navy who performed acts of gallantry in the presence of the enemy. As a result of the 1993 Review of gallantry awards and resultant changes to the operational gallantry award system, the DSO is now awarded for "Leadership" — theoretically to all ranks (it is not awarded posthumously). The Conspicuous Gallantry Cross is now the equivalent reward for specific acts of gallantry.*

Second award bar

VALUE:	Unnamed single	Attributable group	*Miniature*
Victoria, gold (153)	£4500–6000	From £8500	£100–150
Victoria, silver-gilt (18ct gold centre) (1170)	£1500–2000	From £3500	£60–80
Edward VII (78)	£2000–2500	From £5500	£85–150 (gold)
George V (9900)	£1000–1500	From £2000	£45 (gilt), £120 (gold)
George VI 1st type 1938–48 (4880)	£1500–2000	From £3500	£45–65 (gilt)
George VI 2nd type 1948–52 (63)	£2000–2500	From £5500	£45–65 (gilt)
Elizabeth II	£3000–3500	From £6500	£65–75 (gilt)

28. IMPERIAL SERVICE ORDER

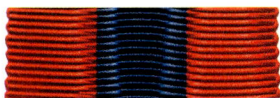

Instituted: August 1902.
Ribbon: 38mm, three equal sections of crimson, blue and crimson.
Metal: Silver with gold overlay.
Size: Height 61mm; max. width 55mm.
Description: The badge consists of a circular gold plaque bearing the royal cypher and surrounded by the words FOR FAITHFUL SERVICE. This plaque is then superimposed on a seven-pointed silver star surmounted by a crown and ring for suspension. The badge of the ISO awarded to women is similar but has a laurel wreath instead of the star-shaped base.
Comments: *Instituted by King Edward VII as a means of rewarding long and faithful service in the Administrative and Clerical grades of the Civil Service at home and overseas. Women were admitted to the order in 1908. The order was awarded after at least 25 years service at home, 20 years and 6 months (India) and 16 years in the tropics, but in exceptional cases awards were made for "eminently meritorious service" irrespective of qualifying period. No UK awards have been made since 1995 but some Commonwealth awards continue to this day. The George VI issue comes in two types: the early ones with GRI cypher and the later GVIR.*

VALUE:			*Miniature*
Edward VII	Gentleman (489)	£350–450	£25–30
	Lady (4)	£2500–3000	£200–300
George V	Gentleman (909)	£350–400	£20–25
	Lady (2)	£2500–3000	£200–300
George VI (608 Gentleman and 8 Lady)			
1st type	Gentleman	£350–450	£15–20
	Lady	£1500–2000	£200–300
2nd type	Gentleman	£350–450	£15–20
	Lady	£1500–2000	£200–300
Elizabeth II	Gentleman (2,153)*	£300–350	£10–15
	Lady (114)*	£1000–1500	£150–200

29. IMPERIAL SERVICE MEDAL

Instituted: August 1902.
Ribbon: 38mm, three equal sections of crimson, blue and crimson
Metal: Silver and bronze.
Size: 32mm
Description: Originally similar to the ISO but with a silver plaque and bronze star or wreath. In 1920 the ISM was transformed into a circular medal of silver with the sovereign's effigy on the obverse and a reverse depicting a naked man resting from his labours, with FOR FAITHFUL SERVICE in the exergue.
Comments: *Instituted at the same time as the ISO but intended for junior grades of the Civil Service.*

VALUE:		*Miniature*
Edward VII, 1903–10 (c. 4,500)		
Star (Gentleman)	£85–150	£15–20
Wreath (Lady)	£500–600	£200–300
George V, 1911-20 (c. 6,000)		
Star (Gentleman)	£85–1505	£12–15
Wreath (Lady)	£500–600	£200–300
George V Circular type		
Coinage profile, 1920–31 (c. 20,000)	£35–45	£10–15
Crowned bust, 1931–37 (c. 16,000)	£35–45	£10–15
George VI		
Crowned bust INDIAE:IMP, 1938–48 (c. 36,000)	£35–45	£10–15
Crowned bust FID:DEF, 1949–52 (c. 16,000)	£35–45	£10–15
Elizabeth II		
Tudor crown BRITT:OMN, 1953–54 (c. 9,000)	£30–35	£15–20
Tudor crown DEI:GRATIA, 1955– (c. 150,000)	£25–35	£15–20

30. INDIAN ORDER OF MERIT

Military

Civil

Instituted: 1837 (by the Honourable East India Company).
Ribbon: Dark blue with crimson edges (military) or crimson with dark blue edges (civil).
Metal: Silver and gold.
Size: Height 41mm; max. width 40mm.
Description: An eight-pointed star with a circular centre surrounded by a laurel wreath and containing crossed sabres and the relevant inscription. The star is suspended by a curvilinear suspension bar. The different classes were denoted by the composition of the star, noted below.
Comments: *The oldest gallantry award of the British Empire, it was founded in 1837 by the Honourable East India Company. Twenty years later it became an official British award when the administration of India passed to the Crown after the Sepoy Mutiny. Originally known simply as the Order of Merit, it was renamed in 1902 following the introduction of the prestigious British order of that name. There were three classes of the order, promotion from one class to the next being the reward for further acts of bravery. A civil division (also in three classes) was introduced in 1902. Ten years later the military division was reduced to two classes, when troops of the Indian Army became eligible for the VC. The civil division became a single class in 1939 and the military in 1945. Both divisions came to an end with the British Raj in 1947.*

VALUE:
Military Division
1837–1912 Reward of Valour

1st class in gold (42)	£6500–8500
2nd class in silver and gold (130)	£3500–4500
3rd class in silver (2740)	£1250–1750

1912–39 Reward of Valour

1st class in silver and gold (26)	£5000–6500
2nd class in silver (1215)	£500–750 continued

Reverse

30. INDIAN ORDER OF MERIT continued

1939-44 Reward of Gallantry		
1st class in silver and gold (2)		Rare
2nd class in silver (332)		£1000–1500
1945-47 Reward of Gallantry (44mm diameter)		£1850–2750
Civil Division		
1902-39 For Bravery (35mm diameter)		
1st class in gold (0)		—
2nd class in silver and gold (0)		—
3rd class in silver (39)		£1500–1850
1939-47 For Bravery (26mm diameter)		
Single class (10)		£3500–4500
Miniature		**£150–250**

NB *These prices represent unattributable pieces. Values can climb rapidly when in company with related campaign medals, particularly for the Victorian era.*

30A. CONSPICUOUS GALLANTRY CROSS

Instituted: October 1993.
Ribbon: White with blue edges and a red central stripe.
Metal: Silver.
Size: Max. width 44.3mm.
Description: A cross pattée imposed on a wreath of laurel, with the royal crown in a circular panel in the centre. Suspended by a ring from a plain suspension bar.
Comments: *As part of the decision to remove distinctions of rank in awards for bravery, this decoration replaced the DSO for specific acts of gallantry as well as the Conspicuous Gallantry Medal and the Distinguished Conduct Medal. It was first awarded in 1995 to Corporal Wayne Mills of the Duke of Wellington's Regiment and in 1996 to Colour Sergeant Peter Humphreys of the Royal Welch Fusiliers, both for gallantry in action during service with the UN Peacekeeping Forces in Bosnia. Two awards were made in respect of gallantry by members of the SAS and SBS in Sierra Leone in May–June 2000. A further two awards were made to members of the SAS and two awards to members of the SBS in Afghanistan in October 2001–March 2002, while awards to Justin Thomas, RM, and Lance Corporal Michael Flynn, Blues and Royals, both for gallantry in Iraq, were gazetted in October 2003, and that to Sqdn Ldr I. J. McKechnie, Royal Air Force, was gazetted on 9 September 2005, making a total of 11 in the first decade. Since then other awards have been made, including a collective award to the Royal Irish Regiment (retroactively to one of its forebears the Ulster Defence Regiment), which appeared in the LG Supplement, December 18, 2006, and three posthumous awards.*

VALUE: From £65,000   *Miniature* £20–25

31. ROYAL RED CROSS

First Class obverse

Second award bar

Instituted: 27 April 1883.

Ribbon: 25mm dark blue edged with crimson, in a bow.

Metal: Gold (later silver-gilt) and silver.

Size: Height 41mm; max. width 35mm.

Description: (Obverse) The *1st class* badge was originally a gold cross pattée, enamelled red with gold edges, but from 1889 silver-gilt was substituted for gold. At the centre was a crowned and veiled portrait, with the words FAITH, HOPE and CHARITY inscribed on three arms, and the date 1883 on the lower arm. Subsequently the effigy of the reigning monarch was substituted for the allegorical profile; (reverse) crowned royal cypher. *2nd Class:* in silver, design as the 1st class but the inscriptions on the arms appear on the reverse. Awards from 1938 have the year of issue engraved on the reverse of the lower arm.

Comments: *This decoration had the distinction of being confined to females until 1976. It is conferred on members of the nursing services regardless of rank. A second class award was introduced in November 1915. Bars for the first class were introduced in 1917. Holders of the second class are promoted to the first class on second awards. Holders of the first class decoration are known as Members (RRC) while recipients of the second class are Associates (ARRC). The second type GVI award is surprisingly scarce as only 50 first class and 100 second class were awarded.*

VALUE:

	First class (RRC)	Miniature	Second class (ARRC)	Miniature
Victoria, gold	£1250–1850	£100–150	—	—
Victoria, silver-gilt	£500–600	£60–70	—	—
Edward VII	£800–1000	£100–120	—	—
George V	£300–350	£25–35	£150–175	£12–25
George V, with bar	£450–550	£50–60	—	
George VI GRI	£300–350	£25–35	£220–250	£12–25
George VI GVIR	£350–450	£25–35	£250–300	£12–25
Elizabeth II	£300–350	£25–35	£200–250	£35–45

32. DISTINGUISHED SERVICE CROSS

Second award bar

Instituted: June 1901.

Ribbon: 36mm three equal parts of dark blue, white and dark blue.

Metal: Silver.

Size: Height 43mm; max. width 43mm.

Description: A plain cross with rounded ends. (Obverse) crowned royal cypher in the centre, suspended by a ring; (reverse) plain apart from the hallmark. From 1940 onwards the year of issue was engraved on the reverse of the lower limb.

Comments: *Known as the Conspicuous Service Cross when instituted, it was awarded to warrant and subordinate officers of the Royal Navy who were ineligible for the DSO. Only 8 EVII issued. In October 1914 it was renamed the Distinguished Service Cross and thrown open to all naval officers below the rank of lieutenant-commander. Bars for subsequent awards were authorised in 1916 and in 1931 eligibility for the award was enlarged to include officers of the Merchant Navy. In 1940 Army and RAF officers serving aboard naval vessels also became eligible for the award. Since 1945 fewer than 100 DSCs have been awarded. As a result of the 1993 Review of gallantry awards and resultant changes to the operational gallantry award system, this award is now available to both officers and other ranks, the DSM having been discontinued. Since 1 January 1984 the award has been issued named.*

VALUE:

	Unnamed single	Attributable group	Miniature
Edward VII	—	From £25,000	£200–250
George V	£1000–1500	From £2500	£25–35
George VI GRI	£1000–1500	From £2000	£15–25
George VI GVIR	—	From £3000	£25–35
Elizabeth II	—	From £7500	£15–25

33. MILITARY CROSS

Instituted: 31 December 1914.

Ribbon: 34mm three equal stripes of white, deep purple and white.

Metal: Silver.

Size: Height 46mm; max. width 44mm.

Description: An ornamental cross with straight arms terminating in broad finials decorated with imperial crowns. The royal cypher appears at the centre and the cross is suspended from a plain silver suspension bar.

Comments: *There was no gallantry award, lesser than the VC and DSO, for junior Army officers and warrant officers until shortly after the outbreak of the First World War when the MC was instituted. Originally awarded to captains, lieutenants and warrant officers of the Army (including RFC), it was subsequently extended to include equivalent ranks of the RAF when performing acts of bravery on the ground and there was even provision for the Royal Naval Division and the Royal Marines during the First World War. Awards were extended to majors by an amending warrant of 1931. Bars for second and subsequent awards have a crown at the centre. The MC is always issued unnamed, although since 1937 the reverse of the cross or bar is officially dated with the year of issue. As a result of the 1993 Review of gallantry awards and resultant changes to the operational gallantry award system, this award is now available to both officers and other ranks, the Military Medal having been discontinued. Since 1 January 1984 the award has been issued named.*

Second award bar

VALUE:	Unnamed single	Attributable group	Miniature
George V 1914–20 (37,000)	£600–750	From £1000	£25–30
one bar (3000)	—	From £1500	
two bars (170)	—	From £3500	
three bars (4)	—	From £8500	
George V 1921–36 (350)	—	From £2000	
one bar (31)	—	From £3000	
George VI GRI 1937–46 (11,000)	£700–750	From £1500	£25–30
one bar (500)	£1000–2000	From £3500	
George VI GVIR (158)	—	From £3500	£30–35
Elizabeth II	£850–1000	From £8000	£20–25

34. DISTINGUISHED FLYING CROSS

Instituted: June 1918.

Ribbon: 30mm originally horizontal but since June 1919 diagonal alternate stripes of white and deep purple.

Metal: Silver.

Size: Height 60mm; max. width 54mm.

Description: (Obverse) a cross flory terminating with a rose, surmounted by another cross made of propeller blades charged in the centre with a roundel within a laurel wreath. The horizontal arms bear wings and the crowned RAF monogram at the centre; (reverse) the royal cypher above the date 1918. The cross is suspended from a bar decorated with a sprig of laurel.

Comments: *Established for officers and warrant officers of the RAF in respect of acts of valour while flying in active operations against the enemy. The DFC is issued unnamed, but Second World War crosses usually have the year of issue engraved on the reverse of the lower limb. After WWII it was expanded to include aviation officers of other services. As a result of the 1993 Review of gallantry awards and resultant changes to the operational gallantry award system, this award is now available to both officers and other ranks, the Distinguished Flying Medal having been discontinued. Since 1 January 1984 the award has been issued named.*

Second award bar

Original ribbon.

Post-1919 ribbon.

VALUE:	Unnamed single	Attributable group	Miniature
George V 1918–20 (1100)	£2000–2500	From £3500	£25–35
one bar (70)	£2000–3000	From £6500	
two bars (3)	—	—	
George V 1920–36 (130)	—	—	
one bar (20)	—	—	
two bars (4)	—	—	
George VI GRI 1939–45 (20,000)	£2000–2500	From £4000	£25–35
one bar (1550)	£2500–3500	From £5000	
two bars (42)	—	—	
George VI GVIR 1948–52 (65)	—	—	£30–45
Elizabeth II	£2000–2500	From £6500	£20–25

(in silver add £5)

35. AIR FORCE CROSS

Instituted: June 1918.

Ribbon: 30mm originally horizontal but since June 1919 diagonal alternate stripes of white and crimson.

Metal: Silver.

Size: Height 60mm; max. width 54mm.

Description: (Obverse) the cross consists of a thunderbolt, the arms conjoined by wings, base bar terminating in a bomb, surmounted by another cross of aeroplane propellers, the finials inscribed with the royal cypher. A central roundel depicts Hermes mounted on a hawk bestowing a wreath; (reverse) the royal cypher and the date 1918.

Comments: *This decoration, awarded to officers and warrant officers of the RAF was instituted in June 1918 for gallantry on non-operational missions and for meritorious service on flying duties. After WWII it was expanded to include aviation officers of other services. Since the 1993 Review of gallantry awards it is now available to all ranks for non-operational gallantry in the air only (no longer for meritorious service also). Since 1 January 1984 the award has been issued named.*

Second award bar

Original ribbon.

Post-1919 ribbon.

VALUE:	Unnamed single	Attributable group	Miniature
George V 1918-20 (678)	£1000–1250	From £2500	£25–35
one bar (12)	—	—	
two bars (3)	—	—	
George V 1920-36 (111)	£1500–2000	From £2500	
George VI GRI (2605)	£1250–2000	From £2500	£25–35
one bar (36)	£2000–2500	From £3500	
two bars (1)	—	—	
George VI GVIR (411)	£1000–1250	From £2000	£35–45
Elizabeth II	£1500–1750	From £2500	£20–25

(in silver add £5)

36. ORDER OF BRITISH INDIA

Instituted: 1837 by the Honourable East India Company.

Ribbon: Worn around the neck, the base colour of the ribbon was originally sky blue but this was altered to crimson in 1838, allegedly because the hair oil favoured by Indians of all classes would soon have soiled a light ribbon. From 1939 onwards the first class ribbon had two thin vertical lines of light blue at the centre, while the second class ribbon had a single vertical line. Originally these distinctive ribbons were only worn in undress uniform (without the insignia itself), but from 1945 they replaced the plain crimson ribbons when worn with the decoration.

Metal: Gold.

Size: Height 42mm; max. width 38mm.

Description: The first class badge consists of a gold star with a crown between the upper two points and a blue enamelled centre bearing a lion surrounded by the words ORDER OF BRITISH INDIA enclosed in a laurel wreath. The second class badge is smaller, with dark blue enamel in the centre and with no crown.

Comments: *Intended for long and faithful service by native officers of the Indian Army, it was thrown open in 1939 to officers of the armed forces, frontier guards, military police and officers of the Indian native states. There were two classes, promotion to the first being made from the second. Recipients of both classes were entitled to the letters OBI after their names, but holders of the first class had the rank of Sardar Bahadur, while those of the second were merely Bahadur. A few awards were made by Pakistan to British officers seconded to the Pakistani forces at the time of independence.*

Original ribbon.

1838 ribbon.

1st class, post-1939 ribbon.

2nd class, post-1939 ribbon.

VALUE:		Miniature
1st class, light blue centre and dark blue surround	£1750–2000	£200–250
1st class, sky blue centre and surround (1939)	£1450–1750	£200–250
2nd class	£1250–1450	£200–250

NB The prices quoted are for unattributable awards.

37. ORDER OF BURMA

Instituted 1940.
Ribbon: 38mm dark green with light blue edges.
Metal: Gold.
Size: Height 52mm; max. width 38mm.
Description: The badge consists of a gold-rayed circle with a central roundel charged with a peacock in his pride azure, surmounted by an imperial crown.
Comments: *Instituted by King George VI, three years after Burma became independent of British India. Only 24 awards were made, to Governor's Commissioned Officers for long, faithful and honourable service in the army, frontier force and military police of Burma. By an amendment of 1945 the order could also be awarded for individual acts of heroism or particularly meritorious service. It was abolished in 1947.*

VALUE: £4500–5500   *Not known in miniature*

38. KAISAR-I-HIND MEDAL

Instituted: May 1900.
Ribbon: 37mm bluish green.
Metal: Gold, silver or bronze.
Size: Height 61mm; max. width 34mm.
Description: An oval badge surmounted by the imperial crown. (Obverse) the royal cypher set within a wreath; (reverse) FOR PUBLIC SERVICE IN INDIA round the edge and KAISAR-I-HIND (Emperor of India) on a scroll across the centre against a floral background.
Comments: *Queen Victoria founded this medal for award to those, regardless of colour, creed or sex, who had performed public service in India. Originally in two classes George V introduced a 3rd Class in bronze. The medals were originally large and hollow but were changed to smaller in diameter and solid during the reign of George V.*

Victoria obv.   *Victoria rev.*

Second award bar

VALUE:	1st class (gold)	Miniature	2nd class (silver)	Miniature	3rd class (bronze)	Miniature
Victoria	£2000–2500	£175–250	£450–500	£85–100	—	
Edward VII	£2000–2500	£175–250	£350–475	£85–100	—	
George V 1st	£1850–2250	£125–175	£350–475	£35–50	—	
George V 2nd	£1500–2000	£100–150	£300–450	£35–50	£150–175	£25–30
George VI	£1500–2000	£150–200	£350–475	£50–80	£150–175	£25–30

39. ALBERT MEDAL

2nd class land service medal.

2nd class land and sea service ribbons (until 1904).

1st class land service ribbon.

2nd class land service ribbon.
See also ribbon chart

Instituted: 7 March 1866.

Ribbons:

Gold (1st Class) Sea
16mm blue with two white stripes (1866)
35mm blue with four white stripes (1867–1949)

Gold (1st Class) Land
35mm red with four white stripes (1877–1949)

Bronze (2nd Class) Sea
16mm blue with two white stripes (1867–1904)
35mm blue with two white stripes (1904–71)

Bronze (2nd Class) Land
16mm red with two white stripes (1877–1904)
35mm red with two white stripes (1904–71)

Metal: Gold (early issues gold and bronze); bronze.

Size: Height 57mm; max. width 30mm.

Description: The badge consists of an oval enclosing the entwined initials V and A. The sea medals have, in addition, an anchor. The oval is enclosed by a bronze garter with the words FOR GALLANTRY IN SAVING LIFE, with AT SEA or ON LAND as appropriate, and enamelled in blue or crimson respectively. The whole is surmounted by a crown pierced by a ring for suspension. The first class medal was originally worked in gold and bronze and later in gold alone, the second class in bronze alone.

Comments: *Named in memory of the Prince Consort who died in 1861, this series of medals was instituted for gallantry in saving life at sea. An amendment of 1867 created two classes of medal and ten years later awards were extended to gallantry in saving life on land. In 1917 the title of the awards was altered, the first class becoming the Albert Medal in Gold and the second class merely the Albert Medal. It was last awarded in gold to a living recipient in April 1943, the last posthumous award being in May 1945. The last bronze medal awarded to a living recipient was in January 1949, and posthumous in August 1970. In 1949 the Medal in Gold was abolished and replaced by the George Cross and henceforward the Albert Medal (second class) was only awarded posthumously. In 1971 the award of the medal ceased and holders were invited to exchange their medals for the George Cross. Of the 69 eligible to exchange, 49 did so. In recent months (2019) the prices for the AM have softened a little as a large private collection came on to the market.*

VALUE:

	Civilian	Service	Miniature
Gold Sea (25)	From £12,000	From £15,000	£75–100*
Bronze Sea (211)	From £8,000	From £10,000	£50–75
Gold Land (45)	From £12,000	From £15,000	£75–100*
Bronze Land (290)	From £8,000	From £10,000	£50–75

*assumed gilt

40. UNION OF SOUTH AFRICA KING'S/ QUEEN'S MEDAL FOR BRAVERY (WOLTEMADE MEDAL)

Instituted: 1939 by the Government of the Union of South Africa.

Ribbon: Royal blue with narrow orange edges.

Metal: Gold or silver.

Size: 37mm.

Description: (Obverse) an effigy of the reigning sovereign; (reverse) a celebrated act of heroism by Wolraad Woltemade who rescued sailors from the wreck of the East Indiaman *De Jong Thomas* which ran aground in Table Bay on 17 June 1773. Seven times Woltemade rode into the raging surf to save fourteen seamen from drowning, but on the eighth attempt both rider and horse perished.

Comments: *This medal was awarded to citizens of the Union of South Africa and dependent territories who endangered their lives in saving the lives of others. It was awarded very sparingly, in gold or silver.*

VALUE:

		Miniature
George VI Gold (1)	—	£250–300
George VI Silver (34)	£2000–3000	£150–200
Elizabeth II Silver (1)	—	£150–200

41. DISTINGUISHED CONDUCT MEDAL

1st type obv.

Instituted: 1854.
Ribbon: 32mm crimson with a dark blue central stripe.
Metal: Silver.
Size: 36mm.
Description: (Obverse) originally a trophy of arms but, since 1902, the effigy of the reigning sovereign; (reverse) a four-line inscription across the field FOR DISTINGUISHED CONDUCT IN THE FIELD.
Comments: *The need for a gallantry medal for other ranks was first recognised during the Crimean War, although previously the Meritorious Service Medal (qv) had very occasionally been awarded for gallantry in the field. The medals have always been issued named, and carry the number, rank and name of the recipient on the rim, together with the date of the act of gallantry from 1881 until about 1901. Bars are given for subsequent awards and these too were dated from the first issued in 1881 until 1916 when the more usual laurelled bars were adopted. Since 1916 it has ranked as a superior decoration to the Military Medal. As a result of the 1993 Review of gallantry awards and resultant changes to the operational gallantry award system, the decoration has been replaced by the Conspicuous Gallantry Cross.*

VALUE*:

Crimea (800)	**From £3500**
Indian Mutiny (17)	**From £7000**
India general service 1854–95	**From £4000**
Abyssinia 1867–68 (7)	**From £6500**
Ashantee 1873–64 (33)	**From £5500**
Zulu War 1877–79 (16)	**From £10,000**
Afghanistan 1878–80 (61)	**From £4500**
First Boer War 1880–81 (20)	**From £9000**
Egypt & Sudan 1882–89 (134)	**From £5000**
India 1895–1901	**From £5000**
Sudan 1896–97	**From £4500**
Second Boer War 1899–1902 (2090)	**From £1500**
Boxer Rebellion 1900	**From £8000**
Edward VII	**Many rarities**
George V 1st type (25,000)	**From £1000**
ditto, unnamed (as issued to foreign recipients)	**From £350**
George V 2nd type 1930–37 (14)	**From £6000**
George VI, IND IMP 1937–47	**From £4000**
ditto, unnamed (as issued to foreign recipients)	**From £500**
George VI, 2nd type 1948–52 (25)	**From £12,000**
Elizabeth II, BR: OMN:	**From £10,000**
Elizabeth II, DEI GRATIA	**From £20,000**

Miniature (in silver add £5)

Victoria	**£75–85**
Edward VII	**£50–75**
George V	**Type I £35–45, II £70–100**
George VI	**Type I £15–20, II £25–40**
Elizabeth II	**£15–20**

*Awards for some specific actions such as the Charge of the Light Brigade command a much higher premium than the figures quoted.

Second award bar — type i

Second award bar — type ii

42. DISTINGUISHED CONDUCT MEDAL (DOMINION & COLONIAL)

Instituted: 31 May 1895.
Ribbon: 32mm crimson with a dark blue central stripe.
Metal: Silver.
Size: 36mm.
Description: As above, but the reverse bears the name of the issuing country or colony round the top.
Comments: *A separate DCM for warrant officers, NCOs and men of the colonial forces. Medals were struck for the Cape of Good Hope, New Zealand, New South Wales, Queensland, Tasmania, Natal and Canada, but only the last two actually issued them and the others are known only as specimens.*

VALUE:

Victoria Canada (1)	**Rare**
Victoria Natal (1)	**Rare**
Edward VII Natal (9)	**Rare**

43. DISTINGUISHED CONDUCT MEDAL (KAR & WAFF)

Instituted: early 1900s.
Ribbon: Dark blue with a central green stripe flanked by crimson stripes.
Metal: Silver.
Size: 36mm
Description: As no. 42, with either King's African Rifles or West Africa Frontier Force around the top of the reverse.
Comments: *Separate awards for gallantry were instituted in respect of the King's African Rifles (East Africa) and the West Africa Frontier Force (Nigeria, Sierra Leone, Gambia and the Gold Coast). These were issued until 1942 when they were superseded by the British DCM. An unnamed version of a George VI KAR DCM is known.*

VALUE:	Attributable groups
Edward VII KAR (2)	Rare
Edward VII WAFF (55)	£3500–4500
George V KAR (190)	£2250–2500
George V WAFF (165)	£2250–2500

44. CONSPICUOUS GALLANTRY MEDAL

Instituted: 1855.
Ribbon: 31mm white (RN) or sky blue (RAF) with dark blue edges. The Royal Navy ribbon was originally dark blue with white central stripe.
Metal: Silver.
Size: 36mm.
Description: (Obverse) the effigy of the reigning monarch; (reverse) the words FOR CONSPICUOUS GALLANTRY in three lines within a crowned laurel wreath.
Comments: *Conceived as the naval counterpart to the DCM, it was instituted for award to petty officers and seamen of the Royal Navy and to NCOs and other ranks of the Royal Marines. Originally awarded only for gallantry during the Crimean War, it was revived in 1874 to recognise heroism during the Ashantee War and has since been awarded, albeit sparingly, for other wars and campaigns. The Crimean issue utilised the dies of the Meritorious Service Medal which had the date 1848 below the truncation of the Queen's neck on the obverse. The raised relief inscription MERITORIOUS SERVICE on the reverse was erased and the words CONSPICUOUS GALLANTRY engraved in their place. When the decoration was revived in 1874 a new obverse was designed without a date while a new die, with the entire inscription in raised relief, was employed for the reverse. In 1943 the CGM was extended to NCOs and other ranks of the RAF. Both naval and RAF medals are identical, but the naval medal has a white ribbon with dark blue edges, whereas the RAF award has a pale blue ribbon with dark blue edges. It ranks as one of the rarest decorations: the only three medals issued in the reign of Queen Elizabeth II were awarded to Cpl. J. D. Coughlan, RAAF, for gallantry in Vietnam (1968), to Staff-Sergeant James Prescott, RE, during the South Atlantic War (1982) (posthumous) and to CPO Diver Philip Hammond, RN, during the Gulf War (1991). As a result of the 1993 Review and resultant changes to the operational gallantry award system, the decoration has been replaced by the Conspicuous Gallantry Cross.*

Second award bar.

RN first type ribbon

RN

RAF

VALUE:		Attributable groups
Victoria 1st type (11)		From £10,000
Victoria 2nd type (50)		From £10,000
Edward VII (2)		—
George V (110)		From £8000
George VI Navy/RM (80)		From £12,000
George VI RAF (103)	Immediate	From £12,000
	Non-immediate	From £7500
Elizabeth II (3)		—
Miniature		
Victoria		£50–80
Edward VII		£50–80
George V		£25–35
George VI		£15–20
Elizabeth II		£15–20

45. GEORGE MEDAL

Instituted: 1940.
Ribbon: 32mm crimson with five narrow blue stripes.
Metal: Silver.
Size: 36mm.
Description: (Obverse) the effigy of the reigning monarch; (reverse) St George and the Dragon, modelled by George Kruger Gray, after the bookplate by Stephen Gooden for the Royal Library, Windsor.
Comments: *Awarded for acts of bravery where the services were not so outstanding as to merit the George Cross. Though primarily a civilian award, it has also been given to service personnel for heroism not in the face of the enemy. Of the approximately 2,000 medals awarded, just over half have been to civilians. 27 second award bars have been issued.*

Second award bar.

VALUE:

	Civilian	Service
George VI 1st type 1940–47	From £3500	From £4000
George VI 2nd type 1948–52	From £3500	From £4500
Elizabeth II 1st type 1953	From £3000	From £4500
Elizabeth II 2nd type	From £3000	From £4500

Miniature
George VI, 1st type	£20–25
2nd type	£25–30
Elizabeth II, 1st type	£15–25
2nd type	£15–25

Silver add £5

46. KING'S POLICE MEDAL

Instituted: 7 July 1909.
Ribbons: 36mm. Originally deep blue with silver edges, but in 1916 a central silver stripe was added. Gallantry awards have thin crimson stripes superimposed on the silver stripes.
Metal: Silver.
Size: 36mm.
Description: (Obverse) the monarch's effigy; (reverse) a standing figure with sword and shield inscribed TO GUARD MY PEOPLE. The first issue had a laurel spray in the exergue, but in 1933 two separate reverses were introduced and the words FOR GALLANTRY or FOR DISTINGUISHED SERVICE were placed in the exergue.
Comments: *Instituted to reward "courage and devotion to duty" in the police and fire services of the UK and overseas dominions. Recognising the bravery of the firemen during the Blitz, the medal was retitled the King's Police and Fire Services Medal in 1940, but no change was made in the design of the medal itself. From 1950, the gallantry medals were only awarded posthumously and all medals were discontinued in 1954 when separate awards were established for the two services (see numbers MYB47 and 48).*

Second award bar.

VALUE:

		Miniature
Edward VII (100)	£850–1000	£25–30
George V 1st type coinage head (1900)	£600–850	£20–25
George V 2nd type crowned head	£600–850	£40–50
George V for Gallantry (350)	£1000–1500	£15–20
George V for Distinguished Service	£550–600	£15–20
George VI 1st type for Gallantry (440)	£850–1250	£15–20
George VI 2nd type for Gallantry (50)	£1500–2000	£15–20
George VI 1st type for Distinguished Service	£500–550	£15–20
George VI 2nd type for Distinguished Service	£500–550	£15–20

KPM

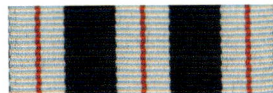

KPM (Gallantry)

47. QUEEN'S / KING'S POLICE MEDAL

Instituted: 19 May 1954.
Ribbon: Three silver stripes and two broad dark blue stripes. Gallantry awards have thin crimson stripes superimposed on the silver stripes.
Metal: Silver.
Size: 36mm.
Description: (Obverse) effigy of the reigning monarch; (reverse) a standing figure (as on the KPM) but the laurel spray has been restored to the exergue and the words FOR GALLANTRY or FOR DISTINGUISHED POLICE SERVICE are inscribed round the circumference.
Comments: *The QPM for Gallantry has been effectively redundant since November 1977 when it was made possible to award the George Medal posthumously. Prior to this the QPM was the posthumous equivalent of the GM for police officers. Issued in New Zealand under Regulations dated November 18, 1959 by the Minister in Charge of Police.*

Gallantry

VALUE:		*Miniature*
Elizabeth II for Gallantry (23)	£1750–2500	£30–40
Elizabeth II for Distinguished Service	£550–750	£15–25
Charles III	—	—

48. QUEEN'S / KING'S FIRE SERVICE MEDAL

Instituted: 19 May 1954.
Ribbon: Red with three yellow stripes (distinguished service) or similar, with thin dark blue stripes bisecting the yellow stripes (gallantry).
Metal: Silver.
Size: 36mm
Description: (Obverse) effigy of the reigning monarch; (reverse) standing figure with sword and shield (as on KPM), laurel spray in the exergue, and inscription round the circumference FOR GALLANTRY or FOR DISTINGUISHED FIRE SERVICE.
Comments: *To date no award of this medal, which can be awarded posthumously, has been made for gallantry.*

VALUE:		*Miniature*
Elizabeth II for Gallantry	—	£30–40
Elizabeth II for Distinguished Service	£600–750	£15–30
Charles III	—	—

Gallantry

48A. QUEEN'S / KING'S VOLUNTEER RESERVES MEDAL

Instituted: 1999.
Ribbon: Dark green with three narrow gold stripes.
Metal: Silver.
Size: 36mm.
Description: (Obverse) effigy of reigning monarch; (reverse) five ribbons containing the words THE QUEEN'S / KING'S VOLUNTEER RESERVES MEDAL. The medal is fitted with a large ring for suspension.
Comments: *Awarded to men and women of any rank in the volunteer reserves of all three services in recognition of outstanding service which formerly would have merited an award within the Order of the British Empire. Holders are entitled to the post-nominal letters QVRM / KVRM.*

VALUE: £350–500   *Miniature   £10–15*

48B. QUEEN'S / KING'S AMBULANCE SERVICE MEDAL FOR DISTINGUISHED SERVICE

Instituted: July 2012.
Branch of Service: Members of the NHS Ambulance Service.
Ribbon: Dark green with central silver stripe and silver edges.
Metal: Silver.
Size: 36mm.
Description: (Obverse) effigy of reigning monarch; (reverse) the inscription FOR DISTINGUISHED AMBULANCE SERVICE around the ambulance service emblem.
Comments: *Issued to recognise exceptional duty and outstanding service of NHS ambulance personnel. The medals are named around the edge and recipients can use the post-nominals QAM / KAM.*

VALUE: £200–250   *Miniature   £15–20*

49. KING'S POLICE MEDAL (SOUTH AFRICA)

Instituted: 24 September 1937.
Ribbon: Silver with two broad dark blue stripes. Red stripes are added for gallantry awards.
Metal: Silver.
Size: 36mm.
Description: (Obverse) effigy of George VI and title including the words ET IMPERATOR (1937-49), George VI minus ET IMPERATOR (1950-52) and Queen Elizabeth II (1953-60). (Reverse) as UK (no. 47 above) but inscribed in English and Afrikaans. Inscribed FOR BRAVERY VIR DAPPERHEID or FOR DISTINGUISHED SERVICE VIR VOORTREFLIKE DIENS.
Comments: *Awarded to members of the South Africa Police for courage and devotion to duty. In 1938 it was extended to cover the constabulary of South West Africa.*

VALUE:
George VI 1st type 1937-49
    for Gallantry (10)   —
    for Distinguished Service (13) —
George VI 2nd type 1950-52
    for Distinguished Service (13) —
Elizabeth II 1953-60
    for Gallantry (20) —
Elizabeth II 1953-69
    for Distinguished Service (3) —
Not seen in Miniature

50. EDWARD MEDAL (MINES)

Instituted: July 1907.
Ribbon: Dark blue edged with yellow.
Metal: Silver or bronze.
Size: 33mm.
Description: (Obverse) the monarch's effigy; (reverse) a miner rescuing a stricken comrade, with the caption FOR COURAGE across the top (designed by W. Reynolds-Stephens).
Comments: *Awarded for life-saving in mines and quarries, in two grades: first class (silver) and second class (bronze). Interestingly, the cost of these medals was borne not by the State but from a fund created by a group of philanthropic individuals led by A. Hewlett, a leading mine-owner. Medals were engraved with the names of the recipient from the outset, but since the 1930s the date and sometimes the place of the action have also been inscribed. Since 1949 the medal was only granted posthumously and in 1971 living recipients were invited to exchange their medals for the GC, under Royal Warrant of 1971. Two silver and eight bronze medallists elected not to do so. This is one of the rarest gallantry awards, only 77 silver and 318 bronze medals having been granted since its inception. Only two second award bars have been awarded—both for mine rescues.*

VALUE:	Silver	Bronze
Edward VII	£2500–3500	£2000–2500
George V 1st type	£2500–3500	£1500–2000
George V 2nd type	£4000–6000	£2500–3000
George VI 1st type	£3500–5000	£3500–4500
George VI 2nd type	—	£4000–5000
Elizabeth II	Not issued	£4000–6000
Miniature		
Edward VII	£80–90	£70–80
George V	£70–80	£60–70
George VI	£70–80	£60–70

51. EDWARD MEDAL (INDUSTRY)

1st type rev.

2nd type rev.

Instituted: December 1909.
Ribbon: As above.
Metal: Silver or bronze.
Size: 33mm.
Description: (Obverse) effigy of the reigning monarch; (reverse) originally a worker helping an injured workmate with a factory in the background and the words FOR COURAGE inscribed diagonally across the top. A second reverse, depicting a standing female figure with a laurel branch and a factory skyline in the background, was introduced in 1912.
Comments: *Awarded for acts of bravery in factory accidents and disasters. Like the Mines medal it was also available in two classes, but no first class medals were awarded since 1948. Since 1949 the medal was only granted posthumously and in 1971 living recipients were invited to exchange their medals for the GC, under Royal Warrant of 1971. Two Silver and three Bronze recipients declined to exchange. A total of 25 silver and 163 bronze awards have been issued. Two awards were made to women, the rarest gallantry award to a lady.*

VALUE:	Silver	Bronze
Edward VII	From £5000	£2500–3500
George V 1st Obv, 1st Rev	Unique	£4500–5000
George V 1st Obv, 2nd Rev	From £5000	£1500–2000
George V 2nd Obv, 2nd Rev	From £5000	£2500–3500
George VI 1st type	Unique	£2500–3500
George VI 2nd type	Not issued	£5000–6000
Elizabeth II 1st type	Not issued	£5000–6000
Elizabeth II 2nd type	Not issued	£5000–6000
Miniature		
George V	£150–200	£100–150
George VI	£70–80	
George VI Modern example	£15–20	

52. INDIAN DISTINGUISHED SERVICE MEDAL

Second award bar.

Instituted: 25 June 1907.
Ribbon: Crimson with broad dark blue edges.
Metal: Silver.
Size: 36mm.
Description: (Obverse) the sovereign's effigy. (Reverse) the words FOR DISTINGUISHED SERVICE in a laurel wreath.
Comments: *Awarded for distinguished service in the field by Indian commissioned and non-commissioned officers and men of the Indian Army, the reserve forces, border militia and levies, military police and troops employed by the Indian Government. An amendment of 1917 extended the award to Indian non-combatants engaged on field service, bars for subsequent awards being authorised at the same time. It was formally extended to the Royal Indian Marine in 1929 and members of the Indian Air Force in 1940. Finally it was extended in 1944 to include non-European personnel of the Hong Kong and Singapore Royal Artillery although it became obsolete in 1947.*

VALUE:		*Miniature*
Edward VII (140)	£1000–1500	£80–90
George V KAISAR-I-HIND (3800)	£800–1200	£50–60
George V 2nd type (140)	£1250–1750	£50–60
George VI (1190)	£1000–1500	£40–50

53. BURMA GALLANTRY MEDAL

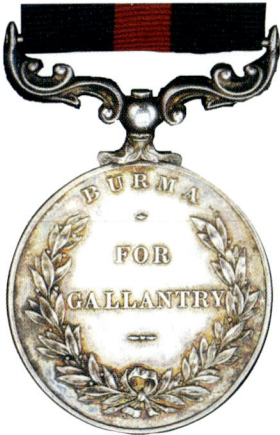

Second award bar.

Instituted: 10 May 1940.
Ribbon: Jungle green with a broad crimson stripe in the centre.
Metal: Silver.
Size: 36mm.
Description: (Obverse) the effigy of King George VI; (reverse) the words BURMA at the top and FOR GALLANTRY in a laurel wreath.
Comments: *As Burma ceased to be part of the Indian Empire in April 1937 a separate gallantry award was required for its armed services. The Burma Gallantry Medal was awarded by the Governor to officers and men of the Burma Army, frontier forces, military police, Burma RNVR and Burma AAF, although by an amendment of 1945 subsequent awards were restricted to NCOs and men. The medal became obsolete in 1947 when Burma became an independent republic and left the Commonwealth. Just over 200 medals and three bars were awarded, mainly for heroism in operations behind the Japanese lines.*

VALUE:	*Miniature*
£4000–5000	£20–25 for late example, contemporary example unknown

54. DISTINGUISHED SERVICE MEDAL

Instituted: 14 October 1914.

Ribbon: Dark blue with two white stripes towards the centre.

Metal: Silver.

Size: 36mm.

Description: (Obverse) the sovereign's effigy; (reverse) a crowned wreath inscribed FOR DISTINGUISHED SERVICE.

Comments: *Awarded to petty officers and ratings of the Royal Navy, NCOs and other ranks of the Royal Marines and all other persons holding corresponding ranks or positions in the naval forces, for acts of bravery in face of the enemy not sufficiently meritorious to make them eligible for the CGM. It was later extended to cover the Merchant Navy and Army, the WRNS and RAF personnel serving aboard ships in the Second World War. Of particular interest and desirability are medals awarded for outstanding actions, e.g. Jutland, Q-Ships, the Murmansk convoys, the Yangtze incident and the Falklands War. First World War bars for subsequent awards are dated on the reverse, but Second World War bars are undated. As a result of the 1993 Review of gallantry awards and resultant changes to the operational gallantry award system, this award has been replaced by the DSC which is now available both to officers and other ranks.*

Second award bar.

VALUE:

		Miniature
George V uncrowned head 1914-30 (4100)	£1000–2000	£20–25
George VI IND IMP 1938-49 (7100)	£1000–2000	£15–20
George VI 2nd type 1949-53	£3500–4500	£30–40
Elizabeth II BR OMN 1953-7	£5000–8000	£10–15
Elizabeth II 2nd type	£5500–8500	£10–15

(in silver add £5)

55. MILITARY MEDAL

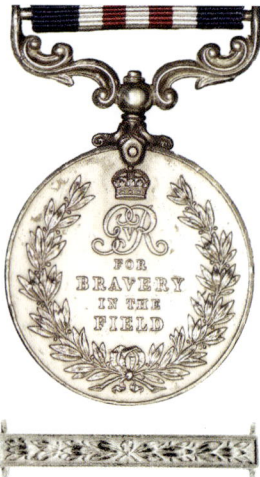

Instituted: 25 March 1916.

Ribbon: Broad dark blue edges flanking a central section of three narrow white and two narrow crimson stripes.

Metal: Silver.

Size: 36mm.

Description: (Obverse) the sovereign's effigy—six types; (reverse) the crowned royal cypher above the inscription FOR BRAVERY IN THE FIELD, enclosed in a wreath.

Comments: *Awarded to NCOs and men of the Army (including RFC and RND) for individual or associated acts of bravery not of sufficient heroism as to merit the DCM. In June 1916 it was extended to women, two of the earliest awards being to civilian ladies for their conduct during the Easter Rising in Dublin that year. Some 115,600 medals were awarded during the First World War alone, together with 5796 first bars, 180 second bars and 1 third bar. Over 16,000 medals were conferred during the Second World War, with 181 first bars and 2 second bar. About 300 medals and 4 first bars were awarded for bravery in minor campaigns between the two world wars, whilst some 932 medals and 8 first bars have been conferred since 1947. As a result of the 1993 Review of gallantry awards and resultant changes to the operational gallantry award system, this award has been replaced by the MC which is now available both to officers and other ranks.*

Second award bar.

VALUE:

		Miniature
George V uncrowned head 1916–30		
Corps/RA—single	£250–450	£15–20
in group	£400–550*	
Regiment—single	£400–550	
in group	£650–1000*	
named to a woman	£5500–6500	
unnamed as awarded to foreign recipients†	£300–400	
George V crowned head 1930–38	£4000–5000	£70–100
George VI IND IMP 1938–48		
Corps	£1000–1800	£15–20
Regiment	£1500–2500	
unnamed as awarded to foreign recipients†	£400–500	
George VI 2nd type 1948-53	£2500–5000	£25–40
Elizabeth II BR: OMN 1953-8	£3500–6000	£15–20
Elizabeth II 2nd type	£5000–8000	£15–20

(in silver add £5)

*Groups to RFC, RAF and RND will be considerably higher and obviously, medals with second (or more) award bars are also worth much more.

†*Note: Some MMs to foreign recipients are found named.*

56. DISTINGUISHED FLYING MEDAL

Instituted: 1918.

Ribbon: Originally purple and white horizontal stripes but since July 1919 thirteen narrow diagonal stripes alternating white and purple.

Metal: Silver.

Size: 42mm tall; 34mm wide.

Description: An oval medal, (obverse) the sovereign's effigy; (reverse) Athena Nike seated on an aeroplane, with a hawk rising from her hand. Originally undated, but the date 1918 was added to the reverse with the advent of the George VI obverse. The medal is suspended by a pair of wings from a straight bar.

Comments: *Introduced at the same time as the DFC, it was awarded to NCOs and men of the RAF for courage or devotion to duty while flying on active operations against the enemy. During the Second World War it was extended to the equivalent ranks of the Army and Fleet Air Arm personnel engaged in similar operations. First World War medals have the names of recipients impressed in large seriffed lettering, whereas Second World War medals are rather coarsely engraved. Approximately 150 medals have been awarded since 1945. After WWII it was expanded to include aviation officers of other services. As a result of the 1993 Review of gallantry awards and resultant changes to the operational gallantry award system, this award has been replaced by the DFC which is now available both to officers and other ranks.*

Second award bar

Pre-1919

Post-1919

VALUE:	Attributable group	Miniature
George V uncrowned head 1918–30 (105)	From £5000	£18–20
George V crowned head 1930–38	From £8000	£70–100
George VI IND IMP 1938–49 (6500)	From £3000	£10–12
George VI 2nd type 1949–53	From £5000	£25–40
Elizabeth II	From £6000	£10–12

(in silver add £5)

Example of WWI impressed naming

WWII engraved naming.

57. AIR FORCE MEDAL

Instituted: 1918.

Ribbon: Originally horizontal narrow stripes of white and crimson but since July 1919 diagonal narrow stripes of the same colours.

Metal: Silver.

Size: 42mm tall; 32mm wide.

Description: An oval medal with a laurel border. (Obverse) the sovereign's effigy; (reverse) Hermes mounted on a hawk bestowing a laurel wreath. The medal is suspended by a pair of wings from a straight bar, like the DFM.

Comments: *Instituted at the same time as the AFC, it was awarded to NCOs and men of the RAF for courage or devotion to duty while flying, but not on active operations against the enemy. About 100 medals and 2 first bars were awarded during the First World War, 106 medals and 3 bars between the wars and 259 medals during the Second World War. After WWII it was expanded to include aviation officers of other services. After the 1993 Review of gallantry awards the AFM was discontinued; the AFC is now available both to officers and other ranks.*

Second award bar

Pre-1919

Post-1919

VALUE:	Attributable group	Miniature
George V uncrowned head 1918–30	From £2500	£25–30
George V crowned head 1930–38	From £5000	£80–100
George VI IND IMP 1939–49	From £3000	£15–20
George VI 2nd type 1949–53	From £3000	£30–40
Elizabeth II	From £3000	£15–20

(in silver add £5)

58. CONSTABULARY MEDAL (IRELAND)

1st type obv.

2nd type obv.

Instituted: 1842.
Ribbon: Originally light blue, but changed to green in 1872.
Metal: Silver.
Size: 36mm.
Description: (Obverse) a crowned harp within a wreath of oak leaves and shamrocks, with REWARD OF MERIT round the top and IRISH CONSTABULARY round the foot. In the first version the front of the harp took the form of a female figure but later variants had a plain harp and the shape of the crown and details of the wreath were also altered. These changes theoretically came in 1867 when the Constabulary acquired the epithet Royal, which was then added to the inscription round the top, although some medals issued as late as 1921 had the pre-1867 title. (Reverse) a wreath of laurel and shamrock, within which are engraved the recipient's name, rank, number, date and sometimes the location of the action.
Comments: *Originally awarded for gallantry and meritorious service by members of the Irish Constabulary. From 1872, however, it was awarded only for gallantry. It was first conferred in 1848 and became obsolete in 1922 when the Irish Free State was established. Bars for second awards were authorised in 1920. About 315 medals and 7 bars were awarded (or, in some cases, second medals—the records are inconclusive), mostly for actions in connection with the Easter Rising of 1916 (23) or the subsequent Anglo-Irish War of 1920 (180) and 1921 (55).*

VALUE:		Miniature
First type	£5000–8000	—
Second type	£5000–8000	£200–250

Original ribbon

Post-1872 ribbon

59. INDIAN POLICE MEDAL

1st type

2nd type (after 1944)

Instituted: 23 February 1932.
Ribbon: Crimson flanked by stripes of dark blue and silver grey. From 1942 onwards additional narrow silver stripes appeared in the centre of the blue stripe intended for the gallantry medal.
Metal: Bronze.
Size: 36mm.
Description: (Obverse) the King Emperor; (reverse) a crowned wreath inscribed INDIAN POLICE, with the words FOR DISTINGUISHED CONDUCT across the centre. In December 1944 the reverse was re-designed in two types, with the words FOR GALLANTRY or FOR MERITORIOUS SERVICE in place of the previous legend.
Comments: *Intended for members of the Indian police forces and fire brigades as a reward for gallantry or meritorious service. The medal became obsolete in 1948 when India became a republic.*

VALUE:

		Miniature
George V	£500–650	£35–45
George VI Distinguished Conduct	£500–650	£35–45
George VI for Gallantry	£850–1000	£45–55
George VI for Meritorious Service	£500–650	£35–45

From 1942 for gallantry

Second award bar.

60. BURMA POLICE MEDAL

Instituted: 14 December 1937.
Ribbon: A wide central blue stripe flanked by broad black stripes and white edges.
Metal: Bronze.
Size: 36mm.
Description: (Obverse) the effigy of George VI; (reverse) similar to the Indian medal (first type) and inscribed FOR DISTINGUISHED CONDUCT, irrespective of whether awarded for gallantry or distinguished service.
Comments: *Introduced following the separation of Burma from India, it was abolished in 1948. All ranks of the police, frontier force and fire brigades, both European and Burmese, were eligible.*

VALUE:

For Gallantry (53)	£1950–2500	*Miniature*	£60–75
For Meritorious Service (80)	£1200–1700		

61. COLONIAL POLICE MEDAL

Instituted: 10 May 1938.
Ribbon: Blue with green edges and a thin silver stripe separating the colours, but the gallantry award had an additional thin red line through the centre of each green edge stripe.
Metal: Silver.
Size: 36mm.
Description: (Obverse) the sovereign's effigy; (reverse) a policeman's truncheon superimposed on a laurel wreath. The left side of the circumference is inscribed COLONIAL POLICE FORCES and the right either FOR GALLANTRY or FOR MERITORIOUS SERVICE.
Comments: *Intended to reward all ranks of the police throughout the Empire for acts of conspicuous bravery or for meritorious service. The number to be issued was limited to 150 in any one year. Only 450 were awarded for gallantry (with nine second award bars), whilst almost 3000 were issued for meritorious service. As from June 14, 2012 this medal was renamed the Overseas Territories Police Medal.*

Second award bar.

Ribbon for gallantry award

VALUE:		*Miniature*
George VI GRI for Gallantry	£850–1250	£40–50
George VI GRI for Meritorious Service	£400–500	£30–40
George VI GVIR for Gallantry	£850–1250	£40–50
George VI GVIR for Meritorious Service	£400–500	£30–40
Elizabeth II 1st type for Gallantry	£850–1250	£40–50
Elizabeth II 1st type for Meritorious Service	£400–500	£30–40
Elizabeth II 2nd type for Gallantry	£850–1250	£40–50
Elizabeth II 2nd type for Meritorious Service	£400–500	£30–40

62. COLONIAL FIRE BRIGADE MEDAL

Instituted: 10 May 1938.
Ribbon: As above.
Metal: Silver.
Size: 36mm.
Description: (Obverse) the effigy of the reigning sovereign; (reverse) a fireman's helmet and axe, with the inscription COLONIAL FIRE BRIGADES FOR GALLANTRY or FOR MERITORIOUS SERVICE.
Comments: *This medal was intended to reward all ranks of the Colonial fire brigades for gallantry or meritorious service but very few were awarded for gallantry. As from June 14, 2012 this medal was renamed the Overseas Territories Fire Brigade Medal.*

VALUE:		*Miniature*
George VI GRI for Gallantry	Rare	£40–50
George VI GRI for Meritorious Service	Rare	£30–40
George VI GVIR for Gallantry	Rare	£40–50
George VI GVIR for Meritorious Service	£350–500	£30–40
Elizabeth II 1st type for Gallantry	From £750	£40–50
Elizabeth II 1st type for Meritorious Service	£350–500	£30–40
Elizabeth II 2nd type for Gallantry	£600–800	£40–50
Elizabeth II 2nd type for Meritorious Service	£300–450	£30–40

63. QUEEN'S / KING'S GALLANTRY MEDAL

Instituted: 20 June 1974.

Ribbon: Blue with a central pearl-grey stripe bisected by a narrow rose-pink stripe.

Metal: Silver.

Size: 36mm.

Description: (Obverse) the Queen's effigy; (reverse) St. Edward's crown above THE QUEEN'S GALLANTRY MEDAL flanked by laurel sprigs.

Comments: *Awarded for exemplary acts of bravery. Although intended primarily for civilians, it is also awarded to members of the armed forces for actions which would not be deemed suitable for a military decoration. With the introduction of the QGM the gallantry awards in the Order of the British Empire came to an end. To date, almost 1,100 QGMs have been awarded, including 18 bars. A bar is added for a second award. A post-1990 SAS QGM and bar group sold at a recent auction for £26,000.*

Second award bar.

VALUE:		Miniature
Service award	From £5000	£15–20
Civilian award	From £3500	

64. ALLIED SUBJECTS' MEDAL

Instituted: November 1920.

Ribbon: Bright red with a light blue centre, flanked by narrow stripes of yellow, black and white (thus incorporating the Belgian and French national colours).

Metal: Silver or bronze.

Size: 36mm.

Description: (Obverse) the effigy of King George V; (reverse) designed by C. L. J. Doman, the female allegory of Humanity offering a cup to a British soldier resting on the ground, with ruined buildings in the background.

Comment: *Shortly after the cessation of the First World War it was proposed that services rendered to the Allied cause, specifically by those who had helped British prisoners of war to escape, should be rewarded by a medal. The decision to go ahead was delayed on account of disagreement between the War Office and the Foreign Office, but eventually the first awards were announced in November 1920, with supplementary lists in 1921 and 1922. Medals were issued unnamed and almost half of the total issue, namely 56 silver and 247 bronze medals, were issued to women.*

VALUE:		Miniature
Silver (134)	£1000–1250	£40–50
Bronze (574)	£500–600	£45–55

NB These prices are for unattributable awards.

65. KING'S MEDAL FOR COURAGE IN THE CAUSE OF FREEDOM

Instituted: 23 August 1945

Ribbon: White with two narrow dark blue stripes in the centre and broad red stripes at the edges.

Metal: Silver.

Size: 36mm.

Description: (Obverse) the crowned profile of King George VI; (reverse) inscribed, within a chain link, THE KING'S MEDAL FOR COURAGE IN THE CAUSE OF FREEDOM.

Comments: *Introduced to acknowledge acts of courage by foreign civilians or members of the armed services "in the furtherance of the British Commonwealth in the Allied cause" during the Second World War. Like its First World War counterpart, it was intended mainly to reward those who had assisted British escapees in enemy-occupied territories. About 3200 medals were issued, commencing in 1947.*

VALUE: £600–700 (unattributable)   *Miniature* £30–40

66. KING'S MEDAL FOR SERVICE IN THE CAUSE OF FREEDOM

Instituted: 23 August 1945.
Ribbon: White with a central red stripe flanked by dark blue stripes.
Metal: Silver.
Size: 36mm.
Description: (Obverse) effigy of King George VI; (reverse) a medieval warrior in armour carrying a broken lance, receiving nourishment from a female.
Comments: *Introduced at the same time as the foregoing, it was intended for foreign civilians who had helped the Allied cause in other less dangerous ways, such as fund-raising and organising ambulance services. 2490 medals were issued.*

VALUE: £250–300 (unattributable)   *Miniature*   £15–20

67. SEA GALLANTRY MEDAL

Instituted: 1855, under the Merchant Shipping Acts of 1854 and 1894.
Ribbon: Bright red with narrow white stripes towards the edges.
Metal: Silver or bronze.
Size: 58mm or 33mm.
Description: (Obverse) Profile of the reigning monarch; (reverse) a family on a storm-tossed shore reviving a drowning sailor. Both obverse and reverse were sculpted by Bernard Wyon.
Comments: *Exceptionally, this group of medals was authorised not by Royal Warrant but by Parliamentary legislation, under the terms of the Merchant Shipping Acts of 1854 and 1894. The 1854 Act made provision for monetary rewards for life saving at sea, but in 1855 this was transmuted into medals, in gold, silver or bronze, in two categories, for gallantry (where the rescuer placed his own life at risk) and for humanity (where the risks were minimal). The gold medal, if ever awarded, must have been of the greatest rarity. These medals, issued by the Board of Trade, were 58mm in diameter and not intended for wearing. The only difference between the medals lay in the wording of the inscription round the circumference of the obverse. In 1903 Edward VII ordered that the medal be reduced to 1.27 inches (33mm) in diameter and fitted with a suspension bar and ribbon for wearing. Both large and small medals were always issued with a minimum of the recipient's name and date of rescue round the rim. The last medal was awarded in 1989 and it appears to have fallen into disuse although the award has not been cancelled. Only one second award clasp has ever been issued—that to Ch.Off. James Whiteley in 1921.*

VALUE:

	Silver	Bronze	*Miniature*
Victoria Gallantry	£1000–1500	£550–750	£100–150
Victoria Humanity (to 1893)	£1000–1250	£500–650	
Edward VII Gallantry (large)	£1750–2000	£1500–1650	
Edward VII Gallantry (small)	£850–1000	£550–650	£100–150
Edward VII (2nd small type)	£750–950	£450–550	
George V	£500–650	£350–450	£50–75
George VI 1st type	£1200–1500	—	
George VI 2nd type	—	—	
Elizabeth II	—	—	

68. SEA GALLANTRY MEDAL (FOREIGN SERVICES)

Type 4 rev.

Instituted: 1841.

Ribbon: Plain crimson till 1922; thereafter the same ribbon as the SGM above.

Metal: Gold, silver or bronze.

Size: 36mm or 33mm.

Description: The large medal had Victoria's effigy (young head) on the obverse, but there were five reverse types showing a crowned wreath with PRESENTED BY (or FROM) THE BRITISH GOVERNMENT inside the wreath. Outside the wreath were the following variants:

1. Individually struck inscriptions (1841-49 but sometimes later).
2. FOR SAVING THE LIFE OF A BRITISH SUBJECT (1849-54)
3. FOR ASSISTING A BRITISH VESSEL IN DISTRESS (1849-54)
4. FOR SAVING THE LIVES OF BRITISH SUBJECTS (1850-54)

There are also unissued specimens or patterns with a Latin inscription within the wreath VICTORIA REGINA CUDI JUSSIT MDCCCXLI.

The small medal, intended for wear, has five obverse types combined with four reverse types: as 2 above (1854-1906), as 3 above (1854-1918), as 4 above (1854-1926), or FOR GALLANTRY AND HUMANITY (1858 to the present day).

Comments: *Although intended to reward foreigners who rendered assistance to British subjects in distress some early awards were actually made for rescues on dry land. Originally a special reverse was struck for each incident, but this was found to be unnecessarily expensive, so a standard reverse was devised in 1849. Medals before 1854 had a diameter of 45mm and were not fitted with suspension. After 1854 the diameter was reduced to 33mm and scrolled suspension bars were fitted. Of the large medals about 100 gold, 120 silver and 14 bronze were issued, while some 10 gold and 24 bronze specimens have been recorded. The small bronze medal is actually the rarest of all, only six medals being issued.*

Original ribbon

Post-1922 ribbon

VALUE:	Gold	Silver	Bronze
Victoria large	—	£650–750	£450–550
Victoria small	£2000–2500	£350–450	—
Edward VII	£2000–2750	£450–550	—
George V	£1750–2000	£350–450	—
George VI	—	—	—
Elizabeth II	—	—	—
Miniature			£175–225

69. BRITISH NORTH BORNEO COMPANY'S BRAVERY CROSS

Instituted: 1890.

Ribbon: Gold (later yellow) watered silk 34mm.

Metal: Silver or bronze.

Size: 36mm.

Description: The cross pattée has a central medallion bearing a lion passant with the Company motto PERGO ET PERAGO (I carry on and accomplish) within a garter. The arms of the cross are inscribed BRITISH NORTH BORNEO with FOR BRAVERY in the lower limb. Three crosses have been recorded with the lower inscription for bravery omitted.

Comments: *Manufactured by Joseph Moore of Birmingham. The silver version bears the Birmingham hallmark for 1890. The reverse of the bronze medal is smooth. The cross was awarded for bravery in some 17 actions between 1883 and 1915, to the Company's Armed Constabulary. Several of these actions involved fewer than 40 combatants, but at the other extreme 144 men took*

69. BRITISH NORTH BORNEO COMPANY'S BRAVERY CROSS *continued*

part in the major battle at Tambunan in 1900. Only five silver and four bronze crosses are known to have been awarded. Jemadar Natha Singh was the only officer to win both bronze (1892) and silver (1897). Examples with the word STERLING on the reverse are modern copies.

VALUE:

Silver	£1000–1500	*Not known in miniature.*
Bronze	£500–750 (but much more in either case if attributable)	
Specimens/Copies	£100–150	

70. KING'S MEDAL FOR NATIVE CHIEFS

Instituted: 1920.
Ribbon: Yellow with two white central stripes (silver-gilt) or a single white stripe (silver).
Metal: Silver or silver-gilt.
Size: Oval 40mm x 34mm or circular 36mm x 32mm.
Description: Originally an oval badge with collar. (Obverse) the crowned effigy of the monarch; (reverse) a warship, symbolic of imperial power. The medals of Elizabeth II come in two versions: the original larger size with collar and the smaller size (1955) fitted with a plain ring for suspension from a yellow watered silk ribbon with or without a narrow central white stripe.

Comments: *Various large silver medals were struck for award to native chiefs in various parts of the world, from the eighteenth century onwards, and of these the awards to American Indian chiefs are probably the best known. In 1920, however, a standard King's Medal for Chiefs was instituted. It was awarded exceptionally in silver-gilt (first class), and usually in silver (second class). The oval medal was worn round the neck from a silver collar. The more modern issues, however, are smaller and intended for wear with a ribbon from the breast. The medal is normally returned on the death of the recipient.*

VALUE:

	Silver-gilt	Silver
George V		
First (couped) type	£1200–1500	£800–1000
Second (larger bust) type	£1000–1200	£750–850
George VI	£1000–1200	£650–750
Elizabeth II		
First type	£1000–1200	£650–750
Second (small) type	£400–500	£350–450

MENTIONS
and Commendations

A description of the various emblems denoting Mentions in Despatches and King's (or later Queen's) Commendations was published as a Supplement to the London Gazette, July 27, 1951. A special emblem to signify a Mention in Despatches was first instituted during World War I and continued to be awarded for active service in that conflict up to August 10, 1920. It was worn on the ribbon of the Victory Medal (no. 170) or the British War Medal if no Victory Medal is awarded and consisted of a bronze spray of oak leaves.

For Mentions in Despatches after August 10, 1920, or a King's Commendation for Brave Conduct or Valuable Service in the Air, a bronze emblem consisting of a single oak leaf was worn on the appropriate medal ribbon, either a General Service Medal or the War Medal, 1939–45. King's or Queen's Commendations for Brave Conduct or Valuable Service in the Air, in cases where no campaign or war medal was awarded, were worn on the breast in the position where an appropriate medal ribbon would have been worn, generally on the uniform tunic after any medal ribbons.

King's or Queen's Commendations in respect of bravery, granted to civilians for acts during or since the Second World War, are denoted by a silver emblem in the form of a spray of laurel leaves (this was originally a plastic oval badge). The emblem was worn on the ribbon of the Defence Medal (no. 185) for bravery in situations earning the medal. Where no medal was awarded, it was sewn directly on to the coat. For civilians the King's or Queen's Commendation for Valuable Service in the Air, during the Second World War and subsequently, consisted of an oval silver badge, worn on the coat below any medals or medal ribbons, or in civil airline uniform, on the panel of the left breast pocket.

Since 2003 all MiD and Commendation emblems may be worn on UK, UN, NATO or EC/EU medal ribbons.

Mention in Despatches emblem 1914–20

Mention in Despatches emblem 1920–94

King's Commendation for Brave Conduct plastic badge for civilians (1942–45).

King's Commendation for Valuable Service in the Air silver badge for civilians (1942–93).

The emblems for Mentions and Commendations were revised in 1994, as shown in the table below.

FOR GALLANTRY			FOR VALUABLE SERVICE
IN ACTION WITH THE ENEMY (ALL ENVIRONMENTS)	NOT IN ACTION WITH THE ENEMY or OUT OF THEATRE (EXCEPT FLYING)	NOT IN ACTION WITH THE ENEMY or OUT OF THEATRE (FLYING)	IN-THEATRE BUT NOT IN ACTION WITH THE ENEMY
MENTION IN DESPATCHES	QUEEN'S / KING'S COMMENDATION FOR BRAVERY	QUEEN'S / KING'S COMMENDATION FOR BRAVERY IN THE AIR	QUEEN'S / KING'S COMMENDATION FOR VALUABLE SERVICE
A single oak leaf in SILVER	A spray of laurel leaves in SILVER	A new emblem in SILVER	A spray of oak leaves in SILVER

MEDAL NEWS

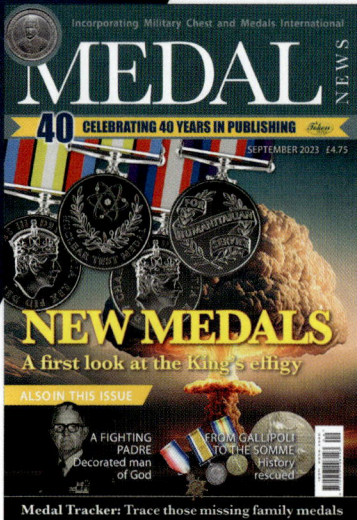

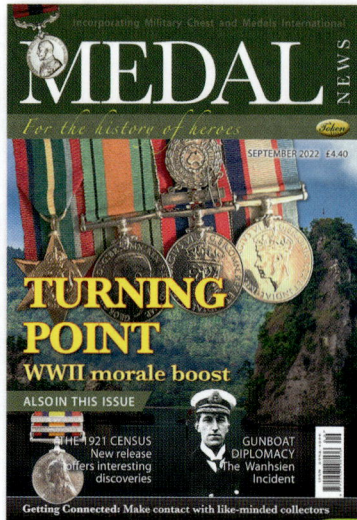

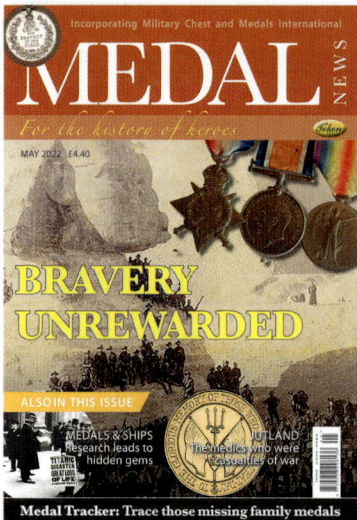

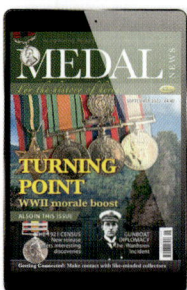

CAMPAIGN
Medals

The evolution of medals struck to commemorate, and later to reward participants in, a battle or campaign was a very gradual process. The forerunner of the modern campaign medal was the Armada Medal, cast in gold or silver, which appears to have been awarded to naval officers and distinguished persons after the abortive Spanish invasion of 1588. The obverse bears a flattering portrait of Queen Elizabeth (thought to have been designed by Nicholas Hilliard, the celebrated miniaturist) with a Latin inscription signifying "enclosing the most precious treasure in the world" (i.e. the Queen herself). On the reverse, the safety of the kingdom is represented by a bay tree growing on a little island, immune from the flashes of lightning which seem to strike it. This medal, and a similar type depicting the Ark floating calmly on a stormy sea, bore loops at the top so that a chain or cord could be passed through it for suspension from the neck of the recipient.

The Civil War produced a number of gallantry medals, mentioned in the previous section; but in 1650 Parliament authorised a medal which was struck in silver, bronze or lead to celebrate Cromwell's miraculous victory over the Scots at Dunbar. This was the first medal granted to all the participants on the Parliamentary side, and not restricted to high-ranking officers, or given for individual acts of heroism.

The Dunbar Medal thus established several useful precedents, which were eventually to form the criteria of the campaign medal as we know it today. After this promising start, however, the pattern of medals and their issue were much more restrictive. Naval medals were struck in gold for award to admirals and captains during the First Dutch War (1650–53), while the battle of Culloden (1746) was marked by a medal portraying the "Butcher" Duke of Cumberland, and granted to officers who took part in the defeat of the Jacobites.

In the second half of the eighteenth century there were a number of medals, but these were of a private or semi-official nature. The Honourable East India Company took the lead in awarding medals to its troops. These medals were often struck in two sizes and in gold as well as silver, for award to different ranks. The siege of Gibraltar (1779–83) was marked by an issue of medals to the defenders, but this was made on the initiative (and at the expense) of the garrison commanders, Generals Eliott and Picton, themselves.

During the French Revolutionary and Napoleonic Wars several medals were produced by private individuals for issue to combatants. Alexander Davison and Matthew Boulton were responsible for the medals granted to the officers and men who fought the battles of the Nile (1798) and Trafalgar (1805). Davison also produced a Trafalgar medal in pewter surrounded by a copper rim; it is recorded that the seamen who received it were so disgusted at the base metal that they threw it into the sea! At the same time, however, Government recognition was given to senior officers who had distinguished themselves in certain battles and engagements and a number of gold medals were awarded. The events thus marked included the capture of Ceylon (1795–96) and the battles of Maida, Bagur and Palamos.

Towards the end of the Napoleonic Wars an Army Gold Medal was instituted in two sizes—large (generals) and small (field officers). Clasps for second and third battles and campaigns were added to the medal, but when an officer became eligible for a third clasp the medal was exchanged for a Gold Cross with the names of the four battles engraved on its arms. Clasps for subsequent campaigns were then added to the cross (the Duke of Wellington receiving the Gold Cross with nine clasps). A total of 163 crosses, 85 large and 599 small medals were awarded, so that, apart from their intrinsic value, these decorations command very high prices when they appear in the saleroom.

The first medal awarded to all ranks of the Army was the Waterloo Medal, issued in 1816 shortly after the battle which brought the Napoleonic Wars to an end. No action was taken to grant medals for the other campaigns in the Napoleonic Wars until 1847 when Military and Naval General Service Medals were awarded retrospectively to veterans who were then still alive. As applications were made, in some cases, in respect of campaigns more than fifty years earlier, it is hardly surprising that the number of medals awarded was comparatively small, while the number of clasps awarded for certain engagements was quite minute. The Military General Service Medal was restricted to land campaigns during the Peninsular War (1808–13), the American War (1812–14) and isolated actions in the West Indies, Egypt and Java, whereas the Naval GSM covered a far longer period, ranging from the capture of the French frigate La Cleopatra by HMS Nymphe in June 1793, to the naval blockade of the Syrian coast in 1840, during the British operations against Mehemet Ali. Thus Naval Medals with the clasp for Syria are relatively plentiful (7057 awarded) while in several cases clasps were awarded to one man alone, and in seven cases there were no claimants for clasps at all. It is worth bearing in mind that applications for the medals and clasps resulted mainly from the publicity given by printed advertisements and notices posted up all over the country. With the poor general standard of literacy prevalent at the time, many people who were entitled to the medals would have been quite unaware of their existence.

The Naming of Medals

The Military and Naval GSMs, with their multitudinous combinations of clasps, have long been popular with collectors, but the other campaign medals of the past century and a half have a strong following as well. With the exception of the stars and medals awarded during World War II, all British campaign medals have usually borne the name of the recipient and usually his (or her) number, rank and regiment, unit or ship as well. This brings a personal element into the study of medals which is lacking in most other branches of numismatics. The name on a medal is very important for two reasons. It is a means of testing the genuineness, not only of the medal itself, but its clasp combination, and secondly it enables the collector to link the medal not only with the man who earned it, but with his unit or formation, and thus plays a vital part in the development of naval or military history, if only a small part in most cases.

Much of the potential value of a medal depends on the man who won it, or the unit to which he belonged. To form a coherent collection as opposed to a random accumulation of medals, the collector would be well advised to specialise in some aspect of the subject, restricting his interests perhaps to one medal (the Naval GSM) or a single group (British campaigns in India), or to medals awarded to the men of a particular regiment. The information given on the rim or back of a medal is therefore important in helping to identify it and assign it to its correct place. Even this has to be qualified to some extent. Some regiments are more popular than others with collectors and much depends on the part, active or passive, played by a unit in a particular battle or campaign for which the medal was awarded. Then again, the combination of event with the corps or regiment of the recipient must also be considered.

At one extreme we find the Royal Regiment of Artillery living up to its motto Ubique (everywhere) by being represented in virtually every land action (and not a few naval actions, as witness the Atlantic Star worn by former Maritime Gunners), so that a comprehensive collection of medals awarded to the RA would be a formidable feat.

At the other extreme one finds odd detachments, sometimes consisting of one or two men only, seconded from a regiment for service with another unit. The Indian IGS medal with clasp Hazara 1891, was also issued to five men of the 1st Dragoon Guards, these men were part of the "Government Telegraph Department", Punjab Division, whose names appear on Roll WO100/75 page 269, together with other soldiers serving as Signallers from other regiments. Whereas a specimen of the IGS medal with this clasp is not hard to find named to a soldier in one of the Bengal units, it constitutes a major rarity when awarded to one of the "odd men" and its value is correspondingly high.

As the personal details given on a medal regarding the recipient are so important, it is necessary for the collector to verify two facts — that the person whose name is on the medal was actually present at the action for which either the medal or its clasps were awarded, and

secondly, that the naming of the clasp and the attachment of the clasps is correct and not tampered with in any way. As regards the first, the National Archives at Kew, London, is a goldmine of information for all naval and military campaigns. Apart from despatches, reports and muster rolls covering the actions, there are the medal rolls compiled from the applications for medals and clasps. Transcriptions of the medal rolls are held by regimental museums and also by such bodies as the Military Historical Association and the Orders and Medals Research Society and, of course, many of these can be found on-line. Details of these and other clubs and societies devoted to medal collecting can be found in the later chapters.

The presence of a name on the roll does not mean that a medal or clasp was inevitably awarded; conversely authenticated medals are known to exist named to persons not listed on the medal roll. There are often divergences between the muster and medal rolls. Moreover, discrepancies in the spelling of recipients' names are not uncommon and clasps are sometimes found listed for regiments which were not even in existence when the battle was fought! This is explained, however, by the fact that a man may have been serving with one unit which took part in the campaign and subsequently transferred to another regiment. When claiming his medal he probably gave his present unit, rather than the one in which he was serving at the time of the action.

Unfortunately cases of medals having been tampered with are by no means rare, so it is necessary to be able to recognise evidence of fakery. A common device of the faker is to alter the name and personal details of the recipient and to substitute another name in order to enhance the medal's value. This is done simply by filing the inscription off the rim and adding a new one. In order to check for such alterations a similar medal of proven genuineness should be compared with a pair of fine callipers. Take the measurements at several points round the rim so that any unevenness should soon be apparent.

We cannot stress too much the importance of being closely familiar with the various styles of naming medals. Over the past 150 years an incredible variety of lettering — roman, italic, script, sans-serif, seriffed in all shapes and sizes — has been used at one time or another. In some cases the inscription was applied by impressing in raised relief; in others the inscription was punched in or engraved by hand. If a medal is normally impressed and you come across an engraved example you should immediately be on your guard. This is not an infallible test, however, as medals have been known with more than one style of naming, particularly if duplicates were issued at a much later date to replace medals lost or destroyed.

A rather more subtle approach was adopted by some fakers in respect of the Naval GSM. The three commonest clasps — Algiers (1362), Navarino (1137) and Syria (7057) — were awarded to many recipients possessing common names such as Jones or Smith which can be matched with recipients of some very rare clasps. In the case of the Naval GSM the ship on which the recipient served is not given, thus aiding the fraudulent substitution of clasps. It is necessary, therefore, to check the condition of clasps, even if the naming appears to be correct. Points to watch for are file or solder marks on the rivets which secure the clasps to each other and to the suspender of the medal. This test is not infallible as clasps do occasionally work loose if subject to constant wear (particularly if the recipient was a cavalryman, for obvious reasons). But clasps whose rivets appear to have been hammered should automatically be suspect, until a check of the medal rolls pass them as authentic. Examples of the earlier medals, particularly those awarded to officers may be found with unorthodox coupling. Major L. L. Gordon in his definitive British Battles and Medals, mentions a Naval GSM awarded to one of his ancestors with clasps for Guadaloupe and Anse la Barque in a large rectangular style which must have been unofficial. The medal is quite authentic, so it must be presumed that officers were allowed a certain degree of latitude in the manner in which they altered their medals.

Medals with clasps awarded for participation in subsequent engagements are invariably worth much more than the basic medal. In general, the greater number of clasps, the more valuable the medal, although, conversely, there are a few instances in which single-clasp medals are scarcer than twin-clasp medals. There is no short answer to this and individual rare clasps can enhance the value of an otherwise common medal out of all proportion. Thus the Naval GSM with clasp for Syria currently rates about £1000, but one of the two medals known to have been issued with the Acheron clasp of 1805 would easily rate 12 times as much. Again, relative value can only be determined by reference to all the circumstances of the award.

The person to whom a medal was issued has considerable bearing on its value. If the recipient belonged to a regiment which played a spectacular part in a battle, this generally rates a premium. The rank of the recipient also has some bearing; in general the higher the rank, the more valuable the medal. Medals to commissioned officers rate more than those awarded to NCOs and other ranks, and the medals of British servicemen rate more as a rule than those awarded to native troops. Medals granted to women usually command a relatively good premium. Another grim aspect is that medals issued to personnel who were wounded or killed in the campaign also rate more highly than those issued to servicemen who came through unscathed.

With the collector of British campaign medals the person to whom the medal was awarded tends to become almost as important as the medal itself. It is often not sufficient to collect the medal and leave it at that. The collector feels that he must investigate it and delve into the archives to find out all that he can about the recipient. Nowadays there is a plethora of information available on-line and the National Archives and regimental museums have already been mentioned, but do not overlook the usefulness of such reference tools as the monumental Mormon International Genealogical Index (now on microfiche and available in good public libraries and county record offices). All of these should help you to flesh out the bare bones of the details given in the muster and medal rolls.

Medal Groups

Apart from the combination of clasps on a medal and the significance of the recipient, there is a third factor to be considered in assessing the value of medals, namely the relationship of one medal to another in a group awarded to one person. Just as the number of clasps on a medal is not in itself a significant factor, so also the number of medals in a group is not necessarily important per se. Groups of five or more medals, whose recipient can be identified, are by no means uncommon. For example, a fairly common five medal group would consist of 1914–15 Medal, War Medal and Victory Medal (for World War I) and the Defence Medal and War Medal (for World War II). Thousands of men served throughout the first war survived to do duty, in a less active role, during a part at least of the second, long enough to qualify for the latter pair of medals.

It should be noted that none of the medals awarded for service in World War II was named to the recipient, so that groups comprising such medals alone cannot be readily identified and are thus lacking in the interest possessed by those containing named medals. Six-medal groups for service in World War II are not uncommon, particularly the combination of 1939–45 Star, Africa Star, Italy Star, France and Germany Star, Defence Medal and War Medal awarded to Army personnel who served from any time up to late 1942 and took part in the campaigns of North Africa and Europe.

Conversely it would be possible for troops to have served over a longer period and seen more action and only been awarded the 1939–45 Star, Burma Star (with Pacific clasp) and the War Medal. Naval groups consisting of the 1939–45 Star, Atlantic Star (with clasp for France and Germany), Italy Star and War Medal are less common and therefore more desirable (with, of course, the rider that it must be possible to identify the recipient), while the most desirable of all is the three-medal group of 1939–45 Star (with Battle of Britain clasp), Air Crew Europe Star (with clasp for France and Germany) and the War Medal. Such a group, together with a Distinguished Flying Cross awarded to one of The Few, is a highly coveted set indeed, providing, as always, that one can prove its authenticity. In any event, the addition of a named medal to a World War II group (e.g. a long service award, a gallantry medal, or some other category of medal named to the recipient), together with supporting collateral material (citations, log-books, pay-books, service records, newspaper cuttings, etc), should help to establish the provenance of the group.

The prices quoted in this publication are average figures for medals and decorations as individual items. Combinations with other decorations and campaign medals will produce a value usually well in excess of the aggregate of the individual items. Value will depend to a large extent on the personal factors and circumstances of the award, but where general factors are involved (e.g. the design of the medal, the period of issue or the campaign concerned, or in some cases the branch of the services) these are itemised separately. "—" indicates that either no examples have come onto the market or no examples have been issued. The figure in brackets (where available) is the approximate number awarded. Where the term RARE is used for a value this does not necessarily refer to the scarcity of the award in terms of numbers issued but rather their scarcity to market. It is possible that we have been able to ascertain prices for medals that were only issued in their tens as they regularly come up for sale whereas others, with higher issue numbers, haven't appeared on lists or at auction for some while and thus a true value has been difficult to obtain. Of course, often the term will apply to those medals that rarely come up for sale simply because so few of them were issued!

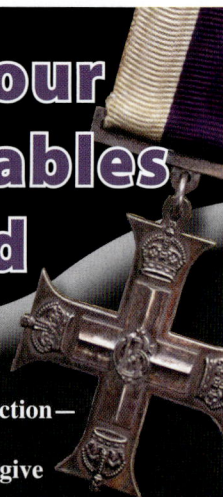

71. LOUISBURG MEDAL

Date: 1758.
Campaign: Canada (Seven Years War).
Branch of Service: British Army and Navy.
Ribbon: 32mm half yellow, half blue, although not originally intended for wear and therefore not fitted with suspension or ribbon.
Metals: Gold, silver or bronze.
Size: 42mm.
Description: (Obverse) the globe surrounded by allegorical figures of victory and flanked by servicemen; (reverse) burning ships in the harbour.
Comments: *More in the nature of a decoration, this medal was only given to certain recipients for acts of bravery or distinguished service in the capture in July 1758 of Louisburg in Canada during the Seven Years War. James Wolfe and Jeffrey Amherst commanded the land forces and Edward Boscawen the fleet.*

VALUE:
Gold	Rare
Silver	£4500–5500
Bronze	£1750–2500

72. CARIB WAR MEDAL

Date: 1773.
Campaign: Carib rebellion, St Vincent.
Branch of Service: Local militia or volunteers.
Ribbon: None.
Metal: Silver.
Size: 52mm.
Description: (Obverse) bust of George III in armour; (reverse) Britannia offering an olive branch to a defeated Carib, the date MDCCLXXIII in the exergue.
Comments: *The Legislative Assembly of St Vincent in the West Indies instituted this award to members of the militia and volunteers who served in the campaign of 1773 which put down a native rebellion that had been fomented by the French.*

VALUE:
Silver	£2500–3500

73. DECCAN MEDAL

Date: 1784.
Campaign: Western India and Gujerat 1778-84.
Branch of Service: HEIC forces.
Ribbon: Yellow cord.
Metals: Gold or silver.
Size: 40.5mm or 32mm.
Description: (Obverse) a rather languid Britannia with a trophy of arms, thrusting a laurel wreath towards a distant fort. (Reverse) an inscription in Farsi signifying "As coins are current in the world, so shall be the bravery and exploits of these heroes by whom the name of the victorious English nation was carried from Bengal to the Deccan. Presented in AH 1199 [1784] by the East India Company's Calcutta Government".
Comments: *The first medals struck by order of the Honourable East India Company were conferred on Indian troops for service in western India and Gujerat under the command of Warren Hastings. They were struck at Calcutta in two sizes; both gold and silver exist in the larger size but only silver medals in the smaller diameter.*

VALUE:
40.5mm gold	£5000–6500
40.5mm silver	£1800–2000
32mm silver	£1200–1400

74. DEFENCE OF GIBRALTAR

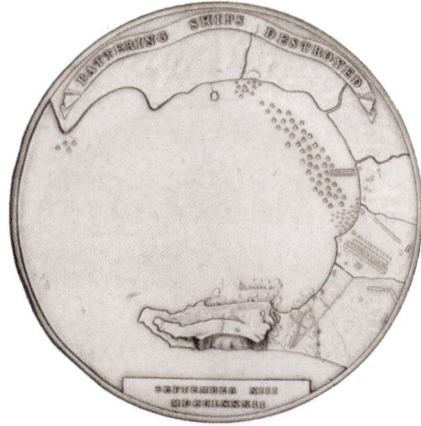

Eliott's medal

Picton's medal

Date: 1783.
Campaign: Siege of Gibraltar 1779–83.
Branch of Service: British and Hanoverian forces.
Ribbon: None.
Metal: Silver.
Size: 49mm (Eliott) and 59mm (Picton) .
Description: Eliott's medal was confined to the Hanoverian troops, hence the reverse inscribed
BRUDERSCHAFT (German for "brotherhood") above a wreath containing the names of the three
Hanoverian commanders and General Eliott. The obverse, by Lewis Pingo, shows a view of the Rock and
the naval attack of 13 September 1782 which was the climax of the siege. Picton's medal, awarded to the
British forces, has a larger than usual diameter, with a map of the Rock on the obverse and a 22-line text—the
most verbose British medal—above a recumbent lion clutching a shield bearing the castle and key emblem of
Gibraltar on the reverse.
Comments: *Several medals of a private nature were struck to commemorate the defence of Gibraltar during the Franco-
Spanish siege of 1779–83, but those most commonly encountered are these silver medals which were provided by George
Augustus Eliott and Sir Thomas Picton, the military commanders.*

VALUE:

Eliott medal	£850–1250
Picton medal	£1000–1500

75. MYSORE MEDAL

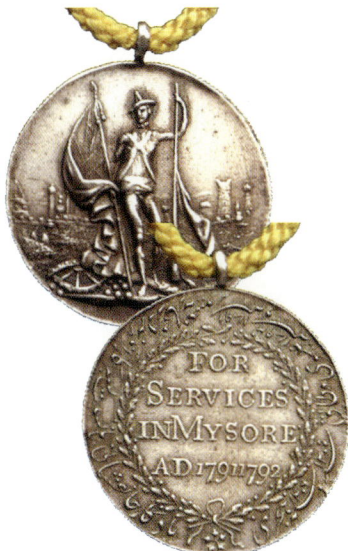

Date: 1792.
Campaign: Mysore 1790-92.
Branch of Service: HEIC forces.
Ribbon: Yellow cord.
Metal: Gold or silver.
Size: 43mm or 38mm.
Description: (Obverse) a sepoy of the HEIC Army holding British and Company flags over a trophy of arms with the fortress of Seringapatam in the background; (reverse) a bilingual inscription (in English and Farsi). The medal has a ring for suspension round the neck by a cord.
Comments: *Indian officers and men who served under Marquis Cornwallis and Generals Abercromby and Meadows received this medal for service in the campaign which brought about the downfall of Tippoo Sultan of Mysore.*

VALUE:

43mm gold (subadars)	£15,000–25,000
43mm silver (jemadars)	£2500–2800
38mm silver (other ranks)	£1500–1800

76. ST VINCENTS BLACK CORPS MEDAL

Date: 1795.
Campaign: Carib rebellion 1795.
Branch of Service: Local militia volunteers.
Ribbon: None.
Metal: Bronze.
Size: 48.5mm.
Description: (Obverse) the winged figure of Victory brandishing a sword over a fallen foe who has abandoned his musket; (reverse) native holding musket and bayonet, BOLD LOYAL OBEDIENT around and H.G.FEC. in exergue.
Comments: *Awarded to the officers and NCOs of the Corps of Natives raised by Major Seton from among the island's slaves for service against the rebellious Caribs and French forces.*

VALUE:

Bronze	£1000–1250

77. CAPTURE OF CEYLON MEDAL

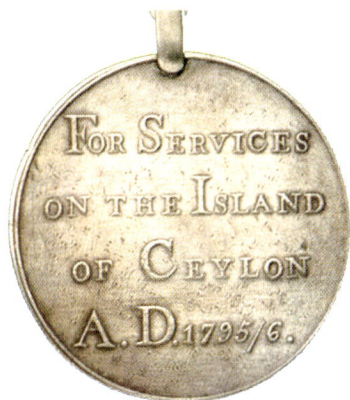

Date: 1796.
Campaign: Ceylon 1795.
Branch of Service: HEIC forces.
Ribbon: Yellow cord.
Metal: Gold or silver.
Size: 50mm.
Description: The plain design has an English inscription on the obverse, and the Farsi equivalent on the reverse.
Comments: *Awarded for service in the capture of Ceylon (Sri Lanka) from the Dutch during the French Revolutionary Wars. It is generally believed that the gold medals were awarded to Captains Barton and Clarke while the silver medals went to the native gunners of the Bengal Artillery.*

VALUE:

Gold (2)	—	
Silver (121)	£2500–3500 (original striking)	£800–1000 (later striking)

78. DAVISON'S NILE MEDAL

Date: 1798.

Campaign: Battle of the Nile 1798.

Branch of Service: Royal Navy.

Ribbon: None, but unofficially 32mm, deep navy blue.

Metal: Gold, silver, gilt-bronze and bronze.

Size: 47mm.

Description: (Obverse) Peace caressing a shield decorated with the portrait of Horatio Nelson; (reverse) the British fleet at Aboukir Bay. The edge bears the lettering "A TRIBUTE OF REGARD FROM ALEX^r DAVISON, ESQ^r ST JAMES'S SQUARE=".

Comments: *Nelson's victory at the mouth of the Nile on 1 August 1798 was celebrated in a novel manner by his prize agent, Alexander Davison, whose name and London address appear in the edge inscription of the medal designed by Kuchler. Originally issued without a suspender, many recipients added a ring to enable the medal to be worn. Admiral Nelson's medal was stolen in 1900 and is believed to have been melted down. Prices quoted below are for unnamed specimens, contemporary engraved medals are usually worth about twice as much.*

VALUE:	
Gold (Nelson and his captains)	**£12,000–15,000**
Silver (junior officers)	**£1500–2000**
Gilt-bronze (petty officers)	**£550–750**
Bronze (ratings)	**£300–450**

79. SERINGAPATAM MEDAL

Date: 1808.

Campaign: Seringapatam, India, 1799.

Branch of Service: HEIC forces.

Ribbon: 38mm gold.

Metal: Gold, silver-gilt, silver, bronze and pewter.

Size: 48mm or 45mm.

Description: (Obverse) the British lion defeating Tiger of Mysore (Tippoo Sultan) with the date of the capture of the fortress IV MAY MDCCXCIX (1799) in the exergue; (reverse) the assault on Seringapatam.

Comments: *The British and native troops who took part in the renewed campaign against Tippoo Sultan were awarded this medal in 1808 in various metals without suspension (a number of different types of suspenders and rings were subsequently fitted by individual recipients). The medal was designed by Kuchler and struck in England (48mm) and Calcutta, the latter version being slightly smaller (45mm). There are several different strikings of these medals.*

VALUE:

British Mint

Gold 48mm (30)	**£8000–10,000**
Silver-gilt 48mm (185)	**£1500–1750**
Silver 48mm (850)	**£1000–1500**
Bronze 48mm (5000)	**£450–550**
Pewter 48mm (45,000)	**£350–450**

Calcutta Mint

Gold 45mm (83)	**£5000–6500**
Silver 45mm (2786)	**£1000–1500**

Miniature	**Silver £230–290**

80. EARL ST. VINCENT'S MEDAL

Date: 1800.   **Campaign:** Mediterranean.
Branch of Service: Royal Navy.
Ribbon: None.
Metal: Gold or silver.   **Size:** 48mm
Description: (Obverse) left-facing bust of the Earl in Admiral's uniform; (reverse) a sailor and marine.
Comments: *A private medal presented by Earl St Vincent, when he struck his flag and came ashore in 1800, to the petty officers and men of his flagship* Ville de Paris *as a token of appreciation to his old shipmates. Contemporary engraved and named pieces with researched provenance are worth at least twice as much as unnamed specimens.*

VALUE:
Gold	£6000–7500
Silver	£850–1000

81. EGYPT MEDAL 1801

Date: 1801.
Campaign: Egypt 1801.
Branch of Service: HEIC forces.
Ribbon: Yellow cord.
Metal: Gold or silver.
Size: 48mm.
Description: (Obverse) a sepoy holding a Union Jack, with an encampment in the background. A four-line Farsi text occupies the exergue; (reverse) a warship and the Pyramids.
Comments: *Issued by the Honourable East India Company to British and Indian troops in the Company's service who took part in the conquest of Egypt under Generals Baird and Abercromby.*

VALUE:
Gold (16)	—	
Silver (2200)	£1800–2000 (original striking)	£400–500 (later striking)

82. SULTAN'S MEDAL FOR EGYPT

Date: 1801.

Campaign: Egypt 1801.

Branch of Service: British forces.

Ribbon: The gold medals were originally suspended by gold hook and chain as shown. The silver medals were hung from a sand-coloured ribbon.

Metals: Gold or silver.

Size: Various (see below).

Description: The very thin discs have an elaborate arabesque border enclosing the *toughra* or sign manual of the Sultan.

Comments: *This medal was conferred by Sultan Selim III of Turkey on the British officers and NCOs who took part in the campaign against the French. It was produced in five gold versions for award to different ranks of commissioned officers, as well as one in silver for award to sergeants and corporals.*

VALUE:

Gold 54mm studded with jewels	—
Gold 54mm plain (less than 100 issued)	£8500–10,000
Gold 48mm	£5500–6500
Gold 43mm	£4500–5500
Gold 36mm	£4000–5000
Silver 36mm	£2500–3500

Miniature	
Gold	£175–230
Silver	£125–175

83. HIGHLAND SOCIETY'S MEDAL FOR EGYPT 1801

Date: 1801.

Campaign: Egypt 1801.

Branch of Service: British forces.

Ribbon: None.

Metals: Gold, silver and bronze.

Size: 49mm.

Description: The medal was designed by Pidgeon. (Obverse) the right-facing bust of General Sir Ralph Abercromby, with a Latin inscription alluding to his death in Egypt; (reverse) a Highlander in combat with the Gaelic inscription NA FIR A CHOISIN BUAIDH SAN EPHAIT(These are the heroes who achieved victory in Egypt) and the date 21 MAR 1801. On the edge is the inscription "On choumun Chaeleach D'on Fhreiceadan Dubh Na XLII RT" (From the London Highland Society to the Black Watch or 42nd Regt.).

Comments: *The Highland and Agricultural Society (now Royal) was founded in 1784 to promote the development of agriculture in Scotland generally and the Highlands in particular. General Abercromby (born at Tullibody, 1734) commanded the British expedition to Egypt, and the landing at Aboukir Bay on 2 March 1801 in the face of strenuous French opposition, is justly regarded as one of the most brilliant and daring exploits of all time. The French made a surprise attack on the British camp on the night of 21 March and Abercromby was struck by a ricochet; he died aboard the flagship seven days later. Medals in gold were presented to the Prince Regent and Abercromby's sons, but silver and bronze medals were later struck and awarded to senior officers of the expedition as well as soldiers who had distinguished themselves in the campaign.*

VALUE:

Gold	—
Silver	£650–850
Bronze	£250–300

84. BOULTON'S TRAFALGAR MEDAL

Date: 1805.
Campaign: Battle of Trafalgar 1805.
Branch of Service: Royal Navy.
Ribbon: None, but unofficially 32mm navy blue (originally issued without suspension).
Metals: Gold, silver, white metal, gilt-bronze or bronze.
Size: 48mm.
Description: (Obverse) bust of Nelson; (reverse) a battle scene.
Comments: *Matthew Boulton of the Soho Mint, Birmingham, originally struck about 15,000 examples of this medal in white metal on his own initiative for presentation to the survivors of the battle of Trafalgar, but bronze and gilt-bronze specimens also exist. It was subsequently restruck on at least two occasions, the first and second strikings have the inscription impressed in large capitals around the rim TO THE HEROES OF TRAFALGAR FROM M:BOULTON, the later having the inscription omitted. As the original dies were used for each striking, they had to be polished before reuse, so the fine detail on Nelson's uniform and in the battle scene is less pronounced in the second and subsequent strikings. Examples of the original striking can sometimes be found engraved in various styles, but great care should be taken over checking the authenticity of such pieces. All gold specimens are restrikes. Silver medals were later ordered from Boulton's successors by officers who wished to have a medal to form a group with the 1848 NGS.*

VALUE:

Gold (c. 1905)	£4500–5500	Gilt-bronze	£750–850
Silver (1820–50)	£1750–2500	Bronze	£250–500
White metal	£450–600		

NB These prices are based on medals issued from the original striking and are dependent on attribution and generally in EF to Mint condition.

85. DAVISON'S TRAFALGAR MEDAL

Date: 1805.
Campaign: Battle of Trafalgar 1805.
Branch of Service: Royal Navy.
Ribbon: None, but unofficially 32mm navy blue.
Metal: Pewter with a copper rim.
Size: 52mm.
Description: (Obverse) bust of Nelson; (reverse) a man-of-war surrounded by an appropriate biblical quotation from Exodus "The Lord is a Man of War" and below: "Victory off Trafalgar over the combined Fleets of France and Spain Oct.21.1805".
Comments: *Alexander Davison, Nelson's prize agent, had this medal struck for award to the ratings of HMS* Victory *who took part in the battle.*

VALUE: £1750–2000

86. CAPTURE OF RODRIGUEZ, ISLE OF BOURBON AND ISLE OF FRANCE

Date: 1810.
Campaign: Indian Ocean 1809-10.
Branch of Service: HEIC forces.
Ribbon: Yellow cord.
Metal: Gold or silver.
Size: 49mm.
Description: (Obverse) a sepoy in front of a cannon with the Union Jack; (reverse) a wreath with inscriptions in English and Farsi.
Comments: *The East India Company awarded this medal to native troops of the Bengal and Bombay Armies for the capture of three French islands in the Indian Ocean (the latter two being better known today as Mauritius and Reunion) between July 1809 and December 1810.*

VALUE:	Original striking	Later striking
Gold (50)	£8500–10,000	—
Silver (2200)	£2000–2500	£550–650

87. BAGUR AND PALAMOS MEDAL

Date: 1811.
Campaign: Peninsular War 1810.
Branch of Service: Royal Navy.
Ribbon: Red with yellow edges (illustration at right has faded ribbon).
Metal: Gold or silver. **Size:** 45mm.
Description: (Obverse) the conjoined crowned shields of Britain and Spain in a wreath with ALIANZA ETERNA (eternal alliance) round the foot; (reverse) inscription in Spanish GRATITUDE OF SPAIN TO THE BRAVE BRITISH AT BAGUR 10 SEPT. 1810, PALAMOS 14 SEPT. 1810.
Comments: *Awarded by the Captain General of Catalonia to General Sir Charles Doyle and the Royal Marines and a limited number of officers and seamen from the British frigate* Cambrian, *for two actions on the coast of Catalonia in September 1810. Only awarded to those who actually went ashore: General Doyle, the Royal Marines, Captain Francis Fane and three of his officers received the medal for their participation in the attack on Bagur, while Lieutenant Benjamin Baynton and the launch crew received the medal for their participation at Palamós. Awarded in gold to officers and silver to other ranks.*

VALUE: Gold (8) £8500–10,000 Silver (72+) £2750–3500

88. JAVA MEDAL

Date: 1811.
Campaign: Java 1811.
Branch of Service: HEIC forces.
Ribbon: Yellow cord.
Metals: Gold or silver.
Size: 49mm.
Description: (Obverse) the assault on Fort Cornelis; (reverse) inscriptions in English and Farsi.
Comments: *Awarded by the HEIC for the seizure of Java from the Dutch. The 750 British officers and men who took part in the operation were not only awarded this medal but were eligible for the Military GSM with Java clasp, issued 38 years later. Senior officers of the Company were given the gold medal, while junior officers, NCOs and sepoys received the silver version.*

VALUE:	Original striking	Later striking
Gold (133)	£8500–10,000	£3500–4000
Silver (6519)	£1600–1800	£500–600

89. NEPAL MEDAL

Date: 1816.
Campaign: Nepal 1814-16.
Branch of Service: HEIC native troops.
Ribbon: Yellow cord.
Metal: Silver.
Size: 51mm.
Description: (Obverse) a fortified mountain-top with a cannon in the foreground; (reverse) Farsi inscription.
Comments: *This medal marked the campaign to pacify Nepal led by Generals Marley, Ochterlony and Gillespie (the last named being killed in action). At the conclusion of the war Ochterlony began recruiting Gurkha mercenaries, a policy which has continued in the British Army to this day. The clasp "Nepaul" was granted with the Army of India Medal to British forces in 1851.*

VALUE: Original striking £2000–2750
          Later striking £450–500 (as illustrated)

90. CEYLON MEDAL

Date: 1818.
Campaign: Ceylon (Sri Lanka) 1818.
Branch of Service: British and HEIC forces.
Ribbon: 38mm deep navy blue.
Metal: Gold or silver.
Size: 35mm.
Description: The very plain design has "Ceylon 1818" within a wreath (obverse) and REWARD OF MERIT at top and bottom of the reverse, the personal details being engraved in the centre.
Comments: *Awarded by the Ceylon government for gallant conduct during the Kandian rebellion. Only selected officers and men of the 19th, 73rd and 83rd Foot, the 1st and 2nd Ceylon Regiments and 7th, 15th and 18th Madras Native Infantry received this medal.*

VALUE:

Gold (2)	—
Silver (45)	£2000–3000

91. BURMA MEDAL

Date: 1826.
Campaign: Burma 1824-26.
Branch of Service: HEIC native forces.
Ribbon: 38mm crimson edged with navy blue.
Metals: Gold or silver.
Size: 39mm.
Description: (Obverse) the Burmese elephant kneeling in submission before the British lion; (reverse) the epic assault on Rangoon by the Irrawaddy Flotilla.
Comments: *Granted to native officers and men who participated in the campaign for the subjugation of Burma. This was the first of the HEIC campaign medals in what was to become a standard 1.5 inch (38mm) diameter. The medal was fitted with a large steel ring for suspension and issued unnamed. British troops in this campaign were belatedly (1851) given the clasp "Ava" to the Army of India Medal.*

VALUE:

		Miniature
Gold (750)	£4500–5500	—
Silver-gilt	£1500–2000	—
Silver (24,000)	£850–1250	£300–350

92. COORG MEDAL

Date: 1837.
Campaign: Coorg rebellion 1837.
Branch of Service: HEIC loyal Coorg forces.
Ribbon: Yellow cord.
Metals: Gold, silver or bronze.
Size: 50mm.
Description: (Obverse) a Coorg holding a musket, with kukri upraised; (reverse) weapons in a wreath with the inscription FOR DISTINGUISHED CONDUCT AND LOYALTY TO THE BRITISH GOVERNMENT COORG APRIL 1837, the equivalent in Canarese appearing on the obverse.
Comments: *Native troops who remained loyal during the Canara rebellion of April-May 1837 were awarded this medal by the HEIC the following August. Bronze specimens were also struck but not officially issued and may have been restrikes or later copies. Bronzed and silvered electrotype copies are also known.*

VALUE:	Original striking	Later striking
Gold (44)	**£7500–8500**	—
Silver (300)	**£2000–2500**	**£500–600**
Bronze	**£300–400**	—

93. NAVAL GOLD MEDAL

Date: 1795.
Campaign: Naval actions 1795-1815.
Branch of Service: Royal Navy.
Ribbon: 44mm white with broad dark blue edges.
Metal: Gold.
Size: 51mm and 38mm.
Description: The medals were glazed on both sides and individually engraved on the reverse with the name of the recipient and details of the engagement in a wreath of laurel and oak leaves. (Obverse) the winged figure of Victory bestowing a laurel wreath on the head of Britannia standing in the prow of a galley with a Union Jack shield behind her, her right foot on a helmet, her left hand holding a spear.
Comments: *Instituted in 1795, a year after Lord Howe's naval victory on "the glorious First of June", this medal was awarded continually till 1815 when the Order of the Bath was expanded into three classes. Large medals were awarded to admirals and small medals went to captains. As medals were awarded for separate actions it was possible for officers to wear more than one; Lord Nelson himself had three. Two miniatures are recorded and would probably fetch at least £1000 if they came on to the market.*

VALUE:	
Large medal (22)	**From £85,000**
Small medal (117)	**From £60,000**
Miniature	**£350–450**

94. NAVAL GENERAL SERVICE MEDAL

Date: 1847.

Campaign: Naval battles and boat actions 1793-1840.

Branch of Service: Royal Navy.

Ribbon: 32mm white with dark blue edges.

Metal: Silver.

Size: 36mm.

Description: (Obverse) the Young Head profile of Queen Victoria by William Wyon; (reverse) Britannia with her trident seated on a sea horse.

Clasps: No fewer than 230 different clasps for major battles, minor engagements, cutting-out operations and boat service were authorised. These either have the name or date of the action, the name of a ship capturing or defeating an enemy vessel, or the words BOAT SERVICE followed by a date. No fewer than 20,933 medals were awarded but most of them had a single clasp. Multi-clasp medals are worth very considerably more. The greatest number of clasps to a single medal was seven (three awards made); four medals had six clasps and 26 medals had five clasps. For reasons of space only those clasps which are met with fairly often in the salerooms are listed below. At the other end of the scale it should be noted that only one recipient claimed the clasps for *Hussar* (17 May 1795), *Dido* (24 June 1795), *Spider* (25 August 1795), *Espoir* (7 August 1798), *Viper* (26 December 1799), *Loire* (5 February 1800), *Louisa* (28 October 1807), *Carrier* (4 November 1807), *Superieure* (10 February 1809), *Growler* (22 May 1812) and the boat actions of 15 March 1793, 4 November 1803, 4 November 1810 and 3-6 September 1814. In several cases no claimants came forward at all. The numbers of clasps awarded are not an accurate guide to value, as some actions are rated more highly than others, and clasps associated with actions in the War of 1812 have a very strong following in the USA as well as Britain. Clasps for famous battles, such as Trafalgar, likewise command a high premium out of all proportion to the number of clasps awarded. A medal to HMS *Victory* would be worth in excess of £15,000.

Comments: *Instituted in 1847 and issued to **surviving** claimants in 1848, this medal was originally intended to cover naval engagements of the French Revolutionary and Napoleonic Wars (1793-1815) but was almost immediately extended to cover all naval actions of a more recent date, down to the expedition to Syria in 1840. It was fitted with a straight suspender.*

VALUE (for the most commonly encountered clasps):

v.	1 June 1794 (583)	£3500–4500	cxxviii.	Guadaloupe (484)		£1500–2000
ix.	14 March 1795 (114)	£3500–4500	cxli.	Lissa (124)		£3000–3500
xv.	23 June 1795 (200)	£3500–4500	cxlvi.	Java (695)		£2000–2500
xxxi.	St Vincent (364)	£3500–4500	clxi.	Shannon wh Chesapeake (42)		£6500–7500
xxxiv.	Camperdown (336)	£4000–5000	clxiii.	St Sebastian (288)		£4000–5000
xxxvi.	Mars 21 April 1798 (26)	£6500–8500	clxv.	Gluckstadt 5 Jany 1814 (45)		£5000–6500
xxxviii.	Lion 15 July 1798 (23)	£6500–8500	clxxvi.	Gaieta 24 July 1815 (89)		£5000–6000
xxxix.	Nile (351)	£3500–4000	clxxvii.	Algiers (1,362)		£1500–2500
xli.	12 Octr 1798 (79)	£4000–5000	clxxviii.	Navarino (1,137)		£1500–2500
xlv.	Acre 30 May 1799 (50)	£4500–5500	clxxix.	Syria (7,057)		£1000–1500
lxii.	Egypt (618)	£2000–2500				
lxiii.	Copenhagen (545)	£4500–6000	**Boat Service**			
lxv.	Gut of Gibraltar (144)	£4000–5000	cxcii.	16 July 1806 (52)		£3500–4500
lxxv.	Trafalgar (1,710)	£8000–8500	ccvi.	1 Novr 1809 (110)		£3000–4000
lxxvi.	4 Novr 1805 (297)	£3000–4000	ccx.	28 June 1810 (27)		£4500–5500
lxxvii.	St Domingo (406)	£3500–4500	ccxxiii.	29 Sepr 1812 (25)		£4500–5500
lxxix.	London 13 March 1806 (27)	£5000–6000	ccxxvii.	Ap and May 1813 (51)		£4500–5500
lxxxv.	Curacao 1 Jany 1807 (67)	£4000–5000	ccxxviii.	2 May 1813 (48)		£4500–5500
xcvii.	Stately 22 March 1808 (31)	£5000–6500	ccxxix.	April 1814 (24)		£5500–6500
cxiii.	Martinique (506)	£2000–2500	ccxxx.	24 May 1814 (14)		£6000–7000
cxvii.	Basque Roads (551)	£3000–3500	ccxxxiii.	14 Decr 1814 (205)		£2500–3000

Miniature Without clasp £125–175, for each clasp add £75+ depending on the action.

Below are listed all of the clasps authorised for wear on the Naval General Service Medal. As they were not issued until some years after the events, in some cases very few were ever claimed and in some instances there were no claimants at all. The numbers issued are indicated in brackets.

i.	Nymphe 18 June 1793 (4)		lxiv.	Speedy 6 May 1801 (7)
ii.	Crescent 20 Octr 1793 (12)		lxv.	Gut of Gibraltar 12 July 1801 (144)
iii.	Zebra 17 March1794 (2)		lxvi.	Sylph 28 Septr 1801 (2)
iv.	Carysfort 29 May 1794 (0)		lxvii.	Pasley 28 Octr 1801 (4)
v.	1 June 1794 (583)		lxviii.	Scorpion 31 March 1804 (4)
vi.	Romney 17 June 1794 (2)		lxix.	Beaver 31 March 1804 (0)
vii.	Blanche 4 Jany 1795 (5)		lxx.	Centurion 18 Septr 1804 (12)
viii.	Lively 13 March 1795 (6)		lxxi.	Arrow 3 Feby 1805 (8)
ix.	14 March 1795 (114)		lxxii.	Acheron 3 Feby 1805 (2)
x.	Astraea 10 April 1795 (2)		lxxiii.	San Fiorenzo 14 Feby 1805 (13)
xi.	Thetis 17 May 1795 (2)		lxxiv.	Phoenix 10 Aug 1805 (29)
xii.	Hussar 17 May 1795 (1)		lxxv.	Trafalgar (1,710)
xiii.	Mosquito 9 June 1795 (0)		lxxvi.	4 Novr 1805 (297)
xiv.	17 June 1795 (42)		lxxvii.	St. Domingo (406)
xv.	23 June 1795 (200)		lxxviii.	Amazon 13 March 1806 (30)
xvi.	Dido 24 June 1795 (1)		lxxix.	London 13 March 1806 (27)
xvii.	Lowestoffe 24 June 1795 (6)		lxxx.	Pique 26 March 1806 (8)
xviii.	Spider 25 August 1795 (1)		lxxxi.	Sirius 17 April 1806 (20)
xix.	Port Spergui (4)		lxxxii.	Blanche 19 July 1806 (22)
xx.	Indefatigable 20 April 1796 (8)		lxxxiii.	Arethusa 23 Aug 1806 (17)
xxi.	Unicorn 8 June 1796 (4)		lxxxiv.	Anson 23 Aug 1806 (11)
xxii.	Santa Margarita 8 June 1796 (3)		lxxxv.	Curacoa 1 Jany 1807 (67)
xxiii.	Southampton 9 June 1796 (8)		lxxxvi.	Pickle 3 Jany 1807 (2)
xxiv.	Dryad 13 June 1796 (6)		lxxxvii.	Hydra 6 Aug 1807 (12)
xxv.	Terpsichore 13 Oct 1796 (3)		lxxxviii.	Comus 15 Aug 1807 (9)
xxvi.	Lapwing 3 Decr 1796 (2)		lxxxix.	Louisa 28 Octr 1807 (1)
xxvii.	Minerve 19 Decr 1796 (4)		xc.	Carrier 4 Novr 1807 (1)
xxviii.	Blanche 19 Decr 1796 (4)		xci.	Ann 24 Novr 1807 (0)
xxix.	Indefatigable 13 Jany 1797 (8)		xcii.	Sappho 2 March 1808 (4)
xxx.	Amazon 13 Jany 1797 (6)		xciii.	San Fiorenzo 8 March 1808 (17)
xxxi.	St Vincent (364)		xciv.	Emerald 13 March 1808 (10)
xxxii.	San Fiorenzo 8 March 1797 (8)		xcv.	Childers 14 March 1808 (4)
xxxiii.	Nymphe 8 March 1797 (5)		xcvi.	Nassau 22 March 1808 (31)
xxxiv.	Camperdown (336)		xcvii.	Stately 22 March 1808 (31)
xxxv.	Phoebe 21 Decr 1797 (5)		xcviii.	Off Rota 4 April 1808 (19)
xxxvi.	Mars 21 April 1798 (26)		xcix.	Grasshopper 24 April 1808 (7)
xxxvii.	Isle St. Marcou (3)		c.	Rapid 24 April 1808 (1)
xxxviii.	Lion 15 July 1798 (23)		ci.	Redwing 7 May 1808 (7)
xxxix.	Nile (351)		cii.	Virginie 19 May 1808 (21)
xl.	Espoir 7 Aug 1798 (1)		ciii.	Redwing 31 May 1808 (7)
xli.	12 Octr 1798 (79)		civ.	Seahorse wh Badere Zaffer (32)
xlii.	Fisgard 20 Octr 1798 (9)		cv.	Comet 11 Aug 1808 (4)
xliii.	Sybille 28 Feby 1799 (12)		cvi.	Centaur 26 Aug 1808 (42)
xliv.	Telegraph 18 March 1799 (0)		cvii.	Implacable 26 Aug 1808 (44)
xlv.	Acre 30 May 1799 (50)		cviii.	Cruizer 1 Novr·1808 (4)
xlvi.	Schiermonnikoog 12 Aug 1799 (9)		cix.	Amethyst wh Thetis (31)
xlvii.	Arrow 13 Sept 1799 (2)		cx.	Off the Pearl Rock 13 Decr 1808 (16)
xlviii.	Wolverine 13 Sept 1799 (0)		cxi.	Onyx 1 Jany 1809 (5)
xlix.	Surprise wh Hermione (7)		cxii.	Confiance 14 Jany 1809 (8)
l.	Speedy 6 Novr 1799 (3)		cxiii.	Martinique (506)
li.	Courier 22 Novr 1799 (3)		cxiv.	Horatio 10 Feby 1809 (13)
lii.	Viper 26 Decr 1799 (2)		cxv.	Supérieure 10 Feby 1809 (1)
liv.	Harpy 5 Feby 1800 (4)		cxvi.	Amethyst 5 April 1809 (27)
lv.	Fairy 5 Feby 1800 (4)		cxvii.	Basque Roads 1809 (551)
lvi.	Peterel 21 March 1800 (2)		cxviii.	Recruit 17 June 1809 (7)
lvii.	Penelope 30 March 1800 (11)		cxix.	Pompee 17 June 1809 (47)
lviii.	Vinciego 30 March 1800 (2)		cxx.	Castor 17 June 1809 (13)
lix.	Capture of the Désirée (24)		cxxi.	Cyane 25 and 27 June 1809 (5)
lx.	Seine 20 August 1800 (7)		cxxii.	L'Espoir 25 and 27 June 1809 (5)
lxi.	Phoebe 19 Feby 1801 (6)		cxxiii.	Bonne Citoyenne wh Furieuse (12)
lxii.	Egypt (618)		cxxiv.	Diana 11 Septr 1809 (8)
lxiii.	Copenhagen 1801 (545)		cxxv.	Anse la Barque 18 Decr 1809 (51)

cxxvi.	Cherokee 10 Jany 1810 (4)
cxxvii.	Scorpion 12 Jany 1810 (8)
cxxviii.	Guadaloupe (484)
cxxix.	Thistle 10 Feby 1810 (0)
cxxx.	Surly 24 April 1810 (1)
cxxxi.	Firm 24 April 1810 (1)
cxxxii.	Sylvia 26 April 1810 (1)
cxxxiii.	Spartan 3 May 1810 (30)
cxxxiv.	Royalist May and June 1810 (3)
cxxxv.	Amanthea 25 July 1810 (23)
cxxxvi.	Banda Neira (68)
cxxxvii.	Staunch 18 Septr 1810 (2)
cxxxviii.	Otter 18 Septr 1810 (8)
cxxxix.	Boadicea 18 Septr 1810 (15)
cxl.	Briseis 14 Octr 1810 (2)
cxli.	Lissa (124)
cxlii.	Anholt 27 March 1811 (40)
cxliii.	Arrow 6 April 1811 (0)
cxliv.	Off Tamatave 20 May 1811 (87)
cxlv.	Hawke 18 Aug 1811 (6)
cxlvi.	Java (695)
cxlvii.	Skylark 11 Novr 1811 (4)
cxlviii.	Locust 11 Novr 1811 (2)
cxlix.	Pelagosa 29 Novr 1811 (74)
cl.	Victorious wh Rivoli (67)
cli.	Weasel 22 Feby 1812 (6)
clii.	Rosario 27 March 1812 (7)
cliii.	Griffon 27 March 1812 (3)
cliv.	Northumberland 22 May 1812 (63)
clv.	Growler 22 May 1812 (1)
clvi.	Malaga 29 May 1812 (18) (the date should have been 29 April 1812)
clvii.	Off Mardoe 6 July 1812 (47)
clviii.	Sealark 21 July 1812 (4)
clix.	Royalist 29 Decr 1812 (4)
clx.	Weasel 22 April 1813 (8)
clxi.	Shannon wh Chesapeake (42)
clxii.	Pelican 14 Aug 1813 (4)
clxiii.	St. Sebastian (288)
clxiv.	Thunder 9 Octr 1813 (9)
clxv.	Gluckstadt 5 Jany 1814 (45)
clxvi.	Venerable 16 Jany 1814 (42)
clxix.	Cyane 16 Jany 1814 (7)
clxx.	Eurotas 25 Feby 1814 (32)
clxxi.	Hebrus wh L'Etoile (40)
clxxii.	Phoebe 28 March 1814 (36)
clxxiii.	Cherub 28 March 1814 (7)
clxxiv.	The Potomac 17 Aug 1814 (108)
clxxv.	Endymion wh President (58)
clxxvi.	Gaieta 24 July 1815 (89)
clxxvii.	Algiers (1,362)
clxxviii.	Navarino (1,137)
clxxix.	Syria (7,057)

BOAT SERVICE

These clasps have the words BOAT SERVICE separating the month and the years of the dates. They were only awarded for actions which culminated in an officer or the senior member present being promoted.

clxxx.	15 March 1793 (1)
clxxxi.	17 March 1794 (29)
clxxxii.	29 May 1797 (3)
clxxxiii.	9 June 1799 (4)
clxxxiv.	20 Decr 1799 (3)
clxxxv.	29 July 1800 (4)
clxxxvi.	29 Aug 1800 (25)
clxxxvii.	27 Octr 1800 (5)
clxxxvii.	21 July 1801 (7)
clxxxviii.	27 June 1803 (5)
clxxxix.	4 Novr 1803 (2)
cxc.	4 Feby 1804 (11)
cxci.	4 June 1805 (10)
cxcii.	16 July 1806 (52)
cxciii.	2 Jan 1807 (3)
cxciv.	21 Jan 1807 (8)
cxcv.	19 April 1807 (0)
cxcvi.	13 Feby 1808 (2)
cxcvii.	10 July 1808 (8)
cxcviii.	11 Aug 1808 (17)
cxcix.	28 Novr 1808 (2)
cc.	7 July 1809 (35)
cci.	14 July 1809 (7)
ccii.	25 July 1809 (36)
cciii.	27 July 1809 (10)
cciv.	29 July 1809 (11)
ccv.	28 Aug 1809 (15)
ccvi.	1 Novr 1809 (100)
ccvii.	13 Decr 1809 (9)
ccviii.	13 Feby 1810 (20)
ccix.	1 May 1810 (15)
ccx.	28 June 1810 (27)
ccxi.	27 Sept 1810 (36)
ccxii.	4 Novr 1810 (1)
ccxiii.	23 Novr 1810 (42)
ccxiv.	24 Decr 1810 (6)
ccxv.	4 May 1811 (10)
ccxvi.	30 July 1811 (4)
ccxvii.	2 Aug 1811 (9)
ccxviii.	20 Sept 1811 (6)
ccxix.	4 Decr 1811 (19)
ccxx.	4 April 1812 (4)
ccxxi.	1st Sept 1812 (21)
ccxxii.	17 Sept 1812 (11) (Bars are known dated 17 Decr 1812 in error)
ccxxiii.	29 Sept 1812 (25)
ccxxiv.	6 Jany 1813 (25)
ccxxv.	21 March 1813 (3)
ccxxvi.	29 April 1813 (2)
ccxxvii.	Ap and May 1813 (51)
ccxxviii.	2 May 1813 (48)
ccxxix.	8 April 1814 (24)
ccxxx.	24 May 1814 (14)
ccxxxi.	Aug and Septr 1814 (1)
ccxxxii.	3 and 6 Septr 1814 (1)
ccxxxiii.	14 Decr 1814 (205)

111

95. ARMY GOLD CROSS

Date: 1813.

Campaigns: Napoleonic and Peninsular War.

Branch of Service: British Army.

Ribbon: 38mm crimson edged with dark blue.

Metal: Gold. **Size:** 38mm.

Description: A cross pattée with a laurel border having a rose at the centre on each of the four flat ends. At the centre of the cross appears a British lion statant. The scrolled top of the cross is fitted with an elaborate ring decorated with laurel leaves looped through a plain swivel ring fitted to the suspender. The arms of the cross on both obverse and reverse bear the names of four battles in relief.

Clasps: Large borders of laurel leaves enclosing the name of a battle in raised relief within an elliptical frame, awarded for fifth and subsequent battles.

Comments: *Arguably the most prestigious award in the campaign series, the Army Gold Cross was approved by the Prince Regent in 1813. It was granted to generals and officers of field rank for service in four or more battles of the Peninsular War. Four crosses were also awarded for Maida, seven Martinique and three Guadeloupe. A total of 164 crosses and 244 clasps were awarded. Three crosses had six clasps, two had seven, while the Duke of Wellington himself had the unique cross with nine clasps, representing participation in thirteen battles.*

VALUE:

Gold cross without clasp (61)	From £25,000
Miniature	£520–635

The Duke of Wellington.

96. MAIDA GOLD MEDAL

Date: 1806.
Campaign: Battle of Maida 1806.
Branch of Service: British Army.
Ribbon: 38mm crimson edged with navy blue.
Metal: Gold.
Size: 39mm.
Description: (Obverse) laureated profile of George III; (reverse) winged figure of Victory hovering with a laurel wreath over the head of Britannia, shield upraised, in the act of throwing a spear. The name and date of the battle appears on Britannia's left, with the *trinacria* or three-legged emblem on the right.
Clasps: None.
Comments: *This small gold medal was authorised in 1806 and awarded to the thirteen senior officers involved in the battle of Maida in Calabria when a small British force under General Sir John Stuart defeated a much larger French army with heavy loss. A small unknown number of gold and silver specimens are known to exist.*

VALUE: From £45,000

97. ARMY GOLD MEDAL

Date: 1810.
Campaigns: Peninsular War 1806-14 and War of 1812.
Branch of Service: British Army.
Ribbon: 38mm crimson edged with navy blue.
Metal: Gold.
Size: 54mm and 33mm.
Description: (Obverse) Britannia seated on a globe, holding a laurel wreath over the British lion and holding a palm branch in her left hand while resting on a shield embellished with the Union Jack. The name of the first action is generally engraved on the reverse.
Clasps: For second and third actions.
Comments: *The Maida medal (no. 96) established a precedent for the series of medals instituted in 1810. The name of the battle was inscribed on the reverse, usually engraved, though that for Barossa was die-struck. These medals were struck in two sizes, the larger being conferred on generals and the smaller on officers of field rank. Second or third battles were denoted by a clasp appropriately inscribed, while those who qualified for a fourth award exchanged their medal and bars for a gold cross. The award of these gold medals and crosses ceased in 1814 when the Companion of the Bath was instituted.*

VALUE*:
Large medal	From £30,000
Small medal	From £18,500

*Medals to British officers in the Portuguese Service generally sell for 20% less. Only one miniature is known to exist.

98. MILITARY GENERAL SERVICE MEDAL

Date: 1847.

Campaigns: French Revolutionary and Napoleonic Wars 1793-1814.

Branch of Service: British Army.

Ribbon: 31mm crimson edged with dark blue.

Metal: Silver.

Size: 36mm.

Description: (Obverse) the Wyon profile of Queen Victoria; (reverse) a standing figure of the Queen bestowing victor's laurels on a kneeling Duke of Wellington. The simple inscription TO THE BRITISH ARMY appears round the circumference, while the dates 1793-1814 are placed in the exergue. Despite this, the earliest action for which a clasp was issued took place in 1801 (Abercromby's Egyptian campaign).

Clasps: Only 29 battle or campaign clasps were issued but multiple awards are much more common than in the naval medal, the maximum being fifteen. While it is generally true to say that multi-clasp medals are worth more than single-clasp medals, there are many in the latter category (noted below) which command higher prices. The figures quoted below are based on the commonest regiments. Clasps awarded to specialists and small detached forces rate more highly than medals to the principal regiment in a battle or campaign. In particular, it should be noted that one naval officer, Lieut. Carroll, received the Military GSM and clasp for Maida, while a few other officers of the Royal Navy and Royal Marines received the medal with the clasps for Guadaloupe, Martinique or Java, and these, naturally, are now very much sought after. Paradoxically, the clasps for Sahagun and Benevente alone are very much scarcer than the clasp inscribed Sahagun and Benevente, awarded to surviving veterans who had participated in both battles. The clasps are listed below in chronological order. Medals to officers rate a premium.

Comments: *Like the Naval GSM, this medal was not sanctioned till 1847 and awarded the following year. Unlike the Naval medal, however, the Military GSM was confined to land actions up to the defeat of Napoleon in 1814 and the conclusion of the war with the United States. The regiment is now having a bearing on price, with medals to the 52nd, 88th or 95th Foot worth a good premium.*

VALUE:

i.	Egypt	£1250–1500	xxi.	Chateauguay	£6000–7000
ii.	Maida	£1550–2000	xxii.	Chrystler's Farm	£7000–8000
iii.	Roleia	£1150–1350	xxiii.	Vittoria	£1000–1250
iv.	Vimiera	£1000–1250	xxiv.	Pyrenees	£1000–1250
v.	Sahagun	£2000–2500	xxv.	St Sebastian	£1100–1300
vi.	Benevente	£4500–6000	xxvi.	Nivelle	£1000–1250
vii.	Sahagun and Benevente	£2000–2500	xxvii.	Nive	£950–1100
viii.	Corunna	£1000–1250	xxviii.	Orthes	£950–1100
ix.	Martinique	£1500–1750	xxix.	Toulouse	£950–1100
x.	Talavera	£1100–1300	2 clasps		from £1250
xi.	Guadaloupe	£1000–1250	3 clasps		from £1500
xii.	Busaco	£1000–1250	4 clasps		from £1750
xiii.	Barrosa	£1000–1250	5 clasps		from £2000
xiv.	Fuentes D'Onor	£1000–1250	6 clasps		from £2250
xv.	Albuhera	£1250–1500	7 clasps		from £2500
xvi.	Java	£1000–1250	8 clasps		from £3000
xvii.	Ciudad Rodrigo	£1000–1250	9 clasps		from £3500
xviii.	Badajoz	£1300–1550	10 clasps		from £4000
xix.	Salamanca	£1000–1250	11 clasps		from £4500
xx.	Fort Detroit	£7000–8000	12 or more clasps		from £7500

Miniature without clasp £125–175, for each clasp add £75+ depending on the action.

99. WATERLOO MEDAL

Date: 1815.
Campaign: Waterloo 1815.
Branch of Service: British Army.
Ribbon: 38mm, crimson edged in dark blue.
Metal: Silver.
Size: 37mm.
Description: (Obverse) the profile of the Prince Regent; (reverse) the seated figure of Victory above a tablet simply inscribed WATERLOO with the date of the battle in the exergue.
Comments: *This was the first medal awarded and officially named to all ranks who took part in a particular campaign. It was also issued, however, to those who had taken part in one or more of the other battles of the campaign, at Ligny and Quatre Bras two days earlier. The ribbon was intended to be worn with an iron clip and split suspension ring but many recipients subsequently replaced these with a more practical silver mount which would not rust and spoil the uniform. Some 39,000 medals were issued. The value of a Waterloo medal depends to a large extent on the regiment of the recipient. Medals awarded to those formations which saw the heaviest action and bore the brunt of the losses are in the greatest demand, whereas medals named to soldiers in General Colville's reserve division which did not take part in the fighting, are the least highly rated.*

VALUE:

Heavy Cavalry	£3750–4750
Scots Greys	£8500–10,000
Light Cavalry	£2750–3750
Royal Artillery	£2500–3000
Royal Horse Artillery	£2500–3000
Foot Guards	£2250–2850
1st, 27th, 28th, 30th, 42nd, 44th, 52nd, 73rd, 79th, 92nd, 95th Foot	£4000–5000
Other Foot regiments	£2250–2750
Colville's division (35th, 54th, 59th, 91st Foot)	£1750–2250
King's German Legion	£1500–1850

Miniature
Original £60–250

100. BRUNSWICK MEDAL FOR WATERLOO

Date: 1817.
Campaign: Battle of Waterloo 1815.
Branch of Service: Brunswick troops.
Ribbon: 38mm wide, yellow with light blue stripes towards the edges.
Metal: Bronze.
Size: 35mm.
Description: (Obverse) Duke Friedrich Wilhelm of Brunswick who was killed in the battle; (reverse) a wreath of laurel and oak leaves enclosing the German text "Braunschweig Seinen Kriegern" (Brunswick to its warriors) and the names of Quatre Bras and Waterloo.
Comments: *The Prince Regent authorised this medal for issue to the contingent from the Duchy of Brunswick who served at Quatre Bras or Waterloo. The next of kin of those killed in action at either battle where awarded the medal disc only with no ring, clip, suspension or ribbon. It is thought that approximately 700 medals are still extant.*

VALUE: £600–800
Casualty £2000–2500

Miniature —

101. HANOVERIAN MEDAL FOR WATERLOO

Date: 1818.
Campaign: Battle of Waterloo 1815.
Branch of Service: Hanoverian troops.
Ribbon: Maroon edged with light blue.
Metal: Silver.
Size: 35mm.
Description: (Obverse) the Prince Regent, his name and title being rendered in German. (Reverse) a trophy of arms below the legend HANNOVERISCHER TAPFERKEIT (Hanoverian bravery), with the name and date of the battle wreathed in the centre.
Comments: *The Prince Regent authorised this medal on behalf of his father George III in his capacity as Elector of Hanover and this was conferred on survivors of the battle. Suspension was by iron clip and ring similar to the British Waterloo Medal.*

VALUE:	£700–800
Miniature	£125–175

102. NASSAU MEDAL FOR WATERLOO

Date: 1815.
Campaign: Battle of Waterloo 1815.
Branch of Service: Nassau forces.
Ribbon: Dark blue edged in yellow.
Metal: Silver.
Size: 28mm.
Description: (Obverse) Duke Friedrich of Nassau; (reverse) the winged figure of Victory crowning a soldier with laurels, the date of the action being in the exergue.
Comments: *Friedrich Duke of Nassau distributed this medal on 23 December 1815 to all of his own troops who had been present at the battle.*

VALUE:	£450–550

103. SAXE-GOTHA-ALTENBURG MEDAL

Date: 1816.
Campaign: Germany and Waterloo 1814-15.
Branch of Service: Saxe-Gotha-Altenburg Foreign Legion.
Ribbon: Green with black edges and gold stripes.
Metal: Gilt bronze or bronze.
Size: 42mm.
Description: (Obverse) a crown with the legend IM KAMPFE FUER DAS RECHT (in the struggle for the right); (reverse) an ornate rose motif with the name of the duchy and the dates of the campaign in roman numerals.
Comments: *Gilded medals were issued to officers, NCOs received bronze medals with gilt raised points and other ranks a bronze version.*

VALUE:	
Gilt-bronze	£1000–1250
Bronze	£650–750

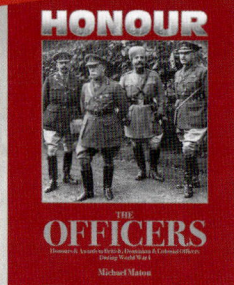
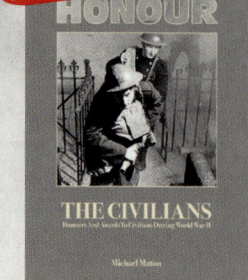

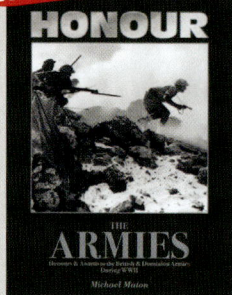
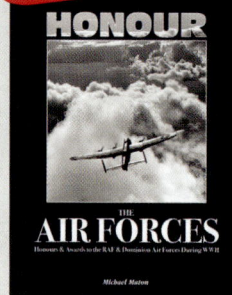

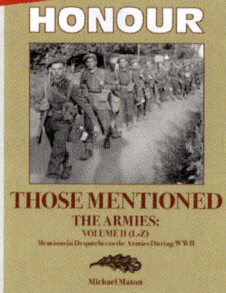
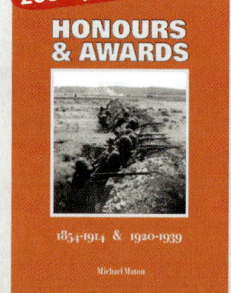
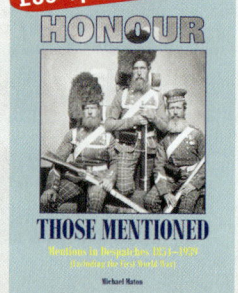
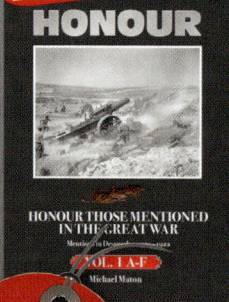
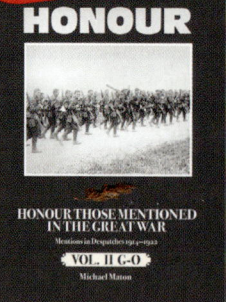
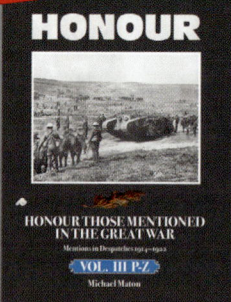
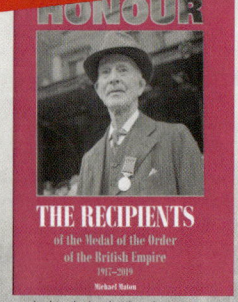

104. ARMY OF INDIA MEDAL

Date: 1851.
Campaigns: India 1803–26.
Branch of Service: British and HEIC troops.
Ribbon: 32mm pale blue.
Metal: Silver.
Size: 35mm.
Description: (Obverse) the Wyon profile of Queen Victoria; (reverse) the seated figure of Victory beside a palm tree, with a wreath in one hand and a laurel crown in the other. The medal is fitted with an ornamental scroll suspender.
Clasps: The medal was not awarded without a campaign clasp and, unusually, in multi-clasp medals, the last clasp awarded was mounted closest to the medal itself, so that the battle roll has to be read downwards. There were two dies of the reverse, leading to the long- or short-hyphen varieties, both of comparable value. In all, some 4500 medals were awarded, but there is a very wide divergence between the commonest and rarest bars. Multi-clasp medals are rare, and medals awarded to Europeans are much scarcer than those to Indian troops.
Comments: *The last of the medals authorised in connection with the Napoleonic Wars, it was instituted and paid for by the Honourable East India Company in March 1851 for award to surviving veterans of the battles and campaigns in India and Burma between 1803 and 1826. Despite the dates 1799–1826 in the exergue, the medal was in fact awarded for service in one or other of four wars: the Second Mahratta War (1803–4), the Nepal War (1814–16), the Pindaree or Third Mahratta War (1817–18) and the Burmese War (1824–26), together with the siege of Bhurtpoor (1825–26). The medal is scarce, and examples with the clasps for the Second Mahratta War are much sought after, partly because few veterans were still alive 48 years after the event to claim their medals, and partly because of the war's association with Arthur Wellesley, the Duke of Wellington, who died in the very year in which the medal was awarded. Medals to the Royal Navy with the Ava clasp are very rare.*

Rev. die a, short hyphen

Rev. die b, long hyphen

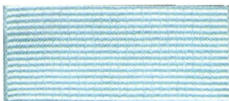

VALUE:
Prices for medals bearing the following clasps are for European recipients. Medals to Indians are generally less expensive.

i.	Allighur (66)	£3000–3500
ii.	Battle of Delhi (40)	£3500–4500
iii.	Assye (87)	£3000–3500
iv.	Asseerghur (48)	£3500–4500
v.	Laswarree (100)	£3000–3500
vi.	Argaum (126)	£2500–3000
vii.	Gawilghur (110)	£3000–3500
viii.	Defence of Delhi (5)	—
ix.	Battle of Deig (47)	£3500–4500
x.	Capture of Deig (103)	£3000–3500
xi.	Nepaul (505)	£1500–1800
xii.	Kirkee (5)	—
xiii.	Poona (75)	£3000–3500
xiv.	Kirkee and Poona (88)	£3000–3500
xv.	Seetabuldee (2)	—
xvi.	Nagpore (155)	£2500–3000
xvii.	Seetabuldee and Nagpore (21)	£6000–8000
xviii.	Maheidpoor (75)	£3000–3500
xix.	Corygaum (4)	£6000–10,000
xx.	Ava (2325)	£1000–1200 (Army)
xxi.	Bhurtpoor (1059)	£1200–1500
2 clasps (300)		from £3500
3 clasps (150)		from £7500
4 clasps (23)		from £10,000
5 or more clasps (10 x 5, 2 x 6, 1 x 7)		—
Glazed gilt specimen		£850–1000

Miniature*

One clasp Ava	£275–300
Further clasps	£125–175 each

*Note there are many silver reproductions and clasps on the market, value £10–20.

105. GHUZNEE MEDAL

Date: 1839.

Campaign: Ghuznee 1839.

Branch of Service: British and HEIC forces.

Ribbon: 35mm half crimson, half dark green (originally green and yellow)

Metal: Silver.

Size: 37mm.

Description: (Obverse) the impressive gateway of the fortress of Ghuznee; (reverse) a mural crown enclosed in a laurel wreath with the date of capture.

Comments: *This was the second medal awarded for a particular campaign (after Waterloo) and was granted to both British and Indian troops who took part in the assault on Ghuznee in July 1839 which brought the first Afghan War to a close, overthrew the pro-Russian Dost Mohamed and restored Shah Soojah who instituted the Order of the Dooranie Empire (awarded to British generals and field officers) in appreciation. The Ghuznee medal was issued unnamed by the Honourable East India Company, but many recipients subsequently had their names impressed or engraved in various styles. No clasps were issued officially, but unauthorised clasps are occasionally encountered.*

VALUE:

British recipient	£850–1000
Indian recipient	£750–850
Unnamed as issued	£500–600
Miniature	£175–330

Original type ribbon.

Taking the Ghuznee fortress.

105A. BRITISH LEGION MEDAL

Date: 1836.
Campaign: First Carlist War.
Branch of Service: British Auxiliary Legion, plus a battalion of Royal Artillery seconded to the forces loyal to Queen Isabella.
Ribbon: Broad blue with narrow yellow stripes towards the edges.
Metal: Silver or white metal.
Size: 36mm.
Description: (Obverse) A cross pattee with the word TUJO in a laurel wreath at the centre; (reverse) ESPANA / AGRADECIDA (Grateful Spain) with a British lion enclosed by the cordon of the Golden Fleece. The medal is fitted with a ring for suspension from a double-looped bar and has a brooch fitment at the top of the ribbon. The medal was struck in Birmingham.
Comments: *The British Auxiliary Legion, commanded by General Sir George De Lacey Evans (1787–1870), volunteered for service in Spain in support of Isabella II who, at the age of three (1833) succeeded her father as monarch. Her uncle, Don Carlos, opposed this and triggered off a war which lasted till 1840 and was largely fought in the northern provinces. The inscription on the obverse alludes to the battle at Laguna del Tujo near Castilla la Mancha.*

VALUE:	Silver	£400–450
	(one Continental size miniature example with engraved details to reverse is known)	
	White metal	£150–200

106. ST. JEAN D'ACRE MEDAL

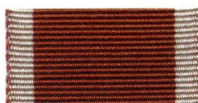

Date: 1840.
Campaign: Syria 1840.
Branch of Service: Royal Navy, Royal Marines and British Army.
Ribbon: Red with white edges.
Metal: Gold (22gms), silver or copper (bronzed).
Size: 30mm.
Description: (Obverse) a fortress flying the Ottoman flag, with six five-pointed stars round the top. A commemorative inscription and date in Arabic appear at the foot; (reverse) the Toughra of the Sultan in a laurel wreath.
Comments: *Awarded by the Sultan of Turkey to British, Austrian and Turkish forces under Sir Charles Napier, taking part in the liberation of this important city on the Syrian coast after eight years of Egyptian occupation. The medal has a plain ring suspension. The clasp "Syria" to the Naval GSM was awarded in 1848 in respect of this operation, and this medal generally accompanies the St Jean d'Acre medal.*

VALUE:		Miniature
Gold (captains and field officers)	£4500–5000	—
Silver (junior officers)	£400–450	£200–250
Copper (petty officers, NCOs and other ranks)	£200–250	—

107. CANDAHAR, GHUZNEE, CABUL MEDAL

Date: 1842.
Campaign: Afghanistan 1841–42.
Branch of Service: British and HEIC troops.
Ribbon: 40mm watered silk of pink, white, yellow, white and blue representing an eastern sky at sunrise.
Metal: Silver.
Size: 36mm.
Description: Although the medals have a uniform obverse, a profile of the Queen captioned VICTORIA VINDEX, reverses are inscribed with the names of individual battles, or combinations thereof, within wreaths surmounted by a crown.
Comments: *The Honourable East India Company instituted this series of medals in 1842 for award to both HEIC and British troops who took part in the First Afghan War. The issue of this medal to units of the British Army, to Europeans serving in the Company's forces, and to Indian troops is further complicated by the fact that unnamed medals are generally common. In addition, the medal for Cabul is known in two versions, with the inscription CABUL or CABVL, the latter being a major rarity as only fifteen were issued. Only 160 medals with Candahar reverse were issued to Europeans. Beware of modern copies of the Candahar and Cabul medals.*

VALUE:	Imperial Regiments	Indian Units	Unnamed
i. Candahar	£850–1000	£500–650	£400–550
ii. Cabul	£650–850	£450–650	£400–550
iii. Cabvl (15)	—	—	—
iv. Ghuznee/Cabul	£850–1000	£500–650	£400–550
v. Candahar/Ghuznee/ Cabul	£1200–1500	£500–650	£400–550
Miniature	from £265 (depending on reverse)		

108. JELLALABAD MEDALS

Type 1

Date: 1842.
Campaign: Afghanistan 1841-42.
Branch of Service: British and HEIC forces.
Ribbon: 44mm watered silk red, white, yellow, white and blue representing an eastern sky at sunrise.
Metal: Silver.
Size: 39mm and 35mm.
Description: There are two different types of this medal, awarded by the HEIC to surviving defenders of the fortress of Jellalabad between 12 November 1841 and 7 April 1842. The first, struck in Calcutta, has a mural crown and JELLALABAD on the obverse, with the date of the relief of the garrison on the reverse; the second type shows the Wyon profile of Victoria (obverse) and the winged Victory with mountain scenery in the background and JELLALABAD VII APRIL round the top and the year in roman numerals in the exergue (reverse).
Comments: *The first type, struck in Calcutta, was considered to be unsuitable and holders were invited to exchange their medals for the second, more attractive, issue which was produced in London, although very few recipients took up the offer. The latter type was also awarded to the next of kin of soldiers killed in action.*

VALUE:	Imperial Regiments	Indian Units	Unnamed	*Miniature*
i. First type (Crown)	£850–1000	£750–850	£600-800	£350–400
ii. Second type (Victory)	£1200–1500	—	£900–1000	£250–350

109. MEDAL FOR THE DEFENCE OF KELAT-I-GHILZIE

Date: 1842.
Campaign: Afghanistan 1842.
Branch of Service: European and native troops, HEIC.
Ribbon: 40mm watered silk red, white, yellow, white and blue representing an eastern sky at sunrise.
Metal: Silver.
Size: 36mm.
Description: (Obverse) a shield bearing the name of the fort, surmounted by a mural crown and encircled by laurels; (reverse) a trophy of arms above a tablet inscribed INVICTA (unbeaten) and the date in roman numerals.
Comments: *Awarded to those who took part in the defence of the fort at Kelat-i-Ghilzie in May 1842, it is the rarest medal of the First Afghan War. No British imperial regiments took part, but 55 Europeans in the Company's service received the medal. It was also awarded to 877 native troops (including a contingent supplied by Shah Soojah) but few of their medals appear to have survived.*

VALUE:
European recipients	£5500–6500
Indian recipients	£3500–4500
Unnamed	£1800–2000
Miniature	£500–600

110. CHINA WAR MEDAL

Date: 1842.
Campaign: China 1841-42.
Branch of Service: British and HEIC forces.
Ribbon: 39mm crimson with deep yellow edges the heraldic colours of Britain and China respectively.
Metal: Silver.
Size: 35mm.
Description: The medal has the usual Wyon obverse, but the reverse was to have shown a British lion with its forepaws on a dragon. This was deemed to be offensive to the Chinese and was replaced by an oval shield bearing the royal arms and a palm tree flanked by a capstan, anchor and naval cannon representing the Royal Navy (left) and a field gun, drum and regimental flag representing the Army (right), with the Latin motto ARMIS EXPOSCERE PACEM (to pray for peace by force of arms) round the top and CHINA 1842 in the exergue.
Comments: *Originally intended for issue to all ranks of the Honourable East India Company, it was subsequently awarded by the British government in 1843 to all who had taken part in the campaign in China popularly known as the First Opium War which ended with the seizure of Nanking.*

Issued reverse

VALUE:
Royal Navy	£850–1250
Indian and Bengal marine units	£650–750
British imperial regiments	£750–850
Indian Army	£600–700
Specimens of the original reverse	£800–1000
Miniature	£200–275

111. SCINDE MEDAL

Date: 1843.

Campaign: Scinde 1843.

Branch of Service: HEIC forces and 22nd Foot.

Ribbon: 44mm watered silk red, white, yellow, white and blue representing an eastern sky at sunrise.

Metal: Silver.

Size: 36mm.

Description: The usual Wyon profile obverse was married to three different reverse types showing a crowned laurel wreath inscribed with the name of one or two campaigns and the date.

Comments: *Authorised in September 1843, this silver medal marked Sir Charles Napier's conquest of Scinde. The two major battles in the campaign, at Meeanee and Hyderabad, accomplished the complete rout of the forces of the Amirs of Scinde. The medals were originally issued with steel suspenders but the commanding officer of the 22nd Foot had the medals awarded to his men fitted with silver suspenders, at his own expense. Medals to the Indus Flotilla are particularly sought after by collectors.*

VALUE:

	22nd Foot	Indian units	HEIC ships
i. Meeanee	£1200–1500	£650–750	£1750–2500 (38)
ii. Hyderabad	£1100–1500	£650–750	£1750–2500 (52)
iii. Meeanee/Hyderabad	£1200–1500	£650–750	—
Miniature	£175–275		

112. GWALIOR STAR

Date: 1843.

Campaign: Gwalior 1843.

Branch of Service: British and HEIC forces.

Ribbon: 44mm watered silk red, white, yellow, white and blue representing an eastern sky at sunrise.

Metals: Bronze, with a silver centre.

Size: Max. width 45mm; max. height 52mm.

Description: Six-pointed bronze star with a silver centre star. The silver stars in the centre bear the name of one or other of the battles and the date 29 December 1843 on which both battles were fought. The plain reverse bears the name and regiment of the recipient.

Comments: *Bronze from guns captured at the battles of Maharajpoor and Punniar during the Gwalior campaign was used in the manufacture of these stars, thus anticipating the production of the Victoria Cross in the same manner. They were presented by the Indian government to all ranks who took part in these actions. When first issued, these stars were fitted with hooks to be worn like a breast decoration, but later ornate bar or ring suspensions were fitted to individual fancy and worn with the standard Indian ribbon of the period.*

VALUE:

	British units	Indian units	*Miniature*
i. Maharajpoor	£750–850	£800–1000	£250–350
ii. Punniar	£750–850	£800–1000	£350–450

113. SUTLEJ MEDAL

Date: 1846.
Campaign: Sutlej 1845-46.
Branch of Service: British and HEIC forces.
Ribbon: Dark blue with crimson edges.
Metal: Silver.
Size: 36mm.
Description: (Obverse) Wyon profile of Queen Victoria; (reverse) standing figure of Victory holding aloft a laurel crown, with a pile of captured weapons at her feet. The legend ARMY OF THE SUTLEJ appears round the top. The medal was fitted with an ornamental scroll suspender.
Clasps: Mounted above the suspender with roses between: Ferozeshuhur, Aliwal or Sobraon.
Comments: *The practice of issuing medals inscribed with different battles now gave way to the style of medals with specific battle or campaign clasps which set the precedent for the Naval and Military GSMs and later awards. As a compromise, however, the exergue of the reverse bears the name and date of the action for which the medal was first granted, and thus several different types are known.*

VALUE:	British regiments	Europeans in HEIC units	Indian units
i. Moodkee	£400–475	£300–500	£325–375
Moodkee 1 clasp	£500–575	£400–550	£375–425
Moodkee 2 clasps	£700–825	£600–750	£475–575
Moodkee 3 clasps	£1500–1800	£950–1150	£750–950
ii. Ferozeshuhur	£400–475	£300–400	£325–375
Ferozeshuhur 1 clasp	£500–575	£400–500	£375–425
Ferozeshuhur 2 clasps	£700–825	£600–750	£475–575
iii. Aliwal	£350–425	£300–400	£325–375
Aliwal 1 clasp	£500–575	£400–550	£375–475
iv. Sobraon	£400–525	£350–450	£375–475
Glazed gilt specimen	£500–750		
Miniature	£125–175, for each clasp add £50		

114. PUNJAB MEDAL

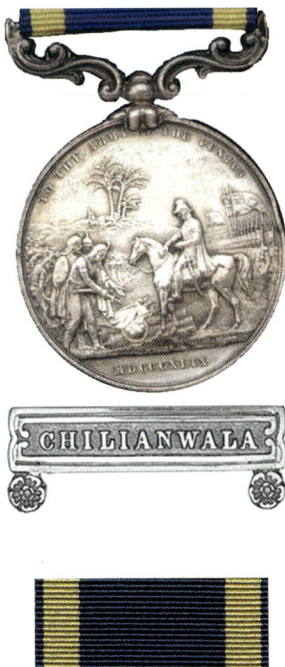

Date: 1849.
Campaign: Punjab 1848-49.
Branch of Service: British and HEIC forces.
Ribbon: Dark blue with yellow stripes towards the edges.
Metal: Silver.
Size: 36mm.
Description: (Obverse) Wyon profile of Queen Victoria; (reverse) Sir Walter Gilbert receiving the Sikh surrender. TO THE ARMY OF THE PUNJAB appears round the top and the year in roman numerals in the exergue. The medal has a scroll suspender.
Clasps: Mooltan, Chilianwala, Goojerat. Unusually the clasps read downwards from top to bottom
Comments: *This medal was granted to troops taking part in the campaigns which ended in the annexation of the Punjab. Unlike the Sutlej medal, however, this silver medal had a standard design. Large numbers of this medal were awarded to native troops, however many were melted down and therefore surprisingly few remain on the market in comparison with medals to European recipients.*

VALUE:	British units	Europeans in HEIC units	Indian units
No clasp	£400–450	£400–450	£350–375
i. Mooltan	£450–550	£400–450	£375–400
ii. Chilianwala	£450–550	£400–450	£375–400
iii. Goojerat	£450–550	£400–450	£375–400
iv. Mooltan/Goojerat	£650–750	£650–700	£475–550
v. Chilianwala/Goojerat	£650–750	£650–700	£475–550
24th Foot casualty at Chilianwala	£1200–1650	—	—
Glazed gilt specimen	£350–500		
Miniature	£90–125, for each clasp add £25		

115. SOUTH AFRICA MEDAL

Date: 1854.

Campaigns: Southern Africa 1834–53.

Branch of Service: Royal Navy and Army.

Ribbon: Gold with broad and narrow deep blue stripes towards each end.

Metal: Silver.   **Size:** 36mm.

Description: (Obverse) Wyon profile of Queen Victoria; (reverse) an African lion crouching in submission beside a protea shrub, the date 1853 being in the exergue.

Clasps: None.

Comments: *Authorised in November 1854, this medal was awarded in respect of three campaigns in southern Africa: 1834–35, 1846–47 and 1850–53, but as the medal was issued with a standard reverse and no campaign clasps it is impossible to tell when and where the recipient served without reference to the medal rolls. The majority of recipients were British troops but several hundred sailors of the Royal Navy also received the medal and a much smaller number of local forces. Medals to proven recipients who took part in well-known sieges or battles such as the siege of Port Natal (1842), Fort Cox (1850) or the battles of Zwartkopje (1845) or Boomplaats (1848) for example, are worth a considerable premium. Also of particular interest are medals awarded to men who survived the sinking of the troopship* Birkenhead *on its way to the Eastern Cape from Simons Town and medals awarded to those in clashes with Boer forces.*

VALUE:

British Army	**£550–650**
Royal Navy	**£700–800**
HMS *Birkenhead*	**From £2000**
Local forces (levies, burghers and colonial units)	**From £550**
Miniature	*£90–125*

116. SIR HARRY SMITH'S MEDAL FOR GALLANTRY

Date: 1851.

Campaign: Eighth Kaffir War 1850-51.

Branch of Service: Army and Colonial Forces.

Ribbon: Dark blue with crimson edges.

Metal: Silver.

Size: 34mm.

Description: (Obverse) British lion passant gardant with a laurel wreath over its head; date 1851 in the exergue. (Reverse) PRESENTED BY round top and FOR GALLANTRY IN THE FIELD round the foot. HIS EXCELLENCY SIR H. G. SMITH and the name of the recipient appear across the centre.

Comments: *Sir Harry Smith (1787–1860) served with distinction in the Kaffir War of 1834–35, gained his KCB in the Gwalior campaign and a baronetcy for his decisive victory at Aliwal in the Sikh War. In 1847 he returned to South Africa as governor of Cape Colony. Although short of troops he conducted the eighth Kaffir War (1850–53) with great resourcefulness but was recalled to England in 1852 before the Xhosas had been subdued. Harrismith in the Orange Free State was named in his honour, while Ladysmith in Natal was named after his beautiful and spirited Spanish wife Juanita, the forces' sweetheart of her day. Sir Harry had this medal struck at his own expense and, according to unconfirmed accounts, awarded to troopers of the Cape Mounted Rifles who took part in the epic ride through the enemy lines from Fort Cox to Kingwilliamstown in 1851. Only 31 medals were presented, of which 22 are believed to be still extant.*

VALUE:

Unnamed	**£3000–4000**
Named and appearing on 1853 medal roll or muster rolls	**£7500–10,000**
One contemporary miniature example is known	

117. INDIA GENERAL SERVICE MEDAL

Date: 1854.

Campaigns: Indian 1854-95.

Branch of Service: British and Indian forces.

Ribbon: Three crimson and two dark blue stripes of equal width.

Metal: Silver or bronze.

Size: 36mm.

Description: (Obverse) Wyon profile of Queen Victoria; (reverse) Victory crowning a semi-nude seated warrior.

Clasps: 24 (see below).

Comments: *This medal was the first of four general service medals issued to cover minor campaigns in India. It was instituted in 1854 and continued for forty-one years, retaining the original Wyon profile of Queen Victoria throughout the entire period. Although the medal itself is quite common, some of its clasps are very rare, notably Kachin Hills 1892–93 awarded to the Yorkshire Regiment and Chin Hills 1892–93 awarded to the Norfolk Regiment. The maximum number of clasps to one medal recorded is seven. At first the medal was awarded in silver to all ranks regardless of race or branch of the services, but from 1885 onwards it was issued in bronze to native support personnel such as bearers, sweepers and drivers.*

VALUE:		RN/RM	British Army	Indian Army	Bronze
i.	Pegu	£350–450	£300–350	£225–300*	—
ii.	Persia	—	£650–850	£350–400	—
iii.	Northwest Frontier	—	£300–360	£225–275	—
iv.	Umbeyla	—	£325–375	£225–275	—
v.	Bhootan	—	£360–385	£225–275	—
vi.	Looshai	—	—	£400–550	—
vii.	Perak	£350–450	£360–385	£250–275	—
viii.	Jowaki 1877–8	—	£300–350	£200–250	—
ix.	Naga 1879–80	—	—	£375–450	—
x.	Burma 1885–7	£350–450	£185–250	£150–175	£150–185
xi.	Sikkim 1888	—	£380–440	£175–200	£200–250
xii.	Hazara 1888	—	£235–260	£175–200	£160–200
xiii.	Burma 1887–89	—	£200–230	£165–185	£160–200
xiv.	Burma 1887–9	—	£225–275	—	—
xv.	Chin Lushai 1889–90	—	£300–350	£200–250	£220–275
xvi.	Lushai 1889-92	—	£600–650	£225–275	£425–500
xvii.	Samana 1891	—	£300–350	£185–200	£175–200
xviii.	Hazara 1891	—	£250–300	£185–200	£175–200
xix.	NE Frontier 1891	—	£385–425	£175–200	£175–200
xx.	Hunza 1891	—	—	£500–550	£850–1000
xxi.	Burma 1889–92	—	£200–250	£175–200	£150–185
xxii.	Chin Hills 1892–93	—	£1100–1300	£385–475	£875–1000
xxiii.	Kachin Hills 1892–93	—	£850–1000	£400–500	£875–1000
xxiv.	Waziristan 1894–95	—	£275–300	£175–200	£175–200

Miniature £25–35, for each clasp add £15–20 (*Hunza, Chin Hills* **and** *Kachin Hills* **clasps are rare**)

* In addition a number of Indian ships were present—medals to Indian naval or marine recipients are rare.

118. BALTIC MEDAL

Date: 1856.
Campaign: Baltic Sea 1854–55.
Branch of Service: Royal Navy, Royal Marines and Royal Sappers and Miners.
Ribbon: Yellow with light blue edges.
Metal: Silver.
Size: 36mm.
Description: (Obverse) Wyon profile of Queen Victoria; (reverse) Britannia seated on a plinth decorated by a cannon, with a coastal scene in the background and BALTIC round the top.
Comments: *Authorised in 1856, this medal was granted to officers and men of the Royal Navy and Royal Marines for operations against Russia in the Baltic at the same time as the war in the Crimea. It was also awarded to about 100 members of the Royal Sappers and Miners engaged in the demolition of Russian fortifications of Bomarsund and Sveaborg. Medals were generally issued unnamed but often privately named afterwards, the exception being medals to the Sappers and Miners which were officially impressed.*

VALUE:

Unnamed	£200–250
Privately named	£200–250
Officially impressed to Sappers and Miners	£1000–1500
Miniature	£75–100

119. CRIMEA MEDAL

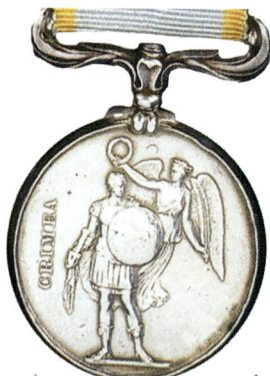

Date: 1854.
Campaign: Crimea 1854–56.
Branch of Service: Royal Navy and Marines, British Army.
Ribbon: Pale blue with yellow edges.
Metal: Silver.
Size: 36mm.
Description: (Obverse) Wyon profile of Queen Victoria; (reverse) a Roman soldier, armed with circular shield and short sword, being crowned by a flying Victory.
Clasps: Unusually ornate, being shaped like oak leaves with acorn finials: Alma, Balaklava, Inkerman, Sebastopol, Azoff, but the maximum found on any medal is four. Recipients of the Balaklava clasp were invariably entitled to other clasps. Unofficial clasps for Traktir, Mamelon Vert, Malakoff, Mer d'Azoff and Kinburn are sometimes found on medals awarded to French troops.
Comments: *Medals may be found unnamed, unofficially or regimentally named, or officially impressed. Medals awarded to participants in the most famous actions of the war—the Thin Red Line (93rd Foot) and the Charge of the Light and Heavy Brigades—rate a very high premium. The prices quoted are for medals named to the Army. Clasps awarded to the Royal Navy and Royal Marines (Azoff, Balaklava, Inkerman, Sebastopol) rate a good premium, especially those named to personnel on board HM Ships* London, Niger, Rodney *and* Wasp.* *No fewer than 19 VCs were awarded for gallantry at Inkerman alone, the largest number for a single action.*

VALUE :	Unnamed	Engraved	Regimentally impressed	Officially impressed Army
No clasp	£150–200	£175–200	£175–200	£200–250
i. Alma	£150–200	£200–250	£200–250	£250–350
ii. Balaklava	£200–250	£200–250	£200–250	£350–400
93rd Foot*	—	£500–575	£800–1000	£1000–1500
Heavy Brigade*	—	£850–1500	£1000–1750	£1500–2000
Light Brigade (Charger)*	—	£2500–3500	£4500–5500	£10,000–15,000
iii. Inkerman	£175–200	£200–250	£200–250	£225–275
iv. Sebastopol	£175–200	£200–250	£200–250	£275–350
v. Azoff	£300–375	£350–400	—	£525–650
2 clasps	£250–300	£300–350	£300–375	£450–600
3 clasps	£325–400	£400–450	£400–475	£750–1000
4 clasps	£400–500	£500–750	£565–700	£1500–2000
Miniature	£25–35, for each clasp add £15			

*It is always difficult to price scarce or rare medals such as those marked * as we have seen many engraved or Depot-style impressing that were probably named in the past 30 to 40 years. Also an engraved Crimea, together with a Mutiny and/or LS&GC would be worth considerably more than the prices indicated. Buyer beware!*

120. TURKISH CRIMEA MEDAL

Date: 1855.
Campaign: Crimea 1855-56.
Branch of Service: British, French and Sardinian forces.
Ribbon: Crimson with green edges (originally 18mm wide).
Metal: Silver.
Size: 36mm.
Description: (Obverse) a cannon, weapons and the four Allied flags with the name and date in the exergue; (reverse) the Toughra and Arabic date according to the Moslem calendar.
Clasps: None.
Comments: *Instituted by the Sultan of Turkey, this silver medal was conferred on troops of the three Allies who fought in the Crimea. The obverse types differed in the arrangement of the flags, corrsponding with the inscription in English, French or Italian in the exergue. Although the medals were intended to be issued to British, French and Sardinian troops respectively, they were issued haphazardly due to most of the British version being lost at sea. They were unnamed, but many were privately engraved or impressed later. There are a number of dangerous copies known to be circulating.*

VALUE:		Miniature
i. CRIMEA (British Issue)	£150–175	£45–50
ii. LA CRIMEE (French Issue)	£220–250	Not seen
iii. LA CRIMEA (Sardinia Issue)	£125–150	£35–45

120A. TURKISH MEDAL FOR GLORY

Date: 1853.
Campaign: Crimea.
Branch of Service: British forces.
Ribbon: Crimson with green edges.
Metal: Gold or silver.
Size: 31mm.
Description: (Obverse) the Sultan's cypher in a beaded ring below a star and crescent with flags and wreath around; (reverse) a star with a smaller star in the centre, an arabic inscription below which reads "Medal for Glory". With ring suspension.
Clasps: None.
Comments: *Instituted by the Sultan of Turkey, it was awarded to officers and men of British forces who fought in the war against Russia, at Silistria and Giurgevo. Gold medals were awarded to high ranking officers and silver to others.*

VALUE:	
Gold	£1000–1500
Silver	£500–750

120B. TURKISH MEDAL FOR THE DEFENCE OF SILISTRIA

Date: 1854.
Campaign: Crimea.
Branch of Service: British and Turkish forces.
Ribbon: Crimson with green edges.
Metal: Gold or silver.
Size: 36mm.
Description: (Obverse) the Sultan's cypher within in a wreath; (reverse) a depiction of the fortress of Silistria with a flag flying from the ramparts with the river Danube in the foreground, an inscription in Turkish script below which reads "Silistria 1271 AH (1854)". With ring suspension
Clasps: None.
Comments: *Instituted by the Sultan of Turkey, it was awarded to officers and men of British forces who were present during the actual siege by 30,000 Russian troops. Only seven British officers were there at the time and qualified for the medal but the medal was issued unnamed.*

VALUE:
Gold	£1000–1500
Silver	£500–750

120C. TURKISH MEDAL FOR THE DEFENCE OF KARS

Date: 1855.
Campaign: Crimea.
Branch of Service: British and Turkish forces.
Ribbon: Crimson with green edges.
Metal: Silver.
Size: 36mm.
Description: (Obverse) the Sultan's cypher within in a wreath; (reverse) a depiction of the city of Kars with a flag flying from the citadel and the words "Kars 1272 AH (1855)" in Turkish script below. With simple ring suspension.
Clasps: None.
Comments: *Instituted by the Sultan of Turkey, it was awarded to officers and men of British forces who were present at the siege of Kars by 50,000 Russian troops. The silver medal was awarded to the British officers present including the British Commissioner, Brigadier General Sir William Fenwick Williams. Lt C. C. Teesdale was sawarded the VC for his part in the action. The medals were issued unnamed.*

VALUE: £2000–3000

121. INDIAN MUTINY MEDAL

Date: 1858.

Campaign: Sepoy Mutiny, India 1857–58.

Branch of Service: Royal Navy, British Army and Indian forces. It was also awarded to many civilians who took part in suppressing the Mutiny.

Ribbon: White with two red stripes, representing blood and white bandages.

Metal: Silver.

Size: 36mm.

Description: (Obverse) Wyon profile of Queen Victoria; (reverse) the standing figure of Britannia bestowing victor's laurels, with the British lion alongside. INDIA appears round the top with the dates 1857–1858 in the exergue.

Clasps: Delhi, Defence of Lucknow, Relief of Lucknow, Lucknow, Central India. The maximum recorded for a single medal is four (Bengal Artillery) or three (imperial troops, 9th Lancers).

Comments: *This medal was awarded to troops who took part in operations to quell the Sepoy mutiny which had been the immediate cause of the uprising, although it also served to focus attention on the Honourable East India Company's conduct of affairs and led directly to the transfer of the administration of India to the Crown. Medals with the clasp for the defence of Lucknow awarded to the original defenders rate a considerable premium, as do medals awarded to members of the Naval Brigade which witnessed most of the fighting in the mopping-up operations. Medals to Indian recipients although scarcer on the market, generally bring a little less than their British counterparts although verified four-clasp medals to the Bengal Artillery are much sought after.*

VALUE:

	Royal Navy	British Army	Miniature
No clasp	£800–1000*	£250–350	£30-40
i. Delhi	—	£550–650	£50–60
ii. Defence of Lucknow			
original defender	—	£1750–1850	£70–95
first relief force	—	£800–1000	
iii. Relief of Lucknow	£1800–2000	£450–550	£50–60
iv. Lucknow	£1800–2000	£450–550	£60–70
v. Central India	—	£450–550	£60–70, add
2 clasps	£2000–2500	£550–750	£15 for each
3 clasps (9th Lancers)	—	£1850–2000	additional clasp
4 clasps (Bengal Arty.)	—	£3500–4500	

66 medals to HMS Shannon and 253 to HMS Pearl.

122. SECOND CHINA WAR MEDAL

Original ribbon.

Second type ribbon.

Date: 1861.

Campaign: Second China War 1857-60.

Branch of Service: Royal Navy and British Army.

Ribbon: 33mm crimson with yellow edges (originally five equal stripes of green, white, red, yellow and blue, edged with red).

Metal: Silver.

Size: 36mm.

Description: As the First China War Medal (no. 110), but without the year 1842 at the foot.

Clasps: Fatshan 1857, Canton 1857, Taku Forts 1858, Taku Forts 1860, Pekin 1860.

Comments: *This medal was awarded to British sevicemen who took part, alongside the French, in the campaign against China which had been provoked by hostile acts against European nationals. The Royal Navy, under Admiral Sir Michael Seymour, destroyed a Chinese flotilla at Fatshan Creek, preparing the way for the attack on Canton whose capture brought the first phase to an end in June 1858. Reinforcements were meanwhile diverted to help put down the Indian mutiny. Fighting broke out again and this time large numbers of troops were involved in the assault on the Taku forts and the sack of Pekin (Beijing). Examples of the China medal of 1842, with or without clasps for 1857-60, have been recorded to recipients who fought in the Second China War. Medals may be found unnamed or with names officially engraved (Indian Army) or impressed (British Army, Indian Navy). Although those to the Navy were all issued unnamed, they are occasionally encountered unofficially named.*

VALUE:

	Unnamed	Army/Navy officially impressed	Miniature
No clasp	£150–180	£250–350	£45–50
i. China 1842	—	—	£130–160
ii. Fatshan 1857	£200–275	£450–500	£70–80
iii. Canton 1857	£275–300	£375–450	£70–80
iv. Taku Forts 1858	£275–300	£375–400	£70–80
v. Taku Forts 1860	£275–300	£375–400	£70–80
vi. Pekin 1860	£275–300	£375–400	£70–80
2 clasps	£350–450	£550–650	For each
3 clasps	£450–550	£650–800	clasp add
4 clasps	£600–700	—	£15
5 clasps	£650–750	—	

The storming of the Taku forts.

123. NEW ZEALAND MEDALS

Date: 1869.

Campaigns: First and Second Maori Wars 1845–47 and 1860–66.

Branch of Service: Army, Navy and local volunteers.

Ribbon: Blue with a central orange stripe.

Metal: Silver.

Size: 36mm.

Description: (Obverse) Veiled head of Queen Victoria. (Reverse) Date of service in a wreath, with NEW ZEALAND round the top and VIRTUTIS HONOR (honour of valour) round the foot. Suspender ornamented with New Zealand fern fronds.

Comments: *These medals were unusual in having the recipient's dates of service die-struck on the centre of the reverse, though medals were also issued without dates. As the medal was only awarded to surviving veterans, the numbers issued in respect of the earlier conflict are understandably small. Many of the dates are very scarce, especially those issued to naval personnel in the first war when only naval personnel received dated medals. Medals to locally-raised units are worth a considerable premium. A hitherto unknown 1845-dated medal appeared at auction in January 2010 when it sold for a hammer price of £12,800. This medal was named to Captain David Robertson, HMS* Hazard.

VALUE:		Army	RN/RM
First war			
i.	Undated	£500–600	—
ii.	1845–46 (155)	—	£1300–1600
iii.	1845–47 (36)	—	£1400–1700
iv.	1846–47 (69)	—	£1300–1600
v.	1846 (10)	—	£1500–2000
vi.	1847 (20)	£800–1000	£1500–2000
Second war			
vii.	Undated	£450–550	—
viii.	1860	£750–850	—
ix.	1860–61	£475–575	£650–750
	(to Australians)	£2000–2300	—
x.	1860–63	From £1550	—
xi.	1860–64	£450–550	—
xii.	1860–65	£450–550	—
xiii.	1860–66	£450–550	—
xiv.	1861	—	—
xv.	1861–63	—	—
xvi.	1861–64	£450–550	—
xvii.	1861–65	—	—
xviii.	1861–66	£450–550	—
xix.	1861–66		
	(Waikato Regt issues)	From £850	—
xx.	1862–66	—	—
xxi.	1863	£450–550	—
xxii.	1863–64	£450–550	£650–750
xxiii.	1863–65	£450–550	—
xxiv.	1863–66	£450–550	—
xxv.	1864	£450–550	—
xxvi.	1864–65	£450–550	—
xxvii.	1864–66	£450–550	—
xxviii.	1865	£450–550	£650–750
xxvix.	1865–66	£450–550	—
xxx.	1866	£450–550	—

Miniature		
Undated	£100–125	
Dated	£85–£95	

124. ABYSSINIAN WAR MEDAL

Date: 1869.
Campaign: Abyssinia (Ethiopia) 1867–68.
Branch of Service: Royal Navy, British and Indian Armies.
Ribbon: Red with broad white edges.
Metal: Silver.
Size: 33mm diameter.
Description: (Obverse) the veiled portrait of Victoria framed by a zigzag pattern with floral ornament alternating with the letters of the name ABYSSINIA. The recipient's name and unit were embossed in the centre of the reverse except most to Indian troops which were impressed. Suspension is by a ring via a large crown standing proud from the top of the medal.
Clasps: None.
Comments: *The imprisonment of British subjects by King Theodore of Abyssinia precipitated a punitive expedition under General Sir Robert Napier involving ships of the Royal Navy, a naval brigade and troops of the British and Indian armies. Because casualties were unusually light (only two killed and 27 wounded), medals from this campaign are not so highly rated as those from other nineteenth century wars.*

VALUE:
British troops	£375–475
Royal Navy	£375–475
RN Rocket Brigade	£575–650
Indian troops	£300–400
Miniature	£125–175

125. CANADA GENERAL SERVICE MEDAL

Date: 1899.
Campaign: Canada 1866–70.
Branch of Service: Royal Navy, British Army and Canadian units.
Ribbon: Three equal stripes of orange-red, white and orange-red.
Metal: Silver.
Size: 36mm.
Description: (Obverse) crowned and veiled Old Head bust of Queen Victoria by Sir Thomas Brock (reflecting the very late issue of the medal). (Reverse) Canadian flag surrounded by maple leaves.
Clasps: Fenian Raid 1866, Fenian Raid 1870, Red River 1870.
Comments: *This medal was not authorised until January 1899, thirty years after the event, and was issued by the Canadian Government to British and Canadian local forces who took part in operations to put down the Fenian raids of 1866 and 1870 and the Red River rebellion of the latter year. Of the 16,100 medals awarded, 15,000 went to local forces. Naval medals command a premium.*

VALUE:
	Canadian forces	British Army	Royal Navy	*Miniature*
i. Fenian Raid 1866	£350–400	£475–600	£650–750	£65–70
ii. Fenian Raid 1870	£350–400	£475–600	—	£70–75
iii. Red River 1870	£3500–4000	£4000–4500	—	£90–115
2 clasps*	£750–850	£950–1000	—	£85–110
3 clasps	Rare	—	—	—

*Two 2-clasp medals were awarded to men of the 1st Bn 60th Foot (KRRC) and ten to the 4th Bn.

126. ASHANTEE MEDAL

Date: 1874.

Campaign: Gold Coast 1873–74.

Branch of Service: Royal Navy, Army and native troops.

Ribbon: Yellow with black stripes at the sides and two narrow black stripes towards the centre.

Metal: Silver.   **Size:** 36mm.

Description: The obverse and reverse are similar to the East and West Africa Medal of 1887–1900, differing solely in thickness and the method of naming. The veiled profile of Victoria graces the obverse while the reverse, designed by Sir Edwin Poynter, shows a skirmish in the jungle between British soldiers and Ashantee warriors.

Clasps: Coomassie.

Comments: *All ranks who took part in operations against King Kalkali of Ashantee, Gold Coast, were awarded this medal, approved in June 1874. The campaign was fought in difficult and hostile terrain, requiring the building of a road through dense rain forest, the construction of many staging posts, camps, bridges and a telegraph. The movement of troops and supplies was met with skirmishes and ferocious battles developed as the column approached Kumasi in the final four weeks and resulted in the award of four VCs. There was also a very high incidence of sickness and disease among the troops, notably the naval contingent. Unusually the medals are named in engraved capitals filled in with black.*

VALUE	Royal Navy	Army	Natives	Miniature
No clasp	£350–400	£350–400	£250–300	£50–55
i. Coomassie	£450–550	£450–550	£300–350	£70–75

127. SOUTH AFRICA MEDAL

Date: 1879.

Campaign: South Africa 1877–79.

Branch of Service: Royal Navy, Army and colonial units.

Ribbon: Gold with broad and narrow deep blue stripes towards each end.

Metal: Silver.

Size: 36mm.

Description: The same design as no. 115, except that the date 1853 in the exergue is replaced by a Zulu shield and four crossed assegais.

Clasps: 1877, 1877–8, 1877–9, 1877–8–9, 1878, 1878–9, 1879.

Comments: *The campaign began in 1877 with an attack on the Fingoes by the Galeka and Gaika tribes and culminated in the showdown between the Zulus and the British when Lord Chelmsford's column was annihilated at Isandhlwana. When the 3,000 Zulus advanced on Rorke's Drift, however, they were checked with heavy losses by a tiny garrison of 139 men. During the defence no fewer than eleven VCs were won—a very large number for a single action. The campaign concluded with the defeat of Cetshwayo's warriors at Ulundi. A number of recipients of the medal stayed on in the country and took part in the first Anglo-Boer War of 1880–81. Medals confirmed to these men, particularly those who took part in the sieges of Wakkerstroom, Rustenburg, Standerton, Marabastadt or Lydenburg or well-known battles such as Swartkoppies, are worth a considerable premium.*

VALUE:	RN	Army	Colonial	Miniature
No clasp	£550–650	£650–750	£550–650	£35–40
i. 1877	—	Unique	£3500–4500	£110–160
ii. 1877–8	£950–1250	£850–1000	£850–950	£70–80
iii. 1877–9	—	Unique	£4500–6000	—
iv. 1877–8–9	£850–1000	£1000–1200	£850–1000	£70–80
v. 1878	—	£850–1200	£850–1000	£70–80
vi. 1878–9	—	£850–1200	£850–1000	£70–80
vii. 1879	£850–1000	£850–1500	£850–1000	£75–85

Isandhlwana casualty	From £10,000
Isandhlwana escapee	From £10,000
Rorke's Drift participant	From £35,000

128. AFGHANISTAN MEDAL

Date: 1881.
Campaign: Afghanistan 1878–80.
Branch of Service: British and Indian Armies.
Ribbon: Dark green, the sacred colour of the prophet with broad crimson edges, the heraldic colour of Britain.
Metal: Silver.
Size: 36mm.
Description: (Obverse) veiled profile of Queen Victoria. (Reverse) a column on the march, with an elephant carrying cannon. The dates 1878–79–80 appear in the exergue.
Clasps: Ali Musjid, Peiwar Kotal, Charasia, Kabul, Ahmed Kel, Kandahar. Maximum number of clasps per medal is four.
Comments: *This medal was awarded to all who took part in the campaigns against Afghanistan known as the Second Afghan War. In 1877 the Amir refused to accept a British resident and the following year raised an army which began harrassing the Indian frontier. A treaty with Russia, however, granting it protective rights in Afghanistan, precipitated an armed response from Britain. In 1880 General Roberts led a column from Kabul to Kandahar to relieve General Burrows and the resulting battle led to the defeat of the Afghans and the conclusion of the war. Medals awarded to the 66th Foot (Berkshire Regiment) and E Battery of B Brigade, Royal Artillery rate a high premium as these units sustained the heaviest casualties at the battle of Maiwand in July 1880.*

VALUE:	British units	Indian units	*Miniature*
No clasp silver	£275–350	£175–250	£25–35
i. Ali Musjid	£375–450	£250–300	£35–45
ii. Peiwar Kotal	£375–450	£250–300	£35–45
iii. Charasia	£375–450	£250–300	£35–45
iv. Kabul	£375–450	£250–300	£30–35
v. Ahmed Khel	£375–450	£250–300	£35–45
vi. Kandahar	£375–450	£250–300	£30–35
2 clasps	£550–650	£350–400	£60–70
3 clasps	£650–850	£400–550	£80–90
4 clasps	£800–1500	£500–850	£95–100
Maiwand casualties:			
66th Foot	£3250–3750	—	
E Bty, B Bde RHA	£2750–3500	—	

Richard Caton Woodville's famous depiction of Saving the Guns at Maiwand.

129. KABUL TO KANDAHAR STAR

Date: 1881.
Campaign: Afghanistan 1878–80.
Branch of Service: British and Indian Armies.
Ribbon: 40mm watered silk of pink, white, yellow, white and blue representing an eastern sky at sunrise.
Metal: Bronze from captured guns.
Size: Height 60mm, width 45mm.
Description: (Obverse) a rayed five-pointed star surmounted by a crown with a ring for suspension. The centre is inscribed KABUL TO KANDAHAR with 1880 at the foot and the VRI monogram of the Queen Empress in the centre. Stars were either issued unnamed, or had the recipient's name impressed (to British) or engraved (to Indian) troops on the reverse.
Clasps: None.
Comments: *This star, struck by Jenkins of Birmingham, was awarded to those who took part in the epic 300-mile march from the Afghan capital to Kandahar, led by General Roberts to relieve the beleaguered forces of General Burrows.*

VALUE:

Unnamed	£200–250
Impressed (British troops)	£400–450
Engraved (Indian troops)	£250–300

Miniature	Early pierced crown £75–85
	Later solid crown £50–65

130. CAPE OF GOOD HOPE GENERAL SERVICE MEDAL

Date: 1900.
Campaign: Uprisings in Transkei, Basutoland and Bechuanaland 1880-97.
Branch of Service: Local forces and volunteers.
Ribbon: Dark blue with a central yellow stripe.
Metal: Silver.
Size: 36mm.
Description: (Obverse) Jubilee bust of Queen Victoria by Sir Joseph Boehm; (reverse) arms of Cape Colony.
Clasps: Transkei, Basutoland, Bechuanaland.
Comments: *Instituted by the Cape government, this medal acknowledged service in putting down the Transkei (September 1880–May 1881), Basutoland (September 1880–April 1881) and Bechuanaland (December 1896–July 1897) rebellions in those areas. The medal was awarded, with one or more campaign clasps, to local forces and volunteer regiments. Recent research has shown that the medal could not be awarded without a clasp. The previously held notion that ten medals were awarded without clasps, was brought about by an error in transcribing the medal rolls.*

VALUE:			*Miniature*
i.	Transkei (562)	£375–450	£50–60
ii.	Basutoland (1589)	£250–350	£50–60
iii.	Bechuanaland (2483)	£225–300	£50–60
2 clasps (585)		£350–475	£65–80
3 clasps (23)		£3000–4000	—

131. EGYPT MEDAL 1882–89

Dated rev.

Undated rev.

Date: 1882.

Campaign: Egypt 1882–89.

Branch of Service: Royal Navy and Army.

Ribbon: Three blue and two white stripes, (the Blue and White Niles).

Metal: Silver.

Size: 36mm.

Description: (Obverse) the veiled profile of Queen Victoria; (reverse) the Sphinx.

Clasps: 14, listed below. Maximum number for one medal is 7, but only one such award was made. Common two-clasp combinations are denoted below by /.

Comments: *British involvement in Egypt deepened after the opening of the Suez Canal in 1869, many British officers being seconded to the Khedive's Army. When the Army mutinied in 1882 and triggered off a general anti-European uprising, an Anglo-French expedition was mounted. Subsequently the French withdrew before a landing was effected. Trouble erupted in the Sudan (under Anglo-Egyptian administration) in 1884 where General Gordon was besieged at Khartoum. Further campaigns aimed at the overthrow of the Mahdi and the reconquest of the Sudan. These prolonged operations created immense logistical problems. Nile transportation in particular was a matter resolved only when Canadian voyageurs were recruited to handle the river-boats. In addition, a contingent of troops from New South Wales "answered the Empire's call" and medals awarded to them for the Suakin campaign of 1885 are much sought after. Except where noted, the prices quoted below are for medals awarded to British Army personnel. Medals awarded to Indian or Egyptian troops are generally worth about 25 per cent less than comparable awards to British Army units.*

VALUE:

			Miniature
i.	No clasp (dated)	£125–200	£30–35
ii.	No clasp (undated)	£125–200	£30–35
iii.	Alexandria 11th July	£275–350	£45–50
iv.	Tel-el-Kebir	£250–300	£45–50
v.	El-Teb	£325–375	£45–50
vi.	Tamaai	£325–375	£45–50
vii.	El-Teb–Tamaai	£300–350	£45–50
viii.	Suakin 1884	£250–300	£45–50
ix.	The Nile 1884–85	£250–300	£45–50
x.	The Nile 1884–85/Abu Klea	£900–1200	£45–50
xi.	The Nile 1884–85/Kirbekan	£350–400	£45–50
xii.	Suakin 1885	£250–300	£45–50
xiii.	Suakin 1885/Tofrek	£350–400	£45–50
xiv.	Gemaizah 1888	£300–350	£45–55
xv.	Toski 1889	£450–650	£55–65
xvi.	Gemaizah 1888/Toski 1889		
	Egyptian troops	£260–300	
	20th Hussars	£350–450	
2 clasps		£275–350	Add £15
3 clasps		£375–475	for each
4 clasps		£475–600	clasp
5 clasps		£1250–2000	—
Canadian boatmen		£2500–3000	
NSW units (Suakin 1885)		£2600–2900	

132. KHEDIVE'S STAR

Date: 1882.
Campaign: Egypt 1882–91.
Branch of Service: Royal Navy and Army.
Ribbon: 37mm deep blue.
Metal: Bronze.
Size: Height 60mm; width 45mm.
Description: A five-pointed star with a circular centre showing the Sphinx and Pyramids surrounded by a band inscribed EGYPT followed by a year round the top, with "Khedive of Egypt" and the year in the Moslem calendar in Arabic at the foot. (Reverse) the Khedive's monogram surmounted by a crown. The star is suspended by a ring from an ornamental clasp in the centre of which is a star and crescent.
Clasps: Tokar.
Comments: *This star, struck by Jenkins of Birmingham, was conferred by Khedive Tewfik of Egypt on those who qualified for the Egypt medal and it was invariably worn alongside, to the detriment of the silver medal which suffered abrasion from the points of the star. There was also an undated version found with or without a campaign clasp for Tokar, awarded in 1891. These stars were issued unnamed.*

VALUE:			Miniature
i.	1882	£80–100	£15–20
ii.	1884	£80–100	£14–18
iii.	1884-86	£80–100	£20–25
iv.	Undated	£80–100	£20–25
v.	Undated with Tokar bar	£250–300	£75-120

133. GENERAL GORDON'S STAR FOR THE SIEGE OF KHARTOUM

Date: 1884.
Campaign: Mahdist uprising, Sudan 1884.
Branch of Service: British and Sudanese forces.
Ribbon: Deep blue or red.
Metal: Silver or pewter.
Size: Height 80mm; maximum width 54mm.
Description: Star with three concentric circles and seven groups of rays on which are superimposed seven crescents and stars. Suspension by a ring from a Crescent and Star ornament.
Clasps: None.
Comments: *To boost the morale of the defenders Charles Gordon, commanding the garrison at Khartoum, had this star cast locally in a sand mould, using his own breast star of the Order of Mejidieh as the model. Exceptionally, recipients had to purchase their medals, the proceeds going to a fund to feed the poor.*

VALUE:	
Silver gilt	£1500–2000
Silver	£1000–1200
Pewter	£1000–1200

134. NORTH WEST CANADA MEDAL

Date: 1885.

Campaign: Riel's rebellion 1885.

Branch of Service: Mainly local forces.

Ribbon: Blue-grey with red stripes towards the edges.

Metal: Silver.

Size: 36mm.

Description: (Obverse) bust of Queen Victoria; (reverse) the inscription NORTH WEST CANADA 1885 within a frame of maple leaves.

Clasps: Saskatchewan,

Comments: *Paradoxically, while the medal for the Fenian Raids of 1866–70 was not sanctioned till 1899, this medal for service in the North West was authorised immediately after the conclusion of operations against the Metis led by Louis Riel. It was issued unnamed, with or without the clasp for Saskatchewan where the bulk of the action took place. Of particular interest are medals to officers and men aboard the steamship Northcote involved in a boat action; exceptionally, their medals were impressed. Other medals may be encountered with unofficial naming. The medal was awarded to sixteen British staff officers but the majority of medals (5600 in all) went to local forces.*

VALUE:			Miniature
i.	No clasp named	£900–1200	—
ii.	No clasp unnamed	£500–600	£65–75
iii.	Saskatchewan	£2000–2500	£80–100
Northcote recipient		£3500–4000	

135. ROYAL NIGER COMPANY'S MEDAL

Date: 1899.

Campaign: Nigeria 1886–97.

Branch of Service: Officers and men of the Company's forces.

Ribbon: Three equal stripes of yellow, black and white.

Metal: Silver or bronze.

Size: 39.5mm.

Description: (Obverse) the Boehm bust of Queen Victoria; (reverse) the Company's arms in a laurel wreath.

Clasps: Nigeria 1886-97 (silver), Nigeria (bronze).

Comments: *This medal was issued in silver to Europeans and bronze to natives for service in the vast territories administered by the Royal Niger chartered company. Silver medals were impressed in capitals, but those in bronze were more usually stamped with the recipient's service (constabulary) number. Specimens of both versions were later struck from the original dies but these lack name or number.*

VALUE:		Miniature
Silver named (85)	£3000–4000	no clasp £175–220
Silver specimen	£80–100	—
Bronze oficially numbered (250)	£650–850	Nigeria clasp £210–260
Bronze specimen	£60–80	—

136. IMPERIAL BRITISH EAST AFRICA COMPANY'S MEDAL

Date: 1890.
Campaign: East Africa (Kenya and Uganda) 1888–95.
Branch of Service: Company forces.
Ribbon: Plain dark blue.
Metal: Silver.
Size: 40mm.
Description: (Obverse) the Company badge, a crowned and radiant sun, with a Suaheli inscription in Arabic round the foot signifying "the reward of bravery"; (reverse) plain except for a wreath. Suspension is by a plain ring or an ornamental scroll.
Comments: *The rarest of the medals awarded by the chartered companies, this medal was originally intended solely as a gallantry award; but after the BEA Company was wound up in 1895 further issues were authorised by the Foreign Office for service in Witu (1890) and the Ugandan civil war (1890-91). Fewer than thirty medals are known.*

VALUE: £4000–5000   *Miniature* £330–460

137. EAST AND WEST AFRICA MEDAL

Date: 1892.
Campaigns: East and West Africa 1887–1900.
Branch of Service: Royal Navy, Army and native forces.
Ribbon: As 126.
Metal: Silver or bronze.
Size: 36mm.
Description: As the Ashantee Medal (no. 126), distinguished only by its clasps.
Clasps: 22 (see below). A 22nd operation (Mwele, 1895–96) was denoted by engraving on the rim of the medal.
Comments: *This medal was awarded for general service in a number of small campaigns and punitive expeditions. Though usually awarded in silver, it was sometimes struck in bronze for issue to native servants, bearers and drivers. British regiments as such were not involved in any of the actions, but individual officers and NCOs were seconded as staff officers and instructors and their medals bear the names of their regiments. Units of the Royal Navy were also involved in many of the coastal or river actions. Especially sought after are naval medals with the bar for Lake Nyassa 1893 in which the ships* Pioneer *and* Adventure *were hauled in sections overland through 200 miles of jungle.*

VALUE:		Royal Navy	Europeans	Natives	Miniature
i.	1887–8	£850–1250	£425–625	£400–450	£45–50
ii.	Witu 1890	£200–250	£200–250	£150–180	£50–55
iii.	1891–2	£225–275	£200–250	£150–180	£50–55
iv.	1892	£1250–1500	£200–250	£150–180	£50–55
v.	Witu August 1893	£225–250	—	£150–180	£65–75
vi.	Liwondi 1893	£2500–3500	—	—	—
vii.	Juba River 1893	£3000–4000	—	—	—
viii.	Lake Nyassa 1893	£3000–4000	—	—	—
ix.	1893–94	£750–900	£200–250	£150–180	£55–65
x.	Gambia 1894	£325–375	—	£150–180	£55–65
xi.	Benin River 1894	£350–400	£200–250	£150–180	£45–55
xii.	Brass River 1895	£325–375	—	—	£50–55
xiii.	M'wele 1895–6	£400–450	£300–350	£200–250	£110
	(Bronze)			£800–1000	
xiv.	1896–98	—	£375–475	£220–300	£35–50
xv.	Niger 1897	—	£375–425	£220–300	£50–60
xvi.	Benin 1897	£300–350	£200–250	£220–300	£40–50
xvii.	Dawkita 1897	—	—	—	£110
xviii.	1897–98	—	£325–425	£220–250	£50–55
xix.	1898	£725–950	£325–425	£220–250	£50–55
xx.	Sierra Leone 1898–9	£225–275	£325–425	£220–250	£50–55
xxi.	1899	£925–1250	£325–375	£500–700	£50–55
xxii.	1900	—	£325–375	£220–250	£50–55
	2 clasps	£475–525	£325–375	£250–300	
	3 clasps	£575–675	—	£350–400	—
	4 clasps	—	—	£450–500	—

138. BRITISH SOUTH AFRICA COMPANY'S MEDAL

1st type rev.

Mashonaland (2nd) rev.

Date: 1896.
Campaign: South Africa 1890-97.
Branch of Service: British Army and colonial units.
Ribbon: Seven equal stripes, four yellow and three dark blue.
Metal: Silver.
Size: 36mm.
Description: (Obverse) the Old Head bust of Queen Victoria; (reverse) a charging lion impaled by a spear, with a mimosa bush in the background and a litter of assegais and a shield on the ground.
Clasps: Mashonaland 1890, Matabeleland 1893, Rhodesia 1896, Mashonaland 1897.
Comments: *Originally instituted in 1896 for award to troops taking part in the suppression of the Matabele rebellion of 1893, it was later extended to cover operations in Rhodesia (1896) and Mashonaland (1897). The medal, as originally issued, had the inscription MATABELELAND 1893 at the top of the reverse. The medal was re-issued with RHODESIA 1896 or MASHONALAND 1897 inscribed on the reverse, but holders of medals for their first campaign only added clasps for subsequent campaigns. Rather belatedly, it was decided in 1927 to issue medals retrospectively for the Mashonaland campaign of 1890; in this instance the name and date of the campaign were not inscribed on the reverse though the details appeared on the clasp. Although 705 men were entitled, only 200 claimed the medal and clasp. An unusually ornate suspender has roses, thistles, shamrocks and leeks entwined. Only two medals are known with all four clasps, while only fifteen medals had three clasps.*

VALUE:		Miniature
a. Undated reverse with		
Mashonaland 1890 clasp	£850–1000	£55–65
i. Matabeleland 1893	Rare	—
ii. Rhodesia 1896	Rare	—
iii. Mashonaland 1897	Rare	—
b. Matabeleland 1893 rev.	£350–400	£45–50
ii. Rhodesia 1896	£500–600	£55–65
iii. Mashonaland 1897	£500–600	£55–65
with 2 clasps	£850–1000	£70–80
c. Rhodesia 1896 rev.	£350–400	£55–65
iii. Mashonaland 1897	£600–700	£65–75
d. Mashonaland 1897	£350–400	£55–65
Shangani Patrol confirmed member £1800–2200		

139. HUNZA NAGAR BADGE

Date: 1891.
Campaign: Hunza and Nagar 1891.
Branch of Service: Jammu and Kashmir forces.
Ribbon: Large (46mm x 32mm) with a broad red diagonal band and white centre stripe and green upper left and lower right corners.
Metal: Bronze.
Size: 55mm x 27mm.
Description: A uniface rectangular plaque featuring three soldiers advancing on the crenellated hill fort of Nilt, with mountains in the background. The inscription HUNZA NAGAR 1891 appears lower right. It was intended to be worn as a brooch at the neck but subsequently many were fitted with a suspender for wear with a red and green ribbon. The reverse is impressed "Woodstock St."
Clasps: None.
Comments: *Gurney of London manufactured this badge which was awarded by the Maharajah of Jammu and Kashmir to his own troops who served in the operation against the border states of Hunza and Nagar and qualified for the Indian general service medal with clasp for Hunza 1891. The punitive expedition was led by Colonel A. Durand in response to the defiant attitude of the Hunza and Nagar chiefs towards the British agency at Gilgit.*
VALUE: £500–650

140. CENTRAL AFRICA MEDAL

Date: 1895.
Campaigns: Central Africa 1891–98.
Branch of Service: Mainly local forces.
Ribbon: Three equal stripes of black, white and terracotta representing the Africans, Europeans and Indians.
Metal: Silver or bronze.
Size: 36mm.
Description: Obverse and reverse as the East and West Africa (Ashantee) medal, distinguished only by its ribbon.
Clasps: Originally issued without a clasp but one for Central Africa 1894–98 was subsequently authorised.
Comment: *Though generally issued in silver, a bronze version was awarded to native servants. The first issue of this medal had a simple ring suspension and no clasp. For the second issue a clasp, Central Africa 1894–98 was authorised and the medal was issued with a straight bar suspender, which is very rare.*

VALUE:

		Miniature
Without clasp (ring suspension)		£75–100
To natives	£800–1200	
To Europeans	£2000–3000	
With clasp (ring suspension)		£85–120
To natives	£1500–2000	
To Europeans	£2500–3500	
With clasp (bar suspension)	£1200–1500	£85–120
To Navy native	£2500–3000	
Bronze, unnamed	From £500	—

141. HONG KONG PLAGUE MEDAL

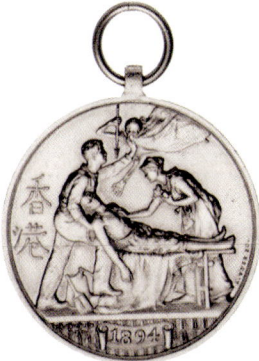

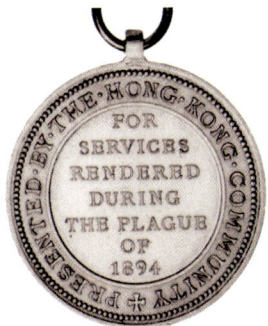

Date: 1894.
Campaign: Hong Kong, May-September 1894.
Branch of Service: Royal Navy, Royal Engineers, KSLI and local personnel.
Ribbon: Red with yellow edges and two narrow yellow stripes in the centre.
Metal: Silver.
Size: 36mm.
Description: (Obverse) a Chinese patient lying on a trestle table being supported by a man warding off the winged figure of Death while a woman tends the sick man. The year 1894 appears on a scroll in the exergue, while the name of the colony in Chinese pictograms is inscribed on the left of the field. (Reverse) inscribed PRESENTED BY THE HONG KONG COMMUNITY round the circumference, and FOR SERVICES RENDERED DURING THE PLAGUE OF 1894 in seven lines across the centre. It was fitted with a plain ring for suspension.
Clasps: None.
Comments: *The colonial authorities in Hong Kong awarded this medal to nurses, civil servants, police, British Army and Royal Navy personnel who rendered assistance when the crown colony was stricken by a severe epidemic of bubonic plague in May 1894. Despite stringent measures, over 2500 people died in the ensuing three months. About 400 medals were issued in silver and awarded to 300 men of the King's Shropshire Light Infantry, 50 petty officers and ratings of the Royal Navy and NCOs and other ranks of the Royal Engineers, as well as about the same number of police and junior officials, while 45 were struck in gold for award to officers, nursing sisters and senior officials. However, the medal was not authorised for wear on uniform by British troops.*

VALUE:

		Miniature
Gold (45)	£6500–10,000	£225–310
Silver (400)	£1600–1800	£175–250

142. INDIA MEDAL

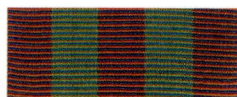

Date: 1896.
Campaign: India 1895–1902.
Branch of Service: British and Indian forces.
Ribbon: Crimson with two dark green stripes—the heraldic colour of Britain and the sacred colour of the prophet.
Metal: Silver or bronze.
Size: 36mm.
Description: Issued with two different obverses, portraying Queen Victoria (1895–1901) and King Edward VII in field marshal's uniform (1901–02). (Reverse) British and Indian soldiers supporting a standard. The Edward VII reverse is undated.
Clasps: Seven, mainly for actions on the North West Frontier (see below).
Comments: *This medal replaced the India GSM which had been awarded for various minor campaigns over a period of four decades from 1854. Combatant troops were given the medal in silver but native bearers and servants received a bronze version. Although the clasp Waziristan 1901–2 is rare to British recipients it was awarded to a number of regiments.*

VALUE:

		British regiments	Indian Army	Bronze	Miniature
i.	Defence of Chitral 1895	£3500–4500	£2400–3000	£3500–4500	£90–110
ii.	Relief of Chitral 1895	£200–225	£175–200	£135–185	£30–35
iii.	Punjab Frontier 1897–98	£200–225	£175–200	£125–160	£25–30
iv.	Malakand 1897*	£500–700	£200–275	£160–225	£55–65
v.	Samana 1897*	£200–225	£185–225	£125–160	£40–45
vi.	Tirah 1897–98*	£200–250	£185–225	£125–160	£50–55
vii.	Waziristan 1901–2	£350–450	£185–225	£125–160	£60–70
3 clasps		£275–350	£275–350	£185–260	£55–65
4 clasps		—	£325–375	—	£65–85

These clasps are always paired with clasp iii.

143. JUMMOO AND KASHMIR MEDAL

Date: 1895.
Campaign: Defence of Chitral 1895.
Branch of Service: Native levies.
Ribbon: White with red stripes at the edges and a central green stripe.
Metal: Bronze, silver.
Size: 35mm high; 38mm wide.
Description: This medal, by Gurney of London, has a unique kidney shape showing the arms of Jummoo (Jammu) and Kashmir on the obverse. (Reverse) a view of Chitral fort with troops in the foreground.
Clasps: Chitral 1895.
Comments: *Awarded by the Maharajah of Jummoo (Jammu) and Kashmir to the Indian troops who participated in the defence of Chitral (a dependency of Kashmir) during the siege of 4 March to 20 April by Chitralis and Afghans led by Umra Khan and Sher Afzul. It always comes with the clasp. with the name of the maker (GURNEY LONDON) on the back. The medal in bronze was presumably awarded to other ranks and those in silver to officers.*

VALUE:	Silver	Bronze
Named	—	£500–700
Unnamed	1200–1600	£400–600

144. ASHANTI STAR

Date: 1896.
Campaign: Gold Coast 1896.
Branch of Service: British forces.
Ribbon: Yellow with two black stripes.
Metal: Bronze.
Size: 44mm.
Description: A saltire cross with a four-pointed star in the angles, surmounted by a circular belt inscribed ASHANTI 1896 around a British crown. The plain reverse is simply inscribed FROM THE QUEEN.
Clasps: None.
Comments: *Issued unnamed, but the colonel of the West Yorkshire Regiment had the medals of the second battalion engraved at his own expense. Some 2000 stars were awarded to officers and men serving in the expedition led by Major-General F.C. Scott against the tyrannical King Prempeh. It is believed that the star was designed by Princess Henry of Battenberg whose husband died of fever during the campaign.*

VALUE:
Unnamed	£200–250
Named to West Yorkshire Regiment	£650–750
In attributable group	£850–1000
Miniature	£50–60

145. QUEEN'S SUDAN MEDAL

Date: 1899.
Campaign: Reconquest of the Sudan 1896–97.
Branch of Service: Royal Navy, Army and local forces.
Ribbon: Half-yellow and half-black representing the desert and the Sudanese nation, divided by a thin crimson stripe representing the British forces.
Metal: Silver or bronze.
Size: 36mm.
Description: (Obverse) the bust of Queen Victoria similar to the Jubilee bust but with sceptre; (Reverse) a seated figure of Victory holding palms and laurels with flags in the background, the word SUDAN appearing on a tablet at her feet.
Clasps: None.
Comments: *Unusually, no clasps were granted for individual actions which included the celebrated battle of Omdurman in which young Winston Churchill charged with the cavalry. Medals named to the 21st Lancers are especially desirable on that account.*

VALUE:
Bronze	
unnamed	£250–300
named	£300–350
Silver	
unnamed	£225–275
named to British Regt	£375–450
Indian Regt	£325–375
21st Lancers	£2500–3500
Confirmed charger*	£3500–4000
RN/RM (46)	£3000–3500
War correspondent	£1500–2000

* Dependent on which Company the recipient served in.

Miniature	£40–50

146. KHEDIVE'S SUDAN MEDAL 1896–1908

(reverse)

Date: 1897.

Campaign: Sudan 1896-1908.

Branch of Service: Royal Navy and British and Egyptian Armies.

Ribbon: 38mm yellow with a broad central deep blue stripe, symbolising the desert and the River Nile.

Metal: Silver or bronze.

Size: 39mm.

Description: (Obverse) an elaborate Arabic inscription translating as 'Abbas Hilmi the Second' and the date 1314 (AD 1897); (reverse) an oval shield surrounded by flags and a trophy of arms. Bar suspender.

Clasps: Fifteen (see below) but medals with more than the two clasps 'The Atbara' and 'Khartoum' are unusual. Inscribed in English and Arabic to British recipients.

Comments: *Instituted by the Khedive of Egypt in February 1897 and granted to those who served in the reconquest of Dongola province in the Sudan (1896-8) as well as in subsequent operations for the pacification of the southern provinces. It was awarded to officers and men of the British and Egyptian Armies and Royal Navy personnel who served on the Nile steamboats. In addition, the crews of the Royal Naval ships HMS Melita (139) and HMS Scout (149) were awarded silver medals with no clasps for Dongola 1896 (but were* not *awarded the Queen's Sudan Medal 1896–98). Medals to Royal Naval personnel with clasps are rare and command a high premium: Hafir (16), The Atbara (6), Sudan 1897 (12), Khartoum (33), Gedaref (9), Gedid (5) and Sudan 1899 (6).*

VALUE:

No clasp silver		
Unnamed	£130–150	
named to British regt	£200–250	
named to Indian regt	£160–185	
named to Royal Navy	£375–475	
No clasp bronze	£160–185	
i. Firket	£160–185	
ii. Hafir	£160–185	
iii. Abu Hamed	£160–185	
iv. Sudan 1897	£160–185	
v. The Atbara	£155–175	
vi. Khartoum	£250–275	
vii. Gedaref	£160–185	
viii. Gedid	£160–185	

ix. Sudan 1899	£160–185	
x. Bahr-el-Ghazal 1900–2	£195–235	
xi. Jerok	£160–185	
xii. Nyam-Nyam	£185–210	
xiii. Talodi	£185–210	
xiv. Katfia	£185–210	
xv. Nyima	£185–210	
2 clasps	£200–250	
3 clasps	£250–275	
4 clasps	£275–350	
5 clasps	£375–450	
6 clasps	£400–500	
7 clasps	£500–550	
8 clasps	£525–600	

Miniature

No clasp silver	£40–55
With any single clasp	£55–85
Add £15 for each additional clasp	

A young, fresh-faced Winston Churchill aged 24 poses in his brand new 4th Hussars dress uniform. He was to be involved in action in the Sudan and his detailed accounts of his experiences there provide an important eye-witness view of this turbulent time in the history of the British Empire.

147. EAST AND CENTRAL AFRICA MEDAL

Date: 1899.
Campaigns: East and Central Africa 1897–99.
Branch of Service: British, Indian and local forces.
Ribbon: Half yellow, half red.
Metal: Silver or bronze.
Size: 36mm.
Description: (Obverse) the bust of Queen Victoria similar to the Jubilee bust but with sceptre; (reverse) a standing figure of Britannia with the British lion alongside.
Clasps: Four (see below).
Comments: *Instituted for service in operations in Uganda and the southern Sudan, it was awarded in silver to combatants and in bronze to camp followers. Most of the medals were awarded to troops of the Uganda Rifles and various Indian regiments. The few British officers and NCOs were troop commanders and instructors seconded from their regiments and their medals are worth very much more than the prices quoted, which are for native awards.*

VALUE:

	Europeans	Natives	Miniature
No clasp			
silver	—	£260–285	£50–60
bronze	—	£335–435	—
i. Lubwa's (with clasp Uganda 1897–98)	—	£750–900	£80–90
ii. Uganda 1897–98	£800–1000	£450–550	£70–80
iii. 1898 (silver)	—	£450–550	£70–80
iv. 1898 (bronze)	—	£550–650	—
v. Uganda 1899	—	£450–550	£70–80

147A. UGANDA STAR

Instituted: 1897–98.
Campaign: Mutiny of Sudanese troops in Uganda.
Branch of Service: African civilians and soldiers.
Ribbon: None.
Metal: Silver.
Description: An eight-pointed uniface star surmounted by a crown, with the dates 1897 and 1898 on a circular rim enclosing the Old Head or Veiled Bust of Queen Victoria. Brooch-mounted. Manufactured by Carrington of London and issued in a blue plush-lined case.
Comments: *This award, approved by the Foreign Office and sanctioned by Queen Victoria, acknowledged the loyalty of African tribal leaders but, in a few cases, was also awarded to Sudanese troops (one, in fact, a Tunisian) who fought gallantly in quelling the serious mutiny of Sudanese troops of the Uganda Rifles. It was for this action that British, Indian and Local forces were awarded the East and Central Africa Medal with the bar for Lubwa's (see above). Only 39 stars were awarded.*

VALUE: From £2500

148. BRITISH NORTH BORNEO COMPANY'S MEDAL 1888–1916

Instituted: 1897.

Campaign: North Borneo (now Sabah, Malaysia), 1897-1916.

Ribbon: Initially gold (later yellow) watered silk 32mm, replaced in 1917 by a 32mm ribbon with maroon edges, two yellow stripes and a dark blue central stripe. The central stripe was originally 6mm wide but modern ribbons have a 10mm stripe.

Metal: Silver or bronze.

Size: 38mm, with a thickness of 5mm.

Description: (Obverse) the shield of the Company, supported by a warrior on either side. The Company motto at the foot is PERGO ET PERAGO (I carry on and accomplish); (reverse) the British lion facing left, standing in front of a bush adorned with the Company flag, with a small wreath in the exergue.

Clasps: Punitive Expedition (1897), Punitive Expeditions (1898-1915), Rundum (1915). The Punitive Expeditions clasp was awarded to those who took part in two or more actions, but it also replaced the earlier single Expedition clasp in due course.

Comments: *These medals were awarded for service in the 15 minor expeditions between 1883 and 1915, excluding the major action at Tambunan. The manufacturers, Spink, supplied 12 silver medals in 1898–9 for award to officers (only three being named). In 1906 a further 74 silver medals were issued, to be exchanged for the bronze medals initially awarded to other ranks. A further 11 silver medals were supplied later on, all unnamed. A total of 75 bronze medals were supplied, 25 of them stamped with a name and sometimes rank and number as well, and issued, both stamped and engraved, to other ranks.*

First type ribbon.

Second type ribbon.

VALUE:

	Type	Officially named	Unnamed original	Stamped "Specimen"	*Miniature*
i. Punitive Expedition	Silver	£1500–2000	£350–500	£60–80	£180–200
	Bronze	£1500–2000	£350–500	£60–80	
ii. Punitive Expeditions	Silver	£1500–2000	£350–500	£60–80	£180–200
	Bronze	£1500–2000	£350–500	£60–80	
iii. Rundum	Silver	£1500–2000	£350–500	£60–80	£180–200

148A. BRITISH NORTH BORNEO COMPANY'S MEDAL 1899–1900

Instituted: 1900.

Campaign: The final expedition in the Tambunan Valley against Mat Salleh.

Ribbon: 32mm yellow with a 10mm green stripe down the centre.

Metal: Silver or bronze.

Size: 38mm. Officially named medals are 5mm thick.

Description: (Obverse) the shield of the British North Borneo Company with BRITISH NORTH BORNEO round the top and the date 1900 below; (reverse) a wreath enclosing a device of one clothed and one naked arm supporting the Company's flag. The motto PERGO ET PERAGO is inscribed outside the wreath. The inscription SPINK & SON, LONDON appears in very tiny lettering at the foot.

Clasps: Tambunan.

Comments: *Instituted for award to those officers and men who took part in the expedition of January-February 1900 against Mat Salleh who had roused the Tegas against the Tiawan Dusuns in the Tambunan Valley. Salleh was killed on February 1, 1900 when Company forces stormed his stronghold and his followers were dispersed or killed. Eight silver medals were originally awarded to officers, but in 1906 some 106 were issued to be exchanged for the bronze medals initially issued to other ranks. A further 22 silver medals were later supplied, unnamed. A total of 125 bronze medals were supplied, 118 of them stamped with a name and sometimes also a rank and number, and issued, both stamped and engraved, to other ranks. Only 36 are recorded as replaced by silver medals, but it is known that some of these bronze medals were not returned to the authorities.*

VALUE:

Type	Officially Named	Unnamed original	Spink copy	Stamped "Specimen"
Silver	£1800–2000	£300–500	£50–60	£60–80
Bronze	£1000–1500	£300–500	£50–60	£60–80

Miniature   £175–200

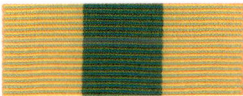

149. SULTAN OF ZANZIBAR'S MEDAL

Date: 1896.

Campaign: East Africa 1896.

Branch of Service: Sultan's forces.

Ribbon: Plain bright scarlet.

Metal: Silver.

Size: 36mm.

Description: (Obverse) a facing bust of Sultan Hamid bin Thwain surrounded by a Suaheli inscription in Arabic; (reverse) same inscription set in four lines.

Clasps: Pumwani, Jongeni, Takaungu, Mwele (inscribed only in Arabic).

Comments: *Awarded to the Zanzibari contingent who served under Lieut. Lloyd-Matthews RN in East Africa alongside British and Imperial forces.*

VALUE: £400–500   *Miniature*   £580–680

150. QUEEN'S SOUTH AFRICA MEDAL

Date: 1899.

Campaign: Anglo-Boer War 1899-1902.

Branch of Service: British and Imperial forces.

Ribbon: Red with two narrow blue stripes and a broad central orange stripe.

Metal: Silver or bronze.

Size: 36mm.

Description: (Obverse) the Jubilee bust of Queen Victoria; (reverse) Britannia holding the flag and a laurel crown towards a large group of soldiers, with warships offshore. The words SOUTH AFRICA are inscribed round the top.

Clasps: 26 authorised but the maximum recorded for a single medal is nine to the Army and eight to the Navy.

Comments: *Because of the large number of British and imperial forces which took part and the numerous campaign and battle clasps awarded, this is one of the most popular and closely studied of all medals, offering immense scope to the collector. A total of 250,000 medals were awarded. Numerous specialist units were involved for the first time, as well as locally raised units and contingents from India, Canada, Australia and New Zealand. Of particular interest are the medals awarded to war correspondents and nurses which set precedents for later wars. Although nurses received the medal they were not issued with clasps to which they were entitled. A small number of bronze medals without a clasp were issued to bearers and servants in Indian units. The original issue of the QSA depicts Britannia's outstretched hand pointing towards the R of AFRICA and bears the dates 1899–1900 on the reverse field. Less than 70 of these were issued to Lord Strathcona's Horse who had returned to Canada before the war ended, but as the war dragged on the date was removed before any other medals were issued, although some medals can be found with a "ghost" of this date still to be seen. On the third type reverse there is again no date but Britannia's hand points towards the F. The prices for clasps given overleaf are for clasps issued in combination with others. Some clasps are much scarcer when issued singly than combined with other clasps and conversely some clasps are not recorded on their own. Verified ten-clasp medals to South African units are known. It is important to note that the following list is very basic and represents the value of straightforward medals and clasps. Confusion can sometimes occur as single clasps and combinations of two or three clasps can command higher premiums than medals with a greater number of clasps. It is beyond the remit of this book to give the value of every possible combination of clasps. A very rough guide would be to take the most valuable clasp as a starting point and add 25% of this value for each Battle clasp and 10% for each State clasp, however, this is by no means infallible. An example would be to take a three-clasp medal which has Elandslaagte (£350–400), Belfast (£80–100) and Relief of Kimberley (£200–275) which as a simple 3-clasp medal would be valued at £100–165—however, on the rough guide system it would be valued at c. £650. Certain clasp combinations will always command a higher premium, for example Relief of Ladysmith/ Relief of Mafeking, Defence of Ladysmith/Relief of Mafeking, Elandslaagte/Defence of Ladysmith, Defence of Kimberley/Paardeberg, etc. Clasps for Natal and Cape Colony cannot appear on the same medal.*

1st type rev.

2nd type rev.
(occasionally ghost dates can be seen)

3rd type rev.

150. QUEEN'S SOUTH AFRICA MEDAL *continued*

VALUE:	RN	British Army	SA/Indian	Aus/NZ	Canadian
No clasp bronze	—	—	£150–250	—	—
No clasp silver	£150–160	£75–85	£85–150	£150–200	£125–175
i. Cape Colony	£180–200	£75–85	£80–100	£150–200	£125–175
ii. Rhodesia	£1000–1250	£400–450	£300–350	£375–450	£350–400
iii. Relief of Mafeking	—	—	£400–450	£425–550	£400–450
iv. Defence of Kimberley	—	£350–450	£250–300	—	—
v. Talana	—	£350–400	£250–350	—	—
vi. Elandslaagte	—	£350–450	£300–350	—	—
vii. Defence of Ladysmith	£750–850	£375–500	£200–250	—	—
viii. Belmont	£300–350	£125–150	—	£250–300	—
ix. Modder River	£300–350	£125–150	—	£250–300	—
x. Tugela Heights	£300–350	£100–125	—	—	—
xi. Natal	£300–350	£100–160	£120–150	—	£220–250
xii. Relief of Kimberley	£750–950	£200–275	£85–100	£150–185	—
xiii. Paardeberg	£250–300	£100–125	£85–100	£125–175	£175–200
xiv. Orange Free State	£180–225	£85–125	£75–100	£125–175	£175–200
xv. Relief of Ladysmith	£450–500	£125–150	£80–100	—	—
xvi. Driefontein	£240–260	£85–125	—	£125–175	£225–275
xvii. Wepener	—	£800–1000	£400–450	—	—
xviii. Defence of Mafeking	—	—	£1500–2250	—	—
xix. Transvaal	£450–600	£85–100	£75–100	£120–155	£225–275
xx. Johannesburg	£250–300	£85–100	£85–100	£125–175	£125–175
xxi. Laing's Nek	£500–650	£85–100	—	—	—
xxii. Diamond Hill	£250–300	£85–100	£85–100	£125–175	£200–225
xxiii. Wittebergen	£1000–1200	£85–100	£85–100	£125–175	—
xxiv. Belfast	£250–300	£85–100	£85–100	£125–175	£125–175
xxv. South Africa 1901	£125–150	£75–90	£75–85	£85–125	£100–150
xxvi. South Africa 1902	£750–800	£75–90	£65–75	£85–125	£100–150
2 clasps (*see Comment above*)	£200–250	£150–200	£100–150	£175–200	£175–200
3 clasps "	£250–280	£100–175	£125–175	£185–225	£185–225
4 clasps	£300–350	£150–275	£130–185	£225–275	£225–275
5 clasps*	£380–450	£150–200	£130–185	£275–300	£225–275
6 clasps*	£550–650	£165–250	£225–275	£325–375	£325–375
7 clasps*	£800–900	£475–550	£450–500	£850–1000	—
To Royal Marines	£1600–1800				
8 clasps*	£1800–2000	£850–1000	£2000–3000	—	—
9 clasps	—	—	£3500–4000	—	—
Relief dates on reverse					
(Lord Strathcona's Horse)	—	—	—	—	£4000–5000
Nurses	—	£500–650	—	—	—
War Correspondents	—	£1500–1750	—	—	—

* excluding date clasps

Miniature

**From £20 with no clasp to £50 with 6 fixed clasps—"slip-on" style clasps approx. 20% less.
With dated reverse £125–175**

151. QUEEN'S MEDITERRANEAN MEDAL

Date: 1899.
Campaign: Mediterranean garrisons 1899-1902.
Branch of Service: British militia forces.
Ribbon: Red with two narrow dark blue stripes and a central broad orange stripe (as for Queen's South Africa Medal).
Metal: Silver.
Size: 36mm.
Description: Similar to the Queen's South Africa Medal but inscribed MEDITERRANEAN at the top of the reverse.
Clasps: None.
Comments: *Awarded to officers and men of the militia battalions which were sent to Malta and Gibraltar to take over garrison duty from the regular forces who were drafted to the Cape.*

VALUE:

Silver (5,000)	£350–400	*Miniature*	£75–85

152. KING'S SOUTH AFRICA MEDAL

Date: 1902.
Campaign: South Africa 1901–02.
Branch of Service: British and imperial forces.
Ribbon: Three equal stripes of green, white and orange.
Metal: Silver.
Size: 36mm.
Description: (Obverse) bust of King Edward VII in field marshal's uniform; (reverse) as for Queen's medal.
Clasps: Two: South Africa 1901, South Africa 1902.
Comments: *This medal was never issued without the Queen's medal and was awarded to all personnel engaged in operations in South Africa in 1901–02 when fighting was actually confined to numerous skirmishes with isolated guerrilla bands. Very few medals were awarded to RN personnel as the naval brigades had been disbanded in 1901. Apart from about 600 nurses and a few odd men who received the medal without a clasp, this medal was awarded with two clasps—most men were entitled to both clasps, single clasp medals being very rare. Only 137 were awarded to New Zealand troops.*

VALUE:

No clasp (Conductors and associated ranks in the ASC (106) and nurses (587))	£300–400
Two clasps:	
i. South Africa 1901	
ii. South Africa 1902	
RN (33)	£1500–1800
Army	£95–125
Canada (160)	£175–200
Australia (*not issued on its own, in a pair with any QSA to an Australian*)	£2500–2600
New Zealand	£300–350
South African units	£85–125
St John Ambulance Brigade (12)	£300–350
Single clasp 1902 (ii) (502 to Imperial troops, none known for Colonial troops)	From £200
Miniature	
No clasp	£15–20
2 clasps	£20–25

152A. ST ANDREW'S AMBULANCE ASSOCIATION MEDAL FOR SOUTH AFRICA

Date: 1902.
Campaign: South Africa 1899–1902.
Branch of Service: St Andrew's Ambulance Association.
Ribbon: Plain white silk.
Metal: Silver.
Size: 31x20mm.
Description: An oval medal: (obverse) the Geneva cross surmounted on a rayed star in red enamel with SOUTH AFRICA above and 1900 below surrounded by the inscription SCOTTISH NATIONAL RED CROSS HOSPITAL; (reverse) the arms of the Association: St Andrew in front of the cross, with ST ANDREW'S AMBULANCE ASSOCIATION around.
Clasps: None.
Comments: *This small medal was awarded in 3 classes, Bronze, Silver and Gold. The Gold medal was given to senior staff of the 160-strong Scottish Hospital, including Sir George Cayley (late IMS) who commanded; the Silver to Officers, Nurses, and Civil Surgeons and the Bronze to the OR's who served. The Bronze variety has been seen named in small impressed capitals on the rim at 6 o'clock. All Varieties of the medal are rare.*
VALUE: Rare   Miniature —

153. ST JOHN AMBULANCE BRIGADE MEDAL FOR SOUTH AFRICA

Date: 1902.
Campaign: South Africa 1899–1902.
Branch of Service: St John Ambulance Brigade.
Ribbon: Black with narrow white edges.
Metal: Bronze.
Size: 37mm.
Description: (Obverse) King Edward VII; (reverse) the arms of the Order and SOUTH AFRICA and the dates 1899 and 1902 with the legend in Latin around.
Clasps: None.
Comments: *Issued by the Order of St John of Jerusalem to the members of its ambulance brigade who served during the Boer War or who played an active part in the organisation, mobilisation and supply roles. Medals were engraved on the edge with the recipient's name and unit. It is most often associated with the two South Africa medals, but 14 members who went on from South Africa to serve during the Boxer Rebellion were also awarded the China Medal.*

VALUE: Bronze (1,871) £300–350   Miniature £175–200 *(in silver slightly less)*

153A. NATIONAL FIRE BRIGADE'S UNION MEDAL FOR SOUTH AFRICA

Date: 1902.
Campaign: South Africa 1899–1902.
Branch of Service: National Fire Brigade's Union.
Ribbon: Red with narrow orange edges and two orange stripes near the centre.
Metal: Silver.
Size: 36mm.
Description: (Obverse) King Edward VII; (reverse) A bust of a helmeted fireman with a Geneva cross in the sky above. Around the circumference a spray of laurel leaves between the dates 1899 and 1902 and SOUTH AFRICA at top.
Comments: *Awarded to a small detachment of volunteers of the National Fire Brigades Union (Ambulance Department) who served in South Africa as stretcher bearers and ambulance personnel. Each volunteeer also received the St John Ambulance Medal for South Africa and the Queen's South Africa Medal with the clasp Cape Colony. Only 42 were awarded.*
VALUE: £1200–1500   Miniature (silver) £220–350

154. KIMBERLEY STAR

Date: 1900.
Campaign: Defence of Kimberley 1899–1902.
Branch of Service: British and local forces.
Ribbon: Half yellow, half black, separated by narrow stripes of red, white and blue.
Metal: Silver.
Size: Height 43mm; max. width 41mm.
Description: A six-pointed star with ball finials and a circular centre inscribed KIMBERLEY 1899–1900 with the civic arms in the middle. (Reverse) plain, apart from the inscription MAYOR'S SIEGE MEDAL 1900. Suspended by a plain ring from a scrolled bar.
Clasps: None
Comments: *The Mayor and council of Kimberley awarded this and the following medal to the defenders of the mining town against the Boer forces. Two medals were struck in gold but about 5000 were produced in silver. Those with the "a" Birmingham hallmark for 1900 rate a premium over stars with later date letters.*

VALUE:

Hallmark "a"	£450–550	*Miniature*	£145–175
Later date letters	£350–450		

155. KIMBERLEY MEDAL

Date: 1900.
Campaign: Defence of Kimberley 1899–1900.
Branch of Service: Local forces.
Ribbon: As above.
Metal: Silver
Size: 38mm.
Description: (Obverse) the figure of Victory above the Kimberley Town Hall, with the dates 1899–1900 in the exergue. (Reverse) two shields inscribed INVESTED 15 OCT. 1899 and RELIEVED 15 FEB. 1900. The imperial crown appears above and the royal cypher underneath, with the legend TO THE GALLANT DEFENDERS OF KIMBERLEY round the circumference.
Comments: *Although awarded for the same purpose as MYB154, this silver medal is a much scarcer award.*

VALUE: £1800–2000

156. YORKSHIRE IMPERIAL YEOMANRY MEDAL

Date: 1900.
Campaign: South Africa 1900–02.
Branch of Service: Yorkshire Imperial Yeomanry.
Ribbon: Dark blue with a central yellow stripe.
Metal: Silver.
Size: 38mm.
Description: Three versions were produced. The first two had the numeral 3 below the Prince of Wales's feathers and may be found with the dates 1900–1901 or 1901–1902, while the third type has the figures 66, denoting the two battalions involved. The uniform reverse has the white rose of Yorkshire surmounted by an imperial crown and enclosed in a laurel wreath with the legend A TRIBUTE FROM YORKSHIRE.
Comments: *Many medals were produced locally and awarded to officers and men of county regiments. The medals struck by Spink and Son for the Yorkshire Imperial Yeomanry, however, are generally more highly regarded as they were much more extensively issued, and therefore more commonly met with.*

VALUE:

		Miniature
3rd Battalion 1900–1901	£300–350	£130–150
3rd Battalion 1901–1902	£300–350	£110–130
66th Company 1900–1901	£300–350	Not seen

157. MEDAL FOR THE DEFENCE OF OOKIEP

Date: 1902.
Campaign: Defence of Ookiep 1902.
Branch of Service: British and colonial forces.
Ribbon: Dark brown with a central green stripe.
Metal: Silver or bronze.
Size: 36mm.
Description: (Obverse) a miner and copper-waggon, with the Company name and date of foundation (1888) round the circumference; (reverse) a thirteen-line text. Fitted with a scroll suspender.
Clasps: None.
Comments: *Commonly known as the Cape Copper Co. Medal, this medal was awarded by the Cape Copper Company to those who defended the mining town of Ookiep in Namaqualand when it was besieged from 4 April to 4 May 1902 by a Boer commando led by Jan Christian Smuts, later Field Marshal, Prime Minister of South Africa and a member of the Imperial War Cabinet. The defence was conducted by Lt-Col W. A. D. Shelton, DSO, and Maj J. L. Dean of the Namaqualand Town Guard, the Company's manager. The garrison consisted of 206 European miners, 660 Cape Coloureds, 44 men of the 5th Warwickshire militia and twelve men of the Cape Garrison Artillery.*
VALUE:

Silver (officers)	£6000–8000
Bronze (other ranks)	£1200–1500

158. CHINA WAR MEDAL 1900

Date: 1901.
Campaign: Boxer Rebellion 1900.
Branch of Service: British and imperial forces.
Ribbon: Crimson with yellow edges.
Metal: Silver or bronze.
Size: 36mm.
Description: (Obverse) bust of Queen Victoria; (reverse) trophy of arms, similar to the 1857-60 China Medal but inscribed CHINA 1900 at the foot.
Clasps: Taku Forts, Defence of Legations, Relief of Pekin.
Comments: *Instituted for service during the Boxer Rebellion and the subsequent punitive expeditions, this medal was similar to that of 1857-60 with the date in the exergue altered to 1900. There are three types of naming: in small, impressed capitals for European troops, in large impressed capitals for naval recipients, and in engraved cursive script for Indian forces. The medal was issued in silver to combatants and in bronze to native bearers, drivers and servants. The international community was besieged by the Boxers, members of a secret society, aided and abetted by the Dowager Empress. The relieving force, consisting of contingents from Britain, France, Italy, Russia, Germany and Japan, was under the command of the German field marshal, Count von Waldersee. The British Legation Guard, comprising 80 Royal Marines and a number of "odd men", won the clasp for Defence of Legations, the most desirable of the campaign bars in this conflict.*

VALUE:	Royal Navy	Army	Indian units	*Miniature*
Silver no clasp	£200–250	£250–300	£185–250	£25–30
Australian naval forces	£1500–2000 (approx. 550 issued)			
HMS *Protector*	£4000–4500			
Bronze no clasp	—	—	£185–250	—
i. Taku Forts	£800–1000	—	—	£35–45
ii. Defence of Legations	£9000–12,000	—	—	£55–65
iii. Relief of Pekin:				
Silver	£450–500	£700–750	£285–350	£30–35
Bronze	—	—	£300–350	—
2 clasps	£800–1000	—	—	£45–55
No-clasp medal to a nurse	£1500–2000			
To a war correspondent (9)	£1500–2000			
ditto Relief of Pekin (1)	—			

159. TRANSPORT MEDAL

Date: 1903.
Campaigns: Boer War 1899-1902 and Boxer Rebellion 1900.
Branch of Service: Mercantile Marine.
Ribbon: Red with two blue stripes.
Metal: Silver.
Size: 36mm.
Description: (Obverse) bust of King Edward VII in the uniform of an Admiral of the Fleet; (reverse) HMST *Ophir* below a map of the world with a Latin inscription at the foot OB PATRIAM MILITIBUS PER MARE TRANSVECTIS ADJUTAM (For carrying troops across the sea).
Clasps: S. Africa 1899-1902, China 1900.
Comments: *The last of the medals associated with the major conflicts at the turn of the century, it was instituted for award to the officers of the merchant vessels used to carry troops and supplies to the wars in South Africa and China. The medal was discontinued as from August 4, 1914.*

VALUE:

			Miniature
i.	South Africa 1899–1902 (1219)	£900–1100	£80–110
ii.	China 1900 (322)	£1200–1500	£80–110
	Both clasps (178)	£1500–1700	£110–160

160. ASHANTI MEDAL

Date: 1901.
Campaign: Gold Coast 1900.
Branch of Service: British and local forces.
Ribbon: Black with two broad green stripes.
Metal: Silver or bronze.
Size: 36mm.
Description: (Obverse) bust of King Edward VII in field marshal's uniform. (Reverse) a lion on the edge of an escarpment looking towards the sunrise, with a native shield and spears in the foreground. The name ASHANTI appeared on a scroll at the foot.
Clasps: Kumassi.
Comments: *A high-handed action by the colonial governor provoked a native uprising and the siege of the garrison at Kumassi. The medal was awarded to the defenders as well as personnel of the two relieving columns. Very few Europeans were involved as most were in South Africa fighting the Boers. The medal was awarded in silver to combatants and bronze to native transport personnel and servants.*

VALUE:

	Silver	Bronze	*Miniature*
No clasp	£350–400	£400–500	£45–65
i. Kumassi	£650–750	Rare	£65–80

161. AFRICA GENERAL SERVICE MEDAL

Date: 1902.
Campaigns: Minor campaigns in Africa 1902 to 1956.
Branch of Service: British and colonial forces.
Ribbon: Yellow with black edges and two thin central green stripes.
Metal: Silver or bronze.
Size: 36mm.
Description: (Obverse) effigies of Edward VII, George V and Elizabeth II; (reverse) similar to that of the East and Central Africa medal of 1897–99, with AFRICA in the exergue.
Clasps: 34 awarded in the reign of Edward VII, ten George V and only one Elizabeth II (see below).

continued overleaf

161. AFRICA GENERAL SERVICE MEDAL *continued*

Comments: *This medal replaced the East and West Africa Medal 1887–1900, to which 21 clasps had already been issued. In turn, it remained in use for 54 years, the longest-running British service medal. Medals to combatants were in silver, but a few bronze medals were issued during the 1903–04 operations in Northern Nigeria and the Somaliland campaigns of 1902 and 1908 to transport personnel and these are now much sought after, as are any medals with the effigy of George V on the obverse. With the exception of the 1902–04 Somali campaign and the campaign against the Mau Mau of Kenya (1952–56) European troops were not involved in any numbers, such personnel consisting mostly of detached officers and specialists.*

VALUE:		RN units	British regiments	African/Indian
i.	N. Nigeria	—	—	£200–225
ii.	N. Nigeria 1902	—	—	£180–200
iii.	N. Nigeria 1903	—	—	£170–190
iv.	N. Nigeria 1903–04	—	—	£240–280
v.	N. Nigeria 1903–04 (bronze)	—	—	£230–250
vi.	N. Nigeria 1904	—	—	£225–250
vii.	N. Nigeria 1906	—	—	£200–225
viii.	S. Nigeria	—	—	£280–320
ix.	S. Nigeria 1902	—	—	£240–280
x.	S. Nigeria 1902–03	—	—	£240–280
xi.	S. Nigeria 1903	—	—	£220–260
xii.	S. Nigeria 1903–04	—	—	£280–320
xiii.	S. Nigeria 1904	—	—	£210–230
xiv.	S. Nigeria 1904–05	—	—	£280–320
xv.	S. Nigeria 1905	—	—	£400–500
xvi.	S. Nigeria 1905–06	—	—	£240–280
xvii.	Nigeria 1918	—	—	£180–200
xviii.	East Africa 1902	—	—	£380–420
xix.	East Africa 1904	—	—	£300–350
xx.	East Africa 1905	—	—	£240–280
xxi.	East Africa 1906	—	—	£280–320
xxii.	East Africa 1913	—	—	£280–320
xxiii.	East Africa 1913–14	—	—	£220–240
xxiv.	East Africa 1914	—	—	£280–320
xxv.	East Africa 1915	—	—	£250–270
xxvi.	East Africa 1918	—	—	£220–250
xxvii.	West Africa 1906	—	—	£250–300
xxviii.	West Africa 1908	—	—	£250–300
xxix.	West Africa 1909–10	—	—	£320–370
xxx.	Somaliland 1901	—	—	£320–370
xxxi.	Somaliland 1901 (bronze)	—	—	£300–350
xxxii.	Somaliland 1902–04	£175–225	£220–280	£160–190
xxxiii.	Somaliland 1902–04 (bronze)	—	—	£350–450
xxxiv.	Somaliland 1908–10	£175–225	—	£150–175
xxxv.	Somaliland 1908–10 (bronze)	—	—	£250–300
xxxvi.	Somaliland 1920	£450–550	—	£170–200
	as above but RAF (225 awarded)	—	£700–900	—
xxxvii.	Jidballi (with Somaliland 1902–04)	—	£350–450	£210–270
xxxviii.	Uganda 1900	—	—	£250–300
xxxix.	B.C.A. 1899–1900	—	—	£250–300
xl.	Jubaland	£300–350	—	£210–270
xli.	Jubaland (bronze)	—	—	£550–650
xlii.	Jubaland 1917–18	—	—	£230–250
xliii.	Jubaland 1917–18 (bronze)	—	—	£250–300
xliv.	Gambia	£600–800	—	£300–350
xlv.	Aro 1901–1902	£800–900	—	£250–300
xlvi.	Lango 1901	—	—	£350–400
xlvii.	Kissi 1905	—	—	£400–450
xlviii.	Nandi 1905–06	—	—	£200–250
xlix.	Shimber Berris 1914–15	—	—	£300–350
l.	Nyasaland 1915	—	—	£250–300
li.	Kenya	£350–500	£150–175	£75–125
lii.	Kenya (to RAF)	—	£200–250	—
	2 clasps	£250–300	£350–400	£175–300
	3 clasps	—	—	£250–450
	4 clasps	—	—	£350–500
	5 clasps	—	—	£450–650
	6 clasps	—	—	£850–1200
	Medal to war correspondent	£1200–1500		

Miniature
Range from £35 to £90 depending upon clasp. "Slip-on" clasps are approx. 20% cheaper. Add £15 for each additional clasp.

162. TIBET MEDAL

Date: 1905.
Campaign: Tibet 1903–04.
Branch of Service: British and Indian regiments.
Ribbon: Green with two white stripes and a broad maroon central stripe.
Metal: Silver or bronze.
Size: 36mm.
Description: (Obverse) bust of King Edward VII; (reverse) the fortified hill city of Lhasa with TIBET 1903–04 at the foot.
Clasps: Gyantse.
Comments: *The trade mission led by Colonel Sir Francis Younghusband to Tibet was held up by hostile forces, against whom a punitive expedition was mounted in 1903. This medal was awarded mainly to Indian troops who took part in the expedition, camp followers being awarded the medal in bronze. A clasp was awarded to those who took part in the operations near Gyantse between 3 May and 6 July 1904.*

VALUE:

	British	Indian	Bronze	Miniature
Without clasp	£500–700	£350–400	£125–150	£45–55
i. Gyantse	£1200–1500	£550–650	£350–450	£65–75

163. NATAL REBELLION MEDAL

Date: 1907.
Campaign: Natal 1906.
Branch of Service: Local forces.
Ribbon: Crimson with black edges.
Metal: Silver.
Size: 36mm.
Description: (Obverse) right-facing profile of King Edward VII. (Reverse) an erect female figure representing Natal with the sword of justice in her right hand and a palm branch in the left. She treads on a heap of Zulu weapons and is supported by Britannia who holds the orb of empire in her hand. In the background, the sun emerges from behind storm clouds.
Clasp: 1906.
Comments: *The Natal government instituted this medal for services in the operations following the Zulu rebellion. Local volunteer units bore the brunt of the action and it is interesting to note that one of the recipients was Sergeant-Major M. K. Gandhi who later led India to independence. Medals to officers are engraved in running cursive script.*

VALUE:

		Miniature
No clasp (2000)	£175–200	£45–55
i. 1906 (8000)	£225–275	£55–70
Natal Naval Corps		
without clasp (67)	£175–250	
clasp 1906 (136)	£275–300	

163A. MESSINA EARTHQUAKE COMMEMORATIVE MEDAL

Date: 1908.

Campaign: Messina earthquake relief.

Branch of Service: Royal Navy.

Ribbon: Green with white edges and central white stripe.

Metal: Silver.

Size: 31.5mm.

Description: (Obverse) left-facing profile of King Victor Emanuel III; (reverse) A wreath of oak leaves within which are the words MEDAGLIA COMMEMORATIVA / TERREMOTO CALABRO SICULO 28 DICEMBRE 1908.

Comments: *The King of Italy rewarded Royal Naval and other personnel who went to the aid of victims of the tragic earthquake that hit Messina in December 1908 with this silver medal. Officers and men serving on certain ships were eligible for the award as well as members of the Mercantile Marine and others who were engaged in relief operations. The Admiralty's published list of RN ships is as follows: HMS Duncan, HMS Euralyus, HMS Exmouth, HMS Lancaster, HMS Minerva and HMS Sutlej. However 52 medals were also awarded to personnel from HMS Boxer, which was omitted from the original list and a further 35 medals were awarded to the officers and men of HMS Philomel who had actually "been engaged in work which was directly attributable to the rescue operations". The medal was issued unnamed. In addition to the commemorative medal a special Messina Earthquake Merit Medal was awarded in two sizes (40mm and 30mm) bronze, silver and gold to organisations, vessels and various key individuals who played a part in the rescue operations and examples are known in miniature, in silver.*

VALUE:

		Miniature
Unattributed single medal	£120–150	£65–85
Royal Navy (c. 3500)	£200–300	
Royal Marines (481)	£250–400	
Mercantile Marine (c. 400)	£300–400	
Other	£200–300	
Merit medal	Rare	£125–£155

The aftermath of the devastating earthquake at Messina.

164. INDIA GENERAL SERVICE MEDAL

Date: 1909.
Campaigns: India 1908 to 1935.
Branch of Service: British and Indian forces.
Ribbon: Green with a broad blue central stripe.
Metal: Silver.
Size: 36mm.
Description: Three obverse types were used: Edward VII (1908–10), George V Kaisar-i-Hind (1910–30) and George V Indiae Imp (1930–35). (Reverse) the fortress at Jamrud in the Khyber Pass, with the name INDIA in a wreath at the foot.
Clasps: Twelve, plus two in bronze (see below).
Comments: *This medal was awarded for a number of minor campaigns and operations in India before and after the First World War. The medals were struck at the Royal Mint in London and by the Indian government in Calcutta, the only difference being in the claw suspenders, the former being ornate and the latter plain. Medals with the clasps North West Frontier 1908 and Abor 1911–12 were also issued in bronze to native bearers.*

VALUE:

		British Army	RAF	Indian regiments	*Miniature*
i.	North West Frontier 1908	£150–200	—	£80–100	£25–30
	bronze clasp	—	—	£200–220	
ii.	Abor 1911–12	—	—	£250–300	£30–35
	bronze clasp	—	£275–350	—	
iii.	Afghanistan NWF 1919	£85–100	£150–180	£50–75	£20–25
iv.	Waziristan 1919–21	£125–150	£180–200	£50–75	£20–25
iva*	Mahsud 1919–20	£125–150	£550–650 (175)	£75–100	£20–25
v.	Malabar 1921–22	£175–200	—	£125–175	£35–40
vi.	Waziristan 1921–24	£85–100	£150–180	£50–75	£20–25
vii.	Waziristan 1925 (254)	—	£1400–1600	—	£25–30
viii.	NW Frontier 1930–31	£85–100	£150–180	£50–75	£20–25
ix.	Burma 1930–32	£125–150	£1000–1500	£75–100	£20–25
x.	Mohmand 1933	£200–250	£500–600	£45–65	£20–25
xi.	NW Frontier 1935	£85–100	£150–200	£45–65	£25–30

*Usually found in combination with Waziristan 1919-21, but 10 medals were awarded either with this clasp alone or with the Afghanistan NWF clasp.

Royal Mint striking.

Calcutta striking.

165. KHEDIVE'S SUDAN MEDAL 1910

Date: 1911.
Campaign: Sudan 1910 to 1922
Branch of Service: British and Egyptian forces.
Ribbon: Black with thin red and green stripes on either side.
Metal: Silver or bronze.
Size: 36mm.
Description: (Obverse) an Arabic inscription signifying the name of Khedive Abbas Hilmi and the date 1328 in the Moslem calendar (1910 AD) (type I). He was deposed in December 1914 when Egypt was declared a British protectorate, and succeeded by his nephew who was proclaimed Sultan. Sultan Hussein Kamil changed the Arabic inscription and date to AH 1335 (1916–17) on later issues of the medal (type II). (Reverse) a lion poised on a plinth with the sunrise in the background.
Clasps: 16, inscribed in English and Arabic.
Comments: *Introduced in June 1911 as a replacement for the previous Khedive's Sudan medal of 1896–1908, it was awarded for minor operations in the southern Sudan between 1910 and 1922. The silver medal was issued with clasps to combatants, and without a clasp to non-combatants, while the bronze version was granted to camp followers. The medal is usually found unnamed although a few British recipients' medals are found named in small impressed capitals or Arabic script. The prices below are for unnamed examples.*

VALUE:

Silver without clasp type I	£350–400	
Silver without clasp type II	£300–350	
Bronze without clasp type I	£400–450	
Bronze without clasp type II	£300–350	
i.	Atwot	£450–500
ii.	S. Kordofan 1910	£450–500
iii.	Sudan 1912	£450–500
iv.	Zeraf 1913-14	£450–500
v.	Mandal	£450–500
vi.	Miri	£450–500
vii.	Mongalla 1915-16	£450–500
viii.	Darfur 1916	£450–500
ix.	Fasher	£450–500
x.	Lau Nuer	£450–500
xi.	Nyima 1917-18	£450–500
xii.	Atwot 1918	£450–500
xiii.	Garjak Nuer	£450–500
xiv.	Aliab Dinka	£450–500
xv.	Nyala	£450–500
xvi.	Darfur 1921	£550–600
2 clasps		£600–700
Miniature		
Silver type I		£40–60
Silver type II		£40–60
With any single clasp		£60–95

For each additional clasp add £15–30 (slip-on clasps approx. 20% less)

165A. BRITISH RED CROSS SOCIETY MEDAL FOR THE BALKAN WARS 1912–13

Date: 1913.
Campaign: Balkan Wars 1912–13.
Branch of Service: British Red Cross Society.
Ribbon: White with a central red stripe.
Metal: Silver gilt.
Size: 30mm.
Description: (Obverse) an enamelled design of a red cross on a white shield with the legend THE BRITISH RED CROSS SOCIETY around; (Reverse) blank for naming and hallmark. Ribbon suspended from a top white enamel brooch with indented ends and BALKAN WAR 1912–13, 1912 or 1913. The medal has a swivel scroll bar suspender
Clasps: White enamelled Bulgaria, Greece, Montenegro, Servia, Turkey.
Comments: *This medal, manufactured by J. R. Gaunt of Birmingham, was given to all members of the Society who rendered first aid service to the belligerents also to others who gave help to those units. A total of 198 medals were awarded to members of the Society and a further 72 to others for services rendered. An additional 14 medals were awarded to Turkish nationals but these carried the Red Crescent emblem in place of the Red Cross. A complete roll of all recipients is held by the BRCS.*

VALUE: £250–300

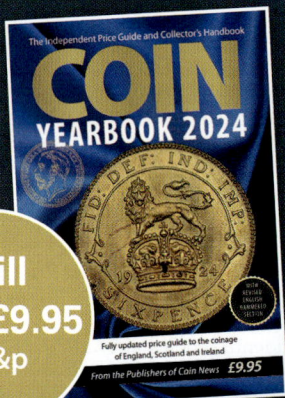

FIRST WORLD WAR MEDALS

The increased popularity in family history research, accompanied by the vast digitisation of records and the on-line resources such as *Ancestry, Find My Past* etc., has gone a long way to encouraging more and more people to find out about their ancestors' military service and as World War I was the first war that touched every family there is plenty of interest in this conflict out there. This interest is inevitably reflected in the prices of World War I medals that have held firm particularly among popular units and whilst the prices we have quoted are broadly similar to previous editions of the *Yearbook*, there are instances of World War I medals being offered for far more than listed here—whether they actually make that amount is a matter of conjecture. Certain medals will command a premium, of course, as with any medals a connection to the more famous actions, in this case particularly the Somme, Gallipoli, the Retreat from Mons, and the battles of Loos and Jutland will increase the price of the group (the prices paid for First Day of the Somme casualties continue to be strong) and gallantry and complete "sets" to casualties all continue to sell exceptionally well. It should also be noted that medals to Imperial forces, particularly Australian, Canadian and New Zealanders are also very popular. As always in the MEDAL YEARBOOK the prices listed in this section are intended as a guide for a non-casualty private in a line regiment. The medals to an officer killed on the First Day of the Somme for example will, of course, be worth more.

166. 1914 STAR

Date: 1917.
Campaign: France and Belgium 1914.
Branch of Service: British forces.
Ribbon: Watered silk red, white and blue.
Metal: Bronze.
Size: Height 50mm; max. width 45mm.
Description: A crowned four-pointed star with crossed swords and a wreath of oak leaves, having the royal cypher at the foot and a central scroll inscribed AUG NOV 1914. Uniface, the naming being inscribed incuse on the plain reverse.
Clasps: 5th Aug.–22nd Nov. 1914. The clasp was sewn on to the ribbon of the medal, the first of this type. A silver rosette is worn on the ribbon strip if the bar was awarded.
Comments: *Awarded to all those who had served in France and Belgium between 5 August and 22 November 1914. In 1919 King George V authorised a clasp bearing these dates for those who had actually been under fire during that period. The majority of the 400,000 recipients of the star were officers and men of the prewar British Army, the "Old Contemptibles" who landed in France soon after the outbreak of the First World War and who took part in the retreat from Mons, hence the popular nickname of Mons Star by which this medal is often known. Approximately 1000 were awarded to members of the Royal Flying Corps of which about 300 received the bar, hence they command a premium. A significant number of Indian Army troops were engaged on the Western Front in 1914 and earned the 1914 Star.*

VALUE:		Miniature
1914 Star	From £75	£5–10
To RN	£225–350	
RM	£125–200	
RND	£175–300	
1914 Star/BWM/Victory trio		
Corps	From £85	
British Regiments	From £125	
Canadian Regiments	From £850	
Australian Regiments	From £1500	
1914 trio with plaque (no. 172)		
Corps	From £200	
Regiments	From £275	
RFC	From £1500	
i. 5th Aug.–22nd Nov. 1914 ("Mons") clasp	From £125	£5–7
Clasp alone	£50–60	

The single 1914 Star named to Private J. Parr of the 4th Battalion Duke of Cambridge's Own (Middlesex Regiment) accepted as being the first fatal casualty of the war, was sold at auction by DNW in August 2021 for £24,000.

167. 1914–15 STAR

Date: 1918.
Campaign: First World War 1914–15.
Branch of Service: British and imperial forces.
Ribbon: Watered silk red, white and blue (as above).
Metal: Bronze.
Size: Height 50mm; max. width 45mm.
Description: As above, but AUG and NOV omitted and scroll across the centre inscribed 1914–15.
Clasps: None.
Comments: *Awarded to those who saw service in any theatre of war between 5 August 1914 and 31 December 1915, other than those who had already qualified for the 1914 Star. No fewer than 2,350,000 were awarded, making it the commonest British campaign medal up to that time.*

VALUE:

1914–15 Star	From £25	*Miniature* £5–8
1914–15 Star/BWM/Victory trio		
Corps	From £50	
RN	From £60	
Regiments	From £65	
1914–15 trio with plaque (no. 172)		
Corps	From £150	
RN	From £200	
Regiments	From £200	

168. BRITISH WAR MEDAL 1914–20

Date: 1919.
Campaign: First World War, 1914–20.
Branch of Service: British and imperial forces.
Ribbon: Orange watered centre with stripes of white and black at each side and borders of royal blue.
Metal: Silver or bronze.
Size: 36mm.
Description: (Obverse) the uncrowned left-facing profile of King George V by Sir Bertram Mackennal. (Reverse) St George on horseback trampling underfoot the eagle shield of the Central Powers and a skull and cross-bones, the emblems of death. Above, the sun has risen in victory. The figure is mounted on horseback to symbolise man's mind controlling a force of greater strength than his own, and thus alludes to the scientific and mechanical appliances which helped to win the war.
Clasps: None.
Comments: *This medal was instituted to record the successful conclusion of the First World War, but it was later extended to cover the period 1919–20 and service in mine-clearing at sea as well as participation in operations in North and South Russia, the eastern Baltic, Siberia, the Black Sea and Caspian. Some 6,500,000 medals were awarded in silver, but about 110,000 in bronze were issued mainly to Chinese, Indian and Maltese personnel in labour battalions. It was originally intended to award campaign clasps, but 79 were recommended by the Army and 68 by the Navy, so the scheme was abandoned as impractical. The naval clasps were actually authorised (7 July 1920) and miniatures are known with them, though the actual clasps were never issued.*

VALUE:		*Miniature*
Silver (6,500,000)	From £15*	£5–10
Bronze (110,000)	£135–155	£15–20
BWM/Victory pair		
Corps	From £25	
Regiments/RN	From £35	
Pair with plaque (no. 172)		
Corps	From £140	
Regiment/RN	From £200	

* Current prices are dictated by world silver markets. The BWM being 1oz of silver, as the price of silver fluctuates so will the minimum price of the BWM.

169. MERCANTILE MARINE WAR MEDAL

Date: 1919.
Campaign: First World War 1914–18.
Branch of Service: Mercantile Marine.
Ribbon: Green and red with a central white stripe, symbolising port and starboard and masthead steaming lights.
Metal: Bronze.
Size: 36mm.
Description: (Obverse) Mackennal profile of King George V; (reverse) a steamship ploughing through an angry sea, with a sinking submarine and a sailing vessel in the background, the whole enclosed in a laurel wreath.
Clasps: None.
Comments: *Awarded by the Board of Trade to members of the Merchant Navy who had undertaken one or more voyages through a war or danger zone.*

VALUE:

Bronze (133,000)	£35–65
To woman	£250–350
With BWM	From £85
With WWI pair	From £125
With 1914–15 trio	From £175
With 1914 trio	From £250
To Australians	Add 50 per cent
To South Africans	Add 75 per cent
With plaque (no. 172)	Add £100+
Miniature	£25–40

170. VICTORY MEDAL

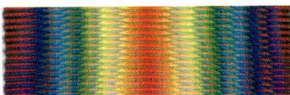

Date: 1919.
Campaign: First World War 1914–19.
Branch of Service: British and imperial forces.
Ribbon: 38mm double rainbow (indigo at edges and red in centre).
Metal: Yellow bronze.
Size: 36mm.
Description: (Obverse) the standing figure of Victory holding a palm branch in her right hand and stretching out her left hand. (Reverse) a laurel wreath containing a four-line inscription THE GREAT WAR FOR CIVILISATION 1914–1919.
Clasps: None.
Comments: *Issued to all who had already got the 1914 or 1914–15 Stars and most of those who had the British War Medal, some six million are believed to have been produced. It is often known as the Allied War Medal because the same basic design and double rainbow ribbon were adopted by thirteen other Allied nations (though the USA alone issued it with campaign clasps). The Union of South Africa produced a version with a reverse text in English and Dutch (not Afrikaans as is often stated).*

VALUE:

British pattern	£10–25
South African pattern	£25–35
Dark "Chocolate" colour issue	£20–25
Miniature	
Normal	£5–6
"CIVILIZATION" variety	£25–30
South African pattern	£75–85

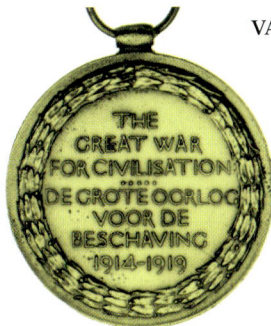

171. TERRITORIAL FORCE WAR MEDAL

Date: 1919.
Campaign: First World War 1914–19.
Branch of Service: Territorial forces.
Ribbon: Watered gold silk with two dark green stripes towards the edges.
Metal: Bronze.
Size: 36mm.
Description: (Obverse) effigy of King George V; (reverse) a wreath enclosing the text FOR VOLUNTARY SERVICE OVERSEAS 1914–19.
Clasps: None.
Comments: *Awarded to all those serving with the Territorial Forces on 4 August 1914, or those who had completed four years service before this date and rejoined on or before 30 September 1914, who served overseas during the course of World War I. Those who had already qualified for the 1914 or 1914–15 Stars, however, were excluded. Around 34,000 medals were awarded, making it by far the scarcest of the First World War medals. The value of individual medals depends on the regiment or formation of the recipient. The totals awarded given below are from "The Great War Medal Collector's Companion" courtesy of Howard Williamson.*

VALUE:

Infantry/Corps (23,762)	£150–300
Artillery (6460)	£120–250
Yeomanry (3271)	£400–500
Cavalry (95)	£850–1000
RFC, RAF, RNAS (505)	£850–1000
Nurses (277)	£650–750
Miniature	£25–35

171A. BRITISH RED CROSS SOCIETY MEDAL FOR WAR SERVICE

Date: 1920.
Campaign: First World War.
Branch of Service: Members of the British Red Cross Society.
Ribbon: Plain white.
Metal: Bronze-gilt.
Size: 31mm.
Description: (Obverse) the Geneva Cross surrounded by a laurel wreath, with the legend BRITISH RED CROSS SOCIETY: FOR WAR SERVICE: 1914–1918 around; (reverse) a wreath enclosing the text INTER/ARMA/CARITAS ("Amidst the arms, charity").
Clasps: None.
Comments: *Granted to all members of the BRCS including Voluntary Aid Detachments who had performed one year or 1,000 hours voluntary service during the war and who did not receive any British War Medal for services rendered in respect of Red Cross war work. The medal was unnamed for wear only on Red Cross or similar uniform.*

VALUE: £15–25   *Miniature* £25–35

For medals awarded by various other organisations for service during World War I see "Miscellaneous Medals" nos. 390 et seq.

172. MEMORIAL PLAQUE

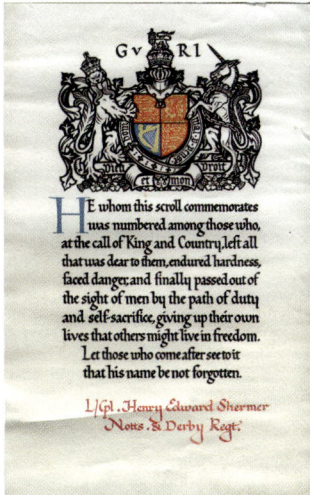

Date: 1919.
Campaign: First World War.
Branch of Service: British forces.
Ribbon: None.
Metal: Bronze.
Size: 120mm.
Description: The plaque shows Britannia bestowing a laurel crown on a rectangular tablet bearing the full name of the dead in raised lettering. In front stands the British lion, with dolphins in the upper field, an oak branch lower right, and a lion cub clutching a fallen eagle in the exergue. The inscription round the circumference reads HE (or SHE) DIED FOR FREEDOM AND HONOVR. A parchment scroll was issued with each plaque giving the deceased's name and unit.
Comments: *Given, with a parchment scroll, to the next of kin of those who lost their lives on active service during the War. Originally it was thought that Naval and Army plaques differed because of the width of the "H" in "HE" however examples of narrow "H" plaques found to Army units and wide "H" plaques to the Navy indicates this to be incorrect. The most likely reason for the narrower "H" is the later decision to add an "S" to allow for female casualty plaques.*

VALUE:	"He died" (1,355,000)	From £65
	"She died" (600)	From £3000
	Parchment scroll (male)	From £35
	ditto (female)	From £1500–2500
Miniature:	Uniface/unnamed (modern manufacture)	£40–50

172A. SILVER WAR BADGE

Date: 12 September 1916.
Campaign: First World War.
Ribbon: None.
Metal: Silver.
Size: 33mm.
Description: A brooch-mounted circular badge with the crowned royal monogram in the centre and edge inscription FOR KING AND EMPIRE + SERVICES RENDERED +.
Comments: *Awarded to service personnel who sustained a wound or contracted sickness or disability in the course of the war as a result of which they were invalided out. It was worn on the lapel in civilian clothes. Each badge was numbered on the reverse. The purpose of the badge was to prevent men of military age but not in uniform from being harassed by women pursuing them with white feathers. Later in the War medical restrictions altered and some men re-enlisted and could wear the badge in uniform. Recently records for these badges have become publicly available and this research potential has inevitably had an effect on prices.*

VALUE:	From £30–40	*Miniature:*	£20–25

172B. CEYLON VOLUNTEER SERVICE MEDAL

Date: 1919.
Campaign: First World War.
Branch of Service: Ceylon volunteer forces.
Ribbon: None.
Metal: Bronze.
Size: 48mm x 44mm.
Description: An upright oval medal. (Obverse) a seated female figure bestowing a laurel crown on a kneeling soldier, with a radiant sun on the horizon; above, a six-line inscription: PRESENTED BY THE GOVERNMENT OF CEYLON TO THOSE WHO VOLUNTARILY GAVE THEIR SERVICES OVERSEAS IN THE GREAT WAR OF with the dates 1914 1919 in two lines on the right of the field; (reverse) the winged figure of Victory seated on a throne above a tablet inscribed with the name of the recipient.
Comments: *Awarded to volunteers from the Ceylon forces who served abroad during the war. Ceylon (now Sri Lanka) was the only British colony to issue such a medal for war service.*

VALUE: £125–175

173. NAVAL GENERAL SERVICE MEDAL 1909–62

Date: 1915.
Campaigns: Naval actions 1909 to 1962.
Branch of Service: Royal Navy.
Ribbon: White with broad crimson edges and two narrow crimson stripes towards the centre.
Metal: Silver.   **Size:** 36mm.
Description: (Obverse) effigy of the reigning monarch (see below). (Reverse) Britannia and two seahorses travelling through the sea.
Clasps: 17 (see below).
Comments: *Instituted for service in minor operations for which no separate medal might be issued. Five different obverses were employed: George V (1915-36), George VI Ind Imp (1936-49), George VI Fid Def (1949-52), Elizabeth II Br Omn (1952-53) and Elizabeth II Dei Gratia (1953-62). Medals issued with the first clasp include the name of the recipient's ship but this lapsed in later awards. The MALAYA clasp was issued with three types of medal: the George VI Fid Def and Elizabeth II Dei Gratia being the most common. The clasp BOMB & MINE CLEARANCE 1945–46 is very rare as it was apparently only awarded to the Royal Australian Navy. The clasp CANAL ZONE was instituted in October 2003 for service between October 1951 and October 1954.*

Bomb & Mine Clearance 1945–53 clasp

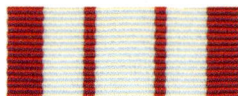

VALUE:			Miniature
i.	Persian Gulf 1909-1914		*(in silver add £5)*
	RN (7,127)	£185–225	
	Army (37)	£800–1000	£20-30
ii.	Iraq 1919-20 (116)	£2000–2500	£20-30
iii.	NW Persia 1919–20 (4)*	Rare	£35–75
iv.	Palestine 1936–39 (13,600)	£125–155	£20-30
v.	SE Asia 1945–46 (2,000)	£250–300	£20-30
vi.	Minesweeping 1945–51 (4,750)	£200–250	£20-30
vii.	Palestine 1945–48 (7,900)	£150–185	£20-30
viii.	Malaya (George VI, Elizabeth II		
	2nd type) (7,800)	£125–155	£20-30
	(Elizabeth II 1st type)	£145–175	£20-30
ix.	Yangtze 1949 (1,450)	£850–1250	£20-30
	to HMS *Amethyst*	£1550–2500	
x.	Bomb & Mine Clearance 1945–53 (145)	£1600–2000	£40–60
xi.	Bomb & Mine Clearance 1945–46	Very rare	£40–60
xii.	Bomb & Mine Clearance		
	Mediterranean (60)	£2000–2500	£40–60
xiii.	Cyprus (4,300)	£155–200	£12–15
xiv.	Near East (17,800)	£100–125	£12–15
xv.	Arabian Peninsula (1,200)	£225–275	£12–15
xvi.	Brunei (900)	£300–375	£12–15
xvii.	Canal Zone	£250–350	—

** The clasp **NW Persia 1920** was withdrawn in favour of the clasp **NW Persia 1919–20**. Recipients were supposed to return their first clasp in exchange for the latter.*

174. GENERAL SERVICE MEDAL 1918–62

Date: 1923.
Campaigns: Minor campaigns 1918 to 1962.
Branch of Service: Army and RAF.
Ribbon: Purple with a central green stripe.
Metal: Silver.
Size: 36mm
Description: (Obverse) six different effigies of the reigning monarch [George V coinage head (1918–30), George V crowned and robed bust (1931–36), George VI Ind Imp (1937–49), George VI Fid Def (1949–52), Elizabeth II Br Omn (1952–54) and Elizabeth II Dei Gratia (1955–62)]. (Reverse) a standing figure of Victory in a Greek helmet and carrying a trident, bestowing palms on a winged sword.
Clasps: 18 (see below).
Comments: *Awarded to military and RAF personnel for numerous campaigns and operations that fell short of full-scale war. It did not cover areas already catered for in the Africa and India general service medals. The George V crowned and robed bust was used only on the medal for Northern Kurdistan in 1931. The clasp CANAL ZONE was instituted in October 2003 for service between October 1951 and October 1954. On 29 July 2014 it was confirmed that those who served in Cyprus between 1955 and 1959 qualify for the clasp CYPRUS, also aircrew who assisted with at least one day's service in the operation between 20 June 1948 and 6 October 1948 qualify for the clasp BERLIN AIRLIFT.*

VALUE:

		British units	RAF	Indian and local units	Miniature (in silver add £5)
i.	S. Persia (Brit. officers)	£275–350	£3000–3500	£75–100	£20-30
ii.	Kurdistan	£125–150	£250–300	£75–100	£20-30
iii.	Iraq	£100–125	£200–250	£75–100	£20-30
iv.	N.W. Persia	£125–150	£300–350	£75–100	£20-30
v.	Southern Desert Iraq	—	£650–750	£1200–1500†	£20–30
vi.	Northern Kurdistan	£350–450	£2000–2500	—	£90–100
vii.	Palestine	£120–150	£150–200	£75–100	£20-30
viii.	S.E. Asia 1945–46	£120–150	£100–150	£65–75	£20-30
ix.	Bomb and Mine Clearance 1945–49	£650–750	£500–600	—	£40–60
x.	Bomb and Mine Clearance 1945–56	—	—	£500–600*	£40–60
xi.	Palestine 1945–48	£75–100	£75–100	£85–100	£20-30
xii.	Malaya (George VI)	£75–100	£75–100	£65–75	£20-30
xiii.	Malaya (Elizabeth II)	£75–100	£75–100	£65–75	£20-30
xiv.	Cyprus	£75–100	£75–100	£65–75	£12–15
xv.	Near East	£85–125	£80–120	—	£12–15
xvi.	Arabian Peninsula	£85–125	£75–100	£65–95	£12–15
xvii.	Brunei	£200–250	£200–250	£125–155	£12–15
xviii.	Canal Zone	£250–300	£250–300	—	£12–15
xvix.	Berlin Airlift	£85–100	£85–100	—	£12–15

†Indian units only *Australian units

174A. IRAQ ACTIVE SERVICE MEDAL

Date: May 1926.
Campaign: Iraq, 1924–38.
Branch of Service: Army and RAF.
Ribbon: 31mm in equal stripes of green, white and green.
Metal: Bronze.
Size: 38mm.
Description: (Obverse) a crescent forming the lower part; with an Arabic inscription above signifying "General Service" in two laurel branches. The medal is superimposed on crossed rifles, with rays in the arc between the muzzles, to which is joined a flattened loop suspender. (Reverse) The name of King Faisal I in Arabic and the date (AH) 1344 (i.e. 1926).
Clasps: Dates 1930–31, 1932, 1935 or 1936 in Arabic numerals with an Arabic inscription on the left.
Comments: *Also known as King Faisal's War Medal, it was awarded to British Army and RAF personnel stationed in Iraq or serving with the Iraq Levies. It was originally issued without a clasp, but clasps denoted subsequent actions or periods of service. By 1931, however, medals were issued with appropriate clasps from the outset.*

VALUE:

Without clasp	£85–125	*Miniature*	£50–80
With clasp	£100–150		

175. INDIA GENERAL SERVICE MEDAL 1936–39

Date: 1938.
Campaign: India 1936–39.
Branch of Service: British and Indian Armies and RAF.
Ribbon: Stone flanked by narrow red stripes, with broad green stripes at the edges.
Metal: Silver.
Size: 36mm
Description: (Obverse) crowned effigy of King George VI; (reverse) a tiger with the word INDIA across the top.
Clasps: North-West Frontier 1936–37, North-West Frontier 1937–39.
Comments: *The fourth and last of the IGS series, it was introduced when the change of effigy from George V to George VI became necessary, anticipating a similarly long life. It was not awarded after the outbreak of the Second World War, while the partition and independence of the Indian sub-continent afterwards rendered it obsolete. The medal was struck at the Royal Mint, London for award to British Army troops and RAF personnel, but the Calcutta Mint struck the medals awarded to the Indian Army.*

VALUE:

	British Army	RAF	Indian Army	*Miniature*
North West Frontier				
i. 1936-37	£100–150	£120–150	£45–50	£20–25
ii. 1937-39	£100–150	£120–150	£45–50	£20–30
2 clasps	£150–200	£180–200	£55–75	£20–35

(slip-on clasps deduct 20%)

176. BRITISH NORTH BORNEO COMPANY'S GENERAL SERVICE MEDAL 1937–1941

Instituted: 1937.
Campaign: British North Borneo (now Sabah), 1937–41.
Branch of Service: British North Borneo Company staff, Constabulary and various civilians.
Ribbon: 35mm, half dark green, half yellow. Gallantry awards were denoted by a thin red central stripe.
Metal: Silver. Copies were made in bronze.
Size: 38mm diameter, with a thickness of 3mm.
Description: (Obverse) the shield of the Company flanked by warriors as supporters. Above the shield are two arms, one clothed and the other naked, supporting the Company's flag. Below the shield is the motto PERGO ET PERAGO (I carry on and accomplish); (reverse) the seated figure of Britannia facing right, holding a trident in her left hand, with her right hand resting on a shield which bears the Union flag. NORTH BORNEO GENERAL SERVICE MEDAL is inscribed round the top and in the exergue is a branch with 11 leaves.
Clasps: None.
Comments: *Only one gallantry award was ever made, to Leong Yew Pong, aged 15, gazetted August 3, 1939. For specially valuable or long and meritorious services 44 were issued, gazetted in 1937, 1938, 1939 and 1941, with one replacement in 1947. Recipients were government officials, armed constabulary, rubber planters, the Archdeacon of North Borneo, the Chairman of the Chamber of Commerce, railway managers, businessmen and local dignitaries.*

VALUE

Medal	Type	Officially named	Unnamed original	Spink copy	Specimen
For Gallantry	Silver	Unique	Rare	£250–300	£300–350
For Service	Silver	£1500–1750	Rare	£150–200	£150–200
Miniature	£210–230				

Ribbon with red stripe denoting gallantry

176A. SUDAN DEFENCE FORCE GENERAL SERVICE MEDAL

Instituted: November 1933.
Campaign: Minor campaigns in the Sudan after 1933.
Branch of Service: Sudan Defence Force (SDF) and Police.
Ribbon: Central stripe of royal blue, edged by two yellow stripes and two black stripes at the edges.
Metal: Silver.
Size: 36mm.
Description: (Obverse) the seal of the Governor-General of the Sudan; (reverse) a stationary group of Sudanese soldiers, with "The Sudan" in Arabic below.
Clasps: None.
Comments: *The medal was awarded on the recommendation of the Kaid el'Amm (SDF Commander) to native personnel of the SDF, Police and other approved Sudanese who served in the field on such operations as might be considered by the Governor-General as being of sufficient importance to warrant the grant of the medal. It was also awarded for action against Italian forces in the southern Sudan from June 1940 to November 1941. About 9,000 were issued.*

VALUE: £175–£250

SECOND WORLD WAR STARS

Nine different campaign stars were issued for the Second World War. Apart from some Commonwealth issues notably Australia, Pakistan and South Africa, these were issued unnamed. In the cases of the Pacific Star, Burma Star and Italy Star naval personnel must have earned the 1939–45 Star before eligibility for those Stars begins. This is the same for the RAF in respect of the Air Crew Europe Star. It was decided that the maximum number of stars that could be earned by any one person was five, although this was increased to six when the Government agreed to the retrospective issue of the Arctic Star in March 2013, while those who qualified for more received a clasp to be sewn on the ribbon of the appropriate star. Only one clasp per ribbon was permitted which was the first to be earned after qualifying for that star, but this rule has been relaxed for the 1939–45 Star to allow for the new *Bomber Command* clasp. Thus the stars could bear the following clasps:

1.	1939–45 Star	Battle of Britain *and/or* Bomber Command
2.	Atlantic Star	Air Crew Europe *or* France and Germany
3.	Arctic Star	None
4.	Air Crew Europe Star	Atlantic *or* France and Germany
5.	Africa Star	North Africa 1942–43, 8th Army *or* 1st Army
6.	Pacific Star	Burma
7.	Burma Star	Pacific
8.	Italy Star	None
9.	France and Germany Star	Atlantic

Most of the ribbons are believed to have been designed by King George VI personally and have symbolic significance in each case. When ribbons alone are worn, the clasp is usually denoted by a silver rosette. However, the Battle of Britain clasp is represented by a gilt rosette and the 8th Army and 1st Army clasps by small silver numerals. As the clasps were sewn on to the ribbon and the stars issued unnamed, it is difficult to put valuations on examples with campaign clasps, however, the prices quoted are for medals with the *original* clasps. When purchasing expensive groups it is advisable that the medals be supported by documentary provenance or form part of a group in which at least one of the medals is named to the recipient.

Many of the medals and stars of the Second World War are still being officially produced, therefore there are a number of different die varieties available. There are also a number of dangerous copies in existence so care should be taken when purchasing expensive items. In the past few years a number of lapel badges or emblems have also been produced for award to veterans—see MYB nos. 242C et seq.

177. 1939–45 STAR

Date: 1945.

Campaign: Second World War 1939–45.

Branch of Service: British and Commonwealth forces.

Ribbon: Equal stripes of dark blue, red and light blue symbolising the Royal and Merchant Navies, Army and RAF respectively. The 1939–43 ribbon was authorised in November 1943 and worn by those awarded this proposed Star which became the 1939–45 Star when finally issued.

Metal: Bronze.

Size: Height 44mm; max. width 38mm.

Description: The six-pointed star has a circular centre with the GRI/VI monogram, surmounted by a crown and inscribed THE 1939-1945 STAR round the foot.

Clasps: Battle of Britain, Bomber Command, sewn directly on to the ribbon.

Comments: *The first in a series of nine bronze stars issued for service in the Second World War, it was awarded to personnel who had completed six months' service in specified operational commands overseas, between 3 September 1939 and 2 September 1945, though in certain cases the minimum period was shortened. Any service curtailed by death, injury or capture overseas also qualified, as did the award of a decoration or a mention in despatches. Clasps were awarded to RAF aircrew who took part in the Battle of Britain and, as a result of constant lobbying, in 2013 a clasp was also granted to aircrew members of Bomber Command. The clasps are denoted by a gilt rosette when the ribbon is worn alone. Surprisingly RAF ground crews who kept the Battle of Britain fighters in the air did not qualify for the 1939–45 Star, although those who assisted with the evacuation of troops from the beaches of Dunkirk did qualify.*

VALUE:

		Miniature
1939–45 Star	£12–15	£5–7
Battle of Britain clasp	£2000–3000	£8–10
Bomber Command clasp	£40–60	£6–8

178. ATLANTIC STAR

Campaign: Atlantic 1939-45.
Branch of Service: Mainly Royal and Commonwealth Navies.
Ribbon: Watered silk blue, white and green representing the ocean.
Metal: Bronze.
Size: Height 44mm; max. width 38mm.
Description: As above, but inscribed THE ATLANTIC STAR.
Clasps: Air Crew Europe, France and Germany.
Comments: *This star was awarded in the Royal Navy for six months' service afloat between 3 September 1939 and 8 May 1945 in the Atlantic or home waters, and to personnel employed in the convoys to North Russia and the South Atlantic. Personnel must have already qualified for the 1939–45 Star with the qualifying period for this not counting towards the Atlantic Star. Merchant Navy personnel also qualified, as did RAF and Army (maritime gunners and air crews—the latter only requiring 2 months service) who served afloat. In the last six months of operational service up to 8 May 1945, the Atlantic Star was awarded but not the 1939–45 Star. Entitlement to the France and Germany or Air Crew Europe stars was denoted by clasps to that effect, if the Atlantic Star was previously awarded. Only one clasp could be worn. Only two awards were made to WRNS: to an officer and a rating.*

VALUE:		Miniature
Atlantic Star	£30–35	£5–7
Air Crew Europe clasp	Add £80-100	£8–10
France and Germany clasp	Add £25–30	£8–10

178A. ARCTIC STAR

Campaign: Arctic convoys 1939–45.
Branch of Service: British and Commonwealth forces.
Ribbon: A central white stripe with fine black edging bordered either side by equal stripes of pale blue, dark blue and red.
Metal: Bronze.
Size: Height 44mm; max. width 38mm.
Description: As above, but inscribed THE ARCTIC STAR.
Clasps: None.
Comments: *As the direct result of constant lobbying by veterans and associated organisations over the years, the Government finally agreed to issue the Arctic Star retrospectively from March 2013. Large numbers of surviving veterans or their next of kin have successfully applied for the medal. The Star is intended primarily to commemorate those who assisted or saw service on the ships of the convoys that sailed to North Russia in support of the Russian allies. Any member of the Royal Navy or Merchant Navy, as well as members of the Army and the RAF and certain civilian units are eligible if they served on or over the Arctic Circle for any length of time.*

VALUE:		Miniature
Arctic Star	£400–500	£8–10

179. AIR CREW EUROPE STAR

Campaign: Air operations over Europe 1939-44.
Branch of Service: RAF and Commonwealth aircrew.
Ribbon: Pale blue (the sky) with black edges (night flying) and a narrow yellow stripe on either side (enemy searchlights).
Metal: Bronze.
Size: Height 44mm; max. width 38mm.
Description: As above, but inscribed THE AIR CREW EUROPE STAR.
Clasps: Atlantic or France and Germany.
Comments: *Awarded for operational flying from UK bases over Europe, for a period of two months between 3 September 1939 and 4 June 1944. Entitlement to either the Atlantic Star or France and Germany Star was denoted by the appropriate bar. This star is by far the most coveted of all the Second World War stars. Officially named stars to South Africans are the rarest of all the Second World War medals.*

VALUE:		Miniature
Air Crew Europe Star	£350–400	£5–10
Atlantic clasp	Add £90	£12–15
France and Germany clasp	Add £25–30	£12–15

180. AFRICA STAR

Campaign: Africa 1940-43.
Branch of Service: British and Commonwealth forces.
Ribbon: Pale buff symbolising the sand of the desert, with a broad red central stripe, a dark blue stripe on the left and a light blue stripe on the right symbolising the three services.
Metal: Bronze.
Size: Height 44mm; max. width 38mm.
Description: As above, but inscribed THE AFRICA STAR.
Clasps: North Africa 1942-43, 8th Army, 1st Army.
Comments: *Awarded for entry into an operational area in North Africa between 10 June 1940 (the date of Italy's declaration of war) and 12 May 1943 (the end of operations in North Africa), but service in Abyssinia (Ethiopia), Somaliland, Eritrea and Malta also qualified for the award. A silver numeral 1 or 8 worn on the ribbon denoted service with the First or Eighth Army between 23 October 1942 and 23 May 1943. A clasp inscribed North Africa 1942-43 was awarded to personnel of the Royal Navy Inshore Squadrons and Merchant Navy vessels which worked inshore between these dates. RAF personnel also qualified for this clasp, denoted by a silver rosette on the ribbon alone.*

VALUE:

		Miniature
Africa Star	£20–25	£3–5
8th Army clasp	Add £20	£8–10
1st Army clasp	Add £20	£8–10
North Africa 1942–43 clasp	Add £20	£10–12

181. PACIFIC STAR

Campaign: Pacific area 1941-45.
Branch of Service: British and Commonwealth forces.
Ribbon: Dark green (the jungle) with a central yellow stripe (the beaches), narrow stripes of dark and light blue (Royal Navy and RAF) and wider stripes of red (Army) at the edges.
Metal: Bronze.
Size: Height 44mm; max. width 38mm.
Description: As above, but inscribed THE PACIFIC STAR.
Clasps: Burma.
Comments: *Awarded for operational service in the Pacific theatre of war from 8 December 1941 to 15 August 1945. Service with the Royal and Merchant navies in the Pacific Ocean, Indian Ocean and South China Sea and land service in these areas also qualified. Personnel qualifying for both Pacific and Burma Stars got the first star and a clasp in respect of the second.*

VALUE:

		Miniature
Pacific Star	£35–40	£3–5
Burma clasp	Add £40	£6–8

182. BURMA STAR

Campaign: Burma 1941-45.
Branch of Service: British and Commonwealth forces.
Ribbon: Three equal bands of dark blue (British forces), red (Commonwealth forces) and dark blue. The dark blue bands each have at their centres a stripe of bright orange (the sun).
Metal: Bronze.
Size: Height 44mm; max. width 38mm.
Description: As above, but inscribed THE BURMA STAR.
Clasps: Pacific.
Comments: *Qualifying service in the Burma campaign counted from 11 December 1941 and included service in Bengal or Assam from 1 May 1942 to 31 December 1943, and from 1 January 1944 onwards in these parts of Bengal or Assam east of the Brahmaputra. Naval service in the eastern Bay of Bengal, off the coasts of Sumatra, Sunda and Malacca also counted.*

VALUE:

		Miniature
Burma Star	£25–30	£3–5
Pacific Clasp	Add £40	£6–8

183. ITALY STAR

Campaign: Italy 1943-45.
Branch of Service: British and Commonwealth forces.
Ribbon: Five equal stripes of red, white, green, white and red (the Italian national colours).
Metal: Bronze.
Size: Height 44mm; max. width 38mm.
Description: As above, but inscribed THE ITALY STAR.
Clasps: None.
Comments: *Awarded for operational service on land in Italy, Sicily, Greece, Yugoslavia, the Aegean area and Dodecanese islands, Corsica, Sardinia and Elba at any time between 11 June 1943 and 8 May 1945.*

VALUE:		Miniature
Italy Star	£20–25	£3–5

184. FRANCE AND GERMANY STAR

Date: 1945.
Campaign: France and Germany 1944-45.
Branch of Service: British and Commonwealth forces.
Ribbon: Five equal stripes of blue, white, red, white and blue (the national colours of the United Kingdom, France and the Netherlands).
Metal: Bronze.
Size: Height 44mm; max. width 38mm.
Description: As above, but inscribed THE FRANCE AND GERMANY STAR.
Clasps: Atlantic.
Comments: *Awarded for operational service in France, Belgium, the Netherlands or Germany from 6 June 1944 to 8 May 1945. Service in the North Sea, English Channel and Bay of Biscay in connection with the campaign in northern Europe also qualified. Prior eligibility for the Atlantic or Air Crew Europe Stars entitled personnel only to a bar for France and Germany. Conversely a first award of the France and Germany Star could earn an Atlantic bar.*

VALUE:		Miniature
France and Germany Star	£20–25	£3–5
Atlantic clasp	Add £90	£6–8

185. DEFENCE MEDAL

Date: 1945.
Campaign: Second World War 1939-45.
Branch of Service: British and Commonwealth forces.
Ribbon: Two broad stripes of green (this green and pleasant land) superimposed by narrow stripes of black (the black-out), with a wide stripe of orange (fire-bombing) in the centre.
Metal: Cupro-nickel or silver.
Size: 36mm.
Description: (Obverse) the uncrowned effigy of King George VI; (reverse) two lions flanking an oak sapling crowned with the dates at the sides and wavy lines representing the sea below. The words THE DEFENCE MEDAL appear in the exergue.
Clasps: None, but the King's Commendation for Brave Conduct emblem is worn on the ribbon.
Comments: *Awarded to service personnel for three years' service at home, one year's service in a non-operational area (e.g. India) or six months' service overseas in territories subjected to air attack or otherwise closely threatened. Personnel of Anti-Aircraft Command, RAF ground crews, Dominion forces stationed in the UK, the Home Guard, Civil Defence, National Fire Service and many other civilian units* qualified for the medal. The medal was generally issued unnamed in cupro-nickel, but the Canadian version was struck in silver.*

VALUE:

			Miniature
Cupro-nickel (32g)		£15–20	£8–10
Silver (Canadian) (36g)		£25–30	£12–15

*The definitive list of eligible recipients was published by the Ministry of Defence in 1992—Form DM1/DM2 and Annexe. This lists 50 different organisations and 90 sub-divisions of eligible personnel.

186. WAR MEDAL 1939–45

Date: 1945.
Campaign: Second World War 1939-45.
Branch of Service: British and Commonwealth forces.
Ribbon: Narrow red stripe in the centre, with a narrow white stripe on either side, broad red stripes at either edge and two intervening stripes of blue.
Metal: Cupro-nickel or silver.
Size: 36mm.
Description: (Obverse) effigy of King George VI; (reverse) a triumphant lion trampling on a dragon symbolising the Axis powers.
Clasps: None.
Comments: *All fulltime personnel of the armed forces wherever they were serving, so long as they had served for at least 28 days between 3 September 1939 and 2 September 1945 were eligible for this medal. It was granted in addition to the campaign stars and the Defence Medal. A few categories of civilians, such as war correspondents and ferry pilots who had flown in operational theatres, also qualified. No clasps were issued with this medal but a bronze oak leaf denoted a mention in despatches. The medal was struck in cupro-nickel and issued unnamed, but those issued to Australian and South African personnel were officially named with SA prefixes (see MYB189). The Canadian version of the medal was struck in silver.*

VALUE:

			Miniature
Cupro-nickel (32g)		£10–15	£8–10
Officially named		£20–25	
Silver (Canadian) (36g)		£25–35	£12–15

186A. KING'S BADGE

Date: 1941.
Campaign: Second World War.
Ribbon: None.
Metal: Silver.
Size: 26mm.
Description: A circular buttonhole badge with the crowned monogram GRI in script capitals in the centre, inscribed FOR LOYAL SERVICE.
Comments: *Awarded to personnel who had been invalided out of the services and were in receipt of a war disablement pension. The badges are not numbered or named. For further information see MEDAL NEWS, September 2008.*

VALUE: £15–20   *Miniature*   £15–20

187. INDIA SERVICE MEDAL

Date: 1945.
Campaign: India 1939-45.
Branch of Service: Indian forces.
Ribbon: Dark blue with two wide and one central thin pale blue stripes. The colours of the Order of the Indian Empire and the Order of the Star of India
Metal: Cupro-nickel.
Size: 36mm.
Description: (Obverse) the effigy of the King Emperor; (reverse) a map of the Indian sub-continent with INDIA at the top and 1939–45 at foot.
Clasps: None.
Comments: *Awarded to officers, men and women of the Indian forces for three years' non-operational service in India. In effect, it took the place of the Defence Medal in respect of Indian forces.*

VALUE: £15–20   *Miniature*   £10–12

188. CANADIAN VOLUNTEER SERVICE MEDAL

Date: 22 October 1943.
Campaign: Second World War 1939-45.
Branch of Service: Canadian forces.
Ribbon: Narrow stripes of green and red flanking a broad central stripe of dark blue.
Metal: Silver.
Size: 36mm.
Description: (Obverse) seven men and women in the uniforms of the various services, marching in step; (reverse) the Canadian national arms.
Clasps: Maple leaf clasp to denote overseas service. A clasp inscribed DIEPPE and surmounted by the Combined Operations emblem, was instituted on 28 April 1994 for award to all servicemen who took part in the Dieppe raid of 19 August 1942. A clasp inscribed Hong Kong, with the letters HK entwined within a circle, was instituted on 28 April 1994 for award to those involved in the Battle of Hong Kong, 8–25 December 1941. A clasp showing an ascending heavy bomber was instituted on 11 April 2013 to be awarded to members of an air crew and non-flying personnel for operational service with a Bomber Command squadron engaged in or supported bombing operations over Continental Europe from September 3, 1939 to May 8, 1945.
Comments: *Awarded for eighteen months' voluntary service in the Canadian forces from 3 September 1939 to 1 March 1947. The seven marching personnel are based on real people taken from National Defence photographs, representing the land, sea and air forces plus a nurse. The individuals are: first row: centre, 3780 Leading Seaman P. G. Colbeck, RCN; left, C52819 Pte D. E. Dolan, 1 Can. Para Bn; right, R95505 F/Sgt K. M. Morgan, RCAF. Second row: centre, W4901 Wren P. Mathie, WRCNS; left, 12885 L/Cpl J. M. Dann, CWAC; right, W315563 LAW O. M. Salmon, RCAF; back row: Lt N/S E. M. Lowe, RCAMC. 650,000 have been awarded including 525,500 with the overseas clasp.*

VALUE:		*Miniature*
Silver medal	£30–35	£8–10
i. Maple Leaf clasp	£30–35	£12–15
ii. Dieppe clasp	£35–45	£15–18
iii. Hong Kong clasp	£35–45	

177

188A. CANADIAN MEMORIAL CROSS

Instituted: 1 December 1919.
Branch of Service: Relatives of deceased Canadian forces.
Ribbon: Violet 11mm with ring suspension only.
Metal: Dull silver.
Size: 32mm.
Description: A Greek cross with the royal cypher at the centre, superimposed on another with arms slightly flared at the ends. Maple leaves adorn three of the arms while the top arm has a crown surmounted by a suspension ring. (Reverse) The service number, rank, initials and name of the person being commemorated are engraved. There is also a sterling mark on the lower arm. Four versions of the cross exist: the original, with GRI cypher (1914–19), with GVIR cypher and ring suspension (1940–45), GVIR cypher with suspension bar (1945–52) and an EIIR version for Korea and later conflicts.
Comments: *Issued to wives and mothers of servicemen who had died during World War I. A second version was introduced in August 1940 for award to widows and mothers of World War II servicemen, but this was extended to include those of merchant seamen and civilian firefighters. Newfoundland service personnel became eligible after April 1, 1949. The current version was introduced in 1950 for the Korean War and peacekeeping operations. All service-related deaths since 7 October 2001 are eligible and up to three Crosses are now granted to persons previously designated by the deceased.*

VALUE:	Named	Unnamed
GVR, ring suspension (58,500)	From £120	£55–65
GVIR, ring suspension } (32,500)	From £120	£55–65
GVIR, bar suspension	From £120	£55–65
EIIR, bar suspension (1,000)	From £150	£65–75

Miniature £70–90

189. AFRICA SERVICE MEDAL

Date: 1943.
Campaign: Second World War 1939-45.
Branch of Service: South African forces.
Ribbon: A central orange stripe, with green and gold stripes on either side.
Metal: Silver.
Size: 36mm.
Description: (Obverse) a map of the African Continent, inscribed AFRICA SERVICE MEDAL on the left and AFRIKADIENS-MEDALJE on the right; (reverse) a leaping Springbok.
Clasps: None, but a Protea emblem is worn on the ribbon by recipients of the King's Commendation.
Comments: *Awarded to Union service personnel who served at home and abroad during the War for at least thirty days. Medals were fully named and gave the service serial number of the recipient, prefixed by various letters, for example N (Native Military Corps), C (Cape Corps), M (Indian and Malay Corps), etc., no prefix indicated a white volunteer.*

VALUE:

Silver medal (190,000)	£25–45	*Miniature* £10–12

Protea emblem.

190. AUSTRALIA SERVICE MEDAL 1939–45

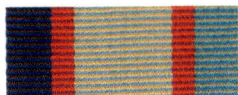

Date: 1949.
Campaign: Second World War 1939-45.
Branch of Service: Australian forces.
Ribbon: Dark blue representing the Royal Australian Navy, Khaki representing the Army, light blue representing the R.A.A.F and red representing the Mercantile Marine.
Metal: Cupro-nickel.
Size: 36mm.
Description: (Obverse) the effigy of King George VI; (reverse) the Arms of the Commonwealth of Australia surrounded by the inscription "THE AUSTRALIA SERVICE MEDAL 1939–45".
Clasps: None.
Comments: *Awarded to all Australian personnel who had seen at least 18 months' full time or three years part-time service. The medals were named to the recipients. In the case of Army personnel, their service numbers were prefixed by the initial of their state or territory of enlistment: D (Northern Territory), N (New South Wales), NG (New Guinea), P (Papua), Q (Queensland), S (South Australia), T (Tasmania), V (Victoria) and W (Western Australia). X prefix is for Volunteer Overseas Services, that is service with the 2nd AIF (Second Australian Imperial Force). In 1996 time served for eligibility was reduced to 30 days full-time, 90 days part-time.*

VALUE:

Cupro-nickel medal (600,000)	£55–65	Miniature £12–15

191. NEW ZEALAND WAR SERVICE MEDAL

Date: 1946.
Campaign: Second World War 1939-45.
Branch of Service: New Zealand forces.
Ribbon: Black with white edges.
Metal: Cupro-nickel.
Size: 36mm.
Description: (Obverse) effigy of King George VI; (reverse) the text FOR SERVICE TO NEW ZEALAND 1939-45 with a fern leaf below. Suspension was by a pair of fern leaves attached to a straight bar.
Clasps: None.
Comments: *Issued unnamed, to all members of the New Zealand forces who completed one month full-time or six months part-time service between September 1939 and September 1945, provided the applicant carried out the prescribed training or duties. This included Home Guard service and Naval Auxiliary Patrol service.*

VALUE:

Cupro-nickel medal (240,000)	£30–35	Miniature £12–15

191A. NZ MEMORIAL CROSS

Instituted: 1960.
Campaign: Second World War, 1939–45.
Branch of Service: Relatives of deceased New Zealand forces personnel.
Ribbon: 12mm royal purple
Metal: Dull Silver.   **Size:** 32 mm.
Description: A cross surmounted by a crown, with fern leaves on each arm, in the centre, within a wreath, the Royal Cypher; (reverse) details of the person in respect of whose death the cross is granted.
Comments: *First announced in the New Zealand Gazette dated at Wellington, September 12, 1947 and approved by the King but not instituted until August 16, 1960. Originally granted to the next-of-kin of persons who had lost their lives on active service with the New Zealand forces during the Second World War, or who had subsequently died of wounds or illness contracted during that conflict. Provision was made for the grant of crosses to the parent(s) as well as the wife or eldest surviving daughter or son. It was subsequently awarded in respect of postwar campaigns: Korea (47), Malaya, South Vietnam (37), and East Timor (3).*

VALUE:	Officially named	Unnamed
	From £100	£75–85

179

192. SOUTH AFRICAN MEDAL FOR WAR SERVICES

Date: 1946.
Campaign: Second World War 1939–46.
Branch of Service: South African forces.
Ribbon: Three equal stripes of red, white and blue, the South African national colours.
Metal: Silver.
Size: 36mm.
Description: (Obverse) South African arms; (reverse) a wreath of protea flowers enclosing the dates 1939 and 1945. Inscribed in English and Afrikaans: SOUTH AFRICA FOR WAR SERVICES on the left and SUID AFRIKA VIR OORLOGDIENSTE on the right.
Clasps: None.
Comments: *Men and women who served for at least two years in any official voluntary organisation in South Africa or overseas qualified for this medal so long as the service was both voluntary and unpaid. Those who already had the Africa Service Medal were ineligible, but exceptions exist. The medals are unnamed but were issued with a named certificate.*

VALUE: Silver (17,500) £40–50   *Miniature* £15–18

192A. SOUTH AFRICAN MEMORIAL PLAQUE

Date: 1946.
Campaign: Second World War 1939–46.
Branch of Service: South African forces.
Metal: Bronze.
Size: Wood backing 135x106.4mm.
Description: The South African arms in a wreath superimposed on a Maltese cross with torches in the angles. Below is a separate panel containing the details of the deceased. Mounted on a wooden panel.
Comments: *The plaque was given to the next of kin to personnel who lost their lives whilst on active service. The name and the cause of death are inscribed thereon. A numbered brooch of a similar design was also issued. Plaques to personnel killed in famous actions or in well-known theatres of war are worth a considerable premium, as are those named to SAAF aircrew, SANF personnel or plaques named to women. Plaques bearing the Star of David signifying that the person was of the Jewish faith are extremely rare.*

VALUE: Plaque from £50, brooch from £25

193. SOUTHERN RHODESIA SERVICE MEDAL

Date: 1946.
Campaign: Second World War 1939-45.
Branch of Service: Southern Rhodesian forces.
Ribbon: Dark green with black and red stripes at each edge.
Metal: Cupro-nickel.
Size: 36mm.
Description: (Obverse) King George VI; (reverse) the Southern Rhodesian national arms. FOR SERVICE IN SOUTHERN RHODESIA round the top and the dates 1939-1945 at the foot.
Clasps: None.
Comments: *This very scarce medal was awarded only to those who served in Southern Rhodesia during the period of the War but who were ineligible for one of the campaign stars or war medals. 5,000 medals were struck but only 3,908 were awarded.*

VALUE:
Cupro-nickel (3908) £300–350   *Miniature* £25–30

194. NEWFOUNDLAND VOLUNTEER WAR SERVICE MEDAL

Date: 1981.
Campaign: Second World War 1939-45.
Branch of Service: Newfoundland forces.
Ribbon: Deep claret with edges of red, white and blue.
Metal: Bronze.
Size: 37mm.
Description: (Obverse) the royal cypher of George VI surmounted by a crown topped by a caribou, the Newfoundland national emblem; (reverse) Britannia on a scallop shell background guarded by two lions.
Comments: *While the Second World War was being fought, Newfoundland was still a separate British colony which did not enter the Canadian Confederation till 1949. Consequently Newfoundland servicemen did not qualify for the Canadian Volunteer Service medal, and this deficiency was not remedied until July 1981 when the Newfoundland provincial government instituted this medal. Those who had served with the Canadian forces, on the other hand, and already held the Canadian medal, were not eligible for this award. The medal could be claimed by next-of-kin of those who died in or since the war.*

VALUE: Bronze (7500) £450–550 *Miniature* £65–75

194A. THE ELIZABETH CROSS

Instituted: 2009.
Campaign: Post World War II.
Branch of Service: Relatives of deceased UK forces personnel.
Ribbon: None.
Metal: Oxidised silver.
Size: 31 mm.
Description: A Greek cross superimposed on another cross, with a crowned Royal cypher at its centre, within a wreath. The arms of the outer cross bear the national emblems of the British Isles: the Rose (England), Thistle (Scotland), Shamrock (Ireland) and the Daffodil (Wales).
Comments: *The Cross was first announced in July 2009 and complements the existing Canadian Memorial Cross (MYB 188A) and the New Zealand Memorial Cross (MYB 191A). Only one Cross will be available to the next of kin of any service personnel who died whilst on operational duty or as a consequence of an act of terrorism. Awards of the Cross have been back-dated to 1 January 1948 to cover deaths that occurred after World War II or as a result of service in Palestine since 27 September 1945. It is accompanied by a memorial scroll, except in the case of Korean War casualties, as a scroll has already been issued for that conflict—in this instance the Cross alone will be issued. Crosses are named to the individual commemorated.*

VALUE: From £400

195. KOREA MEDAL

Date: July 1951.
Campaign: Korean War 1950-53.
Branch of Service: British and Commonwealth forces.
Ribbon: Yellow, with two blue stripes .
Metal: Cupro-nickel or silver.
Size: 36mm.
Description: (Obverse) Right-facing bust of Queen Elizabeth II by Mary Gillick; there are two obverse types, with or without BRITT: OMN; (reverse) Hercules wrestling with the Hydra, KOREA in the exergue.
Clasps: None.
Comments: *Awarded to all British and Commonwealth forces who took part in the Korean War between July 1950 and July 27, 1953. British and New Zealand medals were issued in cupro-nickel impressed in small capitals, medals to Australian forces were impressed in large capitals and the Canadian version was struck in silver and has CANADA below the Queen's bust. Particularly prized are medals issued to the "Glorious Gloucesters" who played a gallant part in the battle of the Imjin River.*

VALUE:		*Miniature*
British		
Regiments	£160–180	£12–15
Corps	£120–150	
RN	£100–150	
RAF	£600–850	
To Gloucester Regiment	£550–750	
Australian or New Zealand naming	£250–300	
Canadian, silver (over 20,000)	£100–150	£15–20

196. SOUTH AFRICAN MEDAL FOR KOREA

Date: 1953.
Campaign: Korea 1950-53.
Branch of Service: South African forces.
Ribbon: Sky blue central stripe flanked by dark blue stripes and edges of orange.
Metal: Silver.
Size: 38mm.
Description: (Obverse) maps of South Africa and Korea with an arrow linking them and the words VRYWILLIGERS and VOLUNTEERS in the field. (Reverse) the then South African arms surmounted by the crowned EIIR.
Clasps: None.
Comments: *Awarded to the 800 personnel in the contingent sent to Korea by the Union of South Africa. Suspension is by a ring and claw.*

VALUE:			
Silver (800)	£450–550	*Miniature*	£40–50
Pilot's issue	£1500–2000		

197. UNITED NATIONS KOREA MEDAL

Date: December 1950.
Campaign: Korea 1950-53.
Branch of Service: All UN forces.
Ribbon: Seventeen narrow stripes alternating pale blue and white.
Metal: Bronze.
Size: 35mm.
Description: (Obverse) the wreathed globe emblem of the UN; (reverse) inscribed FOR SERVICE IN DEFENCE OF THE PRINCIPLES OF THE CHARTER OF THE UNITED NATIONS.
Clasps: Korea.
Comments: *National variants were produced, but the British type was granted to all personnel of the British and Commonwealth forces who had served at least one full day in Korea or in support units in Japan. Moreover, as those who served in Korea after the armistice in July 1953 were also entitled to the UN medal it is sometimes found in groups without the corresponding British medal. The award was extended to cover the period up to July 27, 1954, the first anniversary of the Panmunjom Truce. Issues to Australian, South African and Canadian personnel were named on the rim.*

VALUE: £20–25   *Miniature* £10–15

198. GENERAL SERVICE MEDAL 1962–2007

Date: 1964.
Campaign: Campaigns and operations since 1962.
Branch of Service: British forces.
Ribbon: Deep purple edged with green.
Metal: Silver.
Size: 36mm.
Description: (Obverse) a crowned bust of Queen Elizabeth II; (reverse) an oak wreath enclosing a crown and the words FOR CAMPAIGN SERVICE. It has a beaded and curved suspension above which are mounted campaign clasps.
Clasps: 14. The maximum number of clasps awarded appears to be six.
Comments: *This medal, also commonly known as the Campaign Service Medal 1962, was instituted for award to personnel of all services, and thus did away with the need for separate Army and Navy general service medals. Awards range from a mere 70 for South Vietnam to over 130,000 for service in Northern Ireland. The eligibility for the Northern Ireland clasp ceased at midnight on 31 July 2007—the eligibility period having been from 14 August 1969, almost 38 years, the longest period for any individual clasp. In July 2014 it was confirmed that those who served between 21 December 1963 and 26 March 1964 qualify for the clasp CYPRUS 1963–64.*

VALUE:

			Miniature for silver add £5
i.	Borneo	£85–100	£12–15
ii.	Radfan	£90–120	£12–15
iii.	South Arabia	£75–100	£12–15
iv.	Malay Peninsula	£75–100	£12–15
v.	South Vietnam	Rare	£15–20
vi.	Northern Ireland	£75–100	£12–15
vii.	Dhofar	£220–250	£12–15
viii.	Lebanon	£2000–2500	£12–15
ix.	Mine Clearance, Gulf of Suez (250)	£1800–2000	£12–15
x.	Gulf	£250–300	£12–15
xi.	Kuwait	£400–450	£12–15
xii.	N. Iraq & S. Turkey	£375–475	£12–15
xiii.	Air Operations Iraq	£350–450	£15–20
	2 clasps	£100–125	£15–20
	3 clasps	£150–200	£25–30
	4 clasps	£250–300	£30–35
xiv.	Cyprus 1963–64	£75–95	£15–25

198A. OPERATIONAL SERVICE MEDAL 2000

Date: 1999.

Campaign: Operations after May 5, 2000.

Branch of Service: All branches of the armed forces.

Ribbon: Broad central red stripe, flanked by royal blue and light blue with green edge stripes (Sierra Leone), buff edge stripes (Afghanistan) or ochre edge stripes (Congo). The colours represent the three services.

Metal: Silver.

Size: 36mm.

Description: (Obverse) crowned profile of Queen Elizabeth; (reverse) an eight-pointed star with different crowns impaled on each alternate point, the centre having the Union flag in a circle surrounded by the inscription FOR OPERATIONAL SERVICE. The medal has a scrolled suspender with ornamental finials.

Clasp: Afghanistan (three distinctly different officially issued types), Operation Pitting, D.R.O.C. (Congo), Iraq & Syria, silver rosette.

Comments: *Intended for minor campaigns for which a separate medal is not awarded. It replaces the General Service Medal 1962–2007, except for Northern Ireland and Air Operations Iraq. It has so far been awarded for operations in Afghanistan (from 11 September 2001 to the conclusion of Operation Pitting), Sierra Leone (5 May 2000–31 July 2002), the Democratic Republic of the Congo (14 June–10 September 2003) and Iraq and Syria. The award of a clasp is denoted by the a silver rosette on the ribbon when only the ribbon is worn—for Afghanistan two rosettes can be worn if the two clasps (Afghanistan and Operation Pitting) are awarded. For operations Maidenly and Barras (Sierra Leone) a "South Atlantic" type rosette is worn with the medal, and a smaller version on the ribbon alone. The D.R.O.C. clasp is especially sought after.*

Sierra Leone

Congo

Afghanistan

Iraq & Syria

VALUE:

Cavalry	£400–600
Line regiment	£250–350
Corps	£200–300
Royal Marines	£300–500
Royal Navy	£300–500
RAF	£300–500
RFA	£300–500
Miniature	£12–15 (silver add £5)

198B. ACCUMULATED CAMPAIGN SERVICE MEDAL

Instituted: January 1994.

Branch of Service: All branches of the armed services.

Ribbon: Purple with green edges and a central gold stripe.

Metal: Silver.

Size: 36mm.

Description: (Obverse) crowned effigy of Queen Elizabeth; (reverse) the inscription FOR ACCUMULATED CAMPAIGN SERVICE set within a four-part ribbon surrounded by a branch of oak leaves with laurel and olive leaves woven through the motto ribbon.

Comments: *The ACSM was awarded for aggregated service since August 14, 1969 in those theatres of operations where the General Service Medal (GSM) 1962 with clasp was awarded. The GSM (MYB198) has subsequently been replaced by the Operational Service Medal. The following medals count towards the award: Iraq Medal, GSM 1962–2007 with the clasps for Northern Ireland, Dhofar, Lebanon, Mine Clearance–Gulf of Suez, Gulf, Kuwait, Northern Iraq and Southern Turkey, Air Operations Iraq; the Operational Service Medal awarded since 2000 for Sierra Leone, Afghanistan and the Democratic Republic of Congo. Further periods of 36 months accumulated campaign service are denoted by a clasp, indicated as a silver rosette when the ribbon alone is worn. A gilt rosette is worn on the ribbon alone to denote the award of four silver clasps. A further gilt rosette was awarded for a further three silver clasps and a third gilt rosette for another two silver clasps. Service on UN, NATO EC or EU missions is not allowed to count towards the qualifying service. This was the first British medal put out to competitive tendering, a contract won by the Royal Mint. As such, the medal is not only silver but hallmarked (believed to be the first medal, although hallmarking is a feature of certain decorations and orders). In July 2011 the medal was superseded by the Accumulated Campaign Service Medal 2011 (MYB 198C).*

Accumulated Campaign Service Medal clasp.

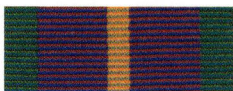

VALUE: £300–350   *Miniature*   £10–12

198C. ACCUMULATED CAMPAIGN SERVICE MEDAL 2011

Instituted: July 2011.
Branch of Service: All branches of the armed services.
Ribbon: Purple with green edges and two central gold stripes.
Metal: Silver.
Size: 36mm.
Description: (Obverse) crowned effigy of Queen Elizabeth; (reverse) the inscription FOR ACCUMULATED CAMPAIGN SERVICE set within a four-part ribbon surrounded by a branch of oak leaves with laurel and olive leaves woven through the motto ribbon.
Comments: *On July 1, 2011 the Accumulated Campaign Service Medal (no. 198B) was superseded by the Accumulated Campaign Service Medal 2011, with the qualifying time to be reduced from 36 months (1,080 days) to 24 months (720 days). Although the medal design remains identical to the previous issue it will not be hallmarked on the rim and the ribbon carries two gold stripes. The range of qualifying service has also been amended to reflect the current operational conditions and the need for medallic recognition. The new medal will mean that holders of an existing operational service medal (whether military, MOD civilian or Contractors on Deployed Operations) or other specifically designated multi-national campaign medal, who are or were serving on or after January 1, 2008 (whether currently serving or retired), are eligible for the ACSM 11 provided they have completed more than 24 months (720 days) campaign service. Bars are to be awarded for each additional period of 720 days approved operational service.*

The following campaign service counts towards the ACSM 11 and holders of the following medals, if they have completed enough service, may be eligible for the new medal: General Service Medal: Northern Ireland August 14, 1969–July 31, 2007; Dhofar October 1, 1969–September 30, 1976; Lebanon February 7, 1983–March 9, 1984; Mine Clearance Gulf of Suez August 15, 1984–October 15, 1984; Gulf November 17, 1986–February 28, 1989; Kuwait March 8, 1991–September 30, 1991; N Iraq & S Turkey April, 6, 1991–July 17, 1991; Air Operations Iraq (South) July 16, 1991–March 18, 2003, and Iraq (North) July 16, 1991–April 30, 2003. Operational Service Medal: Sierra Leone May 5, 2000–July 31, 2002; Afghanistan September 11, 2001 to a date to be decided; Democratic Republic of Congo June 14, 2003– September 10, 2003. The Iraq Medal January 20, 2003–May 22, 2011. And any Multinational campaign medals approved since April 1, 2000. Certain service does not count towards the ACSM 11, this includes any service prior to August 14, 1969, service in Kuwait during Op TELIC after August 10, 2003; service in the Balkans; service in the British Embassy in Iraq; service on Op BANDOG with the exception of Afghanistan; service in the First Gulf War and service in the Falklands Conflict.

VALUE: £300–350   *Miniature*   £10–15

198D. GENERAL SERVICE MEDAL 2008

Date: 2016.
Campaign: Campaigns and Operations since 2008.
Branch of Service: British forces.
Ribbon: 32mm, green with two 5mm purple stripes 5mm from the edges.
Metal: Silver .
Size: 36mm.
Clasps: Southern Asia, Arabian Peninsula, Northern Africa, Western Africa, Eastern Africa, Gulf of Aden.
Description: (Obverse) Effigy of the reigning monarch; with the legend REGINA FID DEF ELIZABETH II DEI GRATIA around; (reverse) A standing figure of Britannia holding a shield and trident, in front of a lion with the words FOR CAMPAIGN SERVICE below, the whole surrounded by a wreath of oak.
Comments: *Instituted for minor campaigns since 2008. The first awards were made by the Secretary of State for Defence, Michael Fallon, in June 2016. The clasps are named for geographic locations as opposed to specific Operations with Southern Asia, Arabian Peninsula each covering two Operations to date.. East Africa covers Operations in Somalia. The Western Africa clasp covers service there in the period 13 January 2013–22 May 2013 with the Northern Africa clasp covering service in that region from 1 November 2012 onwards. The British sailors of HMS Daring who braved the threat of missile attack in the Middle East were the first to receive the Gulf of Aden clasp in August 2018.*

VALUE: —   *Miniature*   £12–15

199. UNITED NATIONS EMERGENCY FORCE MEDAL

Date: 1957.

Campaign: Israel and Egypt 1956–67.

Branch of Service: All UN forces.

Ribbon: Sand-coloured with a central light blue stripe and narrow dark blue and green stripes towards each edge.

Metal: Bronze.

Size: 35mm.

Description: (Obverse) the UN wreathed globe emblem with UNEF at the top; (reverse) inscribed IN THE SERVICE OF PEACE. Ring suspension.

Clasps: None.

Comments: *Awarded to all personnel who served with the UN peace-keeping forces on the border between Israel and Egypt following the Sinai Campaign of 1956. These medals were awarded to troops from Brazil, Canada, Colombia, Denmark, Finland, Indonesia, Norway, Sweden and Yugoslavia.*

VALUE:

Bronze original issue	£35–45	*Miniature* £10–15

200. VIETNAM MEDAL

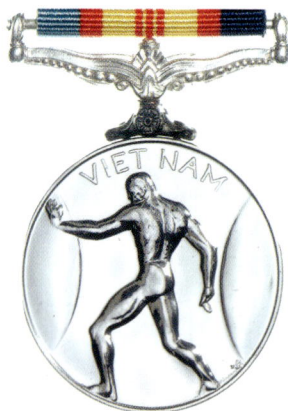

Date: July 1968.

Campaign: Vietnam 1964-73.

Branch of Service: Australian and New Zealand forces.

Ribbon: A broad central stripe of bright yellow surmounted by three thin red stripes (the Vietnamese national colours) and bordered by broader red stripes, with dark and light blue stripes at the edges, representing the three services.

Metal: Silver.

Size: 36mm.

Description: (Obverse) the crowned bust of Queen Elizabeth II; (reverse) a nude male figure pushing apart two spheres representing different ideologies.

Clasps: None.

Comments: *Awarded to personnel who served in Vietnam a minimum of one day on land or 28 days at sea after 28 May 1964. The medal was impressed in large capitals (Australian) or small capitals (New Zealand).*

VALUE:

Australian recipient	£200–250
New Zealand recipient (3,312)	£250–300
Miniature	£10–12

201. SOUTH VIETNAM CAMPAIGN MEDAL

Date: May 12, 1964.

Campaign: Vietnam 1964–72.

Branch of Service: Allied forces in Vietnam.

Ribbon: White with two broad green stripes towards the centre and narrow green edges.

Metal: Bronze.

Size: Height 42mm; max. width 36mm.

Description: A six-pointed star, with gold rays in the angles. The gilt enamelled centre shows a map of Vietnam engulfed in flames; (reverse) a Vietnamese inscription in the centre.

Clasps: 1960 (bronze, cupro-nickel or silver gilt).

Comments: *Awarded by the government of South Vietnam to Australian and New Zealand forces who served at least six months in Vietnam from March 1, 1961. The original issue, of Vietnamese manufacture, was relatively crude and issued unnamed. Subsequently medals were produced in Australia and these are not only of a better quality but bear the name of the recipient. A third version, made in the USA, has the suspension ring a fixed part of the medal. The medal was always issued with a clasp.*

VALUE:

Unnamed	£15–20
Named	£25–35
Miniature	enamels £10–15, painted £5–8

202. RHODESIA MEDAL

Date: 1980.

Campaign: Rhodesia 1979–80.

Branch of Service: British and Rhodesian forces.

Ribbon: Sky blue, with a narrow stripe of red, white and dark blue in the centre.

Metal: Rhodium-plated cupro-nickel.

Size: 36mm.

Description: (Obverse) the crowned bust of Queen Elizabeth II; (reverse) a sable antelope with the name of the medal and the year of issue.

Clasps: None.

Comments: *This medal was awarded to personnel serving in Rhodesia for fourteen days between 1 December 1979 and 20 March 1980, pending the elections and the emergence of the independent republic of Zimbabwe, known as Operation Agila. Medals were issued unnamed or named in impressed capitals. It was officially named to the armed forces and RAF personnel but unnamed to participating British Police. Examples with the word COPY in raised capitals immediately below the suspension fitment are believed to have been issued as replacements for lost medals, although examples with "R" for replacement are also known to exist.There has been some discussion over whether this medal is actually a campaign medal. It seems that the Ministry of Defence includes it in its list of campaign medals whereas the Central Chancery does not include it as a campaign medal but rules that it should be worn after long service awards. Further research may clarify the situation.*

VALUE:

Cupro-nickel (2500)	£450–550	*Miniature*	£15–25

203. SOUTH ATLANTIC MEDAL

Date: 1982.

Campaign: Falkland Islands and South Georgia 1982.

Branch of Service: British forces.

Ribbon: Watered silk blue, white, green, white and blue.

Metal: Cupro-nickel.

Size: 36mm.

Description: (Obverse) crowned profile of Queen Elizabeth II; (reverse) laurel wreath below the arms of the Falkland Islands with SOUTH ATLANTIC MEDAL inscribed round the top.

Clasps: None, but a rosette denoting service in the combat zone.

Comments: *Awarded to all personnel who took part in operations in the South Atlantic for the liberation of South Georgia and the Falkland Islands following the Argentinian invasion. To qualify, the recipient had to have at least one full day's service in the Falklands or South Georgia, or 30 days in the operational zone including Ascension Island. Those who qualified under the first condition were additionally awarded a large rosette for wear on the ribbon. As a result of the Sir John Holmes' Independent medal review in 2012 the 30 day qualifying period for the award of the South Atlantic Medal was extended from 12 July to 21 October 1982. Those who qualify under this condition are not entitled to wear the rosette*

VALUE:	With rosette	Without
Army (7000)	£750–850	£550–750
Scots & Welsh Guards	£1000–1500	
Parachute Regiment	£1750–2500	
Royal Navy (13,000)*	£650–750	£500–650
Royal Marines (3700)	£1200–1500	£750–1000
Royal Fleet Auxiliary (2000)	£475–550	£300–400
RAF (2000)	£550–750	£350–450
Merchant Navy and civilians (2000)	£500–700	£350–450
Gurkhas	£750–850	£500–650
Miniature	£15–20	

*Medals to the crew of HM Submarine Conqueror are worth a considerable premium.

203A. SOVIET 40th ANNIVERSARY MEDAL

Date: 1985.

Campaign: Second World War.

Branch of Service: British and Canadian forces who served mainly in RN or MN ships on Arctic convoys.

Ribbon: One half red, the other orange with three black stripes, edged with pale blue. Later issues have no blue edges. Worn in the Russian style.

Metal: Bronze.

Size: 32mm.

Description: (Obverse) Group of servicemen and women in front of a five-pointed star flanked by oak leaves and the dates 1945–1985 above; (reverse) 40th anniversary of the Victory in the Great Patriotic War 1941–1945, in Russian.

Clasps: None.

Comments: *In 1994 Her Majesty the Queen approved the wearing of this medal, first awarded by the Soviet Government, to selected ex-Servicemen, mostly surviving veterans of the Arctic convoys of World War II. Similar medals have also been issued for the 50th and subsequent five year anniversaries. However, those for the 55th and subsequent anniversaries have not been authorised for wear.*

VALUE:		
British striking	£15–20	
Russian striking	£10–15	
Miniature	£10–15	

40th anniversary

203AA. USHAKOV MEDAL

Date: 2013.
Campaign: Second World War.
Branch of Service: Allied forces who served on the Arctic convoys.
Ribbon: Pale blue moire edged with narrow stripes of white and dark blue. Worn in the Russian style.
Metal: Silver.
Size: 36mm.
Description: (Obverse) Central couped portrait of Marshal Ushakov with Cyrillic wording around and laurel leaves below, the circular medal surmounted on an anchor; (reverse) anchor with serial number.
Clasps: None.
Comments: *Copies of the original Soviet medal were awarded by the Russian Government, on application, to surviving veterans of the Arctic convoys of World War II. Permission to wear was granted in 2013 by HM the Queen.*

VALUE: £35–50

203B. PINGAT JASA MALAYSIA MEDAL

Instituted: 2005.
Ribbon: Central red stripe, flanked by dark blue and yellow.
Metal: Base metal (brass)-coated nickel silver.
Size: 38mm
Description: (Obverse) arms of the Republic of Malaysia with JASA MALAYSIA below; (reverse) map of Malaysia with P.J.M. below, attached to a scrolled suspension bar by two crossed fern fronds.
Comments: *Awarded by the Malaysian Government to members of the British and Commonwealth Armed Forces who were posted on strength of unit or formation and served in the prescribed operational area of Malaysia and Singapore during the "Confrontation" and "Emergency" periods in direct support of operations for: 90 days or more, in Malaysia between August 31, 1957 and December 31 1966 or Singapore between August 31, 1957 and August 9, 1965; or for 180 days for ADF outside the area but in support of operations for the first two dates. Permission to wear was officially granted in time for veterans to wear their medals at the Remembrance Day ceremonies in 2011. Several types are known, with later strikings being of poorer quality than the original and with various minor alterations to the original design.*

VALUE: £35–55   *Miniature*   £10–15

Late striking

203C. KING HUSSEIN MEDAL

Date: 1970.
Campaign: Jordan Civil War.
Branch of Service: British military medical teams.
Ribbon: Plain crimson.
Metal: Silver with red enamel emblem.
Size: 38mm.
Description: (Obverse) Emblem of the Red Cross and Red Crescent. THE HASHEMITE KINGDOM OF JORDAN and its Arabic equivalent, with the date 1970 and Arabic equivalent at the sides; (rev) seven-line inscription across the centre.
Comments: *Awarded to British and American personnel involved in relief operations codenamed Operation Shoveller during and after the Civil War of September 1970. At the end of the deployment all personnel were presented with the medal by King Hussein. Permission to wear it has never been granted.*

VALUE: £50–70

204. GULF MEDAL

Date: 1992.
Campaign: Kuwait and Saudi Arabia 1990-91.
Branch of Service: British forces.
Ribbon: Sand-coloured broad central stripe flanked by narrow stripes of dark blue, red and light blue (left) or light blue, red and dark blue (right) representing the sands of the desert and the three armed services.
Metal: Cupro-nickel.
Size: 36mm.
Description: (Obverse) crowned profile of Queen Elizabeth II; (reverse) an eagle and automatic rifle superimposed on an anchor, symbolising the three armed services. The dates of the Gulf War appear at the foot.
Clasps: 2 Aug 1990, 16 Jan to 28 Feb 1991.
Comments: *Awarded to personnel who had thirty days continuous service in the Middle East (including Cyprus) between 2 August 1990 and 7 March 1991, or seven days between 16 January 1991 and 28 February 1991, or service with the Kuwait Liaison Team on 2 August 1990, the date of the Iraqi invasion. Two clasps were sanctioned and awarded to personnel who qualified for active service with the Liaison Team or in the operations to liberate Kuwait. A rosette is worn on the ribbon alone to denote the campaign clasps. Naming is in impressed capitals. More than 45,000 medals were awarded. See also the Kuwait and Iraq-Turkey clasps awarded to the General Service Medal 1962. About 1,500 civilians, including members of British Aerospace working at Dahran, also received the medal with the clasp 16 Jan to 28 Feb 1991.*

VALUE:

No clasp	£200–250
i. 2 Aug 1990	£2000–3000
ii. 16 Jan to 28 Feb 1991	
Regiments/RN/RAF	£250–350
Corps and Artillery	£200–250
Civilians	£200–250
Miniature	£15–20

204A. BRUNEI GENERAL SERVICE MEDAL

Date: 1968.
Campaign: Service in Brunei.
Branch of Service: British personnel on loan service.
Ribbon: Blue with red edges and a central red stripe.
Metal: Silver.
Size: 40x50mm max.
Description: A radiate star with a central medallion inscribed GENERAL SERVICE MEDAL and its equivalent Pingkat Laila Tugas in Arabic script, the royal insignia of the sultanate appearing in the centre. This insignia has changed several times over the years so varieties are seen. The original versions have a white enamel cross on the star (as illustrated) but the later version has the insignia surrounded by a laurel wreath. Suspended by a plain bar.
Comments: *Awarded to British personnel who completed a minimum of 12 months service. Unrestricted permission to wear the medal has been granted to entitled members of the British forces.*

VALUE: £100–150   *Miniature*   £35–40

204AA. SIERRA LEONE GENERAL SERVICE MEDAL

Date: 1965.
Campaign: Service in Sierra Leone and neighbouring countries.
Branch of Service: British forces on secondment to the Royal Sierra Leone Military Forces.
Ribbon: Broad central red stripe bordered with narrow green, white and dark blue stripes.
Metal: Bronze.
Size: 36mm.
Description: (Obverse) crowned effigy of Queen Elizabeth; (reverse) arms of Sierra Leone with inscription FOR GENERAL SERVICE / SIERRA LEONE. Fitted with a ring for suspension and a brooch bar at the top of the ribbon.
Clasps: Congo.
Comments: *Worn after medals previously earned and before the United Nations' Congo Medal and Sierra Leone Long Service and Independence medals, with restricted permission. UK personnel qualified for this medal if not eligible for any other general service medal for the same service. British personnel who served in the Congo between January 26, 1962 and February 28, 1963 qualified for the clasp.*

VALUE: £55–75   *Miniature*   £15–25

204B. IRAQ MEDAL

Date: 2004.
Campaign: Operation TELIC (the Iraq War).
Branch of Service: All military and civilian personnel, including embedded media, involved in the operations for the liberation of Iraq and the overthrow of Saddam Hussein.
Ribbon: Central narrow stripes of black, white and red (symbolising the Iraq national flag) flanked by broad sand-coloured edges.
Metal: Cupro-nickel.
Size: 36mm.
Description: (Obverse) crowned effigy of Queen Elizabeth; (reverse) image of a Lamassu (ancient Assyrian statue) over the word IRAQ.
Clasps: 19 Mar to 28 Apr 2003.
Comments: *This medal was awarded to all military and civilian personnel involved in Operation TELIC in Kuwait and Iraq from January 20, 2003. Those who took part in the actual combat from March 19, 2003 were awarded the clasp, denoted by a silver rosette on the ribbon alone. The medal is awarded to those who served for 30 days continuously or an aggregate 45 days.*

VALUE:		Miniature
i. With clasp		£10–20
Corps	£300–350	
Regiments/RAF/Navy	£350–400	
Cavalry	£400–450	
ii. No clasp		£10–15
Corps	£150–175	
Regiments/RAF/Navy	£175–250	
Cavalry	£300–350	

204C. IRAQ RECONSTRUCTION SERVICE MEDAL

Instituted: January 2007.
Branch of Service: Civilians and members of the Armed Forces who have seen service in Iraq but do not qualify for the Iraq Medal.
Ribbon: Sand-coloured with a broad green central stripe and narrow blue stripes towards the edges.
Metal: Rhodium-plated cupro-nickel.
Size: 36mm.
Description: (Obverse) Rank-Broadley effigy of the Queen; (reverse) cuneiform tablet translated as 'land bringing forth life' with stylised depiction of two rivers, based on a relief carving from Mesopotamia in the British Museum.
Comments: *The qualifying period for the medal was set at 40 days continuous service since March 19, 2003, or 40 days of service on working visits within Iraq aggregated over a period of one calendar year, for a minimum of 48 hours each. The medal was decommissioned in July 2013.*

VALUE: £300—£450   *Miniature* £15–25

204D. THE CIVILIAN SERVICE MEDAL (AFGHANISTAN)

Instituted: April 2011.
Branch of Service: Civilian.
Ribbon: As 204C but lighter blue stripes.
Metal: Rhodium-plated cupro-nickel.
Size: 36mm.
Description: (Obverse) Rank-Broadley effigy of the Queen; (reverse) a stylised depiction of the mountains of Afghanistan with the name of the country, both in English and Afghan surrounding it.
Comments: *Awarded to recognise the role of civilians and others involved in the transition of Afghanistan to democracy. The qualifying period is 30 days continuous or 45 days aggregate service provided that takes place within a single calendar year and the visits are of at least 48 hours each. Those whose service is curtailed by death or injury are also eligible. Eligible persons include any Crown Servant (including Members of Her Majesty's UK Armed Forces), under Operational Control of the Foreign and Commonwealth Office (but NOT those under the command of the UK joint task force), Police and Contractors. Locally employed civilians are not eligible. Approximately 2,800 awarded.*

VALUE: £600–800   *Miniature*   £15–25

205. SAUDI ARABIAN MEDAL FOR THE LIBERATION OF KUWAIT

Date: 1991.
Campaign: Gulf War 1991.
Branch of Service: British and Allied forces.
Ribbon: Green with edges of red, black and white (the Saudi national colours). The ribbon bar has a gold state emblem (palm tree over crossed scimitars).
Metal: White metal.
Size: approx. 45mm across.
Description: The white metal medal has a star of fifteen long and fifteen short round-tipped rays, surmounted by a bronze circle bearing a crowned and enwreathed globe on which appears a map of Arabia. Above the circle is a palm tree with crossed scimitars, the state emblem of Saudi Arabia. A scroll inscribed in Arabic and English LIBERATION OF KUWAIT appears round the foot of the circle.
Clasps: None.
Comments: *Awarded by the government of Saudi Arabia to all Allied personnel who took part in the campaign for the liberation of Kuwait, although only a few of the 45,000 British servicemen were subsequently given permission by the Foreign and Commonwealth Office to wear it. The contract for production was shared between Spink and a Swiss company, but subsequently a flatter version, more practicable for wear with other medals, was manufactured in the United States.*

Original type

VALUE: Original type   £35–55   *Miniature*   £15–20
             US "flat" type   £25–35

205A. MULTINATIONAL FORCE AND OBSERVERS MEDAL

Civilian

Date: March 1982.

Campaign: Sinai Peninsula.

Ribbon: 36mm orange with central white stripe flanked by 3mm dark green stripes. The civilian award ribbon is orange with two green 8mm stripes and central 8mm white stripe

Metal: Bronze.

Size: 30mm.

Description: (Obverse) a dove clutching an olive branch surrounded by the inscription MULTINATIONAL FORCE & OBSERVERS; (reverse) UNITED IN SERVICE FOR PEACE in five lines.

Comments: *Awarded to personnel of the Multinational Force and Observers (MFO) created in 1979 to monitor the peace agreement between Egypt and Israel. Eligibility for the medal was originally 90 days continuous service in the force, but this was raised to 170 days in March 1985. Subsequent awards for each completed six-month tour are indicated by a silver numeral affixed to the ribbon. It was originally awarded personally by the MFO's first commander, the Norwegian General Fredrik Bull-Hansen. The Force has 3,000 personnel drawn from the armed services of Australia, Canada, Colombia, Fiji, France, Italy, the Netherlands, New Zealand, UK, USA and Uruguay. It is now classed as a Foreign award and can only be worn if authorised, otherwise it may be accepted and retained as a keepsake*

VALUE: £25–30   *Miniature* £15–20

206. KUWAITI LIBERATION MEDALS

4th grade

Date: 1991.

Campaign: Liberation of Kuwait 1991.

Branch of Service: Allied forces.

Ribbon: Equal stripes of green, white and red with a black quadrilateral at the upper edge, representing the Kuwait national flag.

Metal: Various.

Size: Various.

Description: The circular medals have different decorative treatments of the Kuwaiti state emblem on the obverse, enshrined in a five-petalled flower (Second Grade), a five-pointed star with radiate background (Third Grade) and a plain medallic treatment (Fourth Grade). All grades, however, have a straight bar suspender of different designs.

Clasps: None.

Comments: *This medal was issued in five grades and awarded according to the rank of the recipient. The Excellent Grade was only conferred on the most senior Allied commanders, the First Grade went to brigadiers and major-generals, the Second Grade to officers of field rank (colonels and majors), the Third Grade to junior officers (captains, lieutenants and equivalent ranks in the other services), and the Fourth Grade to all other ranks. HM Government has decreed that British personnel may accept their medals as a keepsake but permission to wear them in uniform has so far been refused. The Canadian Government has followed the same policy, but the personnel of other Allied nations are permitted to wear their medals.*

VALUE:		*Miniature*
First Grade	£100–150	£25–30
Second Grade	£40–50	£20–25
Third Grade	£20–30	£20–25
Fourth Grade	£20–30	£20–25 *(silver)*

206A. NATO SERVICE MEDALS

Former Yugoslavia.

Kosovo.

Macedonia.

Eagle Assist.

Active Endeavour.

Non-Article 5.

Afghanistan (ISAF), Africa, Sudan (AMIS), Pakistan, Balkans, Iraq (NATO Training Mission)— denoted by clasp on ribbon.

Instituted: December 1994.

Campaigns: Any theatre or area of operations in the service of the North Atlantic Treaty Organization.

Branch of Service: NATO military and service personnel.

Ribbon: NATO blue with narrow white stripes having central metal threads: For engagements in NATO-led Article 5 operations (gold thread): Eagle Assist (central stripe), Active Endeavour (two stripes towards the edges), Non-Article 5 (central stripe with silver thread, from January 2011 two stripes towards the edges with silver thread denote operations) with clasps.

Metal: Bronze.

Size: 36mm.

Description: (Obverse) the NATO star emblem set in a wreath of olive leaves; (reverse) the title NORTH ATLANTIC TREATY ORGANIZATION and the words IN SERVICE OF PEACE AND FREEDOM in English and French. Two versions of this medal have been recorded: (a) light bronze, broad leaves in wreath, (b) dark bronze, narrow leaves.

Clasps: Former Yugoslavia, Kosovo, Non-Article 5 (superseding the first two clasps), Balkans (replaces last), Ex Yugoslavie, Africa*, OUP Libya/Libye*, NTM-Iraq*, AMIS*, Pakistan*, ISAF*, Article 5 (Eagle Assist & Active Endeavour), Sea Guardian, Afghanistan. *Worn on the same ribbon. A multitour indicator was originally an Arabic numeral, currently it is a bronze square with the number inside.

Comments: *The NATO medal was first instituted to reward personnel who took part in the Alliance operations in the former Yugoslavia. Any person serving under NATO command or operational control is eligible for the award. UK Service personnel cannot qualify for the NATO Medal and the UNPROFOR Medal (no. 207) in respect of the same period of service. The qualifying period for the medal is to be designated by the Secretary-General, however, for the operations in the former Yugoslavia the period has been set as 30 days continuous or accumulated service within the theatre of operations inside the former Yugoslavia and the Adriatic, or 90 days within the area of operations but outside the territory of the former Yugoslavia. The medal takes precedence equal to the General Service Medal in order of date of award. Bronze Arabic numerals are worn on the ribbon to denote multiple tours. The Non-Article 5 medal (ribbon) replaces the three other NATO medals (ribbons) for services anywhere in the Balkans, commencing December 3, 2002. Article 5 of the NATO Charter states that an attack on one member state is an attack on the whole Alliance. Non-Article 5 operations are therefore those outside NATO territory. No clasp was issued for the service in Macedonia (Former Yugoslavia) due to objections from Greece which does not recognise the independent sovereignty of that country. The clasps for Kosovo and Former Yugoslavia have now been superseded by the Non Article 5 clasp. The clasp for Afghanistan bears the initials of the International Security Assistance Force. Those serving more than one tour of duty are authorised to wear a bronze Arabic numeral on their ribbon to indicate this. Eagle Assist, Active Endeavour, Afghanistan and Iraq medals are not approved or authorised for wear by UK personnel, either in full size or in miniature. If presented they may be retained as keepsake(s). NATO ISAF has now been approved for wear by Australian Forces (military and police). Service on awards for these medal(s) does not count as qualifying service towards the Accumulated Campaign Service Medal. Additionally a NATO Meritorious Service Medal has been instituted—see MYB291AA.*

VALUE: £25–£35   *Miniature* £10–12

206B. EUROPEAN COMMUNITY MONITORING MISSION MEDAL

Date: 1995.
Campaigns: Former Yugoslavia.
Branch of Service: EC Community Peacekeeping.
Ribbon: Navy with stripes of white and red and thin yellow.
Metal: Silver.
Size: 36mm.
Description: (Obverse) Outline map of Yugoslavia surmounted by the words EC MONITOR MISSION surrounded by a ring of stars; (reverse) a dove of peace.
Comments: *Awarded for 21 days service between July 27, 1991 and June 30, 1993, in and around the former Yugoslavia. Service for this medal does not count as qualifying service towards the Accumulated Campaign Service Medal.*

VALUE: £30–£35   *Miniature*   £15–20

206C. WESTERN EUROPEAN UNION MISSION SERVICE MEDAL

Date: 1997.
Campaigns: Operations in the Former Yugoslavia.
Branch of Service: Personnel serving with the Western European Union forces.
Ribbon: Bright blue with central broad bright yellow stripe.
Metal: Silver.
Size: 36mm.
Description: (Obverse) capital letters WEU arranged horizontally with U and O above and below the E to signify "Western European Union" and its French equivalent "Union de l'Europe Occidentale". Ten five-pointed stars are ranged around the lower half of the circumference; (reverse) PRO PACE UNUM ("United for peace") in three lines. A clasp signifying the area of service is worn on the ribbon.
Clasp: Ex Yugoslavie.
Comments: *This medal was instituted to award service with missions under the auspices of the Western European Union. It was awarded to personnel who had served at least 30 days in the former Yugoslavia or 90 days in the Adriatic, Hungary or Rumania. The first British recipients (March 6, 1997) were 27 police officers who had served with the WEU Police Force in Bosnia-Herzegovina. A total of 15,982 medals had been awarded by September 2000. This medal is also known as the European Union Police Mission Medal. Service for these medal(s) does not count as qualifying service towards the Accumulated Campaign Service Medal.*

VALUE: £50–70   *Miniature*   £10–15

206D. COMMON SECURITY AND DEFENCE POLICY SERVICE MEDAL

Reverse

Date: 2004.

Campaigns: Any military operations involving the European Union.

Branch of Service: Police.

Ribbon: Bright blue with central yellow stripe for HQ and Forces or with central white stripe for Planning and Support personnel, with an emblem denoting area of service.

Metal: Silver.

Size: 36mm.

Description: (Obverse) Twelve five-pointed stars in a circle; (reverse) PRO PACE UNUM in three lines (roughly translated as "United for peace"). The medal is fitted with a large ring for suspension. A clasp signifying the area of service is worn on the ribbon.

Clasps: Artemis, Concordia, Proxima, Althea, EUPM, EU Copps, EU NAVFOR Atalanta, EUSEC South Sudan, EUBAM Rafah, EUCAP Nestor, EUFOR RD Congo, EUFOR Tchad/RCA, EUPOL-AFG (Afghanistan), EUPOL Copps, EUSEC RD Congo, EUTM Mali, EUTM Somalia, EUMM Georgia, Kosovo (for EULEX Kosovo Mission), AMIS (AMIS EU Mission), Sophia (EUNAVFOR, the European Union Naval Force).

Comments: *This medal has been awarded to police and security personnel serving in any military operation under the auspices of the European Union. It has also been awarded to civilian police missions, as well as Canadian personnel (2005). The clasps denote service in the Democratic Republic of Congo from June to September 2003 (Artemis), with the EU Police mission in Bosnia since January 2003, for service in the former Yugoslav republic of Macedonia from March to December 2003 (Concordia) or December 2003 to December 2004 (Proxima), service in Bosnia since December 2004 (Althea) and Afghanistan since June 2007. Those serving more than one tour of duty are authorised to wear an Arabic numeral on their ribbon to indicate this. Service for these medal(s) does not count as qualifying service towards the Accumulated Campaign Service Medal. The ESDP Medal with clasp Althea has been approved for unrestricted acceptance and wearing by UK personnel—headquarters and units serving in Bosnia and Herzegovina, on this operation. The ESDP medal for planning and support for Operation Althea is not approved for acceptance or wear. Those presented may be retained as a keepsake.*

VALUE: £30–35   *Miniature*   £10–15

207. UNITED NATIONS MEDAL

Date: 1951.
Campaigns: Various supervisory or observation roles since 1948.
Branch of Service: UN forces.
Ribbons: Various (see below).
Metal: Bronze.
Size: 35mm.
Description: (Obverse) the wreathed globe emblem surmounted by the letters UN; (reverse) inscribed "IN THE SERVICE OF PEACE".
Clasps: CONGO, UNGOMAP, OSGAP, UNSMIH, MINUGUA, UNCRO, ONUMOZ, UNSCOM, UNAMIC, UNMIH, UNTMIH, UNOSGI, UNMONUA, UNOCHA, UNAMA.
Comments: *Apart from the UN Korea and UNEF medals, there have been numerous awards to personnel who served in one or other of the UN peace-keeping actions around the world since the end of the Second World War. The all-purpose medal has been awarded with various distinctive ribbons for service in many of the world's trouble spots. Two versions of the medal exist: globe flat (European) and globe raised (US version). Issues to South African Personnel are named. Eligibility is generally 90 days, but some missions were 180 days. Subsequent awards for each six month tour completed with the same mission are indicated by a silver numeral affixed to the ribbon. Those serving more than one tour of duty are authorised to wear an Arabic numeral on their ribbon to indicate this. Service for these medal(s) does not count as qualifying service towards the Accumulated Campaign Service Medal. The missions are listed below in chronological order.*

Style of lettering for clasps.

For the various ribbons for the medal see ribbon charts.

UNTSO United Nations Truce Supervision Organization (Israel, Egypt, Syria since 1948).
Blue ribbon with two narrow white stripes towards the edges.
UNOGIL United Nations Observation Group in Lebanon (1958).
Same ribbon as UNTSO.
ONUC Organisation des Nations Unies au Congo (1960–64).
Originally the same ribbon as UNTSO with clasp CONGO, but a green ribbon, with white and blue edges was substituted in 1963.
UNTEA United Nations Temporary Executive Authority (Netherlands New Guinea, 1962–63).
Blue ribbon with a white central stripe bordered dark green (left) and light green (right).
UNMOGIP United Nations Military Observer Group in India and Pakistan since 1949.
Dark green ribbon shading to light green with white and blue edges.
UNIPOM United Nations India Pakistan Observation Mission (1965–66).
Ribbon as UNMOGIP.
UNYOM United Nations Yemen Observation Mission (1963–64).
Ribbon with brown centre, yellow stripes and light blue edges.
UNFICYP United Nations Force in Cyprus (1964–).
Pale blue ribbon with central white stripe bordered in dark blue. Initially 30, then increased to 90 days.
UNEF 2 United Nations Emergency Force 2 patrolling Israeli-Egyptian cease-fire (1973– 79).
Pale blue ribbon with sand centre and two dark blue stripes.
UNDOF United Nations Disengagement Observer Force, Golan Heights (1974–).
Ribbon of burgundy, white, black and pale blue.
UNIFIL United Nations Interim Force in Lebanon (1978–).
Pale blue ribbon with green centre bordered white and red.
UNGOMAP United Nations Good Offices in Afghanistan and Pakistan.
A bronze bar inscribed UNGOMAP was issued but as the mission was made up from observers from three other missions it can only be found on these ribbons: UNTSO, UNIFIL, UNDOF.
UNIIMOG United Nations Iran-Iraq Monitoring Observation Group.
Pale blue with edges of green, white and red (left) and red, white and black (right) (1988–91).
UNAVEM United Nations Angola Verification Missions: I (1988–91), II (1991–95), III (1995–97).
Pale blue ribbon with yellow edges separated by narrow stripes of red, white and black (same for all three).
ONUCA Observadores de las Naciones Unidas en Centro America (Nicaragua and Guatemala) (1989–92).
Pale blue ribbon with dark blue edges and nine thin central green or white stripes.
UNTAG United Nations Transitional Assistance Group (Namibia, 1989–90).
Sand ribbon with pale blue edges and thin central stripes of blue, green, red, sand and deep blue.
ONUSAL Observadores de las Naciones Unidas en El Salvador (1991–95).
Pale blue ribbon with a white central stripe bordered dark blue.
UNIKOM United Nations Iraq Kuwait Observation Mission (1991–2003).
Sand ribbon with a narrow central stripe of pale blue.

MINURSO Mission des Nations Unies pour la Referendum dans le Sahara Occidental (UN Mission for the Referendum in Western Sahara) (1991–).
Ribbon has a broad sandy centre flanked by stripes of UN blue.

UNAMIC United Nations Advanced Mission in Cambodia (Oct. 1991–March 1992).
Pale blue ribbon with central white stripe bordered with dark blue, yellow and red stripes.

UNTAC United Nations Transitional Authority in Cambodia (March 1992–Sept. 1993).
Green ribbon with central white stripe edged with red, pale blue and dark blue.

UNOSOM United Nations Operations in Somalia (I: 1992–93 and II: 1993–95).
Pale yellow ribbon with central blue stripe edged with green.

UNMIH United Nations Mission in Haiti (1993–96).
Pale blue ribbon with dark blue and red central stripes edged with white.

UNPROFOR United Nations Protection Force (1992–95) operating in the former Yugoslavia, especially Bosnia. *Blue ribbon with central red stripe edged in white and green or brown edges. See also UNCRO below.*

UNOMIL United Nations Observer Mission in Liberia (1993–97).
Pale blue ribbon flanked with white stripes with dark blue or red edges.

UNOMUR United Nations Observer Mission in Uganda/Rwanda (1993–94).
Pale blue central stripe edged by white and flanked by equal stripes of black, orange and red.

UNOMIG United Nations Observer Mission in Georgia (1993–2009). For 180 days service.
Pale blue central stripe flanked by equal stripes of white, green and dark blue.

UNAMIR United Nations Assistance Mission in Rwanda (1993–96).
Pale blue central stripe edged with white and flanked by equal stripes of black, green and red.

UNHQ General service at UN headquarters, New York.
Plain ribbon of pale blue, the UN colour.

UNPREDEP United Nations Preventative Deployment in Yugoslavia (1995–99).
Blue ribbon with central red stripe bearing four yellow lines and flanked by white edging.

UNMOP United Nations Mission of Observers in Pravlaka (1996–2002).
Dark blue ribbon with central yellow stripe edged with white, and two pale blue stripes.

UNTAES United Nations Transitional Authority in Eastern Slavonia. (1996-98)
Pale blue ribbon with yellow, red edged with white, and green stripes.

UNMOT United Nations Peacekeeping Force in Tadjikistan (1994–2000).
Blue ribbon with central green stripe flanked by white stripes.

UNMIBH United Nations Mission in Bosnia Herzegovina (1995–2002).
Blue ribbon with white central stripe, edged with one green and one red stripe.

UNMOGUA United Nations Military Observers in Guatemala (1997).
Blue ribbon with central pale blue stripe and two white stripes each with central green line.

UNSMIH United Nations Support Mission in Haiti (July 1996–97).
Same ribbon as UNMIH above, but with clasp UNSMIH.

UNCRO United Nations Confidence Restoration Operation in Croatia (1994–96).
Same ribbon as UNPROFOR above, but with clasp UNCRO.

MINUGUA Mision de las Naciones Unidas en Guatemala (1997).
Same ribbon as UNMOGUA but clasp with initials in Spanish.

ONUMOZ Operation des Nations Unies pour le referendum dans Mozambique (1992–94).
Pale blue ribbon edged with white and green stripes.

UNSSM United Nations Special Service Medal.
Awarded to personnel serving at least 90 consecutive days under UN control in operations for which no other UN award is authorised. Blue ribbon with white edges. Clasps: UNOCHA, UNSCOM, UNAMA. The medal with no clasp was awarded to Operation Cheshire aircrew who had completed 100 landings at Sarajevo or ground crew who had spent 90 days at Anacona, Split or Zagreb between July 3, 1992 and January 12, 1996.

OSGAP Office of the Secretary General for Afghanistan and Pakistan.
Silver clasp worn by Canadian personnel on the ribbons of UNTSO, UNDOF or UNIFIL.

UNOMSIL United Nations Observer Mission in Sierra Leone. (1998–99)
Awarded for 90 days service. White ribbon with blue edges and the Sierra Leone colours (light blue flanked by green stripes) in the centre. This mission was redesignated UNAMSIL on October 1, 1999.

UNPSG United Nations Police Support Group Medal.
A support group of 180 police monitors created in January 1998 initially to supervise the Croatian police in the return of displaced persons. 90 days qualifying service. White ribbon with a broad blue central stripe and narrow dark grey (left) and bright yellow (right) stripes towards the edges.

MINURCA United Nations Verification Mission in the Central African Republic (1998–2000).
Mission instituted April 15, 1998 to monitor the restoration of peace following the Bangui agreement. 90 days qualifying service. Ribbon has a broad blue central stripe flanked by yellow, green, red, white and dark blue stripes on either side.

UNSCOM United Nations Special Commission.
The UN Special Service Medal with UNSCOM clasp is awarded to personnel with a minimum of 90 days consecutive service or 180 days in all, with UNSCOM in Iraq. Ribbon is UN blue with a white stripe at each edge.

UNMIK United Nations Mission in Kosovo (1999–).
Pale blue ribbon with wide central dark blue stripe edged with white. For 180 days service.

UNAMET United Nations Mission in East Timor (1999).
Pale blue ribbon with wide central white stripe edged with yellow and claret.

UNTAET United Nations Transitional Administration in East Timor (1999–2002).
Pale blue ribbon with wide central white stripe edged with yellow and claret.

207. UNITED NATIONS MEDAL *continued*

UNMISET United Nations Mission of Support in East Timor (2002–05).
Pale blue ribbon with wide central white stripe edged with yellow and claret.
MONUC United Nations Mission in the Congo (1999–2010).
Pale blue ribbon with wide central dark blue stripe edged with yellow.
UNMEE United Nations Mission in Ethiopia and Eritrea (2000–2008).
Pale blue with central band of sand bisected by narrow dark green stripe.
MIPONUH United Nations Civil Police Mission in Haiti (1997–2000).
Central bands of dark blue and red, flanked by narrow silver stripes and broad blue bands
UNTMIH United Nations Transitional Mission in Haiti (July–November 1997).
Same ribbon as MIPONUH but with a bar inscribed UNTMIH.
MICAH International Civilian Support Mission in Haiti (March 2000–01).
Same ribbon as MIPONUH.
UNOSGI The UN Office of the Secretary General in Iraq.
The UN Special Service Medal with UNOSGI clasp issued to a small police group assigned to Baghdad from February 1991 to December 1992.
UNHCR United Nations High Commission for Refugees.
A clasp issued worldwide and still on-going.
UNAMSIL United Nations Medal for Service in Sierra Leone (1999–2005).
Same ribbon as UNOMSIL.
UNAMA United Nations Assistance Mission in Afghanistan (2002–).
This is a political mission. A clasp bearing UNAMA is worn on the UN Special Service Medal.
MINUCI United Nations Mission in Cote d'Ivoire (Ivory Coast) (May 2003–April 2004).
Orange, white and green stripes with blue edges.
UNMIL United Nations Mission in Liberia (September 2003–).
Pale blue with a broad central dark blue stripe edged in red and white.
UNOCI United Nations Operations in Cote d'Ivoire (April 2004–).
Similar to MINUCI but central stripes very narrow and blue edges correspondingly wider.
UNOB United Nations Operations in Burundi (June 2004–07).
Central stripes of white, red, dark green and white, flanked by broad pale blue stripes.
MINUSTAH Mission des Nations Unies Stabilisation dans Haiti (June 2004–).
Narrow central pale blue stripe, flanked by broader equal stripes of white, dark green and dark blue.
UNMIS United Nations Mission in Sudan (March 2005–11).
UN blue with dark blue centre divided by two narrow white stripes.
UNMIT United Nations Integrated Mission in Timor-Leste (August 2006–12)
UN blue with red centre stripe bordered each side with narrow stripes of white, dark blue and yellow.
UNAMID African Union/United Nations Hybrid operation in Darfur (July 2007–)
Yellow with a central stripe of half blue, half white and with dark blue narrow stripes either side or Blue with central white stripe bordered each side by stripes of green and yellow.
MINURCAT United Nations Mission in the Central African Republic and Chad (September 2007–10)
UN blue with five equal narrow stripes of dark blue, white, yellow, green and red.
UNGCI A little-known United Nations Guard Contingent Mission in Iraq (1991–2003)
UN blue with orange stripes at edges divided by black stripes.
MONUSCO United Nations Organisational Stabilisation Mission in the Democratic Republic of the Congo (2010).
Pale blue ribbon with wide central dark blue stripe edged with yellow.
UNISFA United Nations Mission in the Republic of Sudan (2011–).
UN blue with white, green and yellow stripes with central narrow dark blue stripe .
UNMISS United Nations Interim Security Force for Abyei, Sudan (2011–).
UN blue with central green stripe bordered by two white stripes each edged with black.
UNSMIS United Nations Supervision Mission in Syria (2012).
Mission abandoned. Intended ribbon UN blue with red centre stripe bordered each side by thin white stripes divided by a thin green stripe.
MINUSMA United Nations Multidimensional Integrated Stabilisation Mission in Mali (2013).
UN blue edges with central dark blue stripe bordered by thin green, yellow and red stripes at left and single pale yellow stripe at right..
MINUSCA United Nations Multidimensional Integrated Stabilisation Mission in the Central African Republic (2014–).
UN blue with centre narrow stripes of blue, white, red, yellow, green.
MINUJUSTH United Nations Supervision Mission in Haiti (2017–19).
Three equal stripes of Dark blue, light blue and red divided by narrow white stripes..

VALUE:		Miniature
Any current issue medal regardless of ribbon	£25–35	£8–10
Original striking for UNTSO	£30–45	

207A. INTERNATIONAL CONFERENCE ON THE FORMER YUGOSLAVIA MEDAL

Date: 1995.
Campaigns: Former Yugoslavia.
Branch of Service: UN Observers.
Ribbon: Central broad orange stripe, flanked by narrow blue and white stripes and broad red edges, mounted in the Danish style.
Metal: Silver.
Size: 38mm.
Description: (Obverse) the wreathed globe emblem of the United Nations surrounded by 15 five-pointed stars representing the member nations of the conference, with the inscription round the edge: INTERNATIONAL CONFERENCE ON THE FORMER YUGOSLAVIA; (reverse) the Drina River and the mountains of Serbia and Montenegro surmounted by a peace dove in flight, with the words OBSERVER MISSION round the foot.
Comments: *This medal was awarded to about 100 observers who monitored the 17 land and two rail crossings between Serbia and Montenegro and Bosnia-Herzegovina during September 1994.*

VALUE: £80–100   *Miniature*   £12–16

207B. INTERFET MEDAL—International Force East Timor

Instituted: March 7, 2000.
Ribbon: 32mm central thin red stripe, flanked by deep green, white and UN light blue.
Metal: Pewter coloured silver.
Size: 38mm.
Description: (Obverse) central raised stylised dove of peace over the island of Timor, surrounded by raised inscription INTERNATIONAL FORCE EAST TIMOR surmounted by Federation Star and plain suspension bar struck as one unit; (reverse) TOGETHER AS ONE FOR PEACE IN EAST TIMOR around outer circle, inner circle blank for naming.
Method of naming: Pantographed on reverse in capitals with regimental number, initials and surname.
Comments: *The Australian Prime Minister established a specific campaign medal for members of the Australian Defence Force in East Timor. Australia led the coalition of 17 nations and this is the first Australian medal issued to other countries. Awarded for 30 days service during the INTERFET stage of the conflict. 15,046 medals have been issued, including 8,690 to members of the ADF and 6,356 to members of other countries' military establishments.*

**VALUE: To Australian personnel £500–800   *Miniature*   £12–15
                         Others   £700–1000**

207C. UNITAS MEDAL

Instituted: 1994.

Ribbon: 32mm, pale blue with central green stripe of 8mm edged each side by a white stripe of 4mm.

Metal: Lacquered brass.

Size: 38mm.

Description: (Obverse) a seven pointed star with central circle enclosing the Greek letter alpha; (reverse) A small embellished coat of arms of South Africa with date 1994 below. The whole is enclosed by a circle made up of the word "Unity" in all eleven official languages of the new South Africa. Suspender is uniface and struck as one piece with the medal.

Comments: *Awarded to all those who rendered service through being members of a serving force (SA Permanent Force, Citizen Force, Commandos, members of the armed forces of the former self-governing territories, the armed wing of the ANC (the MK) and APLA) during the period of South Africa's first non-racial elections and inauguration of Mr Mandela as the first black State President in South Africa between 27 April and 10 May 1994. Those medals awarded to members of the British Military Advisory Team in South Africa at the time, for which Her Majesty Queen Elizabeth II granted permission for wear, must be considered a rarity.*

VALUE:

			Miniature
SA recipient	£25–35		£15–20
BMA recipient	From £250		

A NOTE ON CAMPAIGN MEDAL CLASPS
Since Worcestershire Medal Services Ltd were awarded the MoD contract for British campaign medals, all campaign clasps have a standard background as per the *Iraq & Syria* clasp on the Operational Service Medal (MYB 198A). This will also apply to all retrospective claims where the medal is produced today; so for example, General Service Medals for Cyprus or Malaya, etc. will now have clasps with the same background as that for Operation Shader—see MEDAL NEWS, December 2019/January 2020 for further details.

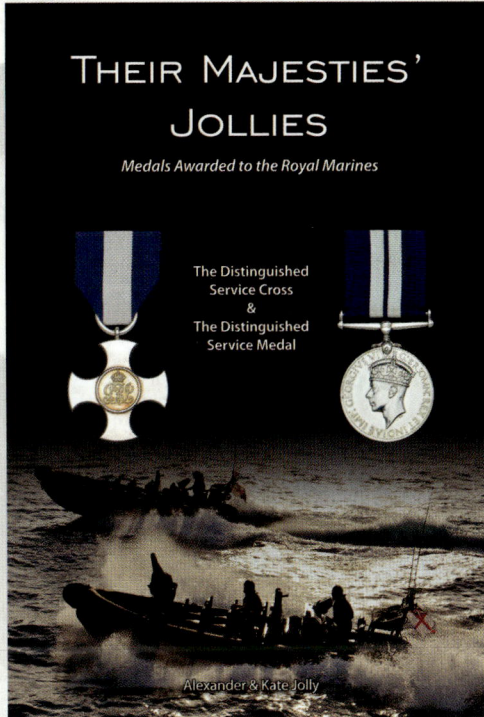

LONG
and Meritorious Service

A large, varied but until recently relatively neglected category comprises the medals awarded for long service and good conduct or meritorious service. Their common denominator is that the grant of such awards is made in respect of a minimum number of years of unblemished service—"undetected crime" is how it is often described in the armed forces. As their title implies, long service and good conduct medals combine the elements of lengthy service with no transgressions of the rules and regulations. Meritorious service, on the other hand, implies rather more. Apart from a brief period (1916–28) when awards were made for single acts of gallantry, MSMs have generally been granted to warrant officers and senior NCOs as a rather superior form of long service medal. Today long service and good conduct medals and meritorious service medals in the services can be awarded to officers as well as other ranks.

Long service and good conduct medals do not appear to excite the same interest among collectors as campaign medals. Perhaps this may be accounted for by their image of stolid devotion to duty rather than the romantic connotations of a medal with an unusual clasp awarded for service in some remote and all but forgotten outpost of the Empire. Nevertheless their importance should not be overlooked. Especially in regard to groups consisting primarily of the Second World War medals, they serve a useful purpose in establishing the provenance of the group, on account of the fact that they are invariably named to the recipient.

Service medals include not only such well known types as the Army LSGC (known affectionately as "the mark of the beast" on account of its high incidence on the chests of sergeant-majors), but also awards to the Territorial and Reserve forces, the auxiliary forces, the nursing services, and organisations such as the Royal Observer Corps and the Cadet Force, the Police, the Red Cross and St John's Ambulance Brigade. The Special Constabulary and Fire Brigades also have their own medals bestowed according to length of service and distinguished conduct. These medals may lack the glamour of naval and military awards but in recent years they have become increasingly fashionable with collectors and will certainly repay further study in their own right.

As many of these medals have been in use for eighty years or more with a standard reverse, variation usually lies in the obverse, changed for each successive sovereign. In addition, considerable variety has been imparted by the use of crowned or uncrowned profiles and busts, and changes in titles.

The following is a summary of the principal obverse types which may be encountered, referred to in the text by their type letters in brackets:

Queen Victoria (A) Young head by William Wyon
Queen Victoria (B) Veiled head by Leonard C. Wyon
Queen Victoria (C) Jubilee head by George W. de Saulles
Queen Victoria (D) Old head by Sir Thomas Brock
Edward VII (A) Bareheaded bust in Field Marshal's uniform
Edward VII (B) Bareheaded bust in Admiral's uniform
Edward VII (C) Coinage profile by George W. de Saulles
Edward VII (D) Crowned profile in Coronation robes
George V (A) Bareheaded bust in Field Marshal's uniform
George V (B) Bareheaded bust in Admiral's uniform
George V (C) Crowned bust in Coronation robes
George V (D) Crowned bust in Delhi Durbar robes
George V (E) Coinage profile by Bertram Mackennal
George VI (A) Crowned profile in Coronation robes
George VI (B) Crowned profile INDIAE: IMP 1937–48
George VI (C) Crowned profile FID: DEF 1949–52
George VI (D) Coinage profile IND: IMP 1937–48
George VI (E) Coinage profile FID: DEF 1949–52
Elizabeth II (A1) Tudor crown BR: OMN 1953–54
Elizabeth II (A) Tudor crown BR: OMN omitted 1954–80
Elizabeth II (B) Coinage bust BRITT: OMN 1953–54
Elizabeth II (C) Coinage bust BRITT OMN omitted 1954–80
Elizabeth II (D) St Edward crown 1955–
Elizabeth II (E) New bust for Diamond Jubilee Medal

PRINCIPAL OBVERSE TYPES:

Queen Victoria (A) Young Head

Queen Victoria (B) Veiled Head

Queen Victoria (C) Jubilee Head

Queen Victoria (D) Old Head

Edward VII (A) Bareheaded bust in Field Marshal's uniform

Edward VII (B) Bareheaded bust in Admiral's uniform

Edward VII (C) Coinage profile by George W. de Saulles

Edward VII (D) Crowned profile in Coronation robes

George V (A) Bareheaded bust in Field Marshal's uniform

George V (B) Bareheaded bust in Admiral's uniform

George V (C) Crowned bust in Coronation robes

George V (D) Crowned bust in Delhi Durbar robes

George V (E) Coinage profile by Bertram Mackennal

George VI (B) Crowned profile with INDIAE: IMP in legend 1937–48

George VI (C) Crowned profile with FID: DEF 1949–52

George VI (D) Coinage profile with IND: IMP 1937–48

George VI (E) Coinage profile with FID: DEF 1949–52

Elizabeth II (A1) Tudor crown with BR.OMN. (1953–54)
Elizabeth II (A) BR.OMN. omitted (as above) 1954–80

Elizabeth II (B) Coinage bust with BRITT: OMN, 1953–54

Elizabeth II (C) Coinage bust without BR: OMN.

Elizabeth II (D) St Edward crown from 1980

Elizabeth II (E) Ian Rank-Broadley coinage bust

Elizabeth II (F) Jody Clark coinage bust

Charles III (A) Crowned head (Tudor crown)

Charles III (B) Uncrowned head

Charles III (C) Crowned with Coronation robes

Charles III (D) in Admiral of the Fleet uniform

Charles III (E) in Field Marshal uniform

Charles III (F) in Air Chief Marshal uniform

208. ROYAL NAVAL MERITORIOUS SERVICE MEDAL

Instituted: 14 January 1919 until 1928 by Order in Council. Reinstituted 1977.

Branch of Service: Royal Navy.

Ribbon: Crimson with three white stripes.

Metal: Silver

Size: 36mm.

Description: (Obverse) effigy of the reigning monarch; (reverse) imperial crown surmounting a wreath containing the words FOR MERITORIOUS SERVICE. The medal was named in large seriffed capitals round the rim.

Comments: *Awarded without annuity or pension to warrant and petty officers of the Royal Navy. Originally it was awarded either for specific acts of gallantry not in the presence of the enemy or for arduous and specially meritorious service afloat or ashore in action with the enemy. Bars were granted for second awards. It was superseded in 1928 by the British Empire Medal for Gallantry or Meritorious Service, but re-instated on 1 December 1977. In this guise it has been awarded to warrant and petty officers of the Royal Navy, warrant officers and senior NCOs of the Royal Marines, and equivalent ranks in the WRNS and QARNNS, who have at least 20 years service and are already holders of the LSGC medal and three good conduct badges. The medal is not awarded automatically when these criteria are satisfied, as no more than 49 medals may be awarded annually. The revived medal is identical to the Army MSM and can only be distinguished by the naming giving rank and name of ship.*

VALUE:

		Miniature
George V (A)	—	—
George V (B) (1020)	£450–550	£25–35
Elizabeth II (B)	£350–450	£18–20

209. ROYAL MARINES MERITORIOUS SERVICE MEDAL

Instituted: 15 January 1849, by Order in Council (although medals dated 1848 are known).

Branch of Service: Royal Marines.

Ribbon: Plain dark blue, but later replaced by the RN MSM ribbon.

Metal: Silver.

Size: 36mm.

Description: (Obverse) effigy of the monarch; (reverse) a crowned laurel wreath enclosing the words FOR MERITORIOUS SERVICE.

Comments: *Annuities not exceeding £20 a year might be granted in addition to the medal for distinguished service. Sergeants with a minimum of 24 years service (the last fourteen as a sergeant), "with an irreproachable and meritorious character" were considered eligible for the award which was extended to discharged sergeants in 1872 when the service qualification was reduced to 21 years. The award of the MSM for gallantry was discontinued in 1874 when the Conspicuous Gallantry Medal was reconstituted. Only six MSMs for gallantry were ever awarded. The medal was identical with the Army MSM, distinguished solely by its ribbon and the naming to the recipient. Under the royal warrants of 1916-19 Marine NCOs became eligible for immediate awards of the MSM for arduous or specially meritorious service. The medals in this case were worn with crimson ribbons with three white stripes and had the obverse showing the King in the uniform of an Admiral or a Field Marshal, depending on whether the award was for services afloat, or with the naval brigades on the Western Front. The use of this medal ceased in 1928 following the institution of the BEM (MYB 19). Although George VI examples are known. The Royal Marines MSM was revived in 1977 solely as a long service award and is the same as the naval MSM already noted, differing only in the details of the recipient.*

Original ribbon.

VALUE:

Victoria (A) dated 1848	£1200–1500	*Miniature*	£50–65
Victoria	£750–1000		£80–90
Edward VII (C)	£600–800		£80–90
George V (A)	£600–800		£45–55
George V (B)	£400–600		£45–55
George VI (E)	£400-600		£35–40
Elizabeth II (B)	£400–600		£30–35

210. ARMY MERITORIOUS SERVICE MEDAL

Instituted: 19 December 1845.
Branch of Service: Army.
Ribbon: Plain crimson (till 1916), white edges added (1916-17), three white stripes (since August 1917).
Metal: Silver.
Size: 36mm.
Description: (Obverse) effigy of the monarch; (reverse) a crowned laurel wreath inscribed FOR MERITORIOUS SERVICE.
Comments: *A sum of £2000 a year was set aside for distribution to recipients in the form of annuities not exceeding £20, paid for life to NCOs of the rank of sergeant and above for distinguished or meritorious service. The number of medals awarded was thus limited by the amount of money available in the annuity fund, so that medals and annuities were only granted on the death of previous recipients or when the fund was increased. Until November 1902 holders were not allowed to wear the LSGC as well as the MSM, but thereafter both medals could be worn, the LSGC taking precedence. In 1979, however, the order of precedence was reversed. Until 1951 the MSM could only be awarded when an annuity became available, but since then it has been awarded without the annuity. From 1956 recipients needed at least 27 years service to become eligible, but this was reduced to 20 years in 2002. What was, in effect, a second type of MSM was introduced in October 1916 when immediate awards for exceptionally valuable and meritorious service were introduced. In January 1917 this was extended to include individual acts of gallantry not in the presence of the enemy. No annuities were paid with the immediate awards which terminated in 1928 with the institution of the Gallantry BEM. Bars for subsequent acts of gallantry or life-saving were introduced in 1916, seven being awarded up to 1928. The standard crown and wreath reverse was used but in addition to the wide range of obverse types swivelling suspension was used until 1926, and immediate and non-immediate awards may be distinguished by the presence or absence respectively of the recipient's regimental number. Recent awards of the Elizabethan second bust medals have reverted to swivelling suspension. By Royal Warrant of February 2002 the annual allocation was a maximum of 201 medals: Royal Navy (49), Royal Marines (3), Army (89) and RAF (60), but these figures are rarely, if ever, attained.*

First type ribbon.

Second type ribbon.

Third type ribbon.

VALUE:

		Miniature
Victoria (A) 1847 on edge (110)	£1000–1200	—
Victoria (A) 1848 below bust (10)	£2000–2500	—
Victoria (A) (990)	£400–450	£35–55
Edward VII (725)	£300–400	£35–45
George V (A) swivel (1050)	£175–250	£20–30
George V (A) non-swivel (400)	£175–250	£15–25
George V (A) Immediate awards 1916–28		
For Gallantry (366+1 bar)	£375–500	—
Meritorious service (25,845+6 bars)	£250–350	—
George V (E) (550)	£350–450	£20–30
George VI (B) (55)	£850–1000	£15–25
George VI (D) (1090)	£250–350	£15–25
George VI (E) (5600)	£250–350	£15–25
Elizabeth II (B) (125)	£450–650	£18–25
Elizabeth II (C) (2750+)	£350–450	£18–25

211. ROYAL AIR FORCE MERITORIOUS SERVICE MEDAL

Instituted: June 1918
Branch of Service: Royal Air Force.
Ribbon: Half crimson, half light blue, with white stripes at the centre and edges. Since 1977 the same ribbon as the Army MSM.
Metal: Silver.
Size: 36mm.
Description: (Obverse) effigy of the monarch; (reverse) a crowned laurel wreath enclosing the words FOR MERITORIOUS SERVICE. Originally medals were named in large seriffed capitals and were issued in respect of the First World War and service in Russia (1918-20), but later medals were impressed in thin block capitals. The RAF version had a swivelling suspension, unlike its military counterpart.
Comments: *Awarded for valuable services in the field, as opposed to actual flying service. This medal was replaced by the BEM in 1928, but revived in December 1977 under the same conditions as the military MSM. No more than 60 medals are awarded annually. The current issue is similar to the naval and military MSMs, differing only in the naming which includes RAF after the service number.*

VALUE:		*Miniature*
George V (E) (854)	£450–550	£25–35
Elizabeth II (C)	£350–450	£12–18

Original ribbon.

212. COLONIAL MERITORIOUS SERVICE MEDALS

Instituted: 31 May 1895.
Branch of Service: Colonial forces.
Ribbon: According to issuing territory (see below).
Metal: Silver.
Size: 36mm.
Description: (Obverse) originally the trophy of arms as MYB 229 but later issues have the head of the reigning monarch; (reverse) as British type, but with the name of the dominion or colony round the top.
Comments: *Awarded for service in the British dominions, colonies and protectorates.*

Canada: Ribbon as for British Army MSM. CANADA on reverse till 1936; imperial version used from then until 1958. No medals with the Victorian obverse were awarded, but specimens exist.
Cape of Good Hope: Crimson ribbon with central orange stripe. Only one or two Edward VII medals issued.
Natal: Crimson ribbon with a central yellow stripe. Exceptionally, it was awarded to volunteers in the Natal Militia. Fifteen Edward VII medals awarded.
Commonwealth of Australia: Crimson ribbon with two dark green central stripes. Issued between 1903 and 1975.
New South Wales: Crimson ribbon with a dark blue central stripe. Issued till 1903.
Queensland: Crimson ribbon with light blue central stripe. Issued till 1903.
South Australia: Plain crimson ribbon. Issued till 1903.
Tasmania: Crimson ribbon with a pink central stripe. Issued till 1903.
New Zealand: Crimson ribbon with a light green central stripe. Issued since 1898 (see also NZ21).

For the various original ribbons see the ribbon charts at the end of this publication.

VALUE	Rare	*Miniature*	*£110–220*

213. INDIAN ARMY MERITORIOUS SERVICE MEDAL 1848

Instituted: 20 May 1848, by General Order of the Indian government.
Branch of Service: Forces of the Honourable East India Company and later the Indian armed services.
Ribbon: Plain crimson.
Metal: Silver.
Size: 36mm.
Description: (Obverse) the Wyon profile of Queen Victoria; (reverse) the arms and motto of the Honourable East India Company.
Comments: *Awarded with an annuity up to £20 to European sergeants, serving or discharged, for meritorious service. It was discontinued in 1873.*

VALUE:		*Miniature*
Undated obverse	£650–750	£240–300
Dated obverse	Rare	—

214. INDIAN ARMY MERITORIOUS SERVICE MEDAL 1888

Instituted: 1888.
Branch of Service: Indian Army.
Ribbon: Plain crimson (till 1917); three white stripes added (1917).
Metal: Silver.
Size: 36mm.
Description: (Obverse) the sovereign's effigy; (reverse) a central wreath enclosing the word INDIA surrounded by the legend FOR MERITORIOUS SERVICE with a continuous border of lotus flowers and leaves round the circumference.
Comments: *For award to Indian warrant officers and senior NCOs (havildars, dafadars and equivalent band ranks). Eighteen years of exceptionally meritorious service was the minimum requirement, subject to the availability of funds in the annuity. At first only one medal was set aside for each regiment and thereafter awards were only made on the death, promotion or reduction of existing recipients. On promotion the medal was retained but the annuity ceased. It became obsolete in 1947.*

Original ribbon.

VALUE:		*Miniature*
Victoria (B)	£250–350	£100–120
Edward VII (A)	£200–250	£100–120
George V (C) Rex Et Indiae Imp	£175–250	£100–120
George V (D) Kaisar-i-Hind	£175–250	£100–120
George VI (B)	£150–200	£100–120

215. AFRICAN POLICE MEDAL FOR MERITORIOUS SERVICE

Instituted: 14 July 1915.

Branch of Service Non-European NCOs and men of the colonial police forces in East and West Africa.

Ribbon: Sand-coloured with red edges.

Metal: Silver.

Size: 36mm

Description: (Obverse) effigy of the sovereign; (reverse) a crown surmounted by a lion passant gardant within a palm wreath and having the legend FOR MERITORIOUS SERVICE IN THE POLICE and AFRICA at the foot.

Comments: *Awarded for both individual acts of gallantry and distinguished, meritorious or long service. In respect of the lastnamed, a minimum of 15 years exemplary service was required. It was superseded by the Colonial Police Medal in 1938.*

VALUE:

George V (A) IND: IMP 1915-31	£700–900
George V (A) INDIAE IMP 1931-7	£700–900
George VI (B) 1938	Rare
Miniature	£100–120

216. UNION OF SOUTH AFRICA MERITORIOUS SERVICE MEDAL

Instituted: 24 October 1914, by Government gazette.

Branch of Service: Service personnel of South Africa, Southern Rhodesia and Swaziland.

Ribbon: Crimson with blue edges and a central white, blue and white band.

Metal: Silver.

Size: 36mm.

Description: As British military MSM.

Comments: *A total of 46 awards were made for 21 years service and 300 meritorious service awards were made up to 1952 when the medal was discontinued. Of these only two were awarded to South Africans in the RNVR.*

VALUE:

George V (A)	Rare
George VI (B)	Rare

217. ROYAL HOUSEHOLD FAITHFUL SERVICE MEDALS

1st type obv.

1st type rev.

Instituted: 1872 by Queen Victoria.
Branch of Service: Royal Household.
Ribbon: Originally Royal Stuart tartan; later, a different ribbon for each monarch: dark blue and red diagonal stripes descending from left to right (George V), the same but descending from right to left (George VI) or dark blue with three red stripes (Elizabeth II).
Metal: Silver.
Size: 27mm (Victoria); 29mm (later awards).
Description: (Obverse) the sovereign's effigy; (reverse) the personal details of the recipient engraved on it. The Victorian medal has a very elaborate suspension ornamented with the crowned royal monogram, with a laurel bar brooch fitting at the top. This medal was not originally intended to be worn with a ribbon, although it had a strip of Royal Stuart tartan behind it. The same medal, but struck in 22 carat gold, was presented to John Brown, the Queen's personal servant. The concept was revived by George V, a silver medal of more conventional appearance being struck with the text FOR LONG AND FAITHFUL SERVICE on the reverse. Thirty, forty and fifty year service bars were also awarded.
Comments: *Originally intended as a reward to servants of the Royal Household for long and faithful service of at least 25 years but during the reign of George V this was changed to 20 years cumulative service. A further 10 years merited a bar. Different ribbons are used for each monarch, corresponding to the crowned cypher joining the medal to the suspension bar on either side of which the recipient's years of service are inscribed.*

VALUE:

		Miniature
Victoria	From £500	Not seen
Edward VII	—	Not seen
George V (E)	From £400	£90–110
George VI (D)	From £400	£80–90
Elizabeth II (C)	From £450	£35–45
Charles III (B)	—	—

Original background ribbon.

2nd type obv. (George V).

2nd type rev.

Charles III obverse.

GV ribbon.

GVI ribbon.

EII ribbon.

CIII Ribbon.

218. ROYAL NAVAL LONG SERVICE AND GOOD CONDUCT MEDAL

1st type obv.

1st type rev.

2nd type rev. wide suspender

Later type ribbon.

2nd type rev. narrow suspender with non-swivelling bar.

Instituted: 24 August 1831, by Order in Council.

Branch of Service: Royal Navy.

Ribbon: Plain dark blue (1831); dark blue with white edges (1848).

Metal: Silver.

Size: 34mm (1831); 36mm (1848).

Description: First type: (Obverse) an anchor surmounted by a crown and enclosed in an oak wreath; (reverse) the recipient's details. Plain ring for suspension.

Second type, adopted in 1848: (Obverse) the sovereign's effigy; (reverse) a three-masted man-of-war surrounded by a rope tied at the foot with a reef knot and having the legend FOR LONG SERVICE AND GOOD CONDUCT round the circumference. This medal originally had a wide suspender bar 38mm, but a narrow suspender was substituted in 1874. Normally the obverse was undated, but about 100 medals were issued in 1849-50 with the obverse of the Naval GSM, with the date 1848 below the Queen's bust. Between 1875 and 1877 a number of medals had the years of service added to the recipient's details, either engraved or impressed on the edge—these medals (about 60 known) are now sought after by collectors. Engraved naming was used from 1875 to 1877, but from then until 1901 impressed naming was adopted. Later medals used the various obverse effigies noted below.

Comments: *Originally awarded for 21 years exemplary conduct, but the period was reduced to 10 years in 1874, then later increased to 15 years. Bars for additional periods of 15 years were instituted by George V. In March 1981 commissioned officers of the naval services became eligible after 15 years service, provided at least 12 years were served in the ranks. Under changes announced in 2015 a clasp is now awarded for every 10 years served and the medal is now available to all ranks.*

VALUE:

		Miniature
Anchor type obv., 1831–47 (644)	£1200–1500	—
Victoria (A):		
1848–75, wide suspender (3572)	£650–850	—
Dated 1848 type (100)	£1500–2000	—
1875–77, narrow suspender, engraved naming (4400)	£175–250	£35–45
Year on edge variety (c. 40)	£450–500	—
1877–1901 impressed naming (18,200)	£175–250	—
Year on edge variety (c. 20)	£400–500	—
Edward VII (B)	£75–100	—
George V (B) 1910–20 swivel	£75–100	£12–18
1920–30 non-swivelling bar	£65–85	£5–12
George V (E) 1931–36	£75–100	£10–15
George VI (D) 1937–48	£85–100	£10–15
George VI (E) 1949–52	£85–100	£10–15
Elizabeth II (B) 1953–54	£75–100	£10–15
Elizabeth II (C) 1954–	£75–100	£10–15

2nd type obv. George V

219. ROYAL NAVAL RESERVE DECORATION

Instituted: 1908.

Branch of Service: Royal Naval Reserve.

Ribbon: Plain green ribbon, white edges being added from 1941 onwards.

Metal: Silver and silver-gilt.

Size: Height 54mm; max. width 33mm.

Description: A skeletal badge with the royal cypher in silver surrounded by an oval cable and reef knot in silver-gilt, surmounted by a crown and suspension ring.

Comments: *Granted for 15 years commissioned service (sub-lieutenant and above) in the Royal Naval Reserve, active service in wartime counting double. Bars are awarded for additional periods of 15 years. Recipients are entitled to the letters RD after their name. This decoration was replaced by the VRSM (No. 242A) in 2000.*

VALUE:		*Miniature*
Edward VII	£150–175	£30–35
George V	£185–200	£30–35
George VI (GRI)	£150–175	£30–35
George VI (GVIR)	£150–175	£30–35
Elizabeth II	£175–190	£15–25

2nd type ribbon.

220. ROYAL NAVAL RESERVE LONG SERVICE AND GOOD CONDUCT MEDAL

Instituted: 1908.

Branch of Service: Royal Naval Reserve.

Ribbon: Plain green, white edges and a central white stripe being added in 1941. On the amalgamation of the RNR and RNVR in 1958 the ribbon was changed to five equal stripes of blue, white, green, white and blue.

Metal: Silver.

Size: 36mm.

Description: (Obverse) effigy of the monarch; (reverse) a battleship with the motto DIUTERNE FIDELIS (faithful for ever) at the foot.

Comments: *Awarded to petty officers and ratings of the RNR for 15 years service, war service counting double, with bars for additional 15 year periods. This medal was replaced by the VRSM (No. 242A) in 2000.*

VALUE:		*Miniature*
Edward VII (B)	£55–65	£30–35
George V (B)	£50–60	£30–35
George V (E)	£35–50	£30–35
George VI (D)	£55–75	£30–35
George VI (E)	£55–75	£30–35
Elizabeth II (B)	£55–75	£10–15
Elizabeth II (C)	£55–75	£10–15

2nd type ribbon.

3rd type ribbon.

221. ROYAL NAVAL VOLUNTEER RESERVE DECORATION

Instituted: 1908.

Branch of Service: Royal Naval Volunteer Reserve.

Ribbon: 38mm originally plain dark green; dark blue with a central green stripe flanked by narrow red stripes (since 1919). Dark blue represents the sea, red represents the Royal Crimson, green represents the Old Volunteer colour

Metal: Silver and silver-gilt.

Size: Height 54mm; max. width 33mm.

Description: Similar to RNR decoration.

Comments: *Awarded to commissioned officers of the RNVR. The qualifying period was 15 years, service in the ranks counting half and war service counting double. In 1966 the decoration was replaced by the RD following the merger of the RNR and RNVR. Holders were entitled to the post-nominals letters VD, until 1947 when the letters VRD were substituted. Additional bars were awarded for each 10 years service.*

VALUE:		*Miniature*
Edward VII	£175–200	£30–35
George V	£150–175	£30–35
George VI GRI	£150–175	£30–35
George VI GVIR	£150–175	£30–35
Elizabeth II	£175–200	£15–25

222. ROYAL NAVAL VOLUNTEER RESERVE LONG SERVICE AND GOOD CONDUCT MEDAL

Instituted: 1908.

Branch of Service: Royal Naval Volunteer Reserve.

Ribbon: Originally plain green, but subsequently a broad central green stripe edged in red with blue stripes at the ends was adopted.

Metal: Silver.

Size: 36mm.

Description: Identical to the RNR medal, but distinguished by the ribbon and the naming which includes the letters RNVR, RCNVR (Canada), RSANVR (South Africa), etc.

Comments: *Awarded to petty officers and ratings for 12 years service with the necessary training, character assessed as "very good" throughout the period. War service counted double. The award was extended to the Colonial Navies during the Second World War.*

VALUE:		*Miniature*
Edward VII (B)	£350–400	£30–35
George V (B)	£50–75	£30–35
George V (E)	£50–75	£30–35
George VI (D, E)	£50–75	£30–35
Elizabeth II (B, C)	£75–100	£10–20

223. ROYAL FLEET RESERVE LONG SERVICE AND GOOD CONDUCT MEDAL

Instituted: 1919.
Branch of Service: Royal Fleet Reserve.
Ribbon: Blue bordered with thin red stripes and white edges.
Metal: Silver.
Size: 36mm.
Description: Similar to the RNR LSGC but with ring suspension instead of a bar suspender.
Comments: *Awarded for 15 years service in the Fleet Reserve. This medal was discontinued in 2000.*

VALUE:		Miniature
George V (B)	£45–55	£30–35
George V (E)	£45–55	£30–35
George VI (D)	£45–55	£30–35
George VI (E)	£45–55	£30–35
Elizabeth II (B)	£55–65	£10–20
Elizabeth II (C)	£55–65	£10–20

224. ROYAL NAVAL AUXILIARY SICK BERTH RESERVE LONG SERVICE AND GOOD CONDUCT MEDAL

Instituted: 1919.
Branch of Service: Royal Naval Auxiliary Sick Berth Reserve.
Ribbon: Plain green but later green with a white central stripe and white edges.
Metal: Silver.
Size: 36mm.
Description: Identical to the RNR equivalent, but the letters RNASBR appear after the recipient's name.
Comments: *Arguably the longest title of any British medal, it continued until the RNASBR was disbanded in 1949. The Auxiliary Sick Berth Reserve was created in 1903, members being recruited from the St John Ambulance Brigade. About 780 medals were granted prior to the Second World War and a further 715 between 1939 and 1949.*

VALUE:		Miniature
George V (B)	£100–120	£30–35
George V (E)	£100–120	£30–35
George VI (D)	£100–120	£30–35

225. ROYAL NAVAL VOLUNTEER (WIRELESS) RESERVE LONG SERVICE AND GOOD CONDUCT MEDAL

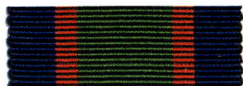

Instituted: 1939.
Branch of Service: Royal Naval Volunteer Wireless Auxiliary Reserve.
Ribbon: A broad central green stripe edged in red with blue stripes at the ends.
Metal: Silver.
Size: 36mm.
Description: Identical to the RNR equivalent, but the letters RNV(W)R after the recipient's name. The last of the service medals with a battleship reverse.
Comments: *Issued till 1957 when the RNWAR was disbanded. It was awarded for 12 years service, only about 200 having been issued.*

VALUE:		Miniature
George VI (D)	£250–350	£30–35
Elizabeth II (C)	£250–350	£30–35

226. ROYAL NAVAL AUXILIARY SERVICE MEDAL

Instituted: July 1965.
Branch of Service: Royal Naval Auxiliary Service (RNXS), formerly the Royal Naval Minewatching Service, disbanded 1994.
Ribbon: Dark blue with a narrow green central stripe and broad white stripes at the edges bisected by thin dark green stripes.
Metal: Cupro-nickel.
Size: 36mm.
Description: (Obverse) the Queen's effigy; (reverse) a fouled anchor in an oak wreath surmounted by a naval crown.
Comments: *Awarded for 12 years service. A bar was awarded for each additional 12 years service. 1,710 were awarded, 131 with one bar and 2 with two bars. Interestingly this medal was the last to be issued with a pure silk ribbon.*

VALUE: Elizabeth II (A) £180–220   *Miniature*   £30–35

227. HM COASTGUARD LONG SERVICE AND GOOD CONDUCT MEDAL

Instituted: 1911 by the Board of Trade.
Branch of Service: Rocket Life Saving Apparatus Volunteers,
Ribbon: Originally pale blue with broad scarlet edges, in 2013 changed to scarlet with one broad central pale blue stripe and two narrow pale blue stripes.
Metal: Silver.
Size: 31mm.
Description: (Obverse) the effigy of the reigning monarch with the date below the truncation. (Reverse) exists in four types. The first refers to the Board of Trade but when that department handed over responsibility to the Ministry of Transport in 1942 the wording was amended to read ROCKET APPARATUS VOLUNTEER MEDAL round the circumference. In 1953 the inscription was changed to COAST LIFE SAVING CORPS, in 1968 to COASTGUARD AUXILIARY SERVICE and in 2012 to HM COASTGUARD.
Comments: *Awarded for 20 years' service.*

First type reverse.

Second award bar.

First type ribbon.

Second type ribbon.

VALUE:		*Miniature*
George V (E)	£175–200	£55–110
George VI (D/E) BoT	£175–200	£55–110
George VI (D/E) Rocket Apparatus	£175–200	£55–110
Elizabeth II (D) Coast Life Saving	£175–200	£55–110
Elizabeth II (D) Coastguard Auxiliary	£175–200	£15–25
Elizabeth II (D) HM Coastguard	£175–200	£15–25

228. HM COASTGUARD COMMENDATION

Instituted: 2000.
Branch of Service: HM Coastguard Service.
Ribbon: None.
Metal: Gilt.
Size: 35mm x 12mm.
Description: Pin badge depicting the emblem of HM Coastguard Service (left) with two-line inscription "HM Coastguard / For Meritorious Service" (right).
Comments: *Awarded to Coastguard, Auxiliary Coastguard and Coastguard rescue teams for rescuing shipwrecked mariners.*

VALUE: —

229. ARMY LONG SERVICE AND GOOD CONDUCT MEDAL

Instituted: 1830.

Branch of Service: Army.

Ribbon: Plain crimson was used till 1917 when white stripes were added to the edges. Dominion and colonial medals formerly had crimson ribbons with a narrow central stripe in dark green (Commonwealth of Australia), dark blue (New South Wales), light blue (Queensland), pink (Tasmania), orange (Cape of Good Hope), yellow (Natal), white (Canada), light green (NZ). New Guinea had a scarlet ribbon with a light blue central stripe and South Australia had no central stripe on a plain crimson ribbon.

Metal: Silver.

Size: 36mm.

Description: Over the long period in which this medal has been in use it has undergone a number of changes. Until 1901 the obverse bore a trophy of arms with the royal arms in an oval shield in the centre while the reverse bore the inscription FOR LONG SERVICE AND GOOD CONDUCT. The first issue had the royal arms with the badge of Hanover on the obverse and small suspension ring with a plain crimson ribbon. A large ring was substituted in 1831. On the accession of Queen Victoria in 1837 the Hanoverian emblem was dropped from the arms. In 1855 a swivelling scroll suspension was substituted and in 1859 small lettering replaced the original large lettering on the reverse. From 1901, however, the effigy of the reigning sovereign was placed on the obverse although the reverse remained the same. In 1920 the swivelling scroll suspension gave way to a fixed suspender. In 1930 the title of the medal was changed to the Long Service and Good Conduct Medal (Military); at the same time the design was modified. A fixed suspension bar was added, bearing the words REGULAR ARMY or the name of a dominion (India, Canada, Australia, New Zealand or South Africa). This replaced the Permanent Forces of the Empire LSGC Medal (see below).

Comments: *Originally awarded to soldiers of exemplary conduct for 21 years service in the infantry or 24 years in the cavalry, but in 1854 the qualifying period was reduced to 18 years and in 1977 to 15 years. Under changes announced in 2015 a clasp is now awarded for every 10 years served. During World War II commissioned officers were permitted to acquire this medal so long as they had completed at least 12 of their 18 years service in the ranks. Canada discontinued the LSGC medal in 1950 when the Canadian Forces Decoration was instituted, while South Africa replaced it with the John Chard Medal later the same year. From 1930 onwards the lettering of the reverse inscription was in tall, thin letters. In 1940 bars for further periods of service were authorised. The LSGC is invariably named to the recipient. The William IV and early Victorian issues (to 1854) were impressed in the style of the Waterloo Medal and also bore the date of discharge and award. The 1855 issue was not dated, while lettering was impressed in the style of the Military General Service Medal. Later Victorian issues, however, were engraved in various styles, while medals from 1901 onwards are impressed in small capitals of various types. Medals to Europeans in the Indian Army are engraved in cursive script. Recent research by Irvin Mortensen, however, reveals that some medals after 1850 were issued unnamed, and this also accounts for various unofficial styles of naming found on later medals. In keeping with the other branches of the armed forces the medal is now available to all ranks.*

1st type obv. Trophy of Arms with badge of Hanover.

2nd type obv. with badge of Hanover omitted and swivel suspender.

GV type C obverse with fixed suspender and "Commonwealth" bar.

Pre-1917 ribbon.

Later ribbon, used from 1917.

VALUE:

		Miniature
William IV small ring 1830–31	£850–1000	—
William IV large ring 1831–37	£750–950	—
Victoria without Hanoverian arms 1837–55	£250–350	—
Victoria swivelling scroll suspension 1855–74	£155–225	£35–45
Victoria small reverse lettering 1874–1901	£100–150	£30–35
Edward VII (A) 1902–10	£75–100	£30–35
George V (A) 1911–20	£65–85	£15–25
George V (A) fixed suspender 1920–30	£65–85	£15–25
George V (C) 1930–36, Regular Army bar	£65–85	£15–25
Commonwealth bar	From £75	£15–25
George VI (C) 1937–48, Regular Army bar	£55–80	£15–25
Commonwealth bar	From £75	£15–25
George VI (E) 1949–52, Regular Army bar	£65–85	£15–25
Elizabeth II 1953–54, Regular Army bar	£65–85	£15–25
Elizabeth II 1954–, Regular Army bar	£65–85	£15–25
Commonwealth bar	From £100	£15–25
To Royal Irish Regiment	£125–175	£15–25

230. ULSTER DEFENCE REGIMENT MEDAL FOR LONG SERVICE AND GOOD CONDUCT

Instituted: 1982.

Branch of Service: Ulster Defence Regiment.

Ribbon: Similar to the Military LSGC medal but with a central green stripe in addition.

Metal: Silver.

Size: 36mm.

Description: (Obverse) the imperial crowned bust of Queen Elizabeth II; (reverse) similar to the Military LSGC medal. Fitted with a fixed suspension bar inscribed UDR.

Comments: *Granted to personnel for 15 years exemplary service after 1 April 1970, with bars for additional 15-year periods. It is also awarded to officers provided that at least 12 of their 15 years service was in the ranks.*

VALUE:

Elizabeth II (B)	£300–450	*Miniature*	£12–18

231. VOLUNTEER OFFICER'S DECORATION

Instituted: 25 July 1892.

Branch of Service: Volunteer Force.

Ribbon: 38mm plain green, suspended from an oak bar brooch. Members of the Honourable Artillery Company were granted a distinctive ribbon in 1906, half scarlet, half dark blue with yellow edges—King Edward's racing colours.

Metal: Silver and silver-gilt.

Size: Height 42mm; max. width 35mm.

Description: An oval skeletal badge in silver and silver-gilt, with the royal cypher and crown in the centre, within a wreath of oak leaves. It is suspended by a plain ring with an oak leaf bar brooch fitted to the top of the ribbon. Although issued unnamed, many examples were subsequently engraved or impressed privately. Two versions of the Victorian decoration were produced, differing in the monogram— VR for United Kingdom recipients and VRI for recipients in the dominions and colonies.

Comments: *The basic qualification was 20 years commissioned service in the Volunteer Force, a precursor of the Territorial Army, non-commissioned service counting half. By Royal Warrant of 24 May 1894 the decoration was extended to comparable forces overseas, the qualifying period for service in India being reduced to 18 years. The colonial VD was superseded in 1899 by the Colonial Auxiliary Forces Officers Decoration and the Indian Volunteer Forces Officers Decoration. In the United Kingdom it was superseded by the Territorial Decoration, on the formation of the TF in 1908. A total of 4,710 decorations were awarded. Awards in Bermuda continued until 1930.*

VALUE:

		Miniature
Victoria VR	£150–175	£40–50
Victoria VRI	£300–350	£95–110
Edward VII	£150–175	£35–45
George V	£150–175	£30–40

HAC ribbon.

232. VOLUNTEER LONG SERVICE MEDAL

Instituted: 1894.

Branch of Service: Volunteer Force.

Ribbon: 32mm plain green, but members of the Honourable Artillery Company were granted a distinctive ribbon in 1906, half scarlet, half dark blue with yellow edges—King Edward's racing colours.

Metal: Silver.

Size: 36mm.

Description: (Obverse) effigy of the reigning monarch; (reverse) a laurel wreath on which is superimposed ribbons inscribed FOR LONG SERVICE IN THE VOLUNTEER FORCE.

Comments: *This medal was awarded for 20 years service in the ranks. Officers could also receive the medal, being eligible on account of their non-commissioned service. Many officers then gained sufficient commissioned service to be awarded either the Volunteer Decoration or (from 1908) the Territorial Decoration. The medal was extended to Colonial Forces in June 1898, the titles of the monarch being appropriately expanded for this version. This medal was superseded by the Territorial Force Efficiency Medal in 1908, although it continued to be awarded until 1930 in Bermuda, India, Isle of Man (Isle of Man Vols.) and the 7th Volunteer Battalion of the King's (Liverpool) Regiment.*

HAC ribbon.

VALUE:

		Miniature
Victoria Regina (C) (UK)	£75–100	
Unnamed	£45–50	£25–30
Victoria Regina et Imperatrix (C) (overseas)	£85–125	£25–30
Edwardus Rex (A)	£85–100	£18–30
Edwardus Rex et Imperator (A) (colonial)	£85–100	£18–30
Edwardus Kaisar-i-Hind (A) (India)	£100–120	£18–30
George V (A)		
India	£85–100	£18–25
Isle of Man	£250–300	£18–25
Bermuda	£150–200	£18–25

233. TERRITORIAL DECORATION

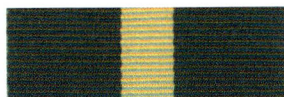

Instituted: 29 September 1908.

Branch of Service: Territorial Force, later Territorial Army.

Ribbon: 38mm plain dark green with a central yellow stripe suspended from an oak bar brooch. Members of the Honourable Artillery Company were granted a distinctive ribbon in 1906, half scarlet, half dark blue with yellow edges—King Edward's racing colours.

Metal: Silver and silver-gilt.

Size: Height 46mm; max. width 35mm.

Description: A skeletal badge with the crowned monogram of the sovereign surrounded by an oval oak wreath, fitted with a ring for suspension.

Comments: *Awarded for 20 years commissioned service, service in the ranks counting half and war service double. It was superseded by the Efficiency Decoration in 1930. A total of 4,783 decorations were awarded.*

VALUE:

		Miniature
Edward VII (585)	£250–275	£18–25
George V (4,198)	£200–250	£18–15

HAC ribbon.

234. TERRITORIAL FORCE EFFICIENCY MEDAL

Instituted: 1908.
Branch of Service: Territorial Force.
Ribbon: Originally 32mm plain dark green with a central yellow stripe but members of the Honourable Artillery Company were granted a distinctive ribbon in 1906, half scarlet, half dark blue with yellow edges—King Edward's household colours. In December 1919 the ribbon was changed to plain dark green with yellow edges.
Metal: Silver.
Size: Height 38mm; max. width 31mm.
Description: An oval medal fitted with claw and ring suspension. (Obverse) the sovereign's effigy; (reverse) inscribed with the name of the medal in four lines.
Comments: *Granted for a minimum of 12 years service in the Territorial Force. It was superseded in 1921 by the Territorial Efficiency Medal when the service was renamed. Bars were awarded for further periods of 12 years service.*

Original ribbon.

HAC ribbon.

VALUE:		Miniature
Edward VII (A) (11,800)	£150–175*	£18–25
Of these:		
With bar (537)	£200–250	
with second bars (64)	£300–350	
George V (A) (37,726)	£75–100	£18–25
George V first clasps	£130–150	

*Medals to Yeomanry regiments command a higher premium.

234A. TERRITORIAL FORCE IMPERIAL SERVICE BADGE

Instituted: 1912.
Branch of Service: Members of the Territorial Force.
Ribbon: None.
Metal: Cupro-nickel or brass.
Size: 10mm x 43mm
Description: A horizontal bar surmounted by a royal crown, the bar inscribed in raised lettering IMPERIAL SERVICE.
Comments: *Awarded to members of the Territorial Force who were prepared to serve outside the United Kingdom in defence of the Empire, mainly during the First World War.*

VALUE: £12–15

235. TERRITORIAL EFFICIENCY MEDAL

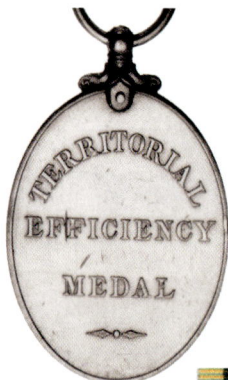

Instituted: 1921.
Branch of Service: Territorial Army.
Ribbon: 32mm plain dark green with yellow edges. Members of the HAC wear the ribbon of the Company as 234 above.
Metal: Silver.
Size: Height 38mm; max. width 31mm.
Description: As above, but with the name amended and inscribed in three lines.
Comments: *Introduced following the elevation of the Territorial Force to become the Territorial Army. It was superseded by the Efficiency Medal in 1930.*

VALUE:			
George V (A)	£85–120	*Miniature*	£10–18

236. EFFICIENCY DECORATION

*Second
?ard bars*

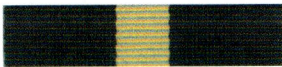

Instituted: 17 October 1930.
Branch of Service: Territorial Army (UK), the Indian Volunteer Forces and the Colonial Auxiliary Forces.
Ribbon: 38mm plain dark green with a central yellow stripe. In 1969, on the introduction of the T&AVR, the ribbon was altered to half blue, half green , with a central yellow stripe. Members of the Honourable Artillery Company wear half blue, half scarlet ribbon, with yellow edges.
Metal: Silver and silver-gilt.
Size: Height 54mm; max. width 37mm.
Description: An oval skeletal badge in silver and silver-gilt with the crowned monogram in an oak wreath, the ring for suspension being fitted to the top of the crown. It differs also from the previous decorations in having a suspender bar denoting the area of service: Territorial (UK), India, Canada, Fiji or other overseas country being inscribed as appropriate, but the previous ribbon was retained.
Comments: *Recipients in Britain were allowed to continue using the letters TD after their names, but in the Commonwealth the letters ED were used instead. The 20-year qualification was reduced to 12 years in 1949, bars for each additional 6 years being added. In 1969 the British suspender bar was changed to T & AVR, on the establishment of the Territorial and Army Volunteer Reserve. In 1982 the title of Territorial Army was resumed, so the inscription on the bar reverted to TERRITORIAL but the blue, yellow and green ribbon was retained. This decoration was superseded in the UK by the VRSM (No. 242A) in 2000. However, it is still current in some Commonwealth countries.*

Original ribbon.

Post-1969 ribbon.

HAC ribbon.

VALUE:

	Territorial	T&AVR	Commonwealth
George V	£150–175	—	From £175
George VI (GRI)	£85–100	—	From £175
George VI (GVIR)	£85–100	—	—
Elizabeth II	£100–125	£120–150	From £175
Miniature	**£20–25**	**£20–25**	**£20–25**

237. EFFICIENCY MEDAL

Instituted: 17 October 1930.
Branch of Service: Territorial Army (UK), Indian Volunteer Forces and Colonial Auxiliary Forces.
Ribbon: 32mm green with yellow edges. In 1969, on the introduction of the T&AVR, the ribbon was altered to half blue, half green, with yellow edges. Members of the Honourable Artillery Company wear half blue, half scarlet ribbon, with yellow edges.
Metal: Silver.

Original ribbon.

Post-1969 ribbon.

HAC ribbon.

237. EFFICIENCY MEDAL *continued*

Aa

Ab

Size: Height 39mm; max. width 32mm.

Description: An oval silver medal. (Obverse) the monarch's effigy; (reverse) inscribed FOR EFFICIENT SERVICE. In place of the simple ring suspension, however, there was now a fixed suspender bar decorated with a pair of palm leaves surmounted by a scroll inscribed TERRITORIAL or MILITIA (for UK volunteer forces), while overseas forces had the name of the country.

Comments: *This medal consolidated the awards to other ranks throughout the volunteer forces of Britain and the Commonwealth. The basic qualification was 12 years continuous efficient service, but war service and peacetime service in West Africa counted double. Additional bars with a crown were awarded for further periods of six years continuous efficient service. The Militia bar was granted to certain categories of the Supplementary Reserve until the formation of the Army Emergency Reserve in 1951. In 1969 the bar inscribed T & AVR was introduced. The bar TERRITORIAL was resumed in 1982 but the half blue, half green ribbon with yellow edges was retained. For the distinctive medal awarded in the Union of South Africa see number 254. Instead of the second obverse of Queen Elizabeth II, Canada adopted a type showing the Queen wearing the Imperial Crown. This medal was superseded in the UK by the VRSM (No. 242A) in 2000, although it is still current in some Commonwealth countries.*

VALUE:	Territorial	Militia	T&AVR	Commonwealth
George V (C)	£75–100	£150–175**	—	From £85*
George VI (Aa)	£60–85	£85–100	—	From £85*
George VI (Ab)	£60–85	£85–100	—	From £85*
Elizabeth II (A1)	£75–100	—	—	From £150*
Elizabeth II (A)	£75–100	—	£85–120	From £150*
Miniature	from £18			£85–95

*These prices are for the commoner Commonwealth types. However, some are extremely rare as can be seen in the table below where the issue numbers are indicated in brackets (where known).
**Only RE (176), R.Signals (94) and RAMC (42).

GEORGE V (C)	GEORGE VI (Aa)	GEORGE VI (Ab)	ELIZABETH II (A1)	ELIZABETH II (A)
—	—	—	Antigua (3)	—
Australia	Australia	Australia	Australia	Australia
Barbados	Barbados	Barbados	Barbados	Barbados
Bermuda	Bermuda	Bermuda	Bermuda	Bermuda
British Guiana (15)	British Guiana	British Guiana	British Guiana	—
British Honduras (1)	British Honduras (23)	British Honduras (3)	British Honduras (13)	—
—	Burma (111)	—	—	—
Canada	Canada	Canada	Canada (Rare)	Canada (Rare)
Ceylon	Ceylon	Ceylon	Ceylon (69)	—
—	Dominica (130)	—	—	—
Falkland Islands (29)	Falkland Islands (29)	—	Falkland Islands	Falkland Islands
Fiji (29)	Fiji (35)	Fiji (9)	Fiji (7)	Fiji (33)
—	—	Gibraltar (15)	Gibraltar	Gibraltar
—	Gold Coast (275)	Gold Coast (35)	—	—
—	Grenada (1)	—	—	—
—	Guernsey (3)	Guernsey (4)	Guernsey (3)	Guernsey (35)
Hong Kong (21)	Hong Kong (50)	Hong Kong (224)	Hong Kong (145)	Hong Kong (268)
India	India	—	—	—
Jamaica	Jamaica	Jamaica	Jamaica	—
—	Jersey (40)	Jersey (7)	—	Jersey (1)

237. EFFICIENCY MEDAL continued

GEORGE V (C)	GEORGE VI (Aa)	GEORGE VI (Ab)	ELIZABETH II (A)	ELIZABETH II (B)
—	Kenya (1)	Kenya (159)	Kenya (36)	—
—	Leeward Islands (49)	Leeward Islands (14)	Leeward Islands (2)	—
—	Malaya	Malaya	Malaya (54)	—
—	Malta (320)	Malta (31)	—	Malta (36)
—	—	—	Mauritius (71)	—
—	—	—	—	Montserrat (6)
New Zealand (71)	New Zealand (34)	New Zealand	New Zealand	New Zealand
Nigeria (1)	—	Nigeria (7)	Nigeria (3)	—
—	—	—	Rhodesia/Nyasaland (7)	—
—	St Lucia (2)	—	St Christopher Nevis (13)	—
—	St Vincent (1)	—	—	—
S. Rhodesia (17)	S. Rhodesia (230)	S. Rhodesia (24)	S. Rhodesia (6)	—
—	Trinidad/Tobago (228)	Trinidad/Tobago (46)	Trinidad/Tobago (5)	—

238. ARMY EMERGENCY RESERVE DECORATION

Instituted: 17 November 1952.
Branch of Service Army Emergency Reserve.
Ribbon: 38mm dark blue with a central yellow stripe.
Metal: Silver and silver-gilt.
Size: Height 55mm; max. width 37mm.
Description: An oval skeletal badge, with the monarch's cypher surmounted by a crown in an oak wreath. Suspension is by a ring through the top of the crown and it is worn with a brooch bar inscribed ARMY EMERGENCY RESERVE.
Comments: *Awarded for 12 years commissioned service. Officers commissioned in the Army Supplementary Reserve or Army Emergency Reserve of Officers between 8 August 1942 and 15 May 1948 who transferred to the Regular Army Reserve of Officers after 10 years service were also eligible. War service counts double and previous service in the ranks counts half. The ERD was abolished in 1967 on the formation of the Territorial and Army Volunteer Reserve.*

VALUE:

Elizabeth II	£150–200	*Miniature*	£20–25

239. ARMY EMERGENCY RESERVE EFFICIENCY MEDAL

Instituted: 1 September 1953.
Branch of Service: Army Emergency Reserve.
Ribbon: 32mm dark blue with three central yellow stripes.
Metal: Silver.
Size: Height 39mm; max. width 31mm.
Description: This oval medal is similar to the Efficiency Medal previously noted but has a scroll bar inscribed ARMY EMERGENCY RESERVE.
Comments: *Awarded for 12 years service in the ranks or for service in the Supplementary Reserve between 1924 and 1948 prior to transferring to the Army Emergency Reserve. War service counted double. It was abolished in 1967 following the formation of the Territorial and Army Volunteer Reserve. .A very small number of awards were issued bearing the George VI effigy.*

VALUE:

Elizabeth II	£150–200	*Miniature*	£15–20

240. IMPERIAL YEOMANRY LONG SERVICE AND GOOD CONDUCT MEDAL

Instituted: December 1904, by Army Order no. 211.
Branch of Service: Imperial Yeomanry.
Ribbon: 32mm plain yellow.
Metal: Silver.
Size: Height 38mm; max. width 31mm.
Description: Upright oval. (Obverse) the sovereign's effigy; (reverse) inscribed IMPERIAL YEOMANRY round the top and the usual long service and good conduct inscription in four lines across the middle.
Comments: *Awarded to NCOs and troopers of the Imperial Yeomanry for 10 years exemplary service. It became obsolete in 1908 when the Territorial Force was created. Nevertheless 48 medals were awarded in 1909, one in 1910, one in 1914 and one in 1917. All medals were issued with the bust of King Edward VII on the obverse.*

VALUE:

Edward VII (A) (1674)	£450–500	*Miniature*	£60–80	

241. MILITIA LONG SERVICE AND GOOD CONDUCT MEDAL

Instituted: December 1904, by Army Order no. 211.
Branch of Service: Militia.
Ribbon: 32mm plain light blue.
Metal: Silver.
Size: Height 38mm; max. width 31mm.
Description: An upright oval medal. (Obverse) the effigy of the monarch; (reverse) similar to the preceding but inscribed MILITIA at the top of the reverse.
Comments: *Qualifying service was 18 years and 15 annual camps. It was superseded by the Efficiency Medal with the Militia bar in 1930. A total of 1,587 medals were awarded between 1905 and 1930 (RGA 341, RE 15, RE Submarine Miners 8, Infantry 988, Channel Islands 89, Malta 131, Bermuda 15).*

VALUE:

		Miniature
Edward VII (A) (1446)	£450–500	£100–130
George V (C) (141)	£600–800	£100–130

242. SPECIAL RESERVE LONG SERVICE AND GOOD CONDUCT MEDAL

Instituted: June 1908, by Army Order no. 126.
Branch of Service: Special Reserve.
Ribbon: Dark blue with a central light blue stripe.
Metal: Silver.
Size: Height 38mm; max. width 31mm.
Description: As the foregoing but inscribed SPECIAL RESERVE round the top of the reverse.
Comments: *Awarded to NCOs and men of the Special Reserve who completed 15 years service and attended 15 camps. A total of 1,078 medals were awarded between 1908 and 1936 with solitary awards in 1947 and 1953. Summary of awards: RA, RFA, RGA 165, RE 9, Royal Anglesey RE 3, Royal Monmouthshire R. 5, RAMC 4, Labour Corps 4, MGC 1. North Irish Horse 16, South Irish Horse 31, King Edward's Horse 14, Infantry 823, Channel Islands 5. Of these, two awards (1 to the RGA, 1 to the South Irish Horse), were subsequently cancelled.*

VALUE:

		Miniature
Edward VII (A) (428)	£500–600	£110–135
George V (C) (650)	£500–600	£110–135

242A. VOLUNTEER RESERVES SERVICE MEDAL

Instituted: 1999.

Branch of Service: Volunteer reserves of all three armed services.

Ribbon: Dark green with three narrow central stripes of dark blue, scarlet and light blue, separated from the green by two narrow stripes of gold. Members of the Honourable Artillery Company wear half blue, half scarlet ribbon, with yellow edges.

Metal: Silver.

Size: Height 38mm; width 32mm.

Description: An oval medal. (Obverse) the sovereign's effigy; (reverse) inscribed FOR SERVICE IN THE VOLUNTEER RESERVES above a spray of oak.

Comments: *Awarded to all ranks of the volunteer reserves who complete ten years of reckonable qualifying service. Bars for additional five-year periods of reckonable qualifying service are also awarded. This medal replaces the Royal Naval Reserve Decoration, the Royal Naval Reserve Long Service and Good Conduct Medal, the Efficiency Decoration, the Efficiency Medal and the Air Efficiency Award. Since 2015 recipients are entitled to use the post-nominals VR, backdated to 1999.*

VALUE:	£250–300	*Miniature*	£10–15

HAC ribbon

242B. ROYAL MILITARY ASYLUM GOOD CONDUCT MEDAL

First type reverse.

Instituted: c.1850.

Branch of Service: Students in the Royal Military Asylum.

Ribbon: Plain red or crimson.

Metal: Silver or bronze.

Size: 36mm.

Description: (Obverse) the royal arms, garnished, crested and with supporters; (reverse) first type ROYAL MILITARY ASYLUM, second type: DUKE OF YORK'S ROYAL MILITARY SCHOOL round the circumference, enclosing a laurel wreath inscribed across the centre FOR GOOD CONDUCT. Fitted with a scrolled suspender and brooch. Engraved in upright capitals with the name of the recipient.

Comments: *The Royal Military Asylum was established for the education of the sons of soldiers who had been killed in action or who had died while in the service. It was renamed the "Duke of York's Royal Military School" in 1892 and subsequent medals are thus inscribed. The actual criteria for the award of the medal are not known.*

VALUE:	"Asylum"	£125–175
	"School"	£100–150

Second type reverse.

242C. ARMED FORCES VETERAN LAPEL BADGE

Date: May 2004.
Branch of Service: Former members of HM Armed Forces, Royal Fleet Auxiliary, Cyprus Regiment, Merchant Navy who took part in a naval action, Home Guard and Polish Forces under UK command.
Ribbon: None.
Description: Badge surmounted by a gold imperial crown with VETERAN on an enamelled scroll at the foot. The badge bears the insignia of the armed services with H.M. ARMED FORCES round the top of the circumference.
Comments: *Originally available to veterans of HM Armed Forces including the Royal Fleet Auxiliary, who served up to December 31, 1954, but later extended. It is intended for any service in the Armed Forces.*

VALUE: £10–15

242D. MERCHANT SEAFARERS VETERAN LAPEL BADGE

Instituted: 2006.
Branch of Service: Personnel of the Merchant Navy.
Ribbon: None.
Description: Similar to 242C but with the badge superimposed on the Red Ensign.
Comments: *Available to surviving veterans of the Merchant Navy who contributed to HM Armed Forces military operations in World War II. Holders of this badge are not eligible for the Armed Forces Veteran badge (242C).*

VALUE: £15–20

242E. ARCTIC EMBLEM

Instituted: 2006.
Branch of Service: Personnel of the Armed Forces and the Merchant Navy
Ribbon: None.
Description: A white five-pointed star edged in gold, with a red centre, above which is a blue arc bearing the words THE ARCTIC.
Comments: *Available to surviving veterans who served north of the Arctic Circle and west of the Urals for at least one day between 3 September 1939 and 8 May 1945. The emblem is also available to the next of kin of deceased veterans.*

VALUE: £20–25

242F. BEVIN BOYS LAPEL BADGE

Date: 2007.
Branch of Service: Former Bevin Boys.
Ribbon: None.
Description: Oval badge enamelled with the outline of a pit-head winch in white on a black background, surrounded by the words BEVIN BOYS VETERANS and with a silhouette of a miner's head with helmet.
Comments: *Available to surviving veterans of the Bevin Boys of World War II.*

VALUE: £10–15

242G. WOMEN'S LAND ARMY AND TIMBER CORPS LAPEL BADGE

Date: 2007.
Branch of Service: Former members of the Women's Land Army or Women's Timber Corps.
Ribbon: None.
Description: Enamelled replica of the original WLA badge surmounted by a crown.
Comments: *Available to surviving veterans of the Women's Land Army and Women's Timber Corps of World War II.*

VALUE: £10–15

242H. AIR TRANSPORT AUXILIARY LAPEL BADGE

Date: 2008.
Branch of Service: Former members of the Air Transport Auxiliary.
Ribbon: None.
Description: Enamelled badge depicting an eagle in flight on a turquoise background surrounded by the words AIR TRANSPORT AUXILIARY on a dark blue ribbon with laurel wreath surround.
Comments: *Available to veterans of the Air Transport Auxiliary of World War II.*

VALUE: £10–15

242 I. GC & CS LAPEL BADGE

Date: 2012.
Branch of Service: Former employees at Bletchley Park and its outstations.
Ribbon: None.
Description: Enamelled badge depicting the GCHQ emblem surrounded by a laurel wreath and the dates 1939-1945, with the legend GC&CS above, BLETCHLEY PARK AND ITS OUTSTATIONS below.
Comments: *Available to surviving personnel who worked at Bletchley Park during World War II.*

VALUE: £20–25

Statue of Women's Land Army and Timber Corps at the National Memorial Arboretum, Alrewas.

242J. MERCHANT NAVY MEDAL

Instituted: 1 June 2005.

Branch of Service: Merchant Navy.

Ribbon: Equal halves of red and green divided by a narrow white stripe. Thin gold edge stripes were added in 2011 to avoid confusion with MYB 169 and to indicate special achievement

Metal: Rhodium plated cupro-nickel.   **Size:** 28mm.

Description: (Obverse) The bust of Admiral Nelson surrounded by the legend "THE MERCHANT NAVY MEDAL" above and "1805 - TRAFALGAR - 2005" below; (reverse) the Merchant Navy logo with the inscription "FOR MERITORIOUS SERVICE" below.

Comments: *This medal was instituted to recognise the meritorious service of British registered Merchant Seafarers. The medal was awarded annually to a maximum of 15 men or women who were judged to have made a significant contribution to merchant shipping, its operations, development, personnel, welfare or safety, or who had performed an act of bravery afloat. The names of recipients were listed in the London Gazette and the award carries the post-nominals MNM. A small silver anchor was added to the ribbon to denote an act of bravery at sea. In 2015 the medal was replaced by MYB242K.*

VALUE: —

242K. QUEEN'S / KING'S MERCHANT NAVY MEDAL FOR MERITORIOUS SERVICE

Instituted: 2016.

Branch of Service: Merchant Navy.

Ribbon: Equal stripes of green, red, white, red, green.

Metal: Rhodium plated cupro-nickel.

Size: 36mm.

Description: (Obverse) uncrowned bust of reigning monarch with the corresponding legend; (reverse) the Merchant Navy logo with the inscription "FOR MERITORIOUS SERVICE" below.

Comments: *Like the previous medal (MYB242J), which it replaces, this medal was instituted to recognise the meritorious service of personnel serving in the Merchant Navy or the Fishing fleets of the United Kingdom, the Isle of Man and the Channel Islands. The medal is awarded annually to a maximum of 20 men or women who are judged to have made a significant contribution to merchant shipping, its operations, development, personnel, welfare or safety and show particularly valuable devotion to duty and exemplary service so as to serve as an outstanding example to others. Recipients will typically have given 20 years of good conduct and exemplary service. The names of recipients are listed in the London Gazette and the award carries the post-nominals QMNM / KMNM.*

VALUE: —   *Miniature*   £12–18

243. INDIAN ARMY LONG SERVICE & GOOD CONDUCT MEDAL FOR EUROPEANS 1848

Instituted: 20 May 1848, by General Order of the Indian Government.
Branch of Service: Indian Army.
Ribbon: Plain crimson.
Metal: Silver.
Size: 36mm.
Description: (Obverse) a trophy of arms, not unlike its British counterpart, but a shield bearing the arms of the Honourable East India Company was placed in the centre. (Reverse) engraved with the recipient's name and service details. In 1859 some 100 medals were sent to India by mistake, these had the Wyon profile of Queen Victoria on the obverse and a reverse inscribed FOR LONG SERVICE AND GOOD CONDUCT within an oak wreath with a crown at the top and a fouled anchor at the foot.
Comments: *Awarded to European NCOs and other ranks of the Indian Army on discharge after 21 years meritorious service. It was discontinued in 1873 after which the standard Army LSGC medal was granted.*

VALUE:		Miniature
HEIC arms	£500–650	£110–165
Victoria (A) (100)	£650–750	£90–110

HEIC arms type.

Victoria type.

244. INDIAN ARMY LONG SERVICE & GOOD CONDUCT MEDAL (INDIAN)

Instituted: 1888.
Branch of Service: Indian Army.
Ribbon: Originally plain crimson but white edges were added in 1917.
Metal: Silver.
Size: 36mm.
Description: (Obverse) the sovereign's effigy; (reverse) the word INDIA set within a palm wreath surrounded by a border of lotus flowers and leaves. The inscription FOR LONG SERVICE AND GOOD CONDUCT appears between the wreath and the lotus flowers.
Comments: *Awarded to native Indian NCOs and other ranks for 20 years meritorious service. The medal became obsolete in 1947 when India achieved independence.*

VALUE:		Miniature
Victoria (B) Kaisar-i-Hind	£150–175	£100–110
Edward VII (A) Kaisar-i-Hind	£100–125	£100–110
George V (D) Kaisar-i-Hind	£90–100	£65–85
George V (C) Rex Et Indiae Imp	£90–100	£65–85
George VI (B)	£90–100	65–85

245. INDIAN VOLUNTEER FORCES OFFICERS' DECORATION

Instituted: May 24, 1894, by extension to the Volunteer Officer Decoration (MYB 231).

Branch of Service: Indian Volunteer Forces.

Ribbon: Plain dark green (see Comments below).

Metal: Silver and silver-gilt.

Size: Height 65mm; max. width 36mm.

Description: An oval skeletal badge with the royal cipher in the centre, surrounded by a band inscribed INDIAN VOLUNTEER FORCES and surmounted by a crown. Designed for a 32mm ribbon, the decoration is fitted with a plain straight suspender behind the crown and hung from a bar brooch with an oak leaf frieze.

Comments: *Awarded for 18 years commissioned service, with service in the ranks counting half and war service double. Replacing the VD with VRI cipher in 1903, the Indian Volunteer Decoration was modelled on the Colonial Auxiliary Forces Decoration (MYB 246) and superseded by the Efficiency Decoration (MYB 236) in 1930. A total of 1,171 decorations are known to have been awarded between 1903 and 1934. Normally issued named, with the recipient's rank, name and unit engraved on the reverse. Seven styles of engraving have been observed over the life of the award. While early and late decorations may be hallmarked, the majority are not.*

VALUE:		Miniature
Edward VII	£300–350	£55–65
George V	£300–350	£35–45

246. COLONIAL AUXILIARY FORCES OFFICERS' DECORATION

Instituted: 18 May 1899.

Branch of Service: Colonial Auxiliary Forces.

Ribbon: Plain green (see Comments below).

Metal: Silver and silver-gilt.

Size: Height 66mm; max. width 35mm.

Description: Similar to the previous decoration, with an oval band inscribed COLONIAL AUXILIARY FORCES.

Comments: *Awarded to officers of auxiliary forces everywhere except in India for 20 years commissioned service. Service in the ranks counting half and service in West Africa counting double. Although issued unnamed, it was usually impressed or engraved privately. Examples to officers in the smaller colonies command a considerable premium. It became obsolete in 1930. The suspension of the medal is by a flattened loop which is only 32mm wide although it was intended to take a 38mm ribbon—the 32mm ribbon is therefore usually worn on the medal and the 38mm on the tunic.*

VALUE:		Miniature
Victoria	£350–375	£90–100
Edward VII	£225–275	£80–90
George V	£175–250	£55–65

247. COLONIAL AUXILIARY FORCES LONG SERVICE MEDAL

Instituted: May 18, 1899.
Branch of Service: Colonial Auxiliary Forces.
Ribbon: Plain green.
Metal: Silver.
Size: 36mm.
Description: (Obverse) the effigy of the reigning monarch; (reverse) an elaborate rococo frame surmounted by a crown and enclosing the five-line text FOR LONG SERVICE IN THE COLONIAL AUXILIARY FORCES.
Comments: *Awarded for 20 years service in the ranks, West African service counting double. It was superseded in 1930 by the Efficiency Medal with the appropriate colonial or dominion bar.*

VALUE:		Miniature
Victoria (D)	£100–125	£30–40
Edward VII (A)	£80–110	£25–30
George V (A)	£80–110	£18–25

248. COLONIAL LONG SERVICE AND GOOD CONDUCT MEDALS

Instituted: May 31, 1895.
Branch of Service: Indian and other Colonial forces.
Ribbon: Crimson with a central stripe denoting the country of service (see no. 212).
Metal: Silver.
Size: 36mm.
Description: Similar to its British counterpart except that the name of the appropriate colony appeared on the reverse. The obverse of the Victorian award for the Colony of Natal depicts the Royal coat of arms.
Comments: *Awarded to warrant officers, NCOs and other ranks for meritorious service and long service and good conduct. Medals of the individual Australian colonies were superseded in 1902 by those inscribed COMMONWEALTH OF AUSTRALIA. The Colonial LSGC medal was replaced in 1909 by the Permanent Forces of the Empire Beyond the Seas LSGC award.*

VALUE:	From £750	Miniature	£85–110

249. PERMANENT FORCES OF THE EMPIRE BEYOND THE SEAS LONG SERVICE AND GOOD CONDUCT MEDAL

Instituted: 1909.
Branch of Service: Colonial and Dominion forces.
Ribbon: Maroon bearing a broad white central stripe with a narrow black stripe at its centre.
Metal: Silver.
Size: 36mm.
Description: (Obverse) the effigy of the reigning sovereign; (reverse) the legend PERMANENT FORCES OF THE EMPIRE BEYOND THE SEAS round the circumference, with FOR LONG SERVICE AND GOOD CONDUCT in four lines across the centre.
Comments: *This award replaced the various colonial LSGC medals, being itself superseded in 1930 by the LSGC (Military) Medal with appropriate dominion or colonial bar. It was awarded for 18 years exemplary service.*

VALUE:		Miniature
Edward VII (A)	£300–400	£65–90
George V (A)	£150–200	£55–65

250. ROYAL WEST AFRICA FRONTIER FORCE LONG SERVICE & GOOD CONDUCT MEDAL

Instituted: September 1903.
Branch of Service: Royal West Africa Frontier Force.
Ribbon: Crimson with a relatively broad green central stripe.
Metal: Silver.
Size: 36mm.
Description: (Obverse) the effigy of the reigning monarch. Two reverse types were used, the word ROYAL being added to the regimental title in June 1928.
Comments: *Awarded to native NCOs and other ranks for 18 years exemplary service.*

VALUE: £300–350   *Miniature*   £30–35

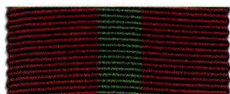

251. KING'S AFRICAN RIFLES LONG SERVICE AND GOOD CONDUCT MEDAL

Instituted: March 1907.
Branch of Service: King's African Rifles.
Ribbon: Crimson with a broad green central stripe.
Metal: Silver.
Size: 36mm.
Description: Very similar to the foregoing, apart from the regimental name round the top of the reverse.
Comments: *Awarded to native NCOs and other ranks for 18 years exemplary service.*

VALUE:		*Miniature*
Edward VII	£650–850	—
George V	£250–300	£55–65
George VI (B)	£250–300	£45–55
Elizabeth II	£500–750	£30–40

252. TRANS-JORDAN FRONTIER FORCE LONG SERVICE AND GOOD CONDUCT MEDAL

Instituted: 20 May 1938.
Branch of Service: Trans-Jordan Frontier Force.
Ribbon: Crimson with a green central stripe.
Metal: Silver.
Size: 36mm.
Description: Similar to the previous medals, with the name of the Force round the circumference.
Comments: *This rare silver medal was awarded for 16 years service in the ranks of the Trans-Jordan Frontier Force. Service in the Palestine Gendarmerie or Arab Legion counted, so long as the recipient transferred to the Frontier Force without a break in service. Only 112 medals were awarded before it was abolished in 1948.*

VALUE: £600–800

253. SOUTH AFRICA PERMANENT FORCE LONG SERVICE AND GOOD CONDUCT MEDAL

Instituted: 29 December 1939.
Branch of Service: South African forces.
Ribbon: Crimson with white stripes.
Metal: Silver.
Size: 36mm.
Description: (Obverse) Crowned effigy of King George VI; (reverse) FOR LONG SERVICE AND GOOD CONDUCT in four lines across the upper half and VIR LANGDURIGE DIENS EN GOEIE GEDRAG in four lines across the lower half. It also differs from its British counterpart in having a bilingual suspension bar.
Comments: *Awarded to NCOs and other ranks with a minimum of 18 years service.*

VALUE:		*Miniature*
George VI (B)	£120–140	£35–45
George VI (C)	£150–170	£35–45

254. EFFICIENCY MEDAL (SOUTH AFRICA)

Instituted: December 1939.
Branch of Service: Coast Garrison and Active Citizen Forces of South Africa.
Ribbon: 32mm plain dark green with yellow edges.
Metal: Silver.
Size: Height 38mm; max. width 30mm.
Description: An oval silver medal rather similar to the Efficiency Medal (number 237) but having a scroll bar inscribed UNION OF SOUTH AFRICA with its Afrikaans equivalent below. The reverse likewise bears a bilingual inscription.
Comments: *Awarded for 12 years non-commissioned service in the Coast Garrison and Active Citizen Forces. A bar, bearing in the centre a crown, was awarded for every six years of additional service. It was replaced in 1952 by the John Chard Medal.*

VALUE:	£65–75	*Miniature*	£35–45

254A. ROYAL HONG KONG REGIMENT DISBANDMENT MEDAL

Instituted: 1995.
Branch of Service: Royal Hong Kong Regiment (Volunteers).
Ribbon: Half red and half blue with a central yellow stripe.
Metal: Cupro-nickel.
Size: 38mm.
Description: (Obverse) Regimental badge with dates 1854 and 1995 either side and ROYAL HONG KONG REGIMENT THE VOLUNTEERS around. (Reverse) Coat of Arms of Hong Kong with DISBANDMENT MEDAL 3rd SEPTEMBER 1995 (date of disbandment) around.
Comment: *Available to those serving with the Regiment as the end of the Crown Colony became imminent. Recipients, however, had to purchase a full size and a miniature medal in a plush case.*

VALUE:	£75–100	*Miniature*	£55–65

255. CANADIAN FORCES DECORATION

Instituted: 15 December 1949.
Branch of Service: Canadian Forces.
Ribbon: 38mm orange-red divided into four equal parts by three thin white stripes.
Metal: Silver-gilt (George VI) or gilded tombac brass or bronze (Elizabeth II).
Size: Height 35mm; max. width 37mm.
Description: A decagonal (ten-sided) medal. The George VI issue has a suspension bar inscribed CANADA and the recipient's details engraved on the reverse, whereas the Elizabethan issue has no suspension bar, the recipient's details being impressed or engraved on the rim and the word "CANADA" appears at the base of the effigy. The reverse has a naval crown at the top, three maple leaves across the middle and an eagle in flight across the foot. The George VI version has the royal cypher superimposed on the maple leaves.
Comments: *Awarded to both officers and men of the Canadian regular and reserve forces for 12 years exemplary service. A bar, gold in colour, bearing the shield from the arms of Canada surmounted by the crown is awarded for each additional 10 years of qualifying service. Approximately 2,400 medals and 3,000 clasps are awarded annually.*

VALUE:

		Miniature
George VI (E)	£75–100	£12–25
Elizabeth II (D)	£30–45	£12–25

256. VICTORIA VOLUNTEER LONG AND EFFICIENT SERVICE MEDAL

1st type obv.

Instituted: 26 January 1881 but not given royal sanction until 21 April 1882.
Branch of Service: Volunteer Forces, Victoria.
Ribbon: White, with broad crimson stripes at the sides.
Metal: Silver.
Size: 39mm.
Description: (Obverse) the crowned badge of Victoria with LOCAL FORCES VICTORIA round the circumference; (reverse) inscribed FOR LONG AND EFFICIENT SERVICE. Two types of obverse exist, differing in the motto surrounding the colonial emblem. The first version has AUT PACE AUT BELLO (both in peace and war) while the second version is inscribed PRO DEO ET PATRIA (for God and country).
Comments: *Awarded to officers and men of the Volunteers in the colony of Victoria for 15 years efficient service. Awards to officers ended in 1894 with the introduction of the Volunteer Officers Decoration. This medal was replaced by the Commonwealth of Australia LSGC medal in 1902.*

VALUE: £800–1200   *Miniature*   £220–330

2nd type obv.

1st and 2nd type rev.

257. NEW ZEALAND LONG AND EFFICIENT SERVICE MEDAL

Instituted: 1 January 1887.
Branch of Service: Volunteer and Permanent Militia Forces of New Zealand.
Ribbon: Originally plain crimson, but two white central stripes were added in 1917.
Metal: Silver.
Size: 36mm.
Description: (Obverse) an imperial crown on a cushion with crossed sword and sceptre and NZ below, within a wreath of oak-leaves (left) and wattle (right) and having four five-pointed stars, representing the constellation Southern Cross, spaced in the field; (reverse) inscribed FOR LONG AND EFFICIENT SERVICE. Plain ring suspension.
Comments: *Awarded for 16 years' continuous or 20 years' non-continuous service in the Volunteer and Permanent Militia Forces of New Zealand. It became obsolete in 1931 following the introduction of the LSGC (Military) medal with bar for New Zealand.*

VALUE: £100–150   *Miniature* £45–55

258. NEW ZEALAND VOLUNTEER SERVICE MEDAL

Instituted: 1902.
Branch of Service: Volunteer Forces, New Zealand.
Ribbon: Plain drab khaki.
Metal: Silver.
Size: 36mm
Description: (Obverse) a right-facing profile of King Edward VII with NEW ZEALAND VOLUNTEER round the top and 12 YEARS SERVICE MEDAL round the foot; (reverse) a kiwi surrounded by a wreath. Plain ring suspension.
Comments: *This rare silver medal (obsolete by 1912) was awarded for 12 years' service. Two reverse dies were used. In type I (1902–04) the kiwi's beak almost touches the ground, whereas in Type II (1905–12) there is a space between the tip of the beak and the ground. Only about 100 of Type I were produced, but 636 of Type II.*

VALUE: Type I   £250–350   *Miniature* £110–130
          Type II   £200–250

259. NEW ZEALAND TERRITORIAL SERVICE MEDAL

Instituted: 1912.
Branch of Service: Territorial Force, New Zealand.
Ribbon: Originally as above, but replaced in 1917 by a ribbon of dark khaki edged with crimson.
Metal: Silver.
Size: 36mm.
Description: (Obverse) left-facing bust of King George V in field marshal's uniform; (reverse) similar to the above.
Comments: *It replaced the foregoing on the formation of the Territorial Force on March 17, 1911, from which date the old Volunteer Force ceased to exist but became obsolete itself in 1931 when the Efficiency Medal with New Zealand bar was adopted.*

VALUE:
   George V   £80–100   *Miniature* £35–55

261. ULSTER DEFENCE REGIMENT MEDAL

Instituted: 1982.
Branch of Service: Ulster Defence Regiment.
Ribbon: Dark green with a yellow central stripe edged in red.
Metal: Silver.
Size: 36mm.
Description: (Obverse) crowned head of Elizabeth II (B); (reverse) crowned harp and inscription ULSTER DEFENCE REGIMENT with a suspender of laurel leaves surmounted by a scroll bar bearing the regiment's initials.
Comments: *Awarded to part-time officers and men of the Ulster Defence Regiment with 12 years' continuous service since 1 April 1970. A bar for each additional six-year period is awarded. Officers are permitted to add the letters UD after their names. This medal is superseded by the Northern Ireland Home Service Medal (MYB 261B).*

VALUE:

Elizabeth II (B)	£350–450	*Miniature*	*£20–25*

261A. ULSTER DEFENCE REGIMENT MEDALLION

Instituted: 1987.
Branch of Service: Relatives of personnel of the Ulster Defence Regiment killed whilst on duty.
Ribbon: Dark green with a yellow central stripe edged in red, as MYB261.
Metal: Silver.
Size: 36mm.
Description: Uniface medal showing a crowned Irish harp flanked by sprays of shamrocks. Ring suspension. Ribbons of awards to widows and other female relatives mounted as a bow with a brooch fitment.
Comments: *Designed by Colour Sergeant Win Clark and struck by Spink & Son, it was commissioned by the Regiment for presentation to the families of UDR personnel killed during the conflict in Northern Ireland as a token of appreciation.*

VALUE: —

261B. NORTHERN IRELAND HOME SERVICE MEDAL

Instituted: 1992.
Branch of Service: Part time members of the Ulster Defence Regiment and the Royal Irish Regiment.
Ribbon: Dark green with a light blue central stripe.
Metal: Silver.
Size: 36mm.
Description: (Obverse) crowned head of Elizabeth II (B); (reverse) a scroll bearing the inscription FOR HOME SERVICE IN NORTHERN IRELAND surmounted by a crown, superimposed on a design of flax with harps below.
Comments: *Awarded to part-time officers and men of the Ulster Defence Regiment or Royal Irish Regiment with 12 years' continuous efficient service after 1 July 1980. A bar for each additional six-year period is awarded. Next of kin of eligible deceased members can apply for the medal.*

VALUE: £300–400 *Miniature* *£15–20*

262. CADET FORCES MEDAL

Instituted: February 1, 1950.
Branch of Service: Cadet Forces.
Ribbon: A broad green central band bordered by thin red stripes flanked by a dark blue stripe (left) and light blue stripe (right, with yellow edges.
Metal: Cupro-nickel.
Size: 36mm.
Description: (Obverse) the effigy of the reigning monarch; (reverse) a hand holding aloft the torch of learning with the words "THE CADET FORCES MEDAL" around. Medals are named to recipients on the rim, in impressed capitals.
Comments: *Awarded to uniformed volunteers of the Cadet Forces in recognition of long and exemplary service in the Cadet Forces. Service may reckon from September 3, 1926, with service between September 3, 1939 and September 2, 1945 counting two-fold. Until June 30, 1971, officers and non-commissioned officers only were awarded the medal, the qualification for which was 12 years' continuous service, with clasps for successive periods of 12 years' service. From July 1, 1971, cadet service over the age of 18 years of age could reckon for the medal and the qualifying period for the clasp was reduced to eight years, which need not be continuous. With effect from April 1, 1999, the qualifying period for the clasp was reduced to six years. Awards are now governed by the Royal Warrant dated November 19, 2001 which consolidates amendments to earlier Royal Warrants and extends the qualification and recognition provisions. Under JSP814 (1st edition) 2006, service for the medal did not have to be continuous; but JSP814 (final dated 31 March 2011) now states service to be continuous. Service for the clasp does not need to be continuous.*

The maximum cadet service is four years; other reckonable services includes the UK Volunteer Services, OTC, University Royal Naval Units and University Air Squadrons (maximum three years and not counted towards the Volunteer Services Medal or its predecessors), and Regular forces (maximum three years and not counted towards a long service award). When the ribbon alone is worn, the award of each clasp is denoted by a silver rose. To denote service beyond the award of three clasps, the following are to be worn: Four clasps—one gold rose, Five clasps—one gold rose and one silver rose, Six clasps—one gold rose and two silver roses, Seven clasps—two gold roses. Award of the medal and clasp is promulgated in the London Gazette. Issued to those qualifying in New Zealand under the terms of a Royal Warrant dated February 1, 1950 and the New Zealand Cadet Forces Medal Regulations dated January 13, 1954.

VALUE:		*Miniature*
George VI (C)	£100–125	£10–12
Elizabeth II (A1, BRITT: OMN)	£125–150	£10–12
Elizabeth II (A, DEI GRATIA)	£85–125	£10–12

263. ROYAL OBSERVER CORPS MEDAL

Instituted: 31 January 1950 but not awarded until 1953.
Branch of Service: Royal Observer Corps.
Ribbon: Pale blue with a broad central silver-grey stripe edged in dark blue.
Metal: Cupro-nickel.
Size: 36mm.
Description: (Obverse) effigy of the reigning monarch; (reverse) an artist's impression of a coast-watcher of Elizabethan times, holding a torch aloft alongside a signal fire, with other signal fires on hilltops in the background with the words "ROYAL OBSERVER CORPS MEDAL" around and the words "FOREWARNED IS FOREARMED" on a scroll below The medal hangs from a suspender of an eagle with outstretched wings. An obverse die with the effigy of George VI was engraved, but no medals were struck from it.
Comments: *Awarded to part-time officers and observers who have completed 12 years' satisfactory service and full-time members for 24 years service. A bar is awarded for each additional 12-year period. Home Office scientific officers and other non Royal Observer Corps members of the United Kingdom Warning and Monitoring Organisation were eligible for the Civil Defence Medal (no. 264) until being stood down on September 30, 1991. This entailed serving for 15 years alongside ROC members who received their own medal for 12 years' service.*

Long Service bar.

VALUE:		*Miniature*
Elizabeth II (B)	£300–350	—
Elizabeth II (C)	£250–300	£20–30

264. CIVIL DEFENCE LONG SERVICE MEDAL

Instituted: March 1961.

Branch of Service: Civil Defence and other auxiliary forces.

Ribbon: Blue bearing three narrow stripes of yellow, red and green.

Metal: Cupro-nickel.

Size: Height 38mm; max. width 32mm.

Description: (Obverse) the effigy of the reigning monarch; (reverse) two types. Both featured three shields flanked by sprigs of acorns and oak leaves. The upper shield in both cases is inscribed CD but the initials on the lower shields differ, according to the organisations in Britain and Northern Ireland respectively—AFS and NHSR (British) or AFRS and HSR (Northern Ireland). After 1968 a new reverse was used incorporating the words CIVIL DEFENCE and LONG SERVICE.

Comments: *Issued unnamed to those who had completed 15 years service in a wide range of Civil Defence organisations. It was extended to Civil Defence personnel in Gibraltar, Hong Kong and Malta in 1965. The medal became obsolescent in the UK after the Civil Defence Corps and Auxiliary Fire Service were disbanded in 1968, but members of the CD Corps in the Isle of Man and Channel Islands are still eligible. A bar is available for additional 15 years' service*

British reverse.

Northern Ireland reverse.

Post-1968 reverse

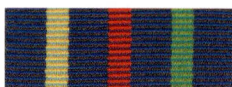

VALUE:

		Miniature
British version	£35–50	£15–25
Northern Ireland version	£85–120	£110–160
Gibraltar	£100–125	
Hong Kong	£100–125	
Malta	£100–125	
Post 1968 reverse	£75–100	

264A. AMBULANCE SERVICE (EMERGENCY DUTIES) LONG SERVICE AND GOOD CONDUCT MEDAL

Instituted: 5 July 1996.
Branch of Service: Ambulance services in England and Wales, Scotland, Northern Ireland, the Isle of Man and the Channel Islands.
Ribbon: Green with, on either side, a white stripe on which is superimposed a narrow green stripe.
Metal: Cupro-nickel.
Size: 36mm.
Description: (Obverse) crowned effigy of the reigning monarch, ELIZABETH II DEI GRATIA REGINA F.D.; (reverse) FOR EXEMPLARY SERVICE round the top, with either the emblem of the Ambulance Services of Scotland or the remainder of the United Kingdom in the centre below. Fitted with a ring for suspension.
Comments: *Both full- and part-time members of Ambulance Services are eligible provided they are employed on emergency duties. Service prior to 1974 in ambulance services maintained by local authorities counts. For paramedics and technicians the qualifying service is 20 years. For ambulance officers and other management grades, at least seven of their 20 years' service must have been spent on emergency duties.*

VALUE: £150–175   *Miniature* £12–20

264B. ASSOCIATION OF CHIEF AMBULANCE OFFICERS SERVICE MEDAL

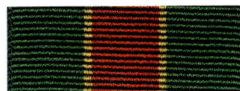

Instituted: —.
Branch of Service: Members of the Ambulance Service.
Ribbon: Dark green with twin central red stripe edged with yellow.
Metal: Bronze.
Size: 36mm.
Description: (Obverse) symbol of the Association (caduceus on a wheel) surrounded by ASSOCIATION OF CHIEF AMBULANCE OFFICERS; (reverse) FOR SERVICE surrounded by a laurel wreath.
Comments: *Issued by members of the Association to ambulance personnel who have performed exemplary service.*

VALUE: £75–85   *Miniature* £55–65

264C. ROYAL FLEET AUXILIARY SERVICE MEDAL

Instituted: July 24, 2001 by Royal Warrant.
Branch of Service: Royal Fleet Auxiliary Service.
Ribbon: Central band of watered royal blue flanked by narrow stripes of cypress green, yellow-gold and purple.
Metal: Cupro-nickel.
Size: 38mm.
Description: (Obverse) the crowned effigy of the Queen; (reverse) the badge of the Royal Fleet Auxiliary Service with the inscription ROYAL FLEET AUXILIARY — FOR LONG SERVICE.
Comments: *The medal is awarded to all officers, petty officers and ratings of the RFA after 20 years' service. Clasps will be granted for a further 10 years' service. The recipient's name and rank, together with date of qualification, are impressed on the rim. The first awards of this medal were made to three petty officers in 2003, a further 400 personnel being eligible.*

VALUE: £200–250   *Miniature*   £12–15

265. (WOMEN'S) ROYAL VOLUNTARY SERVICE LONG SERVICE MEDAL

Instituted: 1961.
Branch of Service: Women's Royal Voluntary Service.
Ribbon: Dark green with twin white stripes towards the end and broad red edges.
Metal: Cupro-nickel.
Size: 36mm.
Description: (Obverse) the interlocking initials WVS in an ivy wreath; (reverse) three flowers, inscribed SERVICE BEYOND SELF round the circumference.
Comments: *Issued unnamed and awarded for 15 years' service. Bars for additional 15 year periods are awarded. Although the majority of the 35,000 (approx.) medals have been awarded to women there has also been a substantial number of male recipients. Since 2013 the WRVS has simply been known as the Royal Voluntery Service. The medal design remains the same.*

VALUE: £15–20   *Miniature*   £35–45

266. VOLUNTARY MEDICAL SERVICE MEDAL

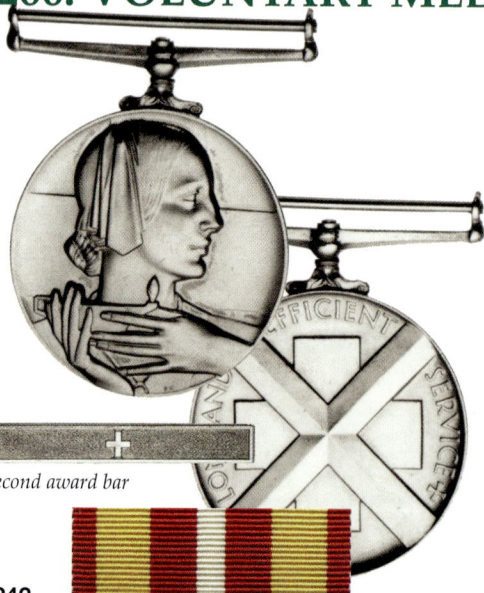

Instituted: 1932.
Branch of Service: British Red Cross Society and the St Andrew's Ambulance Corps (Scotland).
Ribbon: Red with yellow and white stripes.
Metal: Originally struck in silver but since the 1960s it has been produced in cupro-nickel.
Size: 36mm.
Description: (Obverse) the veiled bust of a female holding an oil lamp, symbolic of Florence Nightingale; (reverse) the crosses of Geneva and St Andrew, with the inscription FOR LONG AND EFFICIENT SERVICE.
Comments: *Awarded for 15 years' service, with a bar for each additional period of five years. The service bars are embellished with a Geneva cross or saltire (St Andrew) cross, whichever is the more appropriate.*

Second award bar

VALUE:		*Miniature*
Silver	£25–35	
Cupro-nickel	£15–20	£15–25

267. SERVICE MEDAL OF THE ORDER OF ST JOHN

Original type obverse.

Service Medal in Gold reverse.

Laurel leaf for 52 years' service

Instituted: 1898.

Branch of Service: The Most Venerable Order of the Hospital of St John of Jerusalem.

Ribbon: Three black and two white stripes of equal width. The ribbon for the Service Medal in Gold has a central narrow gold stripe dividing the central black stripe.

Metal: Silver (1898-1947), silvered base metal (1947-60), silvered cupro-nickel (1960-66) and rhodium-plated cupro-nickel (since 1966). The service Medal in Gold is silver-gilt.

Size: 38mm.

Description: (Obverse) an unusual veiled bust of Queen Victoria with her name and abbreviated Latin titles round the circumference. A new obverse was adopted in 1960 with a slightly reduced effigy of Queen Victoria and less ornate lettering. (Reverse) the royal arms within a garter surrounded by four circles containing the imperial crown, the Prince of Wales's feathers and the armorial bearings of the Order and of HRH the Prince of Wales, the first Sub-Prior of the Order. Between the circles are sprigs of St John's Wort. Round the circumference is the Latin inscription MAGNUS PRIORATUS ORDINIS HOSPITALIS SANCTI JOHANNIS JERUSALEM IN ANGLIA in Old English lettering. Since 2019, in keeping with the new Service Medal in Gold, the wording is now in English reading THE MOST VENERABLE ORDER OF THE HOSPITAL OF ST JOHN OF JERUSALEM FOR SERVICE. In Canada the wording in Latin reads VENERABILISSIMI ORDNIS HOSPITALIS SANCTI JOHANNIS HIEROSOLYMITANI-PRO OFFICIO to avoid problems with the dual language in that country.

Comments: *Originally awarded for 15 years' service to the Order in the United Kingdom (12 in the Dominions and 10 in the Colonies) but the qualifying period changed to 12 years and has now been reduced to 10 years' service. The medal was designed in 1898 and first presented in 1900. A silver bar was introduced in 1911 for additional periods of five years. From then until 1924 the bar was inscribed 5 YEARS SERVICE but then a design showing a Maltese cross flanked by sprays of St John's Wort was substituted. Bars for 27 years' and each additional five years' service were subsequently instituted in silver-gilt. In 2004 a gilt laurel leaf was added to the ribbon of the Service Medal for 52 years' service in place of four gilt clasps. In 2019 a new "Gold" award was instituted—the "Service Medal in Gold"—to mark 50 years' service and, as with the silver award, clasps are added for each five years' service—these clasps are gilt. When the ribbon alone is worn a small Maltese cross is attached for each five years' service: silver for the Service Medal and gilt for the Service Medal in Gold. Suspension by a ring was changed in 1913 to a straight bar suspender. The medal is worn on the left breast.*

Although awarded for long service this medal should not be solely referred to as a long service award as it can also be awarded for conspicuous service—when so awarded it was distinguished by the addition of a silver palm leaf on the ribbon. The silver palm was discontinued in 1949, after only three years. It is believed to be the only medal still issued bearing the bust of Queen Victoria (the effigy was first sculpted by HRH Princess Louise, daughter of Queen Victoria).

VALUE:		Miniature
Silver, ring suspension	£35–50	£25–30
Silver, straight bar suspension	£30–45	£15–20
Base metal, first obverse	£20–25	£10–12
Base metal, second obverse	£20–25	£10–12
Silver-gilt	—	£15–20

5-year cross

Palm leaf for conspicuous service

Voluntary Aid Detachment

Military Hospital Reserve

VAD (or MHR) now obsolete. This brooch bar can sometimes be found on the VMS Medal (MYB 266) or could be worn alone

Ribbon bars:

5-year bar (second type)

5-year bar (silver-gilt) type)

Illustrations by M. Thomas.

243

267A. DIPLOMATIC SERVICE MEDAL

Instituted: —
Branch of Service: Royal Diplomatic Service.
Ribbon: Garter Blue (in a bow).
Metal: Silver-gilt.
Size: 39mm×60mm.
Description: (Obverse) Royal cypher within a crowned oval frame bearing the words HER MAJESTY'S DIPLOMATIC SERVICE; (reverse) plain.
Comments: *This medal was pointed out to us by a reader with the one in his collection having apparently been awarded to an erstwhile sergeant in the Royal Tank Regiment who later went on to spend 25 years in the Diplomatic Service. Little is known about its criteria or numbers awarded. We would be pleased to learn more if any reader can help.*

VALUE: £2500–3500

268. ROYAL AIR FORCE LONG SERVICE AND GOOD CONDUCT MEDAL

Instituted: 1 July 1919.
Branch of Service: Royal Air Force.
Ribbon: Dark blue and maroon with white edges.
Metal: Silver.
Size: 36mm.
Description: (Obverse) the effigy of the reigning monarch; (reverse) the RAF eagle and crown insignia.
Comments: *Awarded to NCOs and other ranks of the RAF for 18 years' exemplary service, reduced in 1977 to 15 years. Provision for bars for further periods of service was made from 1944 onwards. A clasp is now awarded for every 10 years served and in keeping with the other armed services the medal is awarded to all ranks. Before 1945 conduct below the required standard was permitted to count if the airman had displayed higher exemplary conduct against the enemy, gallantry or some special service in times of emergency. From 1944 any prior service in the Navy and Army could be counted. Prior to this date only up to four years' service could be counted. In 1947 officers became eligible for the medal provided they had had at least 12 years' service in the ranks. Recipients' details are inscribed on the rim. Since 2016 it has been awarded to all regular members of the RAF including officers who have never served in the ranks. The later issues are of silver-plated base metal.*

VALUE:		Miniature			Miniature
George V (E)	£120–150	£25–35	Elizabeth II (B)	£60–65	£25–35
George VI (D)	£85–100	£25–35	Elizabeth II (C)	£60–65	£25–35
George VI (E)	£85–100	£25–35	RCAF recipient	£300–400	

269. ROYAL AIR FORCE LEVIES LONG SERVICE AND GOOD CONDUCT MEDAL

Instituted: 1948.
Branch of Service: RAF Levies, Iraq.
Ribbon: As the preceding.
Metal: Silver.
Size: 36mm.
Description: Similar to the previous type but was fitted with a clasp inscribed ROYAL AIR FORCE LEVIES IRAQ.
Comments: *Awarded to the locally commissioned officers and men of the RAF Levies in Iraq, for 18 years' service (the last 12 to be of an exemplary nature). The Iraq Levies were raised in 1919 and became the responsibility of the RAF in 1922, maintaining law and order by means of light aircraft and armoured cars. The force was disbanded in 1955 when the RAF withdrew from Iraq. 309 medals were issued, 115 to officers and 194 to airmen.*

VALUE:
George VI (E)	£800–1000
Elizabeth II (B)	£900–1100
Elizabeth II (C)	£900–1100

270. AIR EFFICIENCY AWARD

Instituted: September 1942
Branch of Service: AAF, RAAF and RAFVR.
Ribbon: Green with two light blue stripes towards the centre.
Metal: Silver.
Size: Height 38mm; max. width 32mm.
Description: An oval medal with a suspender in the form of an eagle with wings outspread. (Obverse) the effigy of the reigning monarch; (reverse) inscribed AIR EFFICIENCY AWARD in three lines.
Comments: *Granted for 10 years' efficient service in the Auxiliary and Volunteer Air Forces of the United Kingdom and Commonwealth. A bar was awarded for a further ten-year period. Officers are permitted to add the letters AE after their name. This award was replaced in 2000 by the VRSM (No. 242A). Of the approximately 2,500 awarded 256 were to women.*

VALUE:
George VI (D)	£145–175
George VI (E)	£175–200
Elizabeth II (C)	£150–175
Miniature (all)	£25–35
Named to officers add £40	

Second award bar

271. POLICE LONG SERVICE AND GOOD CONDUCT MEDAL

Instituted: 14 June 1951.
Branch of Service: Police Forces.
Ribbon: Dark blue with twin white stripes towards each end.
Metal: Original issue cupro-nickel, now rhodium plated
Size: 36mm.
Description: The obverse of this medal bears the effigy of the reigning monarch while the reverse has the figure of Justice with scales in her left hand and a wreath in her right surrounded by the inscription 'FOR EXEMPLARY POLICE SERVICE'. The suspender is straight and found in both swivelling and non-swivelling formats
Comments: *Originally awarded to full-time regular police officers within any UK Constabulary for 22 years' service. However, following a national campaign by Warwickshire Police Officer Kenneth Fowler, supported by Chief Officers, the Police Federations and Members of Parliament, the award point of the medal was reduced to 20 years' service on 19 January 2010, bringing it in line with the Fire, Ambulance and Prison Long Service and Good Conduct Medals which are all awarded after 20 years' service. In 1956 this medal was extended to police officers serving in Australia, Papua New Guinea and Nauru. Australia however replaced this medal in 1976 with the National Medal.*

VALUE:

		Miniature
George VI (C)	£40–50	£25–35
Elizabeth II (A)	£40–50	£10–15
Elizabeth II (D)	£40–50	£10–15

272. SPECIAL CONSTABULARY LONG SERVICE MEDAL

Instituted: 30 August 1919.
Branch of Service: Special Constabulary.
Ribbon: A broad red stripe in the centre flanked by black and white stripes.
Metal: Bronze.
Size: 32mm.
Description: (Obverse) the effigy of the reigning monarch; (reverse) a partial laurel wreath with a six-line text inscribed FOR FAITHFUL SERVICE IN THE SPECIAL CONSTABULARY. A second reverse was introduced in 1956 for 15 years' service in the Ulster Special Constabulary, the text being modified to permit the inclusion of the word ULSTER. A third type was introduced in 1982 for 15 years' service in the RUC Reserve and is thus inscribed but, with the name change, in 2001 a fourth type inscribed Police Reserve of Northern Ireland was issued.
Comments: *Awarded to all ranks in the Special Constabulary for 9 years' unpaid service, with more than 50 duties per annum. War service with at least 50 duties counted triple. A clasp inscribed THE GREAT WAR 1914–18 was awarded to those who qualified for the medal during that conflict. Bars inscribed LONG SERVICE, with the date, are awarded for additional ten-year periods (the NI bars are not dated). To qualify during the two world wars a special constable must have served without any pay for not less than three years, and during that period have performed at least 50 duties a year, and be recommended by a chief officer of police as willing and competent to discharge the duties of special constable as required, i.e. in both world wars service counts treble.*

Special Constabulary medal.

1956 Ulster Special Constabulary medal.

Long Service bar.

VALUE:

		Miniature
George V (C)	£20–25	£10–12
With Great War 1914–18 clasp	£30–35	£15–20
George V (E)	£20–25	£10–12
George VI (D)	£20–25	£10–12
George VI (E)	£55–85	£15–20
Elizabeth II (B)	£55–85	£15–20
Elizabeth II (C)	£45–55	£10–12
Northern Ireland types	£250–300	£15–20

273. ROYAL ULSTER CONSTABULARY SERVICE MEDAL

Instituted: 1982.

Branch of Service: RUC and its Reserve.

Ribbon: Green, with narrow central stripes of red, black and dark blue. Following the award of the George Cross to the RUC the ribbon of this medal was modified to reflect the award. The colour of the GC ribbon is now indicated by two vertical blue stripes at the outer edges.

Metal: Cupro-nickel.

Size: 36mm.

Description: (Obverse) the effigy of Queen Elizabeth II; (reverse) the crowned harp insignia of the RUC with the words FOR SERVICE round the foot.

Comments: *Awarded for 18 months continuous service since 1 January 1971, but the award was made immediate on the recipient also being awarded a gallantry decoration or a Queen's commendation.*

VALUE:

Elizabeth II (D)	£200–250	*Miniature*	£10–15

Original ribbon.

Post-2001 ribbon.

273A. POLICE SERVICE OF NORTHERN IRELAND (PSNI) MEDAL

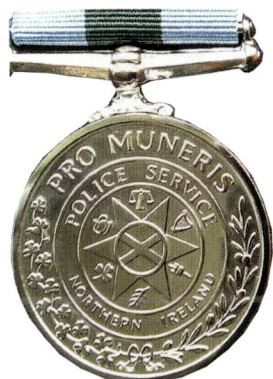

Instituted: 2020

Branch of Service: Police Service of Northern Ireland

Ribbon: Light blue with central dark green stripe

Metal: Cupro Nickel

Size: 36mm

Description: (Obverse) The effigy of the reigning monarch. The QEII version used the Jody Clark coinage profile, possibly the only UK medal to do so. (Reverse) The badge of the PSNI below the motto PRO MUNERIS (For Service) and above a wreath of shamrock and laurel.

Comments: *As part of the Good Friday Agreement of 1998 the Patten review of the following year recommended that the the Royal Ulster Constabulary was disbanded and replaced with the Police Service of Northern Ireland with emphasis on recruiting from both sides of the sectarian divide. The new badge, which appears on this medal, included symbols of the crown, harp and shamrock to represent all of Northern Ireland's inhabitants and it is worth noting that the word "Royal" was dropped from the new name. The PSNI Medal is awarded to all officers of the Police Service of Northern Ireland (PSNI) who have completed five years' service since 25 February 25, 2009. This was the date that the Royal Ulster terrorist threat level was raised from "substantial" to "severe". Those whose service has been curtailed as a result of death, disability or injury caused whilst on active duty are also eligible.*

A similar award, without suspension, the Police Service of Northern Ireland Service Medallion, was instituted at the same time for all police staff who were not serving police officers.

VALUE: *Miniature*

Medal:	—	—
Medallion:	—	

274. COLONIAL POLICE LONG SERVICE MEDAL

Instituted: 1934.

Branch of Service: Colonial police forces.

Ribbon: Green centre bordered with white and broad blue stripes towards the edges.

Metal: Silver.

Size: 36mm.

Description: (Obverse) the effigy of the reigning monarch; (reverse) a police truncheon superimposed on a laurel wreath.

Comments: *Originally awarded to junior officers who had completed 18 years' exemplary service but latterly awarded to officers of all ranks who have the required service qualification. A bar is awarded on completing 25 years' service and a second bar after 30 years. These are represented on the ribbon bar in working dress by silver rosettes. The number (where applicable), rank and name as well as (for George VI and later issues) the relevant force in which the recipient is serving at the time of the award is engraved on the rim, often locally and therefore in a variety of styles.*

VALUE:		*Miniature*
George V (C)	£100–120	£25–35
George VI (B)	£85–100	£25–35
George VI (C)	£85–100	£25–35
Elizabeth II (A)	£85–100	£20–25
Elizabeth II (B)	£85–100	£20–25

274A. OVERSEAS TERRITORIES POLICE LONG SERVICE MEDAL

Following the renaming of this and other Colonial medals in 2012 this medal is now being issued with the inscription "Overseas Territories . . ." in place of "Colonial . . .". In all other respects this medal is identical to MYB 274 above.

275. COLONIAL SPECIAL CONSTABULARY LONG SERVICE MEDAL

Instituted: 1957.
Branch of Service: Colonial Special Constabulary.
Ribbon: Two thin white stripes on a broad green centre, with broad blue edges.
Metal: Silver.
Size: 36mm.
Description: (Obverse) the effigy of the reigning monarch; (reverse) the crowned royal cypher above the words FOR FAITHFUL SERVICE in a laurel wreath.
Comments: *Awarded for nine years' unpaid or 15 years' paid service in a colonial special constabulary. A bar is awarded for further ten-year periods Since June 2012 this medal has been renamed "Overseas Service . . .".*

VALUE:

Elizabeth II (A)	£250–300	*Miniature*	£25–35

276. CEYLON POLICE LONG SERVICE AND GOOD CONDUCT MEDAL (I)

Instituted: 1925.
Branch of Service: Ceylon Police.
Ribbon: Very similar to that of the Special Constabulary Long Service Medal—a broad red stripe in the centre flanked by black and white stripes.
Metal: Silver.
Size: 36mm.
Description: (Obverse) coinage profile of King George V by Sir Bertram Mackennal; (reverse) an elephant surmounted by a crown. Ring suspension.
Comments: *Awarded for 15 years' active service. It was superseded in 1934 by the Colonial Police Long Service Medal.*

VALUE:

George V (E)	£350–400	*Miniature*	£85–95

277. CEYLON POLICE LONG SERVICE AND GOOD CONDUCT MEDAL (II)

Instituted: 1950.
Branch of Service: Ceylon Police.
Ribbon: Dark blue edged with khaki, white and pale blue.
Metal: Cupro-nickel.
Size: 36mm.
Description: (Obverse) the effigy of the reigning monarch; (reverse) similar to the foregoing, but without the crown above the elephant, to permit the longer inscription CEYLON POLICE SERVICE. Straight bar suspender.
Comments: *Awarded for 18 years exemplary service. Bars for 25 and 30 years service were also awarded. It became obsolete when Ceylon (now Sri Lanka) became a republic in 1972.*

VALUE:

		Miniature
George VI (C)	£450–500	£35–45
Elizabeth II (A)	£400–450	£35–45

278. CEYLON POLICE MEDAL FOR MERIT

Instituted: 1950.
Branch of Service: Ceylon Police.
Ribbon: Broad central khaki stripe, flanked by narrow stripes of white, light blue and dark blue.
Metal: Silver.
Size: 36mm.
Description: (Obverse) the effigy of the reigning monarch; (reverse) an Indian elephant with the legend CEYLON POLICE SERVICE at the top and FOR MERIT at the foot.
Comments: *This medal replaced, within Ceylon, the Colonial Police Medal for Meritorious Service (no. 61). It was to be awarded for "valuable service characterised by resource and devotion to duty, including prolonged service marked by exceptional ability, merit and exemplary conduct". The number awarded each year not to exceed 10. Year of issue is included in the naming, e.g. "2/69" signifying the second award of 1969.The medal became obsolete when Ceylon (now Sri Lanka) became a republic in 1972.*

VALUE		*Miniature*
George VI	—	—
Elizabeth II	£400–500	£35–45

278A. CEYLON POLICE MEDAL FOR GALLANTRY

Instituted: 1950.
Branch of Service: Ceylon Police.
Ribbon: As for the Medal for Merit (above) but with the addition of a very narrow red stripe superimposed on the white stripes.
Metal: Silver.
Size: 36mm.
Description: Similar to the Medal of Merit (above) but reverse inscribed FOR GALLANTRY at the foot.
Comments: *The medal became obsolete when Ceylon (now Sri Lanka) became a republic in 1972.*

VALUE:		*Miniature*
George VI	—	£55–65
Elizabeth II	—	£55–65

279. CYPRUS MILITARY POLICE LONG SERVICE AND GOOD CONDUCT MEDAL

Instituted: October 1929.
Branch of Service: Cyprus Military Police.
Ribbon: Yellow, dark green and yellow in equal bands.
Metal: Silver.
Size: 36mm.
Description: (Obverse) King George V; (reverse) the title of the police round the circumference and the words LONG AND GOOD SERVICE in four lines across the middle.
Comments: *Awarded to those who had three good conduct badges, plus six years exemplary service since the award of the third badge, no more than four entries in the defaulters' book and a minimum of 15 years service. Officers who had been promoted from the ranks were also eligible. No more than 7 officers and 54 other ranks were awarded this medal during its brief life before it was superseded in 1934 by the Colonial Police Long Service Medal.*

VALUE: £800–1000

279A. ROYAL FALKLAND ISLANDS POLICE JUBILEE MEDAL

Date: 1996
Branch of Service: Royal Falkland Islands Police
Ribbon: Green with a central blue stripe edged in white.
Metal: Silver.
Size: 36mm.
Description: (Obverse) Elizabeth II (A); (reverse) arms of the colony; ROYAL FALKLAND ISLANDS POLICE round top and double dated 1846-1996 round foot. Fitted with ring suspension and a brooch clasp at the top of the ribbon.
Comments: *Awarded to all officers serving in the Royal Falkland Islands Police on 15 October 1996. Only 27 medals were awarded.*

VALUE: £1000–1500

280. HONG KONG POLICE MEDAL FOR MERIT

Instituted: May 3, 1862.
Branch of Service: Hong Kong Police.
Ribbon: Various, according to class (see below).
Metal: Gold, silver or bronze.
Size: 36mm.
Description: (Obverse) the effigy of the reigning monarch; (reverse) inscribed HONG KONG POLICE FORCE FOR MERIT within a laurel wreath and beaded circle (with various slight modifications). Examples have been recorded with the effigy of Queen Victoria as on the Abyssinian and New Zealand Medals (MY123–124), and King George V types C and E.
Comment: *Exceptionally awarded in five different classes according to the length and type of service. The 1st Class medal was struck in gold and worn with a maroon (VC) ribbon, the 2nd Class in silver with a plain yellow ribbon, the 3rd Class in bronze with a central black stripe on the yellow ribbon, the 4th Class in bronze with two central black stripes in the yellow ribbon, and the 5th Class (confined to the Police Reserve) in bronze had a green ribbon with two black central stripes. The 4th Class was engraved on the reverse above the wreath. These medals were superseded in April 1937 by the Hong Kong Police Silver Medal, only four of which were awarded before it was replaced by the Colonial Police Medal for Meritorious Service 1938.*

VALUE:	1st class	2nd class	3rd class	4th class
Victoria	Rare	£600–700	£500–550	£500–550
Edward VII	Rare	Rare	Rare	Rare
George V (B)	Rare	£500–550	£450–550	£450–500
George V (C)	Rare	£500–550	£450–550	£450–500

Miniature (all, silver or bronze)	Rare

1st Class.

2nd Class.

3rd Class.

4th Class.

280A. HONG KONG DISTRICT WATCH FORCE MERIT MEDAL

Instituted: 1868.
Branch of Service: District Watch Force.
Ribbon: Very dark green with a central deep red stripe.
Metal: Silver or bronze.
Size: 31mm with a prominent rim.
Description: (Obverse) four Chinese characters "Great Britain Hong Kong" above a watchman's lamp, superimposed on a cutlass and police baton, with the Chinese characters for "District Watch Force" and "Medal" at the sides; (reverse) DISTRICT WATCHMEN'S FORCE FOR MERIT within a laurel wreath.
Comment: *While the Hong Kong Police was principally a mixed force of Europeans and Indians, operated in the business and higher class residential areas, and was paid for out of the colony's revenues, the District Watch Force was a purely Chinese organisation, raised by prominent citizens of the colony to patrol and police the Chinese parts of the city. Its members had statutory powers, were uniformed and were trained and functioned in the style of the old parish constables, rather than in the gendarmerie style of the Hong Kong Police which was colonial in nature and imposed on society rather than integrated with it. The District Watch Force ceased to function at the time of the Japanese invasion in 1941 and was not revived on liberation.*

VALUE: £650–700

280B. ROYAL HONG KONG POLICE COMMEMORATIVE MEDAL

Instituted: 1996.
Branch of Service: Royal Hong Kong Police.
Ribbon: Black, magenta and old gold.
Metal: Silver.
Size: 38mm.
Description: (Obverse) the RHKP crest; (reverse) crossed tipstaves inside a laurel wreath with the dates 1844 and 1997.
Comment: *The medal, approved by Commissioner Eddie Hui Ki On, is available on purchase (originally HK$1,000, about £80) to those who served in the Hong Kong Police (1844–1969) and the Royal Hong Kong Police (1969–97). Purchasers' details are often found privately engraved in bold upright capitals in a variety of formats. The medal, worn on the left breast, has the same status as the Royal Hong Kong Regiment Disbandment Medal (254A).*

VALUE: £150–200   *Miniature*   £55–80

280C. ROYAL HONG KONG AUXILIARY POLICE COMMEMORATIVE MEDAL

Instituted: 1996.
Branch of Service: Royal Hong Kong Auxiliary Police.
Ribbon: Black, magenta and old gold.
Metal: Silver.
Size: 38mm.
Description: Similar to the above, but inscribed ROYAL HONG KONG AUXILIARY POLICE FORCE.
Comment: *Similar to the above this medal is available for purchase. Some 5,000 auxiliary policemen and women are eligible for the award.*

VALUE: £150–200   *Miniature*   £55-80

280D. HONG KONG MILITARY SERVICE CORPS MEDAL

Instituted: 1997.

Branch of Service: Hong Kong Military Service Corps.

Ribbon: Red, with a central yellow stripe.

Metal: Silver.

Size: 36mm.

Description: (Obverse) a Chinese dragon on a scroll bearing the initials of the Corps. HONG KONG MILITARY SERVICE CORPS inscribed round the top and 1962-1997 at the foot; (reverse) the British royal arms with inscription round the top TO COMMEMORATE DISBANDMENT and the date 31 March 1997 at the foot.

Comments: *The Military Service Corps was a unit formed in 1962 for defence of the Crown Colony and recruited locally to serve alongside and in support of the British Army. Members of the Corps were presented with this medal following its disbandment prior to the return of Hong Kong to China. A small number were also presented to previous commanding officers.*

VALUE: £100–120

281. HONG KONG ROYAL NAVAL DOCKYARD POLICE LONG SERVICE MEDAL

Instituted: 1920.

Branch of Service: Hong Kong Royal Naval Dockyard Police.

Ribbon: Yellow with two royal blue stripes towards the centre.

Metal: Gilt bronze or silver.

Size: 31mm.

Description: (Obverse) the effigy of the reigning monarch; (reverse) the title of the Police within a laurel wreath. Ring suspension (two sizes).

Comments: *Awarded for 15 years service. Although the Dockyard closed in 1961 men who transferred to other police divisions continued to be awarded the medal up to 1973. About 280 medals in all were issued.*

VALUE:

		Miniature
George V (E)	£400–500	£110–160
George VI (C)	£400–500	£110–160
George VI (D)	£400–500	£110–160
Elizabeth II (C)	£400–500	£110–160

281A. HONG KONG DISCIPLINED SERVICES MEDAL

Instituted: 1986.

Branch of Service: Hong Kong Customs & Excise and Immigration Service.

Ribbon: Green bordered by vertical stripes of dark blue with a strip of sky blue at each edge.

Metal: Silver.

Size: 36mm.

Description: (Obverse) crowned effigy of Queen Elizabeth II (B); (reverse) armorial bearings of Hong Kong, with the inscription "For Long Service and Good Conduct".

Clasps: Awarded after 25 and 30 years, denoted by silver rosettes on riband in working dress.

Comments: *Awarded after 18 years continuous service. Engraved with name and rank on rim. Some 1,739 medals were awarded between 1987 and the return of Hong Kong to China on June 30, 1997. No other long service medal to Customs officers has been awarded in the British system.*

VALUE:

	Customs	Immigration
Medal	£450–£50	£500–£550
1st clasp	£500–£550	£600–£650
2nd clasp	£600–£650	Unique

281B. TIENTSIN BRITISH EMERGENCY CORPS MEDAL

Instituted: —
Branch of Service: British Municipal Emergency Corps.
Ribbon: Buff with a broad central white stripe.
Metal: Silver.
Size: 36mm.
Description: (Obverse) the arms of the colony supported by a sailor and a Chinese worker surrounded by the words TIENTSIN BRITISH MUNICIPAL EMERGENCY CORPS; (reverse) a wreath surrounding a plain panel engraved FOR LONG SERVICE in three lines, with maker's name in small lettering below: STERLING/ARNOLD.
Comments: *The British Emergency Corps was presumably a paramilitary unit recruited locally. Little is known about these medals or the unit but obviously they were awarded for long service.*

VALUE: £175–225

281C. JERSEY HONORARY POLICE LONG SERVICE AND GOOD CONDUCT MEDAL

Instituted: 2014.
Branch of Service: Jersey Police.
Ribbon: Orange with narrow stripes of white, blue and yellow each side.
Metal: Silver.
Size: 36mm.
Description: (Obverse) the effigy of the reigning monarch; (reverse) an outline map of Jersey with the shield of Jersey superimposed on three ceremonial maces with HONORARY POLICE LONG SERVICE JERSEY round the circumference.
Comments: *Awarded to Honorary police officers (Centeniers, Vingteniers and Constable Officers) for 12 years service. A bar will be added for every nine years extra service.*

VALUE: £150–200   *Miniature* £12–15

282. MALTA POLICE LONG SERVICE AND GOOD CONDUCT MEDAL

Instituted: 1921.
Branch of Service: Malta Police.
Ribbon: Dark blue with a narrow central silver stripe.
Metal: Silver.
Size: 36mm.
Description: (Obverse) the effigy of King George V; (reverse) an eight-pointed Maltese cross in a laurel wreath with the title of the service and FOR LONG SERVICE AND GOOD CONDUCT round the circumference.
Comments: *Awarded to sergeants and constables with 18 years exemplary service. Officers who had had 18 years in the ranks were also eligible for the award. It was superseded by the Colonial Police Long Service Medal in 1934. No more than 112 medals were awarded, although only 99 names were published in the Police Commissioner's Annual Reports and in the Malta Gazette.*

VALUE:		*Miniature*
George V (E)	£400–500	£110–130
George V (C)	£400–500	£110–130

282A. MAURITIUS POLICE LONG SERVICE AND GOOD CONDUCT MEDAL: I

Instituted: —.

Branch of Service: Mauritius Police.

Ribbon: Three types: (a) 36mm half black, half white; (b) 33mm white with a broad royal blue central stripe; (c) blue with two narrow white stripes towards the edges.

Metal: Bronze.

Size: Oval, 40x33mm or 39x31mm.

Description: (Obverse) crown surmounting crossed tipstaves with the motto PAX NOBISCUM (Peace be with us) and the legend POLICE DEPARTMENT round the top and MAURITIUS at the foot; (reverse) palm fronds enclosing a three-line inscription FOR GOOD CONDUCT. Fitted with a ring for suspension. Medals with 33mm ribbon fitted at top with a pin brooch by Hunt & Roskill.

Comment: *It is believed that the different ribbons indicated different periods of service, but confirmation is sought. It is presumed that this medal was superseded by no. 282B.*

VALUE:	£200–250	Miniature	£80–110

First type ribbon.

282B. MAURITIUS POLICE LONG SERVICE AND GOOD CONDUCT MEDAL: II

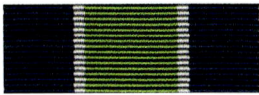

Instituted: —.

Branch of Service: Mauritius Police

Ribbon: Green centre flanked by white stripes and broad blue stripes towards the edges.

Metal: Silver.

Size: 36mm.

Description: (Obverse) the effigy of Queen Elizabeth II; (reverse) police truncheon on a laurel wreath.

Comments: *This medal is identical to the Colonial Police Long Service Medal (no. 274) except that the inscription substituted the name MAURITIUS for COLONIAL. It has been recorded in a medal group of 1976 and may have been introduced in or about 1968 when Mauritius attained independence.*

VALUE:	£200–250	Miniature	£18–20

283. NEW ZEALAND POLICE MEDAL

Instituted: 1886.

Branch of Service: New Zealand Police.

Ribbon: Originally plain crimson but in 1919 it was changed to a pattern very similar to that of the Permanent Forces of the Empire Beyond the Seas LSGC medal (no. 249),

Metal: Silver.

Size: 36mm.

Description: (Obverse) identical to that of the NZ Long & Efficient Service Medal (MY257); (reverse) FOR LONG SERVICE AND GOOD CONDUCT in four lines. Issued with a ring suspender until 1919 when a bar suspender was adopted. Clasps for each additional eight years service were introduced at the same time.

Comments: *Granted to sworn police staff for 14 years service. The clasp qualifying period was reduced to seven years in 1963. This medal was rendered obsolete with the introduction, in 1976, of the New Zealand Police Long Service and Good Conduct Medal (NZ26). It seems that from September 1901 this medal was also awarded to members of the NZ Prison Service and medals have WDR in front of recipient's name.*

First type obverse.

Second type ribbon.

VALUE:		Miniature
Regalia obverse, bar suspension	£120–150	£25–35

283A. SEYCHELLES POLICE LONG SERVICE AND GOOD CONDUCT MEDAL

Instituted: —.
Branch of Service: Seychelles Police.
Ribbon: Crimson.
Metal: Bronze.
Size: Oval, 40x33mm.
Description: (Obverse) crown surmounting crossed tipstaves with legend POLICE DEPARTMENT round the top and SEYCHELLES at the foot; (reverse) palm fronds enclosing a three-line inscription FOR GOOD CONDUCT. Fitted with a ring for suspension.
Comments: *This medal is similar to the Mauritius Police Medal (282A) and it is presumed that this medal also became obsolete on the introduction of the Colonial Police Long Service Medal in 1934. Details of qualifying terms of service and other regulations are sought.*

VALUE: £150–200

284. SOUTH AFRICA POLICE GOOD SERVICE MEDAL

Instituted: 1923.
Branch of Service: South Africa Police.
Ribbon: Broad black centre, flanked by white stripes and green borders.
Metal: Silver.
Size: 36mm.
Description: (Obverse) South African coat of arms; (reverse) bilingual inscriptions separated by a horizontal line. Three versions of the medal have been recorded. In the first version inscriptions were in English and Dutch, the latter reading POLITIE DIENST with VOOR TROUWE DIENST (for faithful service) on the reverse. In the second, introduced in 1932, Afrikaans replaced Dutch and read POLIESIE DIENS and VIR GETROUE DIENS respectively. In the third version, current from 1951 to 1963, the Afrikaans was modified to read POLISIEDIENS and VIR TROUE DIENS.
Comments: *Awarded to other ranks for 18 years exemplary service or for service of a gallant or particularly distinguished character. In the latter instance a bar inscribed MERIT-VERDIENSTE was awarded. The medal was replaced by the South African Medal for Faithful Service.*

VALUE:		
	1st type	£35–40
	2nd type	£30–35
	3rd type	£25–30
	Miniature	£15–20

285. SOUTH AFRICAN RAILWAYS AND HARBOUR POLICE LONG SERVICE AND GOOD CONDUCT MEDAL

Instituted: 1934.
Branch of Service: South African Railways and Harbour Police.
Ribbon: Similar to the Police Good Service Medal but with the colours reversed—a green central stripe flanked by white stripes and blue edges.
Metal: Silver.
Size: 36mm.
Description: (Obverse) the Union arms with S.A.R. & H. POLICE at the top and S.A.S.- EN HAWE POLISIE round the foot, but this was changed in 1953 to S.A.S. POLISIE at the top and S.A.R. POLICE at the foot. (Reverse) six line bilingual inscription.
Comments: *Awarded for 18 years unblemished service. Immediate awards for gallant or especially meritorious service earned a bar inscribed MERIT - VERDIENSTE (later with the words transposed). The medal was superseded in 1960 by the Railways Police Good Service Medal.*

VALUE: 1st type £80–100   2nd type £75–100   *Miniature* £35–45

286. FIRE BRIGADE LONG SERVICE MEDAL

Instituted: 1 June 1954.
Branch of Service: Fire Services.
Ribbon: Red with narrow yellow stripes towards the end and yellow borders.
Metal: Cupro-nickel.
Size: 36mm.
Description: (Obverse) the effigy of reigning monarch; (reverse) two firemen manning a hose. Ring suspension.
Comments: *Awarded to all ranks of local authority fire brigades, whether full- or part-time for 20 years exemplary service. Prior to the institution of this award most local authorities issued their own medals of individual design.*

VALUE:
    Elizabeth II   £45–55   *Miniature*   £12–14

286A. ASSOCIATION OF PROFESSIONAL FIRE BRIGADE OFFICERS LONG SERVICE MEDAL

Instituted: 1902.
Branch of Service: Association of Professional Fire Brigade Officers.
Ribbon: 1902–11 Orange red with narrow yellow stripe near each edge; thereafter a red central stripe flanked by narrow white stripes and broad black edges (silver medal) or grey edges (bronze medal).
Metal: Silver or bronze.
Size: 38mm.
Description: (Obverse) allegorical female figure carrying a palm frond and bestowing a laurel crown on a kneeling fireman; an early fire appliance in the background; blank exergue; (reverse) an oak wreath enclosing a four-line inscription ASSOCIATION OF PROFESSIONAL FIRE BRIGADE OFFICERS FOR LONG SERVICE. Fitted with a swivelling bar suspension.
Comments: *The medal in silver was awarded to professional fire brigade officers for a minimum of 10 years full time service and in bronze for five years, with extra clasps for further service. Engraved on the rim with the rank and name of the officer, together with the year of the award.*

VALUE: Silver £45–55   Bronze £40–50

Ribbon for silver medal 1911 onwards.

286AB. NATIONAL FIRE BRIGADES UNION MEDAL

Instituted: 1895.
Branch of Service: Fire Services.
Ribbon: Mauve (originally with a narrow white central stripe for 20 years' service).
Metal: Silver or bronze.
Size: 38mm.
Description: (Obverse) similar to 286AA but with NATIONAL FIRE BRIGADES UNION round the central motif; (reverse) LONG SERVICE in minuscule lettering inside an oak wreath with space in the centre for the recipient's name. The issue number is impressed on the rim. Fitted with a suspension bar and a brooch bar denoting length of service.
Comments: *The medal in silver was awarded to fire brigade officers for a minimum of 20 years' full time service and in bronze for 10 years' service. Often engraved on the rim with the rank and name of the officer and the medal roll number. When the NFBU became the NFBA in 1918 this medal was replaced by no. 286AA.*

VALUE: Silver £50–75   Bronze £35–55

286AA. NATIONAL FIRE BRIGADES ASSOCIATION LONG SERVICE MEDAL

Instituted: 1918
Branch of Service: Fire Services.
Ribbon: Red with a central dark blue stripe flanked by very thin yellow stripes.
Metal: Silver or bronze.
Size: 38mm.
Description: (Obverse) badge of the Association: a wreathed flag within a circle surmounted by a fireman's helmet and surrounded by ladders and hoses inscribed NATIONAL FIRE BRIGADES ASSOCIATION round the central motif; (reverse) LONG SERVICE in minuscule lettering inside an oak wreath with space in the centre for the recipient's name. Fitted with a plain ring for suspension from a broad bar suspender with a clasp bearing the years of service.
Comments: *The medal in silver was awarded to fire brigade officers for a minimum of 20 years full time service and in bronze for lesser periods. Engraved on the rim with the rank and name of the officer, together with the year of the award and the roll number. The medal replaced no. 286AB.*

VALUE: Silver £45–65   Bronze £35–55

286B. BRITISH FIRE SERVICES ASSOCIATION MEDAL

Instituted: 1949.
Branch of Service: British Fire Services Association.
Ribbon: 33mm with a central silver-blue stripe flanked by black and white stripes and a broad red edge. However, the 10 year medal has a similar ribbon but with the white stripes to the edges to distinguish it from the 20 year ribbon.
Metal: Silver (20 years) or bronze (10 years).
Size: Originally 38mm, now 36mm.
Description: (Obverse) identical to the *obverse* of 286A, i.e allegorical female figure and fireman; (reverse) identical to the *obverse* of 286AA but with FOR LONG SERVICE & EFFICIENCY, round the central motif and THE BRITISH FIRE SERVICES ASSOCIATION round the circumference. The medal originally had an ornamental scrolled suspender with a bar inscribed BFSA, however it now has a simple straight suspender. The recipient's name and service number are engraved on the rim. A bar is added for each additional 5 years of service
Comments: *The British Fire Services Association was formed in 1949 by the amalgamation of the National Fire Brigades Association and the Professional Fire Brigades Association. This medal thus superseded 286A and 286AA. The silver medal of the BFSA was originally awarded for 15 years' service. Bars are awarded for holders of both medals on completion of each additional five years service. A similar medal but with a ribbon with central red stripe flanked with black and white stripes and broad silver-blue edges is awarded for Commendable Service and is not restricted to Association members.*

Original ribbon and current 20 year ribbon.

Current 10 year ribbon.

VALUE: Silver   £45–65   *Miniature* £35–45
              Bronze   £25–35

It should be noted that a number of authorities also issued their own medals for long service and for meritorious service by members of their fire brigades. These medals are invariably well struck and are extremely collectable. However, as they are so many and so varied it is considered that these are outside of the scope of the MEDAL YEARBOOK. For a good example see the article "For Extraordinary Bravery: The London Fire Brigade Silver Medal" by Michael Pinchen in MEDAL NEWS, June/July 2015

286C. BRITISH FIRE SERVICE ASSOCIATION MERITORIOUS SERVICE MEDAL

Instituted: —
Branch of Service: British Fire Services Association.
Ribbon: Silver blue with a broad central stripe edged with thin black stripes *or* watered red with a central white stripe for gallantry.
Metal: Silver.
Size: 45mm x 36mm.
Description: A circular medallion contained within an upright oval laurel wreath suspended from an ornamental suspender with the initials B.F.S.A. on a scroll superimposed on a laurel spray. The central medallion depicts the Union Jack in a wreath with the inscription FOR MERITORIOUS SERVICE round the circumference. Reverse is plain apart from the maker's mark (foot) and the recipient's rank and name engraved on the medallion.
Comments: *Awarded for outstanding service and gallantry in fire-fighting operations. A similar medal inscribed FOR GALLANTRY is awarded for acts of outstanding gallantry.*

VALUE:	Meritorious Service	£250–350
	Gallantry	—

287. COLONIAL FIRE BRIGADE LONG SERVICE MEDAL

Instituted: 1934.
Branch of Service: Colonial Fire Services.
Ribbon: Blue with twin green central stripes separated and bordered by thin white stripes.
Metal: Silver.
Size: 36mm.
Description: (Obverse) the effigy of the reigning monarch; (reverse) a fireman's helmet and axe. Ring suspension.
Comments: *Awarded to junior officers for 18 years full-time exemplary service. Bars are awarded for further periods of service. As from June 14, 2012 this medal was renamed the Overseas Territories Fire Brigade Medal.*

VALUE:		*Miniature*
George V (E)	£300–350	£35–45
George VI (D)	£300–350	£35–45
George VI (E)	£300–350	£35–45
Elizabeth II (C)	£300–350	£15–25
Elizabeth II (D)	£300–350	£15–25

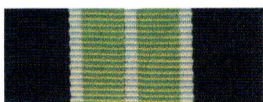

288. CEYLON FIRE BRIGADE LONG SERVICE AND GOOD CONDUCT MEDAL

Instituted: 1950.
Branch of Service: Ceylon Fire Service.
Ribbon: Similar to the Police Medal (MYB277), but with a thin central white stripe through the dark blue band.
Metal: Silver.
Size: 36mm.
Description: As the Police Medal, but with a reverse inscribed CEYLON FIRE SERVICES.

VALUE:	
George VI	£300–400
Elizabeth II	£300–400

288A. NORTHERN IRELAND PRISON SERVICE MEDAL

Instituted: 25 February 2002.
Branch of Service: Northern Ireland Prison Service.
Ribbon: Green with a broad navy blue band having at its centre a sky-blue stripe. Prison grade recipients have a ribbon with an additional thin red stripe bisecting the sky-blue stripe.
Metal: Cupro-nickel.
Size: 36mm.
Description: (Obverse) the crowned profile of the Queen with her name and titles; (reverse) a ring of flax flowers with three keys at the top, enclosing a four line inscription NORTHERN IRELAND PRISON SERVICE. The medal is fitted with a plain bar for suspension. The name of the recipient is stamped on the rim.
Comments: *The medal recognises "those who have rendered professional, committed and brave service as members of and by others in support of the Northern Ireland Prison Service". Up to July 2021 approximately 3,000 medals had been awarded which includes just 250 to civilians.*

VALUE: Civilian issue   £200–250   *Miniature*   £20–25
         Prison service   £250–300

288B. PRISON SERVICE MEDAL

Instituted: 17 December, 2010
Branch of Service: Operational grades in HM Prison Services of England and Wales, Northern Ireland, Jersey, Guernsey, Isle of Man and Scotland.
Ribbon: Black with twin stripes towards each end.
Metal: Cupro-nickel.
Size: 36mm.
Description: (Obverse) The effigy of the reigning monarch; (reverse) a period archway with the wording "For Exemplary Service", within the archway is the Royal cypher surmounted by a crown.
Comments: *Awarded to operational ranks of the Prison Service of the UK, after completing 20 years service on or after 29 April 2008. Naming includes rank, initials, surname and epaulette number, for uniformed ranks. Up to August 2019 almost 15,000 had been awarded.*

VALUE: £140–160   *Miniature*   £12–15

288C. BELFAST HARBOUR POLICE MEDAL

Instituted: 1946.
Branch of Service: Belfast Harbour Police Service.
Ribbon: Deep blue with yellow edges.
Metal: Silver.
Size: 36mm.
Description: (Obverse) A mythical maritime scene—the seal of the Harbour Commissioners—with the words BELFAST HARBOUR COMMISSIONERS around; (reverse) the words WON BY across the centre above the recipient's details with BELFAST HARBOUR POLICE around the edge.
Comments: *The medal is primarily awarded for outstanding meritorious service or when awarded for gallantry a bronze anchor is worn on the ribbon. Since its inception only 16 medals have been awarded, three with the bronze anchor for gallantry, in addition four Harbour Chief Constables have received the medal for long service*

VALUE: £300–500

289. COLONIAL PRISON SERVICE LONG SERVICE MEDAL

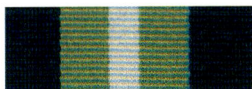

Instituted: October 1955.
Branch of Service: Colonial Prison Services.
Ribbon: Green with dark blue edges and a thin silver stripe in the centre.
Metal: Silver.
Size: 36mm.
Description: (Obverse) Queen Elizabeth II; (reverse) a phoenix rising from the flames and striving towards the sun.
Comments: *Awarded to ranks of Assistant Superintendent and below for 18 years exemplary service. Bars are awarded for further periods of 25 or 30 years service. As from June 14, 2012 this medal was renamed the Overseas Territories Prison Service Medal.*

VALUE:

Elizabeth II	£250–300	*Miniature*	£18–20

290. SOUTH AFRICAN PRISON SERVICE FAITHFUL SERVICE MEDAL

Instituted: September 1922.
Branch of Service: South African Prison Service.
Ribbon: Broad green centre flanked by white stripes and dark blue edges.
Metal: Silver.
Size: 36mm.
Description: (Obverse) arms of the Union of South Africa, of identical design to no. 284 except with GEVANGENIS DIENST round the top and PRISONS SERVICE round the foot. (Reverse) inscribed FOR FAITHFUL SERVICE across the upper half and in Dutch VOOR TROUWE DIENST across the lower half.
Comments: *Awarded to prison officers with 18 years exemplary service. Immediate awards for gallantry or exceptionally meritorious service received the Merit bar. In 1959 this medal was superseded by a version inscribed in Afrikaans.*

VALUE:	£40–50	*Miniature*	£18–20

291. SOUTH AFRICA PRISONS DEPARTMENT FAITHFUL SERVICE MEDAL

Instituted: 1959.
Branch of Service: South African Prisons Department.
Ribbon: Broad dark blue centre flanked by white stripes and green edges.
Metal: Silver.
Size: 36mm.
Description: (Obverse) arms of the Union of South Africa, of identical design to no. 284 except with DEPARTEMENT VAN GEVANGENISSE round the top and PRISONS DEPARTMENT round the foot. (Reverse) VIR TROUE DIENS across the upper half and FOR FAITHFUL SERVICE across the lower half.
Comments: *The conditions of the award were similar to the previous medal, the main difference being the change of title and the substitution of Afrikaans inscriptions for Dutch. This medal was superseded by the Prisons Department Faithful Service Medal of the Republic of South Africa, instituted in 1965.*

VALUE:	£35–50	*Miniature*	£35–45

291AA. NATO MERITORIOUS SERVICE MEDAL

Date: 1994.
Branch of Service: Personnel serving with NATO forces.
Ribbon: NATO blue with white stripes at the edges each having a vertical gold and silver thread.
Metal: Silver.
Size: 36mm.
Description: Obverse and reverse as for the other NATO medals.
Clasps: Silver bar inscribed MERITORIOUS.
Comments: *Awarded for exceptional service to NATO. It is now considered a Foreign award and can be authorised to be accepted and worn. If presented and not authorised it may be retained as a keepsake.*

VALUE: £45–55   *Miniature*   £10–15

291BB. EBOLA MEDAL FOR SERVICE IN WEST AFRICA
(now **MYB 395**—miscellaneous medals section)

291CC. THE NATIONAL CRIME AGENCY LONG SERVICE AND GOOD CONDUCT MEDAL

Instituted: March 2017
Branch of Service: Law Enforcement Agencies.
Ribbon: Central blue column with white edges and yellow stripes.
Metal: Cupronickel.
Size: 36mm
Description: The obverse shows the Ian Rank Broadley effigy of HM Queen Elizabeth II with the standard legend around the edge. The reverse has a crown above a portcullis (representing primacy and compassion) flanked by a griffin and a leopard (representing bravery, truth and valiance). The whole image is surrounded by the words "National Crime Agency" and "For Exemplary Service". Below this is an empty sphere.
Comments: *Awarded to full time members of those involved in law enforcement in the UK. Previous service in HM Revenue and Customs, the Serious Organised Crime Service and the National Crime Squad can count towards the award of this medal. The qualifying period is set at 20 aggregated years of service.*

VALUE: —   *Miniature*   £15–20

291DD. THE ROYAL NATIONAL LIFEBOAT INSTITUTION LONG SERVICE MEDAL

Instituted: 2020
Branch of Service: RNLI Volunteers.
Ribbon: Navy blue with red and yellow stripes at each edge representing the colours of a RNLI Lifeboat hull.
Metal: Cupronickel.
Size: 36mm
Description: (Obverse) the bust of William Hilary founder of the RNLI, surrounded by the name of the Institution; (reverse) a pair of arms, clasped one of which is emerging from the sea symbolising the rescue from water, be it sea, inland or flood by the RNLI operational teams. In the border is the wording WITH COURAGE NOTHING IS IMPOSSIBLE. Clasps: rectangular with a life preserver at each end and the number of years' service in raised lettering, i.e. 30 YEARS, 40 YEARS, 50 YEARS and currently to 60 YEARS.
Comments: *The medal is manufactured by Worcestershire Medal Service Ltd. and is named around the edge with the name of the recipient and year of qualification. It is available to all RNLI Volunteers for 20 years' service with clasps awarded at each additional 10-year period—see also MYB 365*

VALUE: — *Miniature* £12–15

CORONATION
Jubilee and other Royal medals

The first official royal medal was that cast by Henry Basse in 1547 for the accession of the young King Edward VI. It is known cast in gold or silver and is a curious example of bad design and poor workmanship for such an august occasion. No coronation medals were produced in honour of either Mary or Elizabeth I, but under James VI and I there was a small silver medal struck at the Royal Mint to mark the king's accession in 1603. These early medals celebrated the accession of the new sovereign, rather than the act of crowning itself.

To mark the coronation of James I, however, a small silver medalet was struck for distribution among the people who attended the ceremony, and this may be regarded as the forerunner of the modern series. This bore a Latin title signifying that James was Caesar Augustus of Britain and Heir to the Caesars. Thereafter medals in gold, silver or base metals were regularly struck in connection with the coronations of British monarchs. These were purely commemorative and not intended for wear, so they lack rings or bars for suspension.

By the early 19th century medals were being struck by many medallists for sale as souvenirs to the general public. At least fifteen different medals greeted the coronation of William IV in 1830 and more than twice that number appeared seven years later for the coronation of Queen Victoria. That paled into insignificance compared with the number produced for the coronation of Edward VII in 1902. On that occasion numerous civic authorities, organizations, industrial concerns and business firms issued medals in celebration — well over a hundred different medals and medalets were produced.

Sir George Frampton designed two silver medals, and one of these was mounted with a suspender and a blue ribbon with a thin white stripe and scarlet edges. This medal was distributed to notable personages attending the ceremony and established the precedent for subsequent coronation medals which came to be regarded as an award in recognition of services rendered in connection with the coronation, from the Earl Marshal of England to the private soldiers taking part in the ceremonial parades. In more recent times the coronation medal has even been given to people who were not present at the ceremony but who performed notable public service in the coronation year.

Other royal events have been commemorated by medals over the centuries. Royal weddings and the birth of the heir to the throne were regularly celebrated in this manner. Important anniversaries in long reigns have been the subject of numerous commemorative medals. The Golden Jubilee of George III in 1809-10, for example, resulted in over 30 different medals. Five times that number greeted the Golden Jubilee of Queen Victoria in 1887, but among them was an official medal intended for wear by those on whom it was conferred.

Even this, however, was not the first of the royal medals intended to be worn. This honour goes to a very large medal celebrating the proclamation of Victoria as Empress of India in 1877. Although fitted with a suspender bar and worn from a ribbon round the neck, it was not permitted for officers and men to wear this medal while in uniform. Later medals, however, were permitted to be worn when in uniform, but after other orders, decorations and campaign medals.

In the following listing (291A–291N) are the official Coronation Medals of James I, 1603, to Victoria, 1838. All were originally non-wearing, i.e. without suspension or ribbon, although some were later pierced or fitted with suspension for wearing. *Values of these are for silver medals only in VF (lower price) to EF condition.*

291A. JAMES I CORONATION MEDAL

Date: 1603.
Metal: Silver.
Size: 28mm.
Description: (Obverse) Bust of King James I facing right. Legend: IAC: I: BRIT: CAE: AVG: HAE CAESArum cae D.D. (Reverse) Lion rampant facing left. Legend: ECCE PHA(R)OS POPVLIQ(VE) SALVS (Behold a lighthouse and safety of the people)

VALUE: Silver £1500–2500

291B. CHARLES I CORONATION MEDAL

Date: 1626.
Metal: Gold, silver.
Size: 28mm.
Designer: Nicholas Briot.
Description: Bust of Charles I facing right. Legend: CAROLVS. I. DG. MAG. BRITAN. FRAN. ET. HIB. REX. (Reverse) An arm issuing from a cloud and holding a sword. Legend: DONEC. PAX. REDDITA. TERRIS. (As long as Peace returns to the lands).

VALUE: Silver £1200–1800

291C. CHARLES I CORONATION MEDAL

Date: 1633 (Scottish Coronation)
Metal: Gold, silver.
Size: 28mm.
Designer: Nicholas Briot.
Mintage: Gold (3), silver (Unknown)
Description: Bust of Charles I facing left. Legend: CAR-OLVS DG SCOTIAE. ANGLIAE. FR. ET. HIB. REX. (Reverse) A rose bush surmounted by a thistle. Legend: HINC. NOSTRAE. CREVERE. ROSAE (From this our roses abound). Exergue: CORON. 18 JVNII 1633

VALUE: Silver £600–800

291D. CHARLES II CORONATION MEDAL

Date: 1651 (Scottish Coronation).
Metal: Gold, silver.
Size: 31mm.
Designer: Sir James Balfour.
Description: Bust of Charles II facing right. Legend: CAROLVS.2. D.G. SCO. ANG. FRA. ET. HI. REX. FI. DE. cor. i. ia. scon. 1651. (Reverse) Lion rampant facing left, holding a thistle. Legend: NEMO. ME. IMPVNE. LACESSET (No one provokes me with impunity).

VALUE: Silver £3000–4000

291E. CHARLES II CORONATION MEDAL

Date: 1661 (English Coronation).
Metal: Gold, silver.
Size: 30mm.
Designer: Thomas Simon.
Description: Bust of Charles II facing right. Legend: CAROLVS .II.DG ANG. SCO. FR. ET. HI REX. (Reverse) Charles II, wearing royal robe, seated on throne facing left, holding sceptre. Angel hovering over him placing crown on his head. Legend: EVERSO. MISSVS. SVC-CVRRERE. SECLO. XXIII APR. 1661 (the times having been turned upside down, he has been sent to succour us)

VALUE: Silver £400–600

291F. JAMES II CORONATION MEDAL

Date: 1685.
Metal: Gold, silver, copper (?)
Size: 34mm.
Designer: John Roettier.
Mintage: Gold (200), silver (800), copper (Unknown).
Description: Bust of James II facing right, laureate. Legend: JACOBVS. II. D.G. ANG. SCO. FR. ET. HI. REX. (Reverse) Hand holding the crown above a laurel branch resting on a pillow. Legend: A. MILITARI. AD. REGIAM. (from soldiering to the palace). Exergue: INAVGVRAT. 23. AP. 1685.

VALUE: Silver £500–800

291G. WILLIAM AND MARY CORONATION MEDAL

Date: 1689.
Metal: Gold, silver, lead.
Size: 34mm.
Designer: John Roettier.
Mintage: Gold (515), silver (1,200), lead (Unknown).
Description: Conjoint busts of William and Mary facing right. Legend: GVLIELMVS. ET. MARIA. REX. ET. REGINA. (Reverse) Two-horse vehicle lower left, Jove in cloud above right. Legend: NE TOTVS ABSVMATVR. (let not the whole be consumed). Exergue: INAVGVRAT. II. AP. 1689.

VALUE: Silver £400–600

291H. ANNE CORONATION MEDAL

Date: 1702.
Metal: Gold, silver, base metal.
Size: 34mm.
Designer: John Croker.
Mintage: Gold (858), silver (1,200), base metal (Unknown).
Description: Bust of Queen Anne facing left. Legend: ANNA. D:G: MAG: BR. FR. ET. HIB: REGINA. (Reverse) Pallas Athene, left, with shield and lightning bolts, attacking recumbent monster, right. Legend: VICEM GERIT. ILLA. TONANTIS. Exergue: INAVGVRAT. XXIII. AP. MDCCII. (As, making sounds, she conducts herself).

VALUE: Silver   £300–400

291I. GEORGE I CORONATION MEDAL

Date: 1714.
Metal: Gold, silver, base metal.
Size: 34mm.
Designer: John Croker
Mintage: Gold (330), silver (1,200), base metal (Unknown).
Description: Bust of George I facing right. Legend: GEORGIVS. DG. MAG. BR. FR. ET. HIB. REX. (Reverse) Seated King, left, being crowned by Britannia standing right. Exergue: INAVGVRAT. XX. OCT. MDCCXIIII.

VALUE: Silver   £250–350

291J. GEORGE II CORONATION MEDAL

Date: 1727.
Metal: Gold, silver, base metal.
Size: 34mm.
Designer: John Croker
Mintage: Gold (238), silver (800), base metal (Unknown)
Description: Bust of George II facing left. Legend: GEORGIVS. II. D.G. MAG. BR. FR. ET. HIB. REX. (Reverse) King seated on throne, left being crowned by Britannia, standing right. Legend: VOLENTES. PER. POVLOS (through the will of the people) Exergue: CORON. XI. OCTOB. MDCCXXVII.

VALUE: Silver   £250–350

291K. GEORGE III CORONATION MEDAL

Date: 1761.
Metal: Gold, silver, bronze
Size: 34mm.
Designer: Lorenz Natter.
Mintage: Gold (858), silver (800), bronze (unknown)
Description: Bust of George III facing right. Legend: GEORGIVS. III. D.G. M. BRI. FRA. ET. HIB. REX. F.D. (Reverse) Britannia standing left, crowning King seated right. Legend: PATRIAE. OVANTI. (Crowned as the country rejoices). Exergue: CORONAT. XXII. SEPT. CI ƆI ƆCCLXI

VALUE: Silver £500–600

291L. GEORGE IV CORONATION MEDAL

Date: 1821.
Metal: Gold, silver, bronze
Size: 35mm.
Designer: Benedetto Pistrucci.
Mintage: Gold (1,060), silver (800), bronze (unknown, over 1,525)
Description: Bust of George IV, laureate, facing left. Legend: GEORGIVS IIII D.G. BRITAN-NIARUM REX F.D. (Reverse) Three standing ladies, left, facing seated King, right. Behind King stands angel holding crown above his head. Legend: PROPRIO JAM JURE ANIMO PATERNO (already by special right, inaugurated in the spirit of his father). Exergue: INAU-GURATUS DIE JULII. XIX ANNO. MDCCXXI.
Comments: *A slightly smaller and thinner version of this medal was struck and pierced for suspension from a plain maroon ribbon. These medals are invariably named to members of the Buckinghamshire Yeomanry Cavalry Hussars who took part in lining the route of the procession. This is believed to be the first coronation medal designed to be worn.*

VALUE: Silver £350–450

291M. WILLIAM IV CORONATION MEDAL

Date: 1831.
Metal: Gold, silver, bronze
Size: 34mm.
Designer: William Wyon
Mintage: Gold (1,000), silver (2,000), bronze (1,133)
Description: Head of William IV facing right. Legend: WILLIAM THE FOURTH CROWNED SEP: 8 1831 (Reverse) Head of Queen Adelaide facing right. Legend: ADELAIDE. QUEEN CONSORT. CROWNED SEP: 8 1831.

VALUE: Silver £400–500

291N. VICTORIA CORONATION MEDAL

Date: 1838.
Metal: Gold, silver, bronze.
Size: 36mm.
Designer: Benedetto Pistrucci.
Mintage: Gold (1,369), silver (2,209), bronze (1,871)
Description: Head of Queen Victoria facing left. Legend: VICTORIA D.G. BRITANNIARUM REGINA F.D. (Reverse) Three ladies symbolic of England, Scotland and Ireland, standing left, presenting crown to Queen, seated on a dais, right. A lion lies behind her chair. Legend: ERIMUS TIBI NOBILE REGNUM (We shall be a noble Kingdom to you). Exergue: INAUGURATA DIE JUNII XXVIII MDCCCXXXVIII.

VALUE: Silver   £300–400

292. EMPRESS OF INDIA MEDAL

Date: 1877.
Ribbon: 42mm crimson edged in gold.
Metal: Gold or silver.
Size: 58mm.
Description: (Obverse) a left-facing bust of Queen Victoria wearing a veil and a coronet, her name and the date of her elevation being inscribed round the circumference. (Reverse) a broad zigzag border enclosing the words EMPRESS OF INDIA and its equivalent in Urdu and Hindi across the field.
Comments: *Issued to celebrate the proclamation of Victoria as Empress of India on 1 January 1877. It was awarded in gold to Indian princes and high-ranking British officials. Indian civilians and selected officers and men of the various British and Indian regiments serving in India at the time were awarded the silver medal. It was issued unnamed but many examples were subsequently engraved or impressed privately.*

VALUE:		*Miniature*
Gold	£6000–10,000	£275–360
Silver	£650–850	£100–160

292A. VISIT OF THE PRINCE OF WALES TO INDIA MEDAL 1875

(reduced)

Date: 1875–76.
Ribbon: 38mm plain white (gold), pale blue with white edges (silver).
Metal: Gold, silver or white metal with a silver crown.
Size: Oval 48mmx77mm.
Description: (Obverse) left-facing effigy of the Prince of Wales (later King Edward VII) surrounded by a laurel wreath and surmounted by a crown fitted to a suspension ring; (reverse) Prince of Wales's emblem surrounded by the chain of the GCSI.
Comments: *A large oval medal was struck to commemorate the state visit of HRH the Prince of Wales to India. Some 48 medals were struck in gold, 165 in silver and an unknown number in white metal. The gold medals are impressed on the rim with a small numeral, and engraved with the recipient's name in block capitals. The medals were numbered and named in strict order of precedence. The silver medal has a frosted relief on a mirror table. 13 small silver badges were also presented. In addition a small silver medalet was issued to the crews of HMS* Renown *and* Terrible *and the Royal Yacht* Osborne*, with the initials A and E either side of the Prince of Wales' emblem and a reverse inscribed HRH ALBERT EDWARD PRINCE OF WALES INDIA 1875–76 (similar in style to no. 308B).*

VALUE:

Gold (48)	£7000–8000
Silver (165)	£1000–1500
White metal	£200–250
Silver badge (13)	**Rare**
Silver medalet	£100–150

293. JUBILEE MEDAL 1887

Date: 1887.
Ribbon: Broad central blue band with wide white stripes at the edges.
Metal: Gold, silver or bronze.
Size: 30mm.
Description: (Obverse) the bust of Queen Victoria by Sir Joseph Edgar Boehm; (reverse) an elaborate wreath in which are entwined the heraldic flowers of the United Kingdom. This encloses an eight-line inscription surmounted by a crown: IN COMMEMORATION OF THE 50th YEAR OF THE REIGN OF QUEEN VICTORIA 21 JUNE 1887. The reverse was designed by Clemens Emptmayer
Comments: *Struck to celebrate the 50th anniversary of Victoria's accession to the throne. The medal in gold was given to members of the Royal Family and their personal guests. The silver medal was given to members of the Royal Household, government ministers, senior officials, distinguished foreign visitors, naval and military officers involved in the Jubilee parade on 21 June 1887 and the captains of vessels taking part in the great Naval Review at Spithead. The bronze medal was given to selected NCOs and men who took part in the parade or the Spithead Review. All medals were issued unnamed with a ring for suspension. When the Diamond Jubilee was celebrated ten years later holders of the 1887 medal were given a clasp in the form of a cable entwined around the date 1897 and surmounted by an imperial crown. Twin loops at the ends enabled the clasp to be sewn on to the ribbon. Clasp sizes: 28mm (men), 22mm (ladies).*

VALUE:

	Without clasp	With clasp 1897	*Miniature*
Gold (133)	£1350–1500	Rare	£110–160
Silver (1,012)	£200–240	£300–350	£35–40 (add £30 for clasp)
Bronze (600)	£175–200	£300–350	£35–40 (add £30 for clasp)

294. JUBILEE (POLICE) MEDAL 1887

Date: 1887.
Ribbon: Plain dark blue.
Metal: Bronze.
Size: 36mm.
Description: (Obverse) the veiled profile of Queen Victoria; (reverse) a wreath surmounted by a crown and enclosing the inscription: JUBILEE OF HER MAJESTY QUEEN VICTORIA. The year appears at the foot and the name of the force round the top.
Comments: *Issued to all ranks of the Metropolitan and City of London Police and selected civilian staff to celebrate the Jubilee on 21 June 1887. Clasps for the 1897 Jubilee q.v. were issued to recipients of this medal still serving ten years later.*

VALUE:

	Without clasp	With 1897 clasp	*Miniature*
Metropolitan Police (14,000)	£45–55	£55–65	£30–35
City of London Police (900)	£75–100	£100–125	£30–35 (add £10 for clasp)

295. JUBILEE MEDAL 1897

Date: 1897.
Ribbon: Dark blue with two broad white bands and dark blue edges (as for 293).
Metal: Gold, silver or bronze.
Size: 30mm.
Description: This medal is very similar to the 1887 issue, differing solely in the date and anniversary on the reverse. Around 980 medals were awarded to army officers.

VALUE:

		Miniature
Gold (73)	£1500–1750	£150–200
Silver (3040)	£200–250	£35–45
Bronze (890)	£150–200	£25–35

296. JUBILEE MEDAL (MAYORS AND PROVOSTS) 1897

Date: 1897.
Ribbon: White with two broad dark stripes and white edges.
Metal: Gold or silver.
Size: Height 48mm; max. width 40mm.
Description: A diamond-shaped medal with ring suspension, reminiscent of the *Klippe* coinage of central Europe. Both sides had circular centres with trefoil ornaments occupying the angles. (Obverse) the Wyon profile of the young Victoria at the time of her accession; (reverse) Sir Thomas Brock's Old Head veiled bust of the Queen.
Comments: *The gold version was presented to Lord Mayors and Lord Provosts while the silver medal was granted to Mayors and Provosts. Small silver medals of more conventional circular format were produced with these motifs and sold as souvenirs of the occasion.*

VALUE:

		Miniature
Gold (14)	£1000–1500	£820–920
Silver (512)	£350–400	£210–260

297. JUBILEE (POLICE) MEDAL 1897

Date: 1897.
Ribbon: Plain dark blue.
Metal: Bronze.
Size: 36mm.
Description: Very similar to the 1887 issue with the dates suitably amended and the name of the service round the top of the reverse.
Comments: *Separate issues were made in respect of the Police Ambulance service, St John Ambulance Brigade and the Metropolitan Fire Brigade. Holders of the previous medal merely received the 1897 clasp (Metropolitan Police 8708, City of London Police 485).*

VALUE:		Miniature
Metropolitan Police (7481)	£45–55	£55–75
City of London Police (535)	£85–100	£55–75
Police Ambulance (210)	£350–450	£55–75
St John Ambulance Brigade (910)	£75–85	£55–75
Metropolitan Fire Brigade (950)	£75–85	£55–75

298. CEYLON DIAMOND JUBILEE MEDAL 1897

Date: 1897.
Ribbon: Plain red.
Metal: Gold or silver.
Size: 35mm.
Description: (Obverse) the Boehm bust of Queen Victoria with the dates 1837-1897 at the foot. (Reverse) an elephant and a stupa (dome-shaped Buddhist shrine), with two lines of concentric inscriptions: TO COMMEMORATE SIXTY YEARS OF HER MAJESTY'S REIGN and, unusually, THE RT. HON. SIR J. WEST RIDGEWAY K.C.B., K.C.M.G., GOVERNOR. A crown above the rim was fixed to a ring for suspension.
Comments: *Awarded to local dignitaries and leading officials in the Ceylon government.*

VALUE:		Miniature
Gold	£1000–1500	£820–1020
Silver	£200–250	£160–210

299. HONG KONG DIAMOND JUBILEE MEDAL

Date: 1897.
Ribbon: Three equal stripes of dark blue, maroon and dark blue (also known with gold ribbon with central white stripe).
Metal Gold, silver or bronze.
Size: 36mm.
Description: (Obverse) the Boehm bust of Queen Victoria with the date 1897 at the foot; (reverse) a seascape with a British three-masted sailing ship and a Chinese junk in the background and two figures shaking hands in the foreground. The name of the colony appears at the top, while two concentric inscriptions read SIR WILLIAM ROBINSON G.C.M.G. GOVERNOR and TO COMMEMORATE SIXTY YEARS OF HER MAJESTY'S REIGN 1837-1897.
Comments: *Very little is known for certainty about this medal on account of the fact that the colonial records were destroyed during the Japanese occupation. However, it is believed that a small number of gold medals were presented to local high ranking dignitaries, silver to various civil and military personnel and bronze to others.*

VALUE:	
Gold	£2000–2500
Silver	£400–500
Bronze	£180–200

299A. LAGOS DIAMOND JUBILEE MEDAL

Date: 1897.
Ribbon: Dark blue with two broad white stripes towards the edges.
Metal Silver.
Size: 36mm.
Description: (Obverse) the veiled crowned profile of Queen Victoria (similar to the Egypt Medal 1882, No. 131) inscribed VICTORIA QUEEN AND EMPRESS with a Tudor rose at the foot; (reverse) QUEEN'S DIAMOND JUBILEE LAGOS round the circumference, with JUNE 22ND 1897 in the centre.
Comments: *Issued to civil and military personnel associated with the Diamond Jubilee celebrations in the crown colony of Lagos (1886–1906 when it was incorporated in the colony and protectorate of Southern Nigeria).*

VALUE: —

299B. INDIA DIAMOND JUBILEE MEDAL

Date: 1897.
Ribbon: White.
Metal Silver.
Size: 36mm.
Description: (Obverse) the veiled crowned profile of Queen Victoria (similar to the Egypt Medal 1882, No. 131) inscribed VICTORIA QUEEN AND EMPRESS with a Star of India at the foot; (reverse) TO COMMEMORATE THE SIXTIETH YEAR OF THE REIGN OF H.M. QUEEN VICTORIA 1897 within a laurel wreath, with royal arms above and the Star of India below.
Comments: *Issued to civil and military personnel associated with the Diamond Jubilee celebrations in India. It was also issued to Native chiefs in the colony of Natal.*

VALUE: £100–150

300. VISIT TO IRELAND MEDAL 1900

Date: 1900.
Ribbon: Plain dark blue.
Metal: Bronze.
Size: 36mm.
Description: (Obverse) a half-length version of the Boehm bust of Queen Victoria; (reverse) the female allegorical figure of Hibernia looking out over Kingstown (Dun Laoghaire) harbour in which the Royal Yacht can be seen (far left). Unusually, the medal was mounted with a suspension bar decorated with shamrocks.
Comments: *The medal designed by G. W. de Saulles commemorated Queen Victoria's visit to Ireland in 1900. It was awarded to officers of the Royal Irish Constabulary and Dublin Metropolitan Police who were involved in security and policing the various events connected with the visit. The medal was worn with the same ribbon as the Jubilee Police medals.*

VALUE:
Bronze (2285)	£120–150	*Miniature*	£110–130

300A. VISIT TO THE COLONIES MEDAL 1901

Date: 1901.
Ribbon: Unknown.
Metal: Gold and Silver.
Size: Oval 20 x 24mm.
Description: (Obverse) a crowned anchor with the royal garter and rose emblem inset; (reverse) inscribed T.R.H. DUKE & DUCHESS OF CORNWALL & YORK—BRITISH COLONIES 1901 H.M.S. OPHIR.
Comments: *This small medalet was issued to commemorate the visit of the Duke and Duchess of Cornwall and York to the British Colonies aboard HMS Ophir in 1901.*

VALUE: **Gold £500–600**
               Silver £150–200   *Miniature £110–130*

300B. TRHs THE DUKE AND DUCHESS OF YORK MEDAL 1901

Date: 1901.
Ribbon: Dark blue with a central red stripe.
Metal: Silver.
Size: 32mm.
Description: (Obverse) the left-facing conjoined busts of the Duke and Duchess surrounded by a ribboned wreath; (reverse) a crowned anchor surmounted by the garter and rose emblem T.R.H'S THE DUKE & DUCHESS OF YORK'S VISIT TO THE COLONIES 1901 surrounded by a ribboned wreath. With ring suspension
Comments: *It is believed that this attractive medal was awarded to dignitaries on the Royal Tour of 1901.*

VALUE: **£125–150**   *Miniature*   —

301. CORONATION MEDAL 1902

Date: 1902.
Ribbon: Dark blue with a central red stripe and white edges.
Metal: Silver or bronze.
Size: Height 42mm; max. width 30mm.
Description: (Obverse) the left-facing conjoined busts of King Edward VII and Queen Alexandra, both crowned and wearing coronation robes. (Reverse) the crowned royal cypher above the date of the actual ceremony. The medal has an elaborate raised rim decorated with a wreath culminating in a crown through which the ring for suspension was looped.
Comments: *This medal, designed by Emil Fuchs and struck by Messrs. Elkington & Co., celebrated the coronation of King Edward VII on 9 August 1902. It was presented in silver to members of the Royal Family, foreign dignitaries, high officials of the government, senior officials and service officers involved in the celebrations. Selected NCOs and other ranks of the Army and Navy taking part in the parades were awarded the medal in bronze. Both versions were issued unnamed.*

VALUE:		*Miniature*
Silver (3493)	£150–200	£30–35
Bronze (6054)	£100–150	£30–35

302. CORONATION MEDAL (MAYORS AND PROVOSTS) 1902

Date: 1902.
Ribbon: Dark blue with a narrow white central stripe and crimson borders.
Metal: Silver.
Size: 32mm.
Description: (Obverse) conjoined right-facing busts of the King and Queen; (reverse) the crowned cypher and date. It differed from the ordinary medal by having flat, broad borders decorated with the heraldic flowers of the United Kingdom culminating at the top in a simple suspension ring.
Comments: *The medal was designed by Emil Fuchs and struck by Messrs. Elkington & Co.*

VALUE:

Silver	£150–200	*Miniature*	£110–130

303. CORONATION (POLICE) MEDAL 1902

Date: 1902.
Ribbon: Red, with a narrow dark blue central stripe.
Metal: Silver or bronze.
Size: 36mm.
Description: (Obverse) the left-facing bust of King Edward VII; (reverse) a crown above a nosegay of heraldic flowers with the words CORONATION OF HIS MAJESTY KING EDWARD VII 1902 in the upper field. The name or initials of the service appeared round the top, LCC MFB signifying London County Council Metropolitan Fire Brigade.
Comments: *Issued to all ranks of the police and associated services to celebrate the coronation, and awarded in silver or bronze to officers and other ranks respectively. 97 bronze medals were also issued to police civilian staff. The medal was designed by G. W. de Saulles.*

VALUE:	Silver	*Miniature*	Bronze	*Miniature*
Metropolitan Police	£500–600 (51)	£25–35	£25–35 (16,709)	£25–35
City of London Police	£650–850 (5)	£25–35	£65–75 (1060)	£25–35
LCC MFB	£650–850 (12)	—	£55–65 (1000)	£55–65
St John Ambulance Brigade	—	—	£55–65 (912)	£65–75
Police Ambulance Service	Unique	—	£300–350 (204)	£95–110

304. CEYLON CORONATION MEDAL 1902

Date: 1902.
Ribbon: Plain blue.
Metal: Gold.
Size: 35mm.
Description: (Obverse) a crowned left-facing bust of King Edward VII; (reverse) the elephant and stupa motif previously used (MYB298). The concentric inscription on the reverse now tactfully omitted any reference to the governor: IN COMMEMORATION OF THE CORONATION OF H.M. KING EDWARD VII 1902. The medal was fitted with a ring for suspension.
Comments: *Like its predecessor, this rare medal was struck for presentation to local dignitaries and government officials.*

VALUE: — *Miniature* £260–310

305. HONG KONG CORONATION MEDAL 1902

Date: 1902.
Ribbon: None officially designated but it is usually seen with a red, white and blue ribbon.
Metal: Silver or bronze.
Size: 36mm.
Description: (Obverse) conjoined right-facing busts of King Edward VII and Queen Alexandra with their names round the circumference; (reverse) the maritime motif of the Diamond Jubilee medal with new inscriptions in two concentric curves: SIR HENRY A. BLAKE G.C.M.G. GOVERNOR (inner) and TO COMMEMORATE THE CORONATION OF THEIR MAJESTIES THE KING & QUEEN (outer). Usually, but not always, fitted with a suspension ring.
Comments: *Issued to all British and Indian officers and other ranks serving in the colony as well as local police. Some 6,000 medals were produced by Edmonds & Son, London, and issued in cases.*

VALUE
Silver	£150–250
Bronze	£65–85

305A. NATAL CORONATION MEDAL 1902

Date: 1902.
Ribbon: Dark blue with a central claret stripe.
Metal: Silver.
Size: 21mm, 29mm and 51mm.
Description: (Obverse) a right-facing crowned bust of King Edward VII with the inscription TO COMMEMORATE THE CORONATION OF KING EDWARD VII; (reverse) Royal coat of arms above two running wildebeests, inscribed (round top) EDWARDUS DEI GRATIA BRITANNIAR REX F:D and (round bottom) COLONY OF NATAL 26 JUNE 1902. Ring suspension.
Comments: *The small medal was distributed to schoolchildren whereas the large medal was restricted to native chiefs and is relatively scarce. It is believed that the middle-size medal was presented to local dignitaries.*

VALUE:
21mm	£20–30
29mm	£85–100
51mm	£500–600

306. DELHI DURBAR MEDAL 1903

Date: 1903.
Ribbon: Pale blue with three dark blue stripes—the colours of the Order of the Indian Empire and the Order of the Star of India..
Metal: Gold or silver.
Size: 38.5mm.
Description: (Obverse) a right-facing crowned bust of the King Emperor with DELHI DARBAR 1903 on the right side; (reverse) a three-line inscription in Farsi across the field, which translates as "By grace of the Lord of the Realm, Edward, King, Emperor of India, 1901", with an elaborate border of roses, thistles, shamrocks and Indian flowers. Ring suspension.
Comments: *Struck to celebrate the Durbar of the King Emperor at Delhi on 1 January 1903. It was awarded in gold to the rulers of the Indian princely states and in silver to lesser dignitaries, government officials, and officers and other ranks of the armed services actually involved in the celebrations.*

VALUE:		*Miniature*
Gold (140)	£2500–3000	—
Silver (2567)	£250–350	£35–45

307. VISIT TO SCOTLAND MEDAL 1903

Date: 1903.
Ribbon: Plain red.
Metal: Bronze.
Size: 36mm.
Description: Very similar to the Police Coronation medal but the
    year was changed to 1903 and the inscription SCOTTISH POLICE
    appeared round the top of the reverse. The medal was named to the
    recipient on the rim. An ornate clasp decorated with a thistle was
    worn above the suspension bar.
Comments: *This medal was designed by G. W. de Saulles and struck to
    commemorate Their Majesties' post-coronation tour of Scotland in May
    1903. It was awarded to the police and troops involved in parades and
    escort duties, as well as the ancillary services such as the Fire Brigade and
    the St Andrew's Ambulance Association.*

VALUE:
    Bronze (2957)   £100–150   *Miniature*   £45–55

308. VISIT TO IRELAND MEDAL 1903

Date: 1903.
Ribbon: Pale blue.
Metal: Bronze.
Size: 36mm.
Description: (Obverse) bust of King Edward VII; (reverse) as 1900 medal
    with the date altered at the foot. The suspension brooch is ornamented
    with shamrocks.
Comments: *This medal was designed by G. W. de Saulles and struck to mark
    the King's visit to Ireland in July 1903. It was awarded on the same terms as
    the Visit to Ireland Medal 1900.*

VALUE:
    Bronze (7757)   £150–200   *Miniature*   £60–70

308A. VISIT OF THE PRINCE AND PRINCESS OF WALES TO INDIA

Instituted: 1905–06
Ribbon: Neck ribbon 55mm wide, maroon with wide blue stripes
    towards each edge.
Metal: Frosted silver.
Size: 51mm.
Description: (Obverse) conjoined busts of the Prince and Princess
    of Wales (later King George V and Queen Mary), facing right.
    ELKINGTON (manufacturers) inscribed minutely below busts.
    (Reverse) badge of the Prince of Wales surrounded by the chain of
    the GCSI, with legend T.R.H. THE PRINCE & PRINCESS OF WALES
    VISIT TO INDIA 1905–6 around with ELKINGTON LONDON in
    small letters below.
Comments: *Only 72 medals were struck, 70 of which were bestowed on
    British and Indian officials.*

VALUE: £600–800   *Miniature*   £55–65

308B. GEORGE PRINCE OF WALES MEDAL

Instituted: 1905-06.
Ribbon: 15mm, red, white and blue in equal parts.
Metal: Silver or gold.
Size: Oval 20 x 24mm.
Description: (Obverse) the Prince of Wales's plumes surrounded by the Garter and the chain and badge of the GCSI, flanked in the field by the letters G and M; (reverse) inscription T.R.H. GEORGE PRINCE OF WALES & VICTORIA MARY PRINCESS OF WALES with INDIA 1905-6 in the upper centre.
Comments: *The 26 gold medals were given by Their Royal Highnesses to their personal staff, while a total of 1,625 silver medals were presented to all hands aboard HMS* Renown *and* Terrible *and the Royal Yacht* Osborne.

VALUE:

Gold (26)	£1000–1500
Silver (1625)	£120–180

309. CORONATION MEDAL 1911

Date: 1911.
Ribbon: Dark blue with two thin red stripes in the centre.
Metal: Silver.
Size: 32mm.
Description: (Obverse) conjoined left-facing busts of King George V and Queen Mary in their coronation robes within a floral wreath; (reverse) the crowned royal cypher above the date of the coronation itself. Plain ring suspension.
Comments: *Designed by Sir Bertram McKennal, MVO, ARA, these medals were issued unnamed but may sometimes be found with unofficial engraving. Those who were also entitled to the Delhi Darbar Medal received a crowned clasp inscribed DELHI if they had previously been awarded the coronation medal. This was the first occasion that the medal might be awarded to those not actually present at the ceremony itself.*

VALUE:

		Miniature
Silver (15,901)	£80–100	£25–30
With Delhi clasp (134)	£600–800	£55–65

Delhi Durbar 1911.

309A. GUILDHALL CORONATION MEDAL 1911

Date: 1911.
Ribbon: Crimson.
Metal: Silver and enamels.
Size: 37mm.
Description: (Obverse) conjoined left-facing busts of King George V and Queen Mary with their names around, surrounded by a white enamelled ring bearing the words CORONATION RECEPTION . JUNE 1911 with laurel wreath around divided by four shields, surmounted by a crown with three semi-precious stones inset; (reverse) hallmark and pin. Suspended from an ornate clasp (with additional pin) bearing a sword and sceptre.
Comments: *The reception at the Guildhall, London, was a grand affair with members of the Royal family and a number of Heads of State in attendance. The ornate medals were presented in a plush case and were designed to be worn either as a lapel badge or as a conventional medal.*

VALUE: £250–300

310. CORONATION (POLICE) MEDAL 1911

Date: 1911.
Ribbon: Red with three narrow blue stripes.
Metal: Silver.
Size: 36mm.
Description: (Obverse) a crowned left-facing bust of King George V; (reverse) an imperial crown with an ornate surround. The inscription CORONATION 1911 appears at the foot and the name of the service at the top. Ring suspension.
Comments: *By now the number of police and ancillary services had grown considerably, as witness the various reverse types which may be encountered in this medal. The medal was designed by Sir Bertram McKennal, MVO, ARA,*

VALUE:		*Miniature*
Metropolitan Police (19,783)	£35–45	£20–25
City of London Police (1385)	£100–150	£25–30
County and Borough Police (2565)	£90–100	£25–30
Police Ambulance Service (130)	£650–750	£95–110
London Fire Brigade (1374)	£120–150	£95–110
Royal Irish Constabulary (585)	£175–250	£160–210
Scottish Police (1465)	£100–120	£55–65
St John Ambulance Brigade (2755)	£65–85	£65–75
St Andrew's Ambulance Corps (310)	£250–300	£110–160
Royal Parks (120)	£1000–1500	£150–170

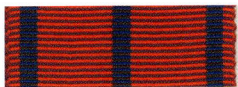

311. VISIT TO IRELAND MEDAL 1911

Date: 1911.
Ribbon: Dark green with thin red stripes towards either end.
Metal: Silver.
Size: 36mm.
Description: Very similar to the foregoing, distinguished only by the reverse which is inscribed CORONATION 1911 round the top, with the actual date of the visit round the foot.
Comments: *This medal was designed by Sir Bertram McKennal, MVO, ARA and was granted to prominent civic dignitaries and members of the Irish police forces involved in the royal visit to Ireland which took place on 7-12 July 1911.*

VALUE:			
Silver (2477)	£75–90	*Miniature*	£75–85

311A. EAST INDIAN RAILWAY COMPANY ROYAL VISIT TO INDIA MEDAL 1911

Date: 1911.

Ribbon: Dark blue with a central maroon stripe flanked by narrow gold stripes.

Metal: Gilded bronze.

Size: 32mm.

Description: (Obverse) the arms of the East Indian Railway Company surrounded by the inscription EAST INDIAN RAILWAY COMPANY with a winged wheel at the foot; (reverse) a ten-line inscription FOR SERVICES RENDERED DURING THE RAILWAY JOURNEYS OF THEIR MAJESTIES THE KING EMPEROR AND QUEEN EMPRESS IN INDIA 1911.

Comments: *Very little is known about this rare medal, but it is believed to have been awarded to members of the Honour Guard of the East Indian Railway Volunteer Rifle Corps and employees of the company present during the tour of India undertaken in 1911 by King George V and Queen Mary. It is believed that no more than 30 medals were issued.*

VALUE: £100–£120

312. DELHI DURBAR MEDAL 1911

Date: 1911.

Ribbon: Dark blue with two narrow red stripes in the middle.

Metal: Gold or silver.

Size: 38.5mm.

Description: (Obverse) the conjoined crowned busts of King George V and Queen Mary in a floral wreath; (reverse) an elaborate Farsi text which translates as "The Durbar of George V, Emperor of India, Master of the British Lands".

Comments: *This medal marked the Delhi Durbar held in the King Emperor's honour in December 1911. Most of the gold medals went to the Indian princely rulers and top government officials, 10,000 of the 30,000 silver medals were awarded to officers and other ranks of the British and Indian Armies for exemplary service, without their necessarily being present at the Durbar itself.*

VALUE:		*Miniature*
Gold (200)	£3000–4000	£320–420
Silver (30,000)	£100–130	£25–30

312AA. DELHI DURBAR MILITARY TOURNAMENT MEDAL 1911

Date: 1911.

Ribbon: None

Metal: Gold, Silver or Bronze.

Size: 44mm.

Description: (Obverse) the left-facing crowned and robed bust of King George V; (reverse) within a wreath of laurel leaves, three tablets engraved with the words DURBAR, TOURNAMENT and the event for which the medal is awarded, e.g. HOCKEY, with the legend DELHI . CORONATION . DURBAR . 1911 around

Comments: *Minted by the Calcutta Mint, and usually named on the edge with the details of the recipient. These very rare medals were awarded for specific events at the Delhi Durbar, but they are rarely seen.*

VALUE:	Gold (6)	£1000–1500
	Silver (15–20)	£350–400
	Bronze (40–50)	£150–200

312A. VISIT OF KING GEORGE V AND QUEEN MARY TO INDIA 1911–12

Date: 1911–12.
Ribbon: None.
Metal: Silver or gold.
Size: Oval 20 x 24mm.
Description: (Obverse): GRI entwined initials as a monogram above the word INDIA; (reverse) MRI monogram and dates 1911–12, suspended from a bar by a simple ring and scroll suspender.
Comments: *Given as a commemorative gift from the King to the crews of the "special service squadron" led by HMS Medina which took the King and Queen to Bombay in 1911 to proceed to Delhi for the Durbar.*

VALUE:	Gold	£750–1000
	Silver	£60–85

312AB. QUEEN ALEXANDRA'S CHILDREN'S BANQUET MEDAL 1914

Date: 28 December 1914.
Ribbon: White, with red stripes at each edge.
Metal: Bronze.
Size: 38mm.
Description: (Obverse) bust of Queen Alexandra facing right with the inscription A GIFT FROM QUEEN ALEXANDRA; (reverse) central inscription FEAR GOD, HONOUR THE KING surrounded by the legend GUILDHALL BANQUET TO OUR SOLDIERS' & SAILORS' CHILDREN 28th DEC. 1914. The suspension is ornate and has the arms of the City of London superimposed.
Comments: *This medal, designed and manufactured by Elkington, was issued unnamed to 1,300 children and a small number of Chelsea pensioners who attended a banquet at the Guildhall on 28 December 1914. The children, between the ages of eight and thirteen, were the sons and daughters of men in the Fleet or on the Western Front. One child was chosen from each family by Sir James Gildea of the Soldiers' and Sailors' Families' Association. Relatively few medals appear to have survived.*

VALUE: £50–£70

312AC. VISIT OF THE PRINCE OF WALES TO NEW ZEALAND 1920

Date: 1920.
Ribbon: Neck ribbon 38mm maroon.
Metal: Silver, with the raised edges of the medal being milled, plain rim.
Size: 50mm.
Description: (Obverse) badge of the Prince of Wales surrounded by the chain of the GCSI; (reverse) the inscription THE VISIT OF H.R.H. THE PRINCE OF WALES TO NEW ZEALAND 1920 in seven lines, surrounded by a laurel wreath, with maker's name ELKINGTON inscribed minutely underneath the base of the wreath. Fitted with a plain suspension ring.
Comments: *This medal was awarded in connection with the visit of HRH the Prince of Wales (later King Edward VIII and Duke of Windsor) to New Zealand in the course of his tour aboard HMS Renown 1919–20.*

VALUE: £100–150

312B. VISIT OF THE PRINCE OF WALES TO INDIA 1921–22

Date: 1921–22.
Ribbon: Neck ribbon 55mm maroon with broad blue stripes towards each edge.
Metal: Frosted silver.
Size: 50mm.
Description: (Obverse) bust of Prince of Wales facing left with inscription EDWARD PRINCE OF WALES INDIA 1921–1922; (reverse) badge of the Prince of Wales surrounded by the chain of the GCSI. Fitted with a plain suspension ring.
Comments: *Only 84 medals were awarded in connection with the visit of HRH the Prince of Wales (later King Edward VIII and Duke of Windsor) to India in the course of his world tour aboard HMS Renown.*

VALUE:	£700–900	*Miniature*	£85–110

312C. WELCOME HOME MEDAL FOR THE PRINCE OF WALES

Date: 1922.
Ribbon: Green with red central stripe.
Metal: Gold, silver and bronze.
Size: Oval 43mm x 34mm.
Description: An oval medal with ornate edges. (Obverse) crowned and robed bust of the Prince of Wales with the inscription EDWARD PRINCE OF WALES KG; (reverse) The Prince of Wales's feathers with the inscription WELCOME HOME 1922. With integral ornate loop for suspension.
Comments: *Struck by F. Bowcher to mark the return of the Prince of Wales to England after his world tour.*

VALUE:	Gold	£850–1000
	Silver	£120–150
	Bronze	£80–100

312D. VISIT OF THE PRINCE OF WALES TO BOMBAY MEDAL 1921

Date: 1921.
Ribbon: Watered blue with central thin white stripe.
Metal: Bronze.
Size: Oval 38mm x 30mm.
Description: An oval medal. (Obverse) bust of the Prince of Wales facing right, with the inscription EDWARD PRINCE OF WALES and surmounted by the Prince of Wales's feathers and motto ICH DIEN; (reverse) VISIT OF HIS ROYAL HIGHNESS BOMBAY NOVEMBER 1921 in six lines.
Comment: *Thought to be presented to the leading military and civil dignitaries present during the visit of the Prince of Wales. New information suggests it was also given to school children although this is unconfirmed. The number issued is not known.*

VALUE: £55–£85

312E. VISIT OF THE PRINCE OF WALES TO PATNA 1921

Date: 1921.
Ribbon: Imperial Purple.
Metal: Bronze.
Size: 40mm.
Description: (Obverse) bust of the Prince of Wales facing right with the inscription EDWARD PRINCE OF WALES, in an oval centre-piece, with an ornate floral decoration either side; (Reverse) centre blank, with the inscription VISIT OF HIS ROYAL HIGHNESS around the top half, and PATNA 22ND. DEC 1921 around the lower half of the reverse.
Comment: *Believed to have been presented to the leading military and civil dignitaries present during the visit of the Prince of Wales. The number issued is not known, but is believed to be very small.*

VALUE : £80–£100

313. JUBILEE MEDAL 1935

Date: 1935.
Ribbon: Red with two dark blue and one white stripes at the edges.
Metal: Silver.
Size: 32mm.
Description: (Obverse) left-facing conjoined half-length busts of King George V and Queen Mary in crowns and robes of state; (reverse) a crowned GRI monogram flanked by the dates of the accession and the jubilee.
Comments: *This medal, designed by Sir William Goscombe John, RA, was issued to celebrate the Silver Jubilee of King George V and widely distributed to the great and good throughout the Empire.*

VALUE:
  Silver (85,234)   £30–45   *Miniature*   £15–20

313A. ISLE OF MAN SILVER JUBILEE MEDAL 1935

Date: 1935.
Ribbon: Three equal stripes of red, white and blue. However some medals had their ribbons substituted with black to mark the death of the King in 1936.
Metal: Nickel-plated brass or silver.
Size: 32mm.
Description: (Obverse) conjoined busts of King George V and Queen Mary in an inner circle surrounded by the legend KING GEORGE V & QUEEN MARY REIGNED 25 YEARS; (reverse) Triskelion emblem with the legend IN COMMEMORATION OF THE SILVER JUBILEE 1935. Suspended from a brooch bar of seven overlapping panels with the centre panel having the royal cypher GvR while the outer panels have two leaves in each.
Comments: *This medal was issued to celebrate the Silver Jubilee and the nickel-plated brass edition was given to all schoolchildren on the island. Just three medals are believed to have been struck in silver for presentation to civic dignitaries or officials. 8,000 medals were struck by James Fenton & Co of Birmingham.*

VALUE: Nickel-plated brass £20–30   Silver (3) £150–200

313B. GUILDHALL JUBILEE MEDAL 1935

Date: 1935.
Ribbon: None.
Metal: Enamelled silver-gilt.
Size: 38mm wide.
Description: (Obverse) Arms of the City of London within a blue enamelled garter with the date 1935 on a white panel, surmounted by the Royal cypher, crown and lion; (reverse) engraved with the date 22nd May 1935. The medal is suspended from a double scroll brooch.
Comments: *This medal was issued to selected dignitaries who attended the banquet at the Guildhall in celebration of the King's Silver Jubilee. It was made by G. Kenning & Son, London.*

VALUE: £250–300

314. CORONATION MEDAL 1937

Date: 1937.
Ribbon: Blue edged with one red and two white stripes.
Metal: Silver.
Size: 32mm.
Description: (Obverse) conjoined busts of King George VI and Queen Elizabeth in their robes of state without any inscription. The stark simplicity of this motif was matched by a reverse showing the crowned GRI over the inscription CROWNED 12 MAY 1937, with the names of the King and Queen in block capitals round the circumference.
Comments: *Issued to celebrate the coronation of King George VI on 12 May 1937.*

VALUE: **Silver (90,000)**   £30–50   *Miniature*   **£15–20**

314A. GUILDHALL CORONATION MEDAL 1937

Date: 1937.
Ribbon: None
Metal: Silver-gilt.
Size: 34mm.
Description: A rectangular medal (obverse) conjoined busts of King George VI and Queen Elizabeth in their robes of state on a shield with palm and vine sprigs below and CORONATION in a tablet. The design struck on a rectangular base with two "steps" at each side in art deco style. Reverse blank, inscribed with the name of recipient. The medal is suspended from an ornate crowned coat of arms of the City of London with GUILDHALL above
Comments: *Issued by the City of London to selected dignitaries who attended the banquet at the Guildhall to celebrate the coronation of King George VI on 12 May 1937.*

VALUE: £150–200

314B. ROYAL VISIT TO SOUTH AFRICA 1947 CHIEFS' MEDALS

Reverse i.

Reverse ii.

Date: 1947.
Ribbon: Yellow.
Metal: Silver.
Size: Oval 25mm x 32mm or 65mm x 55mm.
Description: (Obverse) conjoined busts of King George VI and Queen Elizabeth in their robes of state without any inscription. (Reverse) (i) map of South Africa surmounted by crowned GRE cypher dividing the date 1947 with KONINKLIKE BESOEK above and ROYAL VISIT below; (ii) crowned GRE with the inscription ROYAL VISIT 1947.
Comments: *Issued to celebrate the visit of King George VI to South Africa in 1947. Two distinctly different reverses have been seen but little is known about these medals which were issued in two sizes. These medals were awarded to Native Chiefs/Indabas (perhaps others also) and worn from a neck ribbon (those seen have been yellow although there are reports of others with a red ribbon). It is not known who were awarded the different sizes but it is likely that the bilingual version (Type i) was given to South African chiefs (156 comprising King Williamstown (Ciskei) 7; Umtata (Transkei) 31; Eshowe (Zululand) 40; Pietersburg (Northern Territories) 78). The unilingual version (Type ii) was probably reserved for the Protectorates and possibly Rhodesias. The number awarded is unknown.*

VALUE: **Both types:** **Small £75–100** **Large £125–175**

314C. ROYAL VISIT TO SOUTH AFRICA 1947

Reverse i.

Reverse ii.

Date: 1947.
Ribbon: None
Metal: Silver gilt and silver.
Size: 38mm.
Description: (Obverse) conjoined busts of HM King George VI and HM Queen Elizabeth crowned and robed. Artists initials PM (Percy Metcalfe) on ribbon on King's left shoulder; (Reverse, two types) (i) map of South Africa surmounted by crowned GRE cypher dividing the date 1947 with KONINKLIKE BESOEK above and ROYAL VISIT below; (ii) crowned GRE with the inscription ROYAL VISIT 1947.
Comments: *Type i was issued to celebrate the visit of King George VI to South Africa in 1947. Only six medallions were struck in silver gilt (awarded to the Governor General of the Union of SA, the Prime Minister of SA and the Administrators of the four Provinces of the Union of SA). A total of 394 silver medals in red cases were awarded (Governor General's Staff, Cabinet Ministers in Attendance, Officers commanding Commands, miscellaneous persons, Inter-departmental Committee on Royal Tour, Royal Train, Pilot Train, Railway staff employed at Government Houses, Press, chauffeurs, National/Kruger Park officials, Native Indabas). The medals were distributed by the Prime Minister's Office. Type ii were issued for Northern and Southern Rhodesia as part of the African tour. The medallion, in a blue case, was given to "selected persons who have done special work in connection with the Royal Visit". They were presented to recipients on April 11, 1947, at the Provincial Commissioner's Office in Livingstone. The medallions seem to have been named in seriffed capitals.*

VALUE :
Type i (in red case)	
Silver gilt (6)	£800–1000
Silver (394)	£200–250
Type ii (in blue case)	
Silver gilt (8)	£800–1000
Silver (196)	£200–250

315. CORONATION MEDAL 1953

Date: 1953.
Ribbon: Dark red with two narrow blue stripes in the centre and narrow white edges.
Metal: Silver.
Size: 32mm.
Description: (Obverse) a right-facing bust of Queen Elizabeth II in a Tudor crown and robes of state, the field being otherwise plain. (Reverse) a similar crown over the royal monogram EIIR with the legend QUEEN ELIZABETH II CROWNED 2ND JUNE 1953 round the circumference. Ring suspension.
Comments: *This medal celebrated the coronation of Queen Elizabeth II on 2 June 1953. News that Edmund Hillary and Sherpa Tenzing had successfully attained the summit of Everest reached London on the morning of the Coronation. Subsequently the members of the Hunt Expedition were invited to Buckingham Palace on 16 July 1953 where, on Her Majesty's own initiative, they were presented with coronation medals engraved MOUNT EVEREST EXPEDITION on the rim, following the precedent of the Mwele medals of 1895–96.*

VALUE: *Miniature*
  Silver (129,000)   £50–75   £12–14
  Mount Everest Expedition (37)   £850–1000

315A. ROYAL TOUR OF THE COMMONWEALTH MEDAL 1953–54

Date: 1953
Ribbon: None
Metal: Toned bronze.
Size: 38mm.
Description: (Obverse) Right facing, bare-headed, conjoined busts of HM Queen Elizabeth and Prince Philip, with the inscription "THE ROYAL VISIT" above and "MCMLIII–IV" below; (reverse) the crowned Royal coat of arms, with the Royal cypher above and the roman numerals MCMLIII–IV at the foot.
Comments: *This circular medal, designed by Mary Gillick, was struck by the Royal Mint and issued to mark the Royal Commonwealth Tour of Queen Elizabeth and Prince Philip between November 1953 and May 1954. The medal was issued to the Royal party and to local dignitaries at numerous ports of call throughout the Commonwealth. The total number of medals issued was 1,503.*

VALUE: £75–100

In addition to the official medal illustrated above (MYB 315A), all schoolchildren in New Zealand received a medal suspended from a blue ribbon, together with a folder telling the story of the Royal Family, with pictures of the Coronation regalia, royal palaces and descriptions. For the sake of completeness this medal is included below as MYB 315AA.

Date: 1953.
Ribbon: Dark blue.
Metal: Copper-coloured alloy.
Size: 38mm.
Description: (Obverse) right-facing crowned bust of Queen Elizabeth II wearing Tudor crown; (reverse) the crowned New Zealand coat of arms surrounded by sprays of flowers and the inscription ELIZABETH II ROYAL VISIT 1953–54. The copper-coloured medal is hung by a ring from a scalloped suspender as illustrated.
Comment: *Issued to all New Zealand school-children during the Royal visit, accompanied by a folder. The medals themselves are fairly common, but those with the accompanying folder are quite rare.*

VALUE: £8–12 (with accompanying folder £20–30)

315B. ROYAL VISIT TO MALTA 1954

Date: 1954.
Ribbon: None.
Metal: Gold coloured alloy.
Size: 38mm.
Description: (Obverse) right-facing crowned bust of the Queen; (reverse) shield containing the Maltese flag with the inscription TO COMMEMORATE THE ROYAL VISIT TO MALTA G.C. 1954 round the circumference.
Comments: *Issued to all Maltese schoolchildren, teachers and municipal workers in commemoration of the Royal visit to the island.*

VALUE: £10–15

315C. ROYAL VISIT TO NIGERIA MEDAL 1956

Date: 1956.
Ribbon: None.
Metal: Toned bronze.
Size: 38mm.
Description: (Obverse) Right facing, bare-headed, conjoined busts of HM Queen Elizabeth and Prince Philip, with the inscription "THE ROYAL VISIT" above and "TO NIGERIA 1956" below; (reverse) the crowned Royal coat of arms, with the Royal cypher above and the roman numerals MCMLVI at the foot.
Comments: *This circular medal was struck by the Royal Mint and issued to mark the Royal visit of Queen Elizabeth and Prince Philip to Nigeria, between 28 January and 16 February 1956. The medal was issued to the Royal party and to local dignitaries. A total of 650 medals were issued, each contained in a red leatherette box.*

VALUE: £65–85

315D. ROYAL VISIT TO WEST AFRICA 1961

As above, but dated MCMLXI (1961) on both sides. 500 medals were struck to mark the Royal Visit to Ghana, Sierra Leone and Gambia which was originally to have taken place in 1959 but was postponed pending the birth of Prince Andrew in 1960.

VALUE: £75–100

316. JUBILEE MEDAL 1977

Date: 1977.
Ribbon: White with thin red stripes at the edges, a broad blue stripe in the centre and a thin red stripe down the middle of it.
Metal: Silver.
Size: 32mm.
Description: (Obverse) Right-facing profile of Queen Elizabeth II wearing the St Edward's crown—the first time this design was employed; (reverse) a crown and wreath enclosing the words THE 25TH YEAR OF THE REIGN OF QUEEN ELIZABETH II 6 FEBRUARY 1977. A distinctive reverse was used in Canada, showing the dates of the reign flanking the royal monogram round the foot, CANADA round the top and a large stylised maple leaf in the centre.
Comments: *The 25th anniversary of the Queen's accession was marked by the release of this unnamed medal. The total number of medals issued in the UK was relatively small at 30,000 but they were distributed to a wide range of people including members of the armed forces, crown services and a number of people engaged in important activities including industry, trade, local services, the arts, entertainment, sports, etc..*

VALUE:		*Miniature*
General issue (30,000)	£150–200	£10–12
Canadian issue (30,000)	£100–150	£10–12

318. GOLDEN JUBILEE MEDAL 2002

Date: February 2002.

Ribbon: Royal blue with thin red stripes at the edges, a broad white stripe in the centre and a thin red stripe down the middle.

Metal: Gold-plated cupro-nickel.

Size: 32mm.

Description: (Obverse) a right facing profile of Queen Elizabeth II wearing a crown; (reverse) the royal coat of arms flanked by the dates 1952 and 2002.

Comments: *Issued to celebrate the 50th anniversary of the Queen's accession. It was granted to all personnel of the armed forces who had completed five or more years service on February 6, 2002. Generals who have been Chief of the General Staff and Chief of the Defence Staff or equivalent RN and RAF ranks were awarded the medal even though retired. It was also issued to members of the police, ambulance, coastguard, fire services, RNLI and mountain rescue services, as well as members of the Royal Household including The Queen's Body Guard of the Yeomen of the Guard, who had completed five years service and holders of the VC or GC. One member of HM Customs & Excise was awarded the medal by the Ministry of Defence to mark his close co-operation in work and liaison between the two departments. Almost 400,000 medals were issued.*

VALUE: £75–100   *Miniature*   £10–12

318A. DIAMOND JUBILEE MEDAL 2012

Date: February 2012.

Ribbon: Dark red with royal blue edges and two narrow white stripes in the centre. Medals to Royal Household female recipients have a bow.

Metal: Nickel-silver.

Size: 32mm.

Description: (Obverse) right facing coinage profile of Queen Elizabeth II by Ian Rank-Broadley; (reverse) the crowned royal cypher surmounted on a faceted diamond design, with the dates 1952 – 2012 below.

Comments: *Issued to celebrate the 60th anniversary of HM the Queen's accession. Awarded to members of the armed forces (Regular and Reserve), certain emergency services and operational prison services personnel and Police Community Support Officers who have completed five years service on February 6, 2012, as well as living holders of the VC or GC and members of the Royal Household. Unusually, breaking with tradition the contract to supply the medals was awarded to Worcester Medals. An estimated 438,000 medals were issued. There are copies of this medal which at 32.4mm in diamater are slightly larger than the originals. In addition a special medal with the royal cypher reverse was struck for the Caribbean Realms.*

VALUE: £75–100   *Miniature*   £10–12

318B. DIAMOND JUBILEE MEDAL 2012—CARIBBEAN REALMS

Date: February 2012.
Ribbon: Dark red with royal blue edges, white stripe in the centre bisected by a thin black stripe.
Metal: Nickel-silver.
Size: 32mm.
Description: (Obverse) right facing coinage profile of Queen Elizabeth II by Ian Rank-Broadley with the legend DIAMOND JUBILEE H.M. QUEEN ELIZABETH II around; (reverse) the crowned royal cypher, with CARIBBEAN REALMS above and the dates 1952 – 2012 below.
Comments: *Issued by the Caribbean realms of Antigua and Barbuda (28), the Bahamas (50), Barbados (632), Grenada (5), Jamaica (3,219), Saint Kitts and Nevis (275), Saint Lucia (60), and Saint Vincent and the Grenadines (?) plus 12 to the West Indian Committee and 12 to British citizens, to celebrate the 60th anniversary of HM the Queen's accession. Similar to the British award it was awarded to members of the armed forces, certain emergency services and operational prison services personnel and Police as well as members of the public service sector for outstanding achievement.*

VALUE: £100–150   *Miniature* £12–15

318C. PLATINUM JUBILEE MEDAL 2022

Date: February 2022.
Ribbon: Central stripe of royal blue, two broad red stripes to either side, edged with narrow silver stripes.
Metal: Nickel-silver.
Size: 32mm.
Description: (Obverse) right-facing coinage profile of Queen Elizabeth II by Ian Rank-Broadley; (reverse) the top motif from the Royal Coat of Arms showing the lion statant guardant atop a crowned Royal armorial helmet surrounded by ermine. The dates 1952–2022 appear in the field.
Comments: *Issued to celebrate the 70th Anniversary of HM the Queen's accession. Awarded to serving members of the armed forces (regular and reserve) and selected other uniformed services (including Police and Prison Service personnel) who have completed five years' service on February 6, 2022. Living holders of the VC and GC Association, and members of the Royal Household will also be eligible. It is estimated that over 400,000 will be issued.*

VALUE: —   *Miniature* £10–12

318D. CORONATION MEDAL 2023

Date: 2023.
Ribbon: Blue with a central red stripe edged with white.
Metal: Nickel-plated nickel-silver.
Size: 32mm.
Description: (Obverse) designed by Martin Jennings (who also designed the new King's coinage profile) the obverse features the left-facing, crowned conjoined busts of King Charles III and Queen Camilla. (Reverse) Designed by Phil McDermott (who also designed the ribbon) the features the crowned cypher of His Majesty King Charles III above the date 6 MAY 2023, the whole surrounded by a laurel wreath.
Comments: *Issued to commemorate the Coronation of His Majesty King Charles III at Westminster Abbey on May 6, 2023. The first medals were not actually available until after the Coronation itself, so none were evident on the day.*

VALUE: —   *Miniature*   **£10–12**

MISCELLANEOUS
Medals

Under this heading are grouped a very disparate range of medals whose only common denominator is that they do not fit conveniently into one or other of the preceding categories. They are not without considerable interest and many of them have a very keen following and a buoyant market. They are listed and added to as we have come across them, hence they are in no particular order.

319. KING'S AND QUEEN'S MESSENGER BADGE

Date: 1722.

Ribbon: Garter blue.

Metal: Silver gilt.

Size: Earliest issues variable according to monarch and jeweller; since George V—45mm x 34mm.

Description: (Issues since George V) an upright oval fitted with a plain suspension ring and having a greyhound suspended by a ring from the foot of the rim. (Obverse) the Garter inscribed HONI SOIT QUI MAL Y PENSE enclosing the royal cypher; early issues had the Royal coat of arms; (reverse) plain, engraved with an official number of issue and, on occasion, the name of the messenger.

Comments: *Messengers can be traced back to 1199, but prior to George I badges were not issued. Few of the earlier badges can be found due to a hand in and melt down order instituted by George III in 1762. During the reign of Victoria a number of different shapes and sizes were used for the badges due to a misunderstanding whereby individual messengers obtained their insignia from different jewellers instead of the Jewel Office. Since 1870 Garrards have been responsible for the design, submission and production of Messengers' badges. From 1876 to 1951 the Foreign Office, as Controllers of the Corps of Messengers, purchased and held all badges for issue to those appointed as messengers. Since 1951 messengers, on satisfactorily completing a period of probation, are given a registered number and letter of permission to purchase their badges through the Crown Jewellers. In addition to this badge, on instruction from the Home Office during World War II, a small oval badge bearing the cypher of King George VI was issued to messengers who carried sensitive material between Government departments located in various buildings within the capital city. Garrards produced only 20 of these, thus they are extremely rare.*

VALUE:

George III	£2500–3500
George IV	£2500–3500
William IV	£2500–3500
Victoria official issue	£2500–3000
Victoria unofficial issue	£2000–3000
Edward VII	£2000–3000
George V	£1000–2000
George VI	£1000–2000
Elizabeth II	£1000–2000

King George VI Home Service Messenger Badge.

320. ARCTIC MEDAL 1857

Instituted: 30 January 1857.
Ribbon: 38mm watered white.
Metal: Silver.
Size: Height 46mm; max. width 32mm.
Description: An octagonal medal with a beaded rim, surmounted by a nine-pointed star (representing the Pole Star) through which the suspension ring is fitted. (Obverse) an unusual profile of Queen Victoria, her hair in a loose chignon secured with a ribbon. (Reverse) a three-masted sailing vessel amid icebergs with a sledge party in the foreground and the dates 1818-1855 in the exergue. The medal was issued unnamed, but is often found privately engraved.
Comments: *Awarded retrospectively to all officers and men engaged in expeditions to the polar regions from 1818 to 1855, including those involved in the on-going search for the ill-fated Franklin Expedition of 1845-8. Thus the medal was granted to civilians, scientists, personnel of the French and US Navies and employees of the Hudson's Bay Company who took part in a number of abortive search parties for Sir John Franklin and his crew. Some 1106 medals, out of 1486 in all, were awarded to officers and ratings of the Royal Navy.*

VALUE:

Unnamed	£2000–2400
Named	£3000–3500
Miniature	£1500–2000

321. ARCTIC MEDAL 1876

Instituted: 28 November 1876.
Ribbon: 32mm plain white.
Metal: Silver.
Size: 36mm
Description: A circular medal with a raised beaded rim and a straight bar suspender. (Obverse) a veiled bust of Queen Victoria wearing a small crown, dated 1876 at the foot; (reverse) a three-masted ship icebound.
Comments: *Granted to officers and men of HM ships* Alert *and* Discovery *who served in the Arctic Expedition between 17 July 1875 and 2 November 1876. The medal was later extended to include the crew on the second voyage of the private yacht* Pandora *commanded by Allen Young which cruised in Polar waters between 25 June and 19 October 1875 and from 3 June to 2 November 1876. Medals were engraved with the name, rank and ship of the recipient. Only 155 medals were awarded.*

VALUE:

Named	**From £6000**
Miniature	£400–600

322. POLAR MEDAL

Instituted: 1904.
Ribbon: 32mm plain white.
Metal: Silver or bronze.
Size: 33mm octagonal.
Description: (Obverse) the effigy of the reigning sovereign; (reverse) a view of the Royal Research Ship *Discovery* with a man-handling sledge party in the foreground.
Comments: *Originally issued in silver, with an appropriate clasp, to the officers and men of Captain Scott's 1902–04 Antarctic Expedition, who went out in the* Discovery *and remained throughout the stay of the ship in the Antarctic Regions, from her arrival until her departure, or to any member compulsorily invalided after 3 January 1902, or to any who joined* Discovery *during her second winter in the Antarctic. It was issued in bronze to officers and men who did not remain, for causes other than sickness, throughout the stay of the ship in Antarctic regions; and also to the officers and men of the relief ships* Morning *and* Terra Nova. *These awards continued for subsequent expeditions: the silver medal being usually awarded to officers and to men who landed or who made more than one voyage, whilst the bronze medal was awarded to those not so exposed to the dangers of the polar environment. The bronze medal ceased being awarded after those awarded for Antarctic Research Work during 1929–39. Apart from the bronze medals awarded for the British Antarctic Expedition 1902–04 and the* Aurora *Relief Expedition 1917 where the year of the expedition was on the rim of the medal, the rest all had a clasp with ANTARCTIC and the year(s) of the expedition; the exception to this being those who took part on Shackleton's expedition and who had previously been awarded the bronze medal, received a clasp to their medal. No bronze medals were awarded for the Arctic. Up to December 2005, 271 bronze awards have been made (to 259 individuals, of whom 10 received one or more additional awards); 1038 silver awards have been made (to 948 individuals, of whom 80 received one or more additional awards), 18 recipients have been awarded both the silver and bronze medals. Only six women have been awarded the medal. Names of recipients are engraved on the earlier and most recent issues, and impressed in small capitals on the earlier Elizabethan issues.*

VALUE:	Silver	*Miniature*	Bronze (no clasp)	*Miniature* (no clasp)
Edward VII	From £5000	£125–175	From £6000	£125–160
George V (B)	From £3500	£125–175	From £3000	£125–160
George V (C)	—	£125–175	From £3000	£125–160
George V (E)	From £3500	£125–175	—	£125–160
George VI	From £3000	£125–175	From £3000	£125–160
Elizabeth II	From £3000	£125–175	—	£125–160

Modern examples of miniatures £20–30

323. KING EDWARD VII MEDAL FOR SCIENCE, ART AND MUSIC

Instituted: 1904
Ribbon: 35mm scarlet with a broad central stripe of dark blue and thin white stripes towards the edges.
Metal: Silver.
Size: 32mm.
Description: The raised rim consisted of a laurel wreath and has a ring for suspension. (Obverse) the conjoined busts of King Edward VII and Queen Alexandra; (reverse) the Three Graces engaged in various cultural pursuits.
Comments: *This short-lived medal was discontinued only two years later. It was awarded in recognition of distinguished services in the arts, sciences and music. The medal was struck by Burt & Co.*

VALUE: £1250–1500

324. ORDER OF THE LEAGUE OF MERCY

Modern reverse.

Date: 1898.
Ribbon: 38mm watered white silk with a central broad stripe of black.
Metal: Originally silver, now silver-gilt.
Size: Height 51mm; max. width 39mm.
Description: Originally an enamelled red cross surmounted by the Prince of Wales's plumes enfiladed by a coronet, with a central medallion depicting the emblem of the League, a group of figures representing Charity, set within a laurel wreath. Since 1999: a silver-gilt cross with the emblem in a central medallion. Reverse: a circular plaque inscribed LEAGUE OF MERCY 1999 in four lines.
Comments: *Appointments to the Order were sanctioned and approved by the sovereign on the recommendation of the Grand President of the League of Mercy as a reward for distinguished personal service to the League in assisting the support of hospitals. Ladies and gentlemen who rendered such aid for at least five years were eligible for the award. In 1917 King George V instituted a bar to be awarded to those who gave continuing service over a period of many years after receiving the Order itself. The original Order was last awarded in 1946 and the League itself ceased to exist in 1947. However, in March 1999, 100 years after its institution, the League was re-established and today it awards silver-gilt medals for outstanding voluntary service in health and social care. Over 500 medals have been awarded since 1999.*

VALUE:

Badge of the Order	Original £70–100	Miniature £55–65
	with bar £100–130	

325. QUEEN ALEXANDRA'S IMPERIAL MILITARY NURSING SERVICE CAPE BADGE

Date: 1902–49
Branch of Service: Queen Alexandra's Imperial Military Nursing Service.
Ribbon: Scarlet with two white outer stripes and two black inner stripes.
Metal: Silver.
Size: Oval 55mm by 36mm.
Description: A uniface oval ring surmounted by a Tudor crown fitted to a plain ring for suspension. The ring at the centre has the Cross of the Order of the Dannebrog, with an ornamental cypher of Queen Alexandra. The ring is inscribed in raised lettering QUEEN ALEXANDRA'S IMPERIAL MILITARY NURSING SERVICE.
Comments: *The cape badge was instituted in 1902 and was used until 1949 when the QAIMNS changed its name to the QARANC. It was worn on the right breast on ward dress for commissioned (qualified) nurses. It was issued through stores to each individual.*

VALUE: £80–100   *Miniature* £35–45

325A. QUEEN ALEXANDRA'S IMPERIAL MILITARY NURSING SERVICE RESERVE CAPE BADGE

Date: 1907–50

Branch of Service: Queen Alexandra's Imperial Military Nursing Service Reserve.

Ribbon: Black with two narrow outer white stripes and two inner scarlet stripes.

Metal: Silver.

Size: 38mm or 29mm.

Description: A uniface ring containing a prominent "R" surmounted by a Tudor crown fitted to a plain ring for suspension. The ring is inscribed in raised lettering QUEEN ALEXANDRA'S IMPERIAL MILITARY NURSING SERVICE RESERVE.

Comments: *The cape badge was instituted in 1907 and was used until 1950 when the QAIMNS(R) was incorporated into the QARANC. It was worn on the right breast on ward dress for commissioned (qualified) nurses. It was issued through stores to each individual.*

VALUE:		Miniature
38mm	£40–50	£35–45
29mm	£30–40	£30–35

326. TERRITORIAL FORCE NURSING SERVICE CAPE BADGE

Date: 1907–21.

Branch of Service: Territorial Force Nursing Service.

Ribbon: Scarlet with a narrow central white stripe.

Metal: Silver.

Size: Oval 50mm by 34mm

Description: A uniface oval ring surmounted by a Tudor crown attached to a plain ring for suspension. The ring has at the centre two ornamental letters "A" interlocking and set at an angle. The ring is inscribed in raised lettering: TERRITORIAL FORCE NURSING SERVICE.

Comments: *The cape badge was instituted in 1907 and was used until 1921 when the TFNS was renamed the TANS. It was worn on the right breast on ward dress for commissioned (qualified) nurses. It was issued through stores to each individual.*

VALUE:	£30–£40	Miniature	£30–35

326A. QUEEN ALEXANDRA'S MILITARY FAMILIES NURSING SERVICE CAPE BADGE

Date: 1921–26.
Branch of Service: Queen Alexandra's Military Families Nursing Service.
Ribbon: Black with a wide central scarlet stripe.
Metal: Silver.
Size: Oval 44mm by 34mm
Description: A uniface oval ring containing an ornamental cypher of Queen Alexandra surmounted by a Tudor crown. Three plain rings are attached to the outer edge of the circle for suspension. The ring is inscribed in raised lettering: QUEEN ALEXANDRA'S MILITARY FAMILIES NURSING SERVICE.
Comments: *The cape badge was instituted in 1921 upon formation of the QAMFNS, and was used until 1949 when the QAMFNS was incorporated into the QARANC. It was worn on the right breast on ward dress for commissioned (qualified) nurses. It was issued through stores to each individual.*

VALUE: £80–£100 *Miniature* £25–35

326B. TERRITORIAL ARMY NURSING SERVICE CAPE BADGE

Date: 1921–50.
Branch of Service: Territorial Army Nursing Service.
Ribbon: Scarlet with a narrow central white stripe.
Metal: Silver.
Size: Oval 38mm by 28mm
Description: A uniface oval ring surmounted by a Tudor crown attached to a plain ring for suspension. The ring has at the centre two ornamental letters "A" interlocking and set at an angle. The ring is inscribed in raised lettering: TERRITORIAL ARMY NURSING SERVICE. Beneath, an ornate scroll bearing the Latin inscription: FORTITUDO MEA DEUS.
Comments: *The cape badge was instituted in 1921 upon the formation of the TANS and was used until 1950 when the TANS was incorporated into the QARANC. It was worn on the right breast on ward dress for commissioned (qualified) nurses. It was issued through stores to each individual.*

VALUE: £30–£40 *Miniature* £25–35

326C. QUEEN ALEXANDRA'S ROYAL ARMY NURSING CORPS CAPE BADGE

Date: 1949.
Branch of Service: Queen Alexandra's Royal Army Nursing Corps.
Ribbon: Scarlet with two white outer stripes and two black inner stripes.
Metal: Silver.
Size: Oval 46mm by 32mm.
Description: A uniface oval ring containing the Cross of the Order of the Dannebrog, with an ornamental cypher of Queen Alexandra, surmounted by a Tudor crown, fitted with a plain ring for suspension. The oval ring is inscribed in raised lettering QUEEN ALEXANDRA'S ROYAL ARMY NURSING COPRS.
Comments: *The cape badge was instituted in 1949 and continues to be issued today to all commissioned (qualified) nurses in the QARANC. It is worn on the right breast on ward dress for both female and, since 1992, male commissioned (qualified) nurses. It is issued through stores to each individual.*

VALUE: £80–100   *Miniature* £35–45

327. INDIAN TITLE BADGE

1st Class

2nd Class

3rd Class

Instituted: 12 December 1911.
Ribbon: Light blue edged with dark blue (1st class); red edged with dark red (2nd class); or dark blue edged with light blue (3rd class).
Metal: Silver or silver-gilt.
Size: Height 58mm; max. width 45mm.
Description: A radiate star topped by an imperial crown with a curved laurel wreath below the crown and cutting across the top of a central medallion surrounded by a collar inscribed with the appropriate title. The medallion bears the crowned profile of King George V or King George VI. From the first issue of King George V's Title Badge on June 1, 1912 until 1933, his bust faced right. As from June 1, 1933 his bust faced left for the remainder of the reign. King George VI's Title Badges had his bust facing left. (Reverse) plain, but engraved with the name of the recipient.
Comments: *Introduced by King George V on the occasion of the Delhi Durbar of 1911 and awarded in three classes to civilians and Viceroy's commissioned officers of the Indian Army for faithful service or acts of public welfare. Recipients proceeded from the lowest grade to higher grades, each accompanied by a distinctive title. Each grade was issued in Hindu and Muslim versions, differing in title: Diwan Bahadur (Muslim) or Sardar Bahadur (Hindu), Khan Bahadur (Muslim) or Rai or Rao Bahadur (Hindu) and Khan Sahib (Muslim) or Rai or Rao Sahib (Hindu), in descending order of grade. These title badges took precedence after all British and Indian orders and decorations, and before campaign medals. In miniatures (at least) the George VI versions, which all have his bust facing right, are rarer than those of King George V with left-facing bust.*

VALUE:	Geo. V right	Geo. V left	Geo. VI
First class			
Diwan Bahadur	£150–200	£200–250	£350–400
Sardar Bahadur	£150–200	£200–250	£350–400
Second class			
Khan Bahadur	£100–175	£125–200	£300–350
Rao Bahadur	£100–175	£125–200	£300–350
Third class			
Khan Sahib	£100–175	£125–200	£300–350
Rao Sahib	£100–175	£125–200	£300–350

Miniatures
  George V   £75–85   George VI   £85–95

328. BADGES OF HONOUR (AFRICAN COUNTRIES)

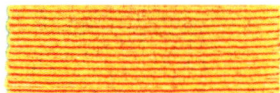

Instituted: 1922.
Ribbon: Plain yellow, 38mm (neck) or 32mm (breast).
Metal: Bronze.
Size: 65mm x 48mm (neck); 45mm x 33mm (breast).
Description: Oval badges with a raised rim of laurel leaves terminating at the top in an imperial crown flanked by two lions. (Obverse) a crowned effigy of the reigning monarch; (reverse) the crowned cypher of the monarch or some emblem symbolic of the particular country with the country name in the exergue.
Comments: *The badge accompanied a certificate of honour awarded to chiefs and other persons of non-European descent who had rendered loyal and valuable service to the government of the territory. The original award was a neck badge suspended by a ribbon, but from 1954 onwards recipients were given the option of taking the award as a neck or breast badge. These awards were quite distinct from the decorations known as the Native Chiefs Medals (see number 70). They were first awarded to Ugandans but later extended to 14 other British territories in East and West Africa as well as the three High Commisson territories in Southern Africa. In particular the Badges issued for Nyasaland under Elizabeth II are rare, as Nyasaland became a Federation with Rhodesia in 1957. They are believed to have fallen into abeyance in the early 1980s.*

VALUE:

George V	£300–400
George VI	£200–275
Elizabeth II (neck)	£175–250
Elizabeth II (breast)	£175–250

329. BADGES OF HONOUR (NON-AFRICAN COUNTRIES)

Instituted: 1926.
Ribbon: 38mm watered silk mustard yellow.
Metal: Silver gilt.
Size: 41mm (George VI) or 32 mm (Elizabeth II).
Description: Circular with a raised rim of laurel leaves bearing a ring for suspension. (Obverse) crowned effigy of the reigning monarch; (reverse) the emblem of the country with the name round the foot.
Comments: *These medals accompanied certificates of honour awarded to indigenous persons who had rendered valuable service to the colony or protectorate. These awards appear to have been in abeyance since the early 1980s. Exceptionally, the New Hebrides badge was awarded to three British officers (Colonel (now General Lord) Guthrie (of Craigiebank), Lieutenant-Colonel C. H. C. Howgill, RM and HRH the Duke of Gloucester) in connection with the "Coconut War" in July 1980 instead of a campaign medal. The reverse types show the badges of 28 colonies or protectorates.*

VALUE:

George V	£1600–1800
George VI	£1800–2500
Elizabeth II	£1500–2000
Miniature	£75–100

329A. GOVERNOR GENERALS' MEDAL OF HONOUR

Instituted: 2014.

Ribbon: Yellow with three central stripes of green / light blue / green

Metal: Nickel silver: gold plated for gold award, nickel plated for silver award. Bronzed brass gilding metal (copper-zinc alloy) for bronze award.

Size: 36mm

Description: (Obverse) Crowned effigy of the reigning Monarch; (reverse) Nine stars representing the nine Caribbean Commonwealth Realms, surrounded by palm fronds with crown above. Designed by Major D Rankin-Hunt, Norfolk Herald of Arms.

Comments: *Awarded in three grades (Gold, Silver and Bronze) on the direct authority of the Governor Generals of the Caribbean realms:*

- **Antigua & Barbuda**
- **The Bahamas**
- **Barbados (Prior to November 30, 2021)**
- **Belize**
- **Grenada**
- **Jamaica**
- **St Christopher and Nevis**
- **St Lucia**
- **St Vincent & The Grenadines**

Used as a gift to reward islanders and others who have shown service to the country or directly in the service of the Governor General, their spouse or the Vice Regal Household.

A second award bar also exists for each grade.

VALUE: —

330. NAVAL ENGINEER'S GOOD CONDUCT MEDAL

Instituted: 1842.
Ribbon: Originally plain dark blue but later broad blue with white edges.
Metal: Silver.
Size: 35mm.
Description: (Obverse) a two-masted paddle steamer with a trident in the exergue; (reverse) a circular cable cartouche enclosing a crowned fouled anchor and the legend FOR ABILITY AND GOOD CONDUCT. Between the cable and the rim the details of the recipient were engraved round the circumference. Considering the rarity of the award, it is even more remarkable that the medals have several unique features. Shaw's medal, for example, had oak leaves in the exergue, flanking the trident, but this feature was omitted from later medals. Medals have been recorded with a straight bar suspender, a steel clip and ring suspender or fixed ring suspension with one or two intermediate rings.
Comments: *This medal was abolished five years after it was instituted, only seven medals being awarded in that period: to William Shaw (1842), William Dunkin (1842), William Johnstone (1843), John Langley (1843), J.P. Rundle (1845), George Roberts (1845) and Samuel B. Meredith (1846). Restrikes were produced in 1875 and at a later date. The original medals have a grooved rim, the 1875 restrikes a diagonal grained rim and the later restrikes a plain, flat rim.*
VALUE:

Original	Rare
1875 restrike	£125–150
Later restrike	£80–100

331. INDIAN RECRUITING BADGE (GEORGE V)

Instituted: 1917.
Ribbon: Plain dark green.
Metal: Bronze.
Size: Height 45mm; max. width 48mm.
Description: A five-pointed star with ball finials, surmounted by a wreathed gilt medallion bearing a left-facing crowned bust of King George V, inscribed FOR RECRUITING WORK DURING THE WAR.
Comments: *Awarded to Indian officers and NCOs engaged in recruitment of troops. It could only be worn in uniform when attending durbars or state functions, but at any time in plain clothes.*

VALUE: George V £100–120 *Miniature* £55–70

332. INDIAN RECRUITING BADGE (GEORGE VI)

Instituted: 1940.
Ribbon: Emerald green divided into three sections interspersed by narrow stripes of red (left) and yellow (right).
Metal: Silver and bronze.
Size: Height 42mm; max. width 39mm.
Description: A multi-rayed silver breast badge surmounted by an imperial crown with a suspension ring fitted through the top of the crown. In the centre is superimposed a bronze medallion bearing the left-facing crowned profile of King George VI, within a collar inscribed FOR RECRUITING.
Comments: *Awarded to selected civilian and military pensioners, full-time members of the Indian Recruiting Organisation, fathers and mothers having at least three children in the armed services, and wives having a husband and at least two children serving in the defence forces.*

VALUE: George VI £70–90 *Miniature* £65–80

333. NAVAL GOOD SHOOTING MEDAL

Instituted: August 1902.
Ribbon: Dark blue with a red central stripe edged in white.
Metal: Silver.
Size: 36mm.
Description: (Obverse) the effigy of the reigning monarch; (reverse) a nude figure of Neptune holding five thunderbolts in each hand. In the background can be seen the bows of a trireme and the heads of three horses, with a trident in the field. The Latin motto VICTORIA CURAM AMAT (Victory loves care) appears round the circumference. Fitted with a straight suspension bar. The recipient's name, number, rank, ship and calibre of gun are impressed round the rim.
Comments: *Instituted to promote excellent gunnery performances in the annual Fleet Competitions, it was first awarded in 1903 but was discontinued in 1914. Subsequent success was marked by the issue of a bar bearing the name of the ship and the date. A total of 974 medals and 62 bars were awarded. 53 men received one bar, three men got two bars and only one achieved three bars.*

Subsequent award bar.

VALUE:		Miniature (in silver)
Edward VII	£350–450	£65–75
George V	£350–450	£65–75
With 1 bar	£600–800	£70–80

334. ARMY BEST SHOT MEDAL

Instituted: 30 April 1869.
Ribbon: Watered crimson with black, white (or buff*) and black stripes at the edges. (*The Regulations state that the stripes should be white but recent medals have been issued with buff stripes.)
Metal: Silver.
Size: 36mm.
Description: (Obverse) the veiled diademmed profile of Queen Victoria; (reverse) Victory bestowing a laurel crown on a naked warrior armed with a quiver of arrows and a bow and holding a target, impaled with arrows, in his other hand. Fitted with a straight suspension bar.
Comments: *This medal, sometimes referred to as the Queen's Medal, was awarded annually to the champion in the Army marksmanship contests held at Bisley. It was originally struck in bronze but was upgraded to silver in 1872. The award ceased in 1882 but was revived in 1923 and thereafter known as the King's Medal. The original reverse was retained, with the appropriate effigy of the reigning sovereign on the obverse. Since 1953 it has been known as the Queen's Medal again. In the post-1923 medals a bar bears the year of the award, with additional year clasps for subsequent awards. Until 1934 a single medal was awarded each year but in 1935 two medals were granted for the champion shots of the Regular and Territorial Armies respectively. Subsequently additional medals have been sanctioned for award to the military forces of India, Canada, Australia, New Zealand, Ceylon, Rhodesia, the British South Africa Police, the Union of South Africa, Pakistan, Jamaica and Ghana.*

VALUE:		Miniature
Victoria bronze	Rare	—
Victoria silver	Rare	—
George V	£1000–1200	£40–50
George VI	£1000–1200	£40–50
Elizabeth II	£1000–1200	£25–30
Charles III	—	—

335. QUEEN'S / KING'S MEDAL FOR CHAMPION SHOTS OF THE ROYAL NAVY AND ROYAL MARINES

Instituted: 12 June 1953.
Ribbon: Dark blue with a broad red central stripe flanked by white stripes.
Metal: Silver.
Size: 36mm.
Description: (Obverse) the effigy of reigning monarch; (reverse) Neptune (as on the Naval Good Shooting Medal).
Comments: *Instituted as the naval counterpart of the Army best shot medal with a bar which bears the year of the award.*

VALUE:

Elizabeth II	£1000–1200	*Miniature*	£20–25
Charles III	—		—

336. QUEEN'S / KING'S MEDAL FOR CHAMPION SHOTS OF THE ROYAL AIR FORCE

Instituted: 12 June 1953.
Ribbon: Broad crimson centre flanked by dark blue stripes bisected by thin light blue stripes.
Metal: Silver.
Size: 36mm.
Description: (Obverse) the effigy of reigning monarch; (reverse) Hermes kneeling on a flying hawk and holding the caduceus in one hand and a javelin in the other. The medal is fitted with a straight bar suspender. A date clasp is attached to the ribbon.
Comments: *Competed for at the annual RAF Small Arms Meeting at Bisley. The medal was issued to the Champion Shot of the RNZAF under the terms of the same Royal Warrant as the RAF.*

VALUE:

Elizabeth II	£1000–1200	*Miniature*	£25–35
Charles III	—		—

337. QUEEN'S / KING'S MEDAL FOR CHAMPION SHOTS OF THE NEW ZEALAND NAVAL FORCES

Instituted: 9 July 1958.
Ribbon: Crimson centre bordered with white and broad dark blue stripes at the edges.
Metal: Silver.
Size: 36mm.
Description: (Obverse) the effigy of reigning monarch; (reverse) similar to that of the Naval Good Shooting Medal of 1903-14. Fitted with a clasp bearing the year of the award and a straight suspension bar.
Comments: *Awards were made retrospective to 1 January 1955. This medal is awarded for marksmanship in an annual contest of the New Zealand Naval Forces. Additional clasps are granted for further success. One contestant, Lt Cdr N. C. G. Peach, RNZN, has won this award ten times*

VALUE:

Elizabeth II	—	*Miniature*	£35–45
Charles III	—		—

338. UNION OF SOUTH AFRICA COMMEMORATION MEDAL

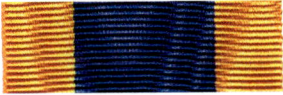

Instituted: 1910.
Ribbon: 38mm orange-yellow with a broad central dark blue stripe.
Metal: Silver.
Size: 36mm.
Description: (Obverse) the uncrowned effigy of King George V; (reverse) Mercury as God of Commerce and Prosperity, bending over an anvil, forging the links of a chain symbolic of the uniting of the four colonies (Cape Colony, Natal, Orange Free State and the Transvaal), with the date 1910 in the exergue and the legend TO COMMEMORATE THE UNION OF SOUTH AFRICA.
Comments: *This was the first medal struck in the reign of George V and resulted from the South Africa Act of 1909. This Act proclaimed the unification on 31 May 1910, of the self-governing four colonies into a legislative Union, becoming provinces of the Union of South Africa. This medal, the obverse of which was designed by Sir Bertram MacKennal, and the reverse by Mr Sydney Marsh, was struck to mark the opening of the first Parliament of the Union by HRH the Duke of Connaught. Awarded to those who took part in the inauguration of the Parliament. Additionally it was awarded to certain officers and men of HMS Balmoral Castle, a Union Castle liner specially commissioned as a man-of-war to convey HRH the Duke of Connaught as the King's representative to South Africa for the celebrations. A total of 551 medals were struck by the Royal Mint, and were issued unnamed, although privately named medals are in existence.*

VALUE:	Named	£600–800
	Unnamed	£600–800
	Miniature	£25–35

339. DEKORATIE VOOR TROUWE DIENST

Instituted: 1920.
Ribbon: A broad dark blue central stripe flanked on one side by a gold stripe with a thin red stripe superimposed towards the edge, and on the other side by a yellow stripe with a thin white stripe towards the edge. Transvaal recipients wore the ribbon with the red to the centre of the chest; Orange Free State recipients wore the ribbon with the white stripe to the centre of the chest.
Metal: Silver.
Size: 36mm.
Description: (Obverse) the arms of the Transvaal; (reverse) the arms of the Orange Free State. Fitted with a fixed suspender. Recipients wore the medal with the appropriate state arms showing.
Comments: *This medal which is correctly named the Dekoratie Voor Trouwe Dienst was awarded by the Union of South Africa to officers of the two former Boer republics for distinguished service during the Second Boer War of 1899-1902. Awards to officers and men of the former Boer Republics had to be individually claimed on prescribed forms and were named with rank, initials and surname of the individual. The late Don Forsyth published a roll listing full names and commandos/units of the recipients. This clearly identifies many recipients but cannot differentiate, for example, between any of the 10 issued ABO medals that were named "Burger P. J. Botha". However, the naming style and type of suspender can help to make positive identification possible.*

The other side is similar to no. 340 illustrated opposite

Medals issued up to October 1937 had a WWI British War Medal (MYB168) suspender and typical SA Mint WWI naming. Between October 1937 and February 1942 the WWI suspender was still used, but the naming was thinner, in a slightly smaller font as on the WWII Africa Service Medal (MYB 189). All subsequent issues have the WWII style naming as well as the "thick-necked" suspender as found on the Africa Service Medal (for details and illustrations see the article by Hent Loots in the OMRS Miscellany of Honours, No. 9, 1992). By comparing the dates on the Medal Application Forms of men with the same initials and surname a particular recipient can sometimes be pinpointed. NB Please note that these medals are often found with the suspender claw flattened to varying degrees: the SA Mint, on occasion, used rather crude methods to "fix" the pin.

VALUE:	Silver (591)	£750–900		
	Paired with matching MYB340	£1100–1500	*Miniature*	£65–75

340. ANGLO-BOERE OORLOG (WAR) MEDAL

Instituted: 1920.
Ribbon: Broad green and yellow stripes with three narrow stripes of red, white and dark blue in the centre. Transvaal recipients wore the ribbon with the green to the centre of the chest, while Orange Free State recipients wore it with the yellow towards the centre.
Metal: Silver.
Size: 36mm.
Description: Both sides inscribed ANGLO-BOERE OORLOG round the top, with the dates 1899-1902 round the foot. Medallions set in a border of a square and quatrefoil show the arms of the Orange Free State on one side and the Transvaal on the other. The medal was worn with the side showing the arms of the appropriate state uppermost. Fitted with a fixed suspender.
Comments: *Correctly named the Anglo-Boere Oorlog Medal, this was awarded by the Union government to officers and men of the former Boer republics for loyal service in the war against the British. To qualify for the medal proof had to be provided that they had fought against the British without surrendering or taking parole or the oath of allegiance prior to May 31, 1902. See note on no. 339 regarding awards to men of the former Boer Republics.*

VALUE: Silver £240–260 Miniature £65–75
Lint Voor Wonden (Wound Ribbon) Certificate value: £30; if with corresponding medal: value: £50.

341. COMMONWEALTH INDEPENDENCE MEDALS

Since the partition of the Indian sub-continent in 1947 and the emergence of the Dominions of India and Pakistan, it has been customary for medals to be issued to mark the attainment of independence. As these medals are invariably awarded to British service personnel taking part in the independence ceremonies, they are appended here in chronological order of institution, the date of the actual award, where later, being given in parentheses. These medals usually have symbolic motifs with the date of independence inscribed. The distinctive ribbons are noted alongside. All are 32mm wide unless otherwise stated.

Pakistan Independence Medal

Ceylon Police Independence Medal.

	VALUE
India 1947 (1948) Three equal stripes of orange, white and green	£20–25
Ceylon Police 1948 Three equal stripes of white, red, white with narrow black edges	£50–75
Pakistan 1947 (1950) Dark green with a central thin white stripe	£15–20
Ghana 1957 Nine alternating stripes of red, yellow and green	£60–65
Nigeria 1960 (1964) Three equal stripes of green, white and green	£25–30
Sierra Leone 1961 Three equal stripes of green, white and blue	£65–75
Jamaica 1962 Black centre flanked by yellow stripes and green edges	£60–65
Uganda 1962 (1963) Six stripes of black, yellow, red, black, yellow, red	£60–65
Kenya 1963 Yellow with two thin black stripes at the edges and a central thin green striope	£60–65

continued

341. COMMONWEALTH INDEPENDENCE MEDALS *continued*

Solomon Islands.

Sierra Leone.

Malawi.

	VALUE
Malawi 1964 Three equal stripes of black, red and green	£65–75
Guyana 1966 Red centre flanked by yellow stripes and broad green edges. The green and yellow separated (left) by a thin black stripe and (right) by a thin pale blue stripe	£60–65
Swaziland 1968 Three equal stripes of red, yellow and blue	£60–65
Fiji 1970 Grey-blue with bars half red, half white, towards each edge	£65–75
Papua New Guinea 1975 Red bordered by thin stripes of yellow and white, with black edges	£65–75
Transkei 1976	£20–25
Solomon Islands 1978 Five equal stripes of blue, yellow, white, yellow and green	£65–75
Gilbert Islands (Kiribati) 1980 Half red, half black, separated by a thin white stripe, and edged in yellow	£50–60
Ellice Islands (Tuvalu) 1980 Equal stripes of red, white and red edged yellow. the white stripe bisected by a thin blue stripe	£30–40
Zimbabwe 1980 Silver or bronze 38mm black centre flanked by red and yellow stripes with edges of green or blue	Silver £30–45 Bronze £20–25
Gambia 1981	£35–45
Vanuatu 1980 (1981) 30mm stripes of red and green with central thinner stripe of yellow edged by black	£20–25
St Christopher, Nevis and Anguilla 1983 Bars of green (left) and red (right) with a black central bar having two thin white stripes, flanked by yellow stripes	£55–75

Papua New Guinea.

Nigeria.

Zimbabwe.

For the various ribbons see ribbon charts on pp. 417 et seq.

342. MALTA GEORGE CROSS 50th ANNIVERSARY COMMEMORATIVE MEDAL

Instituted: 1992.
Ribbon: Dark blue with central stripes of white and red (the Maltese national colours).
Metal: Cupro-nickel.
Size: 36mm.
Description: (Obverse) the crowned arms of the island, which include the George Cross in the upper left corner, with the date 1992 at the foot. (Reverse) a replica of the George Cross with the eight-pointed Maltese Cross at the top and the date 1942 at the foot, with a legend BHALA SHIEDA TA'EROIZMU U DEDIKAZZJONI on one side and TO BEAR WITNESS TO HEROISM AND DEVOTION on the other. Suspension is by a fixed bar decorated with laurels, attached to a ring.
Comments: *Sanctioned by the government of Malta to celebrate the fiftieth anniversary of the award of the George Cross by King George VI to the island for its heroic resistance to prolonged Axis attack during the Second World War. The medal has been awarded to surviving veterans who served in Malta in the armed forces and auxiliary services between 10 June 1940 and 8 September 1943. Permission for British citizens to wear this medal was subsequently granted by the Queen. As a number of veterans applied for the medal after the cut-off date of 15 April 1994, the Maltese Government sanctioned a second striking—these medals carry the word COPY below the right arm of the George Cross.*

VALUE:

Cupro-nickel (original striking)	£90–120	*Miniature* £20–25
Official copy	£50–60	

343. SHANGHAI VOLUNTEER CORPS MEDAL

Date: 1854.
Ribbon: Unknown—details sought.
Metal: Silver.
Size: 38mm
Description: Unknown—details sought.
Comment: *Awarded to the officers and men of the Shanghai Volunteers who took part in the battle of Soo Chow Creek (also known as the battle of Muddy Flats) which took place on April 28, 1854. Examples are of the greatest rarity and the last one to appear at auction was sold in 1991. Further details are sought.*

VALUE: —

344. SHANGHAI JUBILEE MEDAL

Instituted: 1893.
Ribbon: Watered silk half bright red, half white or red with 4mm central white stripe.
Metal: Silver or bronze.
Size: 36mm.
Description: (Obverse) triple-shield arms of the municipality surrounded by a band with thistles, shamrocks and roses round the foot and NOVEMBER 17 1843 round the top. (Reverse) a scrolled shield with the words SHANGHAI JUBILEE and NOVEMBER 17 1843 and inscribed diagonally across the centre with the recipient's name in block capitals. The shield is flanked by Chinese dragons and above is a steamship and the sun setting on the horizon. The rim is engraved "Presented by the Shanghai Municipality". Issued with a small suspension ring, but often replaced by a straight bar. This medal has also been recorded with an ornamental silver brooch bearing the dates 1843–1893.
Comments: *The British settlement in Shanghai was founded in 1843 and formed the nucleus of the International Settlement established in 1854 under the control of an autonomous Municipal Council. In effect the International Settlement functioned as an autonomous City State administered by a Municipal Committee formed from those nations comprising the Settlement. This was abolished when Shanghai was overrun by Imperial Japanese troops in 1941. Recently renewed interest from China and the Far East has vastly inflated the price of these medals at auctions. In February 2023, a silver example hammered at £6,400 at Denhams.*

VALUE:

Silver (625)	£5000–5500
Bronze (100)	£3000–4000

345. SHANGHAI FIRE BRIGADE LONG SERVICE MEDAL

Instituted: Before 1904.
Ribbon: Black with broad crimson borders.
Metal: Silver.
Size: 31mm.
Description: (Obverse) an armorial device featuring a Chinese dragon standing on a symbolic high-rise building on which is displayed a flame on a pole crossed by a hook and ladder, with MIH-HO-LOONG SHANGHAI round the top and the motto "Say the word and down comes your house" round the foot; (reverse) engraved with recipient's details. It seems strange that no Chinese characters appear on the medal. Ring and double claw suspension, with a broad silver brooch bar at the top of the ribbon.
Comment: *Awarded for a minimum of twelve years regular service with the Municipal Fire Brigade. The award was presumably in abeyance following the Japanese invasion in 1937 and the wholesale destruction of the international commercial metropolis.*

VALUE: £500–600   *Miniature*   £95–110

346. SHANGHAI VOLUNTEER FIRE BRIGADE LONG SERVICE MEDAL

Instituted: 1904.
Ribbon: Red with two wide and one narrow (central) white stripes.
Metal: Gold, silver or bronze.
Size: 36mm.
Description: (Obverse) the arms and motto of the Municipality surrounded by a collar inscribed SHANGHAI VOLUNTEER FIRE BRIGADE ESTABLISHED 1866. (Reverse) originally simply engraved with name of unit, later a pair of crossed axes surmounted by a fireman's helmet under which is a horizontal tablet on which are engraved the recipient's dates of service. Round the circumference is inscribed FOR LONG SERVICE (top) and WE FIGHT THE FLAMES (foot) with quatrefoil ornaments separating the two inscriptions. Fitted with a swivelling scroll suspender.
Comments: *The medal in silver was awarded to members of the Volunteer Fire Brigade for five years service, for eight years service a clasp was added to the ribbon and for 12 years service the medal was awarded in gold. Bronze medals exist but are believed to have been specimens only.*

VALUE: £600–700   *Miniature*   £95–110

347. SHANGHAI VOLUNTEER CORPS LONG SERVICE MEDAL

Instituted: 1921.
Ribbon: Equal stripes of red, white and blue, the red bisected by a thin green stripe, the white by black and the blue by yellow.
Metal: Silver.
Size: 36mm.
Description: (Obverse) an eight-pointed radiate star bearing a scroll at the top inscribed 4th APRIL 1854. The arms of the Municipality superimposed on the star and surrounded by a collar inscribed SHANGHAI VOLUNTEER CORPS. Round the foot of the medal is a band inscribed FOR LONG SERVICE. (Reverse) plain, engraved with the name of the recipient and his period of service.
Comments: *The Volunteer Corps was raised in 1853 to protect the British and other foreign settlements. The date on the scroll alludes to the Corps' first engagement, the Battle of Muddy Flat. The Corps was cosmopolitan in structure, although the British element predominated. It was disbanded in September 1942, nine months after the Japanese overran the International Settlement. Awarded for 12 years good service. The last medal was awarded in 1941.*

VALUE: £500–600   *Miniature*   £95–110

348. SHANGHAI MUNICIPAL POLICE DISTINGUISHED CONDUCT MEDAL

Instituted: 1924.
Ribbon: Red with a central blue stripe (1st class); red with a blue stripe at each edge (2nd class).
Metal: Silver or bronze.
Size: 36mm.
Description: (Obverse) arms of the Municipality and the inscription SHANGHAI MUNICIPAL POLICE; (reverse) the words FOR DISTINGUISHED CONDUCT. The recipient's name and rank were engraved around the rim.
Comments: *Awarded to officers and men of the Municipal Police in two classes, distinguished solely by their ribbons and the metal used (silver or bronze). A sliding clasp was fitted to the ribbon to denote a second award; this featured the Municipal crest and was engraved on the reverse with the details of the award. It is believed that a total of 223 medals were awarded up to 1942, including 72 to foreign members of the force.*

VALUE:	Silver	£950–1200	Miniature	£95–110
	Bronze	£700–850		

349. SHANGHAI MUNICIPAL POLICE LONG SERVICE MEDAL

Instituted: 1925.
Ribbon: Brown with a central yellow stripe edged in white.
Metal: Silver.
Size: 36mm.
Description: (Obverse) arms of the Municipality within a collar inscribed SHANGHAI MUNICIPAL POLICE (As MYB 348 above); (reverse) plain apart from the inscription FOR LONG SERVICE in two lines across the centre. The recipient's name and rank were engraved round the rim in upper and lower case lettering. Awards to Indians were named in cursive script with the Hindi equivalent alongside. Fitted with a swivelling scroll suspender.
Comments: *Awarded for 12 years good service in the Shanghai Municipal Police, an international force composed largely of Sikhs, Chinese and White Russians as well as British ex-soldiers and policemen. Dated clasps for further five year periods of service were awarded. The medal was abolished in 1942.*

VALUE:		*Miniature*
Without clasp	£750–1000	£50–55
With clasp	£1500–1750	£55–65
2 clasps	£850–1000	£65–75

350. SHANGHAI MUNICIPAL POLICE (SPECIALS) LONG SERVICE MEDAL

Instituted: 1929.
Ribbon: Dark brown with three white bars, each bisected by a thin yellow stripe.
Metal: Silver.
Size: 36mm.
Description: (Obverse) the arms of the Municipality with the motto OMNIA JUNCTA IN UNO (all joined in one) round the circumference. (Reverse) inscribed SHANGHAI MUNICIPAL POLICE (SPECIALS) FOR LONG SERVICE in six lines. A unique award to A.L. Anderson (1930) was inscribed on the reverse FOR DISTINGUISHED AND VALUABLE SERVICES.
Comments: *Awarded for 12 years active and efficient service in the Special Constabulary. Some 52 medals and 8 clasps for additional service are recorded in the* Shanghai Gazette, *but the actual number awarded was probably greater. The medal was discontinued in 1942.*

VALUE :			
Without clasp	£600–850	With clasp	£1800–2500
Miniature	£210–260		

351. SHANGHAI MUNICIPAL COUNCIL EMERGENCY MEDAL

Instituted: 1937.
Ribbon: 38mm bright red, having a broad white central stripe bordered black and yellow edges separated from the red by thin black stripes.
Metal: Bronze.
Size: 40mm.
Description: An eight-pointed star with ring suspension. (Obverse) a central medallion superimposed on the radiate star with the triple-shield arms of the Municipality surrounded by a collar inscribed SHANGHAI MUNICIPAL COUNCIL. (Reverse) a laurel wreath enclosing the words FOR SERVICES RENDERED - AUGUST 12 TO NOVEMBER 12 1937.
Comments: *Awarded to members of the Police, Volunteer Corps, Fire Brigade and civilians for services during the emergency of August-November 1937 when fighting between the Chinese and Japanese in and around Shanghai threatened to encroach on the International Settlement. Issued unnamed, but accompanied by a certificate bearing the name and unit of the recipient. Examples have been seen with the recipient's name engraved on the reverse.*

VALUE: £300–400   *Miniature* £65–85

351A. CHINESE MARITIME CUSTOMS SERVICE FINANCIAL MEDAL

Instituted:
Ribbon: Green, with yellow stripes.
Metal: Gold, silver or bronze according to class.
Size:
Description: An eight-pointed radiate star suspended by a plain ring, having an oval medallion on the obverse inscribed in Chinese and depicting a Chinese junk; (reverse) a horseshoe scroll inscribed THE CHINESE MARITIME CUSTOMS MEDAL with FINANCIAL across the foot. The recipient's name was engraved in the centre.
Comments: *The Chinese Maritime Customs Service was operated and largely staffed at the higher levels by British personnel from 1854 till 1950. Medals were awarded for five years' service or shorter service of exceptional merit and were granted in three classes, each of three grades, making nine variations in all, distinguished by the respective metals, and awarded according to the rank of the recipient.*

Obverse

VALUE: Very Rare   *Miniature* £100–110

351B. CHINESE MARITIME CUSTOMS SERVICE MERITORIOUS SERVICE MEDAL

Instituted:
Ribbon: Green with yellow stripes.
Metal: Gold, silver or bronze according to grade.
Size:
Description: As above, but FOR MERITORIOUS SERVICE in the tablet on the reverse.
Comments: *Awarded for 25 years continuous service, according to the rank of the recipient, but later awards in silver or gold could be made on promotion to a higher rank, or for exceptional service, notably from 1931 onwards, following the outbreak of hostilities with Japan.*

VALUE: Very Rare

Reverse

352. AUTOMOBILE ASSOCIATION SERVICE CROSS

Date: 1956.
Ribbon: Yellow with three narrow black stripes.
Metal: Silver.
Size: 36mm.
Description: A silver cross flory terminating in scrolls, with the AA emblem surmounted in the centre.
Comments: *Established in commemoration of the Association's Golden Jubilee, the Cross is the highest award to AA patrolmen and other uniformed members of staff for conspicuous acts of bravery involving an imminent risk of personal injury whilst on duty in uniform, or whilst engaged in an action related to duty. To date only 15 crosses have been awarded. A monetary reward accompanies the Cross.*

VALUE: £400–500

353. AUTOMOBILE ASSOCIATION SERVICE MEDAL

Date: 1956.
Ribbon: Half yellow, half black.
Metal: Silver.
Size: 36mm.
Description: A circular medal in the form of the AA badge with wings sprouting from the top and flanking a claw and ring suspension. (Obverse) AA superimposed on a wheel, with the inscription AUTOMOBILE ASSOCIATION/SERVICE MEDAL round the circumference; (reverse) details of the award.
Clasp: A silver-gilt and red enamel clasp inscribed 192064 (ie. 20 years good driving, 1964) has been reported.
Comments: *Like the Cross, the Medal of the Association was instituted in commemoration of the Association's Golden Jubilee. The medal is awarded to members of the uniformed staff for courageous or outstanding initiative and devotion to duty. To date, only 60 medals have been awarded, including four in 1997, mainly for life-saving and bravery in accidents. A monetary reward accompanies the Medal. A Service Citation is also awarded for lesser acts, a total of 63 having been bestowed so far.*

VALUE: £200–250

354. SUFFRAGETTE MEDAL

Instituted: 1909.
Campaign: Votes for women.
Ribbon: Three equal stripes of purple, silver and green.
Metal: Silver.
Size: 20mm.
Clasps: A silver dated bar, or an enamelled bar in the WSPU colours with the date on the reverse, or prison bars surmounted by a broad arrow.
Description: A small silver medal suspended by a ring from a bar with scrolled finials, engraved with the date of the award. A similarly scrolled brooch bar at the top of the ribbon is inscribed FOR VALOUR. The plain medal is engraved HUNGER STRIKE in various styles and hallmarked.
Comments: *This medal was awarded by the Women's Social and Political Union (WSPU) to those militant Suffragettes who were imprisoned for various acts of violence and who went on hunger strike while in prison. At first they were forcibly fed under the most barbaric conditions, as a result of which several died. The Government then introduced the Cat and Mouse Act, whereby hunger strikers at the point of death were released, but were then re-arrested and returned to prison when they had recovered sufficiently from their ordeal. A silver bar was awarded to those who were imprisoned and went on hunger strike whilst an enamel bar was awarded to those who were force fed in prison. The portcullis badge was given to those imprisoned in Holloway and is occasionally seen separately from the medal.*

VALUE: Boxed: From £3500
                   In personally inscribed case: From £6000

355. FLORENCE NIGHTINGALE MEDAL

Date: 1912.
Ribbon: White with narrow yellow and broad red stripes towards the edges.
Metal: Silver with enamels.
Size:
Description: An upright elliptical medal coming to a point at both ends, with a three-quarter length portrait of Florence Nightingale from the Crimean War period, inscribed MEMORIAM FLORENCE NIGHTINGALE 1820–1910 AD. The reverse bears the recipient's name.
Comments: *Instituted by the International Committee of the Red Cross for award to trained nurses, matrons, nursing organisers or voluntary aids for distinguished or exceptional service. Awards are made every other year on the anniversary of Miss Nightingale's birthday. This medal has been awarded very sparingly.*

VALUE: £500–700   *Miniature*   £410–510

356. ANZAC COMMEMORATIVE MEDAL

Date: 1967.
Ribbon: None.
Metal: Bronze.
Size: 76mm x 50mm.
Description: (Obverse) a medallion surmounted by a Royal Crown with a laurel wreath and the word ANZAC in a scroll below. In the field is the date 1915 above a picture of John Simpson and his donkey saving a wounded soldier at Gallipoli (based on a painting by 4/26A Spr Horace Moore-Jones, NZ Engineers. (Reverse) a map of Australia and New Zealand with the Southern Cross constellation. The reverse of the scroll has New Zealand fern leaves.
Comments: *This medal was instituted jointly by the governments of Australia and New Zealand and awarded to surviving veterans of the Australian and New Zealand Army Corps who served in the Gallipoli campaign, all named on the reverse. Designed by Australian artist Raymond Ewers. There is also a half-size lapel badge bearing the obverse design and numbered on the reverse.*

VALUE: Original Medal £150–250   Lapel badge £50–60

357. NEW ZEALAND CADET DISTRICT MEDAL

Date: 1902.
Ribbon: Plain khaki or tan with a central pink flanked by dark green stripes.
Metal: Silver.
Size: 32mm.
Description: (Obverse) profile of Edward VII or George V with inscription FOR KING AND COUNTRY: PUBLIC SCHOOL CADETS, N.Z.; (reverse) DEFENCE NOT DEFIANCE round the top, with DISTRICT PRIZE (or CHALLENGE) MEDAL AWARDED TO in three lines, leaving space for the name of the recipient to be engraved below.
Comments: *These medals were instituted following the establishment of the Public School Cadets in 1902 and were awarded in two classes in Challenge competitions or as prizes in the annual examinations.*

VALUE: District Challenge   £100–150
             District Prize   £90–100

362. CORPS OF COMMISSIONAIRES MEDAL

Date:
Ribbon: Red, white and blue.
Metal: Silver or blackened metal.
Size: 40mm.
Description: A 16-point star bearing a central medallion with the Union Jack in the centre surrounded by the Latin mottoes: VIRTUTE ET INDUSTRIA (top) and LABOR VINCIT OMNIA (foot)—"by ability and industry" and "work conquers all" respectively. Fitted with a plain ring for suspension from the ribbon which bears an elaborate brooch consisting of crossed rifle and sabre on a fouled anchor with a cannon behind, representing the armed forces from which the Corps recruits its members.
Comments: *Awarded by the Corps of Commissionaires for long and exemplary service.*

VALUE: £30–45 *Miniature* £25–30

363. NATIONAL EMERGENCY MEDAL

Date: 1926.
Ribbon: None.
Metal: Gold or bronze.
Size: 50mm.
Description: (Obverse) Britannia seated holding a laurel branch and resting on a shield. Above the inscription across the field FOR SERVICE IN NATIONAL EMERGENCY MAY 1926 appear the national emblems of England and Scotland with the LMS emblem between; (reverse) three female figures with arms outstretched holding locomotives dividing the inscription LARGITAS MUNERIS SALUS REIPUBLICAE (the immensity of the task, the well-being of the country).
Comments: *These medals were designed by Edward Gillick and struck by the Royal Mint on behalf of the London, Midland and Scottish Railway for presentation to those volunteers who had served the company throughout the General Strike of May 1926. The medals were struck in bronze and issued in boxes unnamed to the recipients. According to Mint records, a few medals were also struck in gold, but none has so far been recorded.*

VALUE:
Gold —
Bronze £45–55

364. ROYAL WARRANT HOLDERS ASSOCIATION MEDAL

Original reverse.

1977 "Jubilee" reverse.

Instituted: 1897.
Ribbon: Dark purple with a central yellow stripe.
Metal: Silver, silver-gilt or gold.
Size: 23mm.
Description: (Obverse) crowned profile of the reigning monarch; (reverse) THE ROYAL WARRANT HOLDERS ASSOCIATION round the edge with the name of the Warrant holder engraved in the centre. The medal was surmounted by an imperial crown fitted to a ring for suspension, with a brooch bar at the top of the ribbon, for issues between those of Queen Victoria and George VI. The medal fell into abeyance in 1946 due to the scarcity of silver. In 1897 the Association issued a medal in silver to commemorate the Diamond Jubilee of Queen Victoria. In 1977, for Her Majesty Queen Elizabeth's Silver Jubilee, a new medal was struck, with the dates 1952–1977 appearing below the bust. This medal is surmounted by a Tudor crown and fitted with a ring for suspension from a bar with a brooch bar at the top of the ribbon. This issue has a special reverse bearing the Royal arms—this special reverse was used again in 2002 on the occasion of the Golden Jubilee.

Comments: *This medal was originally instituted by Queen Victoria for individuals who are granted the Royal Warrant and may be worn at formal occasions of the Association. Until 1911 medals were issued in both silver and silver-gilt to members of the Association. However, from 1911 the silver-gilt and gold medals were only awarded to Council members. Miniature medals were also authorised and are believed to have been issued but they are very rare and were discontinued in 1920. Medals were struck for the reign of Edward VIII but were never issued, however unnamed examples do exist. The 1977 Silver Jubilee medal was designed by Alex Styles of Garrard the Crown jewellers. In 2002 Her Majesty the Queen gave approval for the medal to be issued in silver-gilt or gold to mark the Golden Jubilee, but it reverted to silver in 2003. The medal may be purchased by Warrant holders only.*

VALUE:

Victoria Silver-gilt	£200–250
Jubilee	£200–250
Edward VII Silver	£100–150
Silver-gilt	£200–250
George V	£150–200
Edward VIII	£200–250
George VI	£150–200
Elizabeth II	£150–200
1977 Jubilee	£200–250
2002 Jubilee	£200–250

365. ROYAL NATIONAL LIFEBOAT INSTITUTION DECORATION

(see also 291DD and L4)

Type I.

Type II, 2nd class in silver.

Type III lapel badge.

Date: 1901, 1913.

Ribbon: Blue watered silk.

Metal: Gold or silver with enamels.

Size: 27mm (type I) or 36mm (type II).

Description: Type I: a circular uniface medal depicting a lifeboat going to the assistance of a sailing ship in distress, surrounded by a white enamelled lifebelt surmounted by a gilt crown. Type II: A wavy cross in dark blue enamel, with the initials RNLI in the angles interlaced with a rope, surmounted by a Royal Crown, fitted with a ring for suspension. First Class (gold) and Second Class (silver). Type III: an oval enamelled lapel badge depicting the Institution's emblem.

Comments: *The original decoration, suspended from a bow of blue ribbon, designed by Charles Dibdin, the RNLI Secretary, was instituted as a reward for Branch Honorary Secretaries and Lady Auxiliaries for long and devoted service. 36 awards were made initially, followed by 18 other awards in 1902–9. The medal was manufactured by Alstons & Hallam of Bishopsgate. Thereafter a new decoration in the form of a cross, awarded to men and women in two classes, gold and silver, was designed by Mr Burke of the College of Heralds and manufactured by Garrards in 1912. Objections raised by King George V led to the cross being discontinued on May 14, 1914, by which time only ten gold awards had been made and no silver awards. Today long service is rewarded with an enamelled lapel badge as illustrated below.*

VALUE:		
	Type I	—
	Type II	—
	Type III	£20–30

366. MAIDSTONE TYPHOID MEDAL

Date: 1897.
Ribbon: Purple with yellow stripes at the edges.
Metal: Silver
Size: 32mm.
Description: (Obverse) the coat of arms of the town of Maidstone with
MAIDSTONE KENT on a ribbon below; (reverse) an ornate panel engraved
with the recipient's name in the centre and the words WITH GRATITUDE
TO . . . FOR LOVING SERVICES 1897, with an olive branch below.
Comments: *A major epidemic of Typhoid fever broke out in Maidstone, Kent during*
late August 1897. By 9 September 117 cases had been reported, rising to 774 by the
end of the month and by 9 October the number had risen to 1,200, with 42 deaths.
By the end of December when the epidemic was considered to be over a total of 132
people had died. Medals were awarded to the nursing staff who served in the town
during the epidemic. Many were presented by the Mayor of Maidstone at a special
ceremony held at the Museum and Technical School on Wednesday 8 December
1897.

VALUE:	Unnamed	£150–200
	Named	£350–400

367. BOYS' LIFE BRIGADE MEDAL

Date: 1905.
Ribbon: Red.
Metal: Bronze.
Size: 34mm.
Description: (Obverse) A Geneva cross within a crowned circle and a radiate
background, the circle inscribed TO SAVE LIFE; a scroll round the foot
inscribed THE BOYS LIFE BRIGADE; (reverse) personal details of the
recipient. Fitted with a plain suspension ring. The brooch bar is in the form
of a scroll with a laurel wreath superimposed on the middle and a clasp
bearing the date of the award.
Comments: *This medal was awarded for good attendance. The Boys' Life Brigade*
amalgamated with the Boys' Brigade in 1926 and the award of this medal was then
abolished. The BLB Cross for Courage was also abolished at this time having been
awarded only ten times in its history.

VALUE: £20–30

367A. BOYS' BRIGADE SQUAD MEDAL

Date: 1896.
Ribbon: Originally dark blue, later maroon, suspended from an ornate brooch
pin..
Metal: Bronze.
Size: 42mm.
Description: A multi-faceted, eight-pointed star surmounted by the Brigade
badge: an anchor with the word SURE on the top cross-member of the
anchor and STEADFAST on the lower limbs, the initials BB either side.
When the Boys' Brigade amalgamated with the Boys' Life Brigade in 1926
the Geneva cross was added to the design.
Comments: *This medal is believed to have been awarded to the squad who achieved*
the highest average attendance over one year. The Boys' Brigade issued and
continues to issue a large number of badges and medals, most of which are beyond
the scope of this publication..

VALUE: £25–35

368. GIRLS' LIFE BRIGADE MEDAL

Date: 1905.
Ribbon: Red.
Metal: Bronze.
Size: 34mm.
Description: Similar to MYB 367 above, but inscribed THE GIRLS' LIFE BRIGADE.
Comments: *This medal was awarded to members of the Brigade in similar circumstances to those for the Boys' Life Brigade.*

VALUE: £30–40

368A. RSPCA QUEEN VICTORIA MEDAL

Date: 1837.
Ribbon: White with two blue stripes towards each edge.
Metal: Silver.
Size: 34mm.
Description: (Obverse) a group of animals dominated by a standing horse with the legend ROYAL SOCIETY FOR THE PREVENTION OF CRUELTY OF ANIMALS FOUNDED 1824; (reverse) the throned effigy of Queen Victoria with the word PATRON below, surrounded by a floral wreath.
Comments: *This medal is awarded to people who have made a significant contribution to the Society. It was instituted in 1837 and the young Queen Victoria, an enthusiastic supporter of the Society, actually sketched a cat to be included in the reverse design. The name of the recipient is engraved in the exergue below the animals on the obverse.*

VALUE: £70–100

368B. RSPCA MERITORIOUS SERVICE TO ANIMALS MEDAL

Date: Unknown.
Ribbon: White with two blue stripes towards each edge (as 368A).
Size: 38mm.
Description: (Obverse)Two female figures one standing with an outstretched arm bearing a laurel wreath, the other kneeling by a horse with a small group of animals behind and the legend THE ROYAL SOCIETY FOR THE PREVENTION OF CRUELTY TO ANIMALS. (Reverse) A beribboned laurel wreath surmounted by the Royal arms surrounding the words PRESENTED TO (name) FOR MERITORIOUS SERVICE TO ANIMALS.
Comments: *It is uncertain where this medal sits in relation to 368A. It is possible this medal was awarded directly for animal welfare as opposed to contributing to the Society itself for which the RSPCA Queen Victoria Medal would be awarded. Any comments very welcome. See also Medals L31 and L38 in the Life Saving section.*

VALUE: £175–250

368C. RSPCA LONG SERVICE MEDAL

Date: Unknown.
Ribbon: Equal stripes of four blue, three yellow.
Metal: Bronze
Size: 36mm.
Description: (Obverse) A male figure in toga alongside a horse, cow and sheep. The rising sun in the background and the legend LONG SERVICE MEDAL.
Comments: *Little is known at this stage about the medal which was first spotted in a DNW (now Noonan's) Auction in March 2022 (picture courtesy of Noonans). Any further information on it would be gratefully received.*

VALUE: £120–150

369. MARINE SOCIETY REWARD OF MERIT

Date: 1875.
Ribbon: Blue.
Metal: Silver.
Size: 47mm.
Description: (Obverse) a depiction of Britannia holding the hand of a young sailor with seascape behind , with MARINE SOCIETY INSTITUTED MDCCLVI around and INCORPORATED MDCCLXXII in exergue ; (reverse) a wreath of rose, thistle and shamrock enclosing inscription REWARD OF MERIT TO and with the name of the recipient engraved. Suspended from a thin straight bar swivel suspension.
Comments: *The Marine Society was instituted in 1756, at the start of the Seven Years War, by Fowler Walker, Sir John Fielding and Jonas Hanway. Its aim was to encourage poor men and boys to join the Royal and Merchant navies. In this it was successful, and by the end of the war in 1764, it had recruited 5,451 men and 5,174 boys for service at sea. Incorporated by Act of Parliament in 1772 to apprentice poor boys to the Royal and Merchant navies; it clothed them and provided them with an education suitable for their future employment. In 1783, Hanway published a paper promulgating the establishment of schools in every seaport for the training of boys for the sea. So large a concept was beyond the means of the Society but it led the way and in 1786 it commissioned the first pre-sea training ship, the* Beatty, *a sloop which housed 30 boys together with a superintendent, mate, schoolmaster, boatswain and cook. In later years, other organisations followed their example. By 1940, when the Society's training ship* Warspite *was broken up, the Society had trained and equipped some 36,000 boys for the Royal Navy and just under 35,000 for the Merchant Navy. Over the years, the Society was influential in the formation of several related organisations, including The Seamen's Hospital Society, Sail Training Association, Nautical Institute and Sea Cadet Corps. In 1976 the Marine Society merged with a number of other related charities: The Sailors' Home and Red Ensign Club (estab. 1830), The London School of Nautical Cookery (estab. 1893), The Incorporated Thames Nautical Training Trust (HMS Worcester) (estab. 1862), The Seafarers Education Service (estab. 1919), College at Sea (estab. 1938), The Merchant Navy Comforts Service Trust (estab. 1940) and the British Ship Adoption Society (estab. 1936). The Society continues to this day as a charity supporting maritime youth organisations.*

VALUE: £70–100

370. ROYAL BRISTOL VOLUNTEERS MEDAL

Date: 1875.
Ribbon: Plain crimson.
Metal: Silver.
Size: 37mm x 54 max.
Description: (Obverse) Arms of the city of Bristol within a garter bearing the words VIRTUTE ET INDUSTRIA surrounded by ROYAL BRISTOL VOLUNTEERS and IN DANGER READY in scroll below; (reverse) the Volunteers' edict: "IMBODIED FOR THE MAINTENANCE OF PUBLIC ORDER & PROTECTION OF THEIR FELLOW CITIZENS ON THE THREAT OF INVASION BY FRANCE MDCCXCVII. REVIVED AT THE RENEWAL OF HOSTILITIES MDCCCIII. DISBANDED WHEN THE DELIVERANCE OF EUROPE WAS ACCOMPLISHED BY THE PERSEVERENCE & MAGNANIMITY OF GREAT BRITAIN AND HER ALLIES MDCCCXIV" with scroll below bearing the words PRO PATRIA. Suspended from an integral wreath of laurel affixed to an ornamental scroll with the initials GR.
Comments: *This unusual medal was presumably given to all citizens who had volunteered for service when there was the real threat of invasion from France. The medal was worn from the neck on a crimson ribbon.*

VALUE: £150–175

371. GRANTON MEDAL FOR ZEAL

Date: 1915–19
Branch of Service: RN, RNR and RNVR.
Ribbon: Unknown.
Metal: Silver.
Size: 31mm.
Description: A thin medal (1mm) with a simple ring suspension. (Obverse) a raised laurel wreath with the words FOR ZEAL in the centre, in two lines; (reverse) plain, engraved with the recipient's details.
Comments: *Instituted personally by Commodore (later Admiral and an AM recipient) Sir James Startin, SNO of Granton Naval Base, Edinburgh, and selectively awarded to naval personnel under his command who manned the trawlers, sailing ships and coastal trading boats that were involved in extensive mine clearance and Q-ship activities ranging from the North Sea to the Bay of Biscay during the First World War. This medal was awarded to both officers and men for meritorious service in circumstances that would otherwise have gone unrecognised. Although the recipients were mainly from the RNR and RNVR, these medals were awarded at special parades by visiting dignitaries to the base, including King George V, two Prime Ministers (Asquith and Lloyd George) and the Archbishop of Canterbury. Recipients also included Admiral Lord Beatty and Admiral Lord Jellicoe and a gold medal was presented to and accepted by the King. A miniature version of the medal was also available.*

VALUE: £150–200   **Miniature**   £55–80

372. SECURICOR MEDAL FOR LONG SERVICE

Date: —
Ribbon: Yellow with central dark blue stripe and blue edges.
Metal: Silver.
Size: 31mm.
Description: (Obverse) the cross keys of the company's badge with the name SECURICOR above; (reverse) a laurel wreath with centrre panel engraved with the recipient's details.
Comments: *Awarded to employees of the company who exhibit a high standard of devotion to duty over a sustained period.*

VALUE: £35–40

373. SECURICOR MEDAL FOR BRAVERY

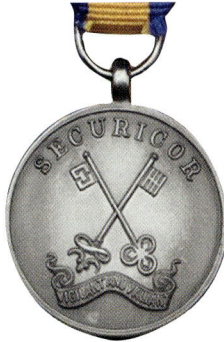

Date: —
Ribbon: Blue with central wide yellow stripe and two thin yellow stripes.
Metal: Silver.
Size: 31mm.
Description: Similar to the above .
Comments: *Awarded to employees of the company who exhibit a particularly high standard of bravery and courage when on duty.*

VALUE: £400–500

373A. SECURICOR MEDAL FOR MERIT

Date: —
Ribbon: Blue with central wide yellow stripe and two thin yellow stripes.
Metal: Silver.
Size: 29mm.
Description: Similar to the above but smaller.
Comments: *Awarded for merit, to employees of the company.*

VALUE: —

374. ST. ANDREW'S ASSOCIATION MEDAL

Date: 1899
Ribbon: Dark red with three narrow yellow stripes.
Metal: Silver.
Size: 36mm.
Description: (Obverse) St Andrew standing before a diagonal cross with the words ST ANDREW'S AMBULANCE ASSOCIATION around the circumference; (reverse) a wreath of thistles surrounding the words FOR SERVICE IN THE ST ANDREW'S AMBULANCE CORPS.
Comments: *Given for long and faithful service in the Association. Originally the medal, in silver or bronze was awarded for bravery in saving life (see MYB L54) but in 1907 the medal was introduced for efficient completion of 15 years service. In 1954 the special medal illustrated left was issued in celebration of the Association's 50th anniversary and Review by HRH the Duke of Edinburgh in Glasgow, inscribed ST ANDREW'S AMBULANCE CORPS 1904–1954, with a yellow ribbon with three narrow red stripes.*

VALUE:	1907 type	£60–75
	1954 issue	£75–100

375. SALVATION ARMY SERVICE MEDAL

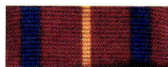

Date: —
Ribbon: Maroon with two narrow blue stripes and a central thin orange stripe.
Metal: Silver.
Size: Various.
Description: An ornate cross surmounted in the centre by the Army's badge in enamels and the words LONG AND FAITHFUL SERVICE on four enamel panels around.
Comments: *Originally awarded for 25 years' service. A silver star is affixed to the ribbon for each additional 10 year period of service. This attractive medal was first instituted by General William Booth and it is believed that the higher the rank, the larger the medal awarded. It was discontinued in favour of a badge after World War II (1957 in the US). There have been other medals awarded by the SA including an extremely rare "Order of the Founder".*

VALUE: From £50

376. ROYAL NORFOLK VETERANS ASSOCIATION MEDAL

Date: 1909
Ribbon: Red ribbon with central thin gold stripe, broad green stripe to the left and broad blue stripe to the right.
Metal: Bronze.
Size: 31mm.
Description: (Obverse) crowned effigy of Edward VII with a laurel branch extending from the bottom of the medal around the left side and the words EDWARD VII on the right; (reverse) the words TO COMMEMORATE THE INSPECTION OF THE ROYAL NORFOLK VETERANS ASSOCIATION BY HIS MAJESTY KING EDWARD VII 25th OCTOBER 1909 in eight lines.
Comments: *This medal was issued to commemorate the inspection of the Association by King Edward VII at Crown Point, Norwich. In 1902 the King had agreed to become Patron of the Association, granting it the Royal title. The King's continued patronage resulted in the inspection of 25 members of the Association at Sandringham in 1907. In 1909 there was a further inspection by the King which resulted in the medal being struck. It is said that the King designed the ribbon for the medal but there is no documentary proof for this. Since 1902 each successive monarch has been the Patron of the Association.*

VALUE: £40–60

377. THE SHIPPING FEDERATION MEDAL FOR MERITORIOUS SERVICE

Date: 1917
Ribbon: None
Metal: Hallmarked gold or silver
Size: 28mm.
Description: (Obverse) a standing figure of Britannia holding a trident and shield, with a submarine on one side and a merchant ship on the other; (reverse) a fouled anchor above a plaque with the words "Presented by the Shipping Federation", flanked by a fish each side. The whole is surrounded by a laurel wreath with a scroll reading "1914 For services During the War 1918" beneath.
Comments: *Awarded by the Shipping Federation for meritorious service during World War I. Each medal has the recipient's name around the rim and the date of the action for which it was awarded.*

VALUE: Gold   £450–550
           Silver   £200–300

378. INNER TEMPLE SERVICE MEDAL 1914–18

Date: 1919.
Campaign: First World War.
Branch of Service: All members of the Inner Temple who participated in the First World War.
Ribbon: None.
Metal: Bronze.
Size: 50mm.
Description: (Obverse) A large Greek cross, with oak leaves in the four corners of the background. Inscription in eight lines: on the upper limb of the cross, in three lines, "The Inner Temple"; across the middle of the cross, in three lines, "To members of the Inn who fought for their country"; on the lower limb of the cross, in two lines, 1914, 1918"; (reverse) The flying figure of Pegasus, over clouds, facing left. Beneath his right front hoof, the dates in roman numerals, MCMXIV—MCMXVIII.
Comments: *Awarded to all members of the Inner Temple who participated in the First World War in any capacity. The name of the recipient is usually found round the edge of the medal, e.g. CAPT. H. F. HALLIFAX, GENL. LIST CAVY. ATTD. 2/8 GURKHA RIFLES AND XX DECCAN HORSE. However, unnamed medals have been seen. The medal was originally issued in a turned wooden box with the recipient's name in calligraphy written on a paper disc glued to the bottom.*

VALUE: £65–100

379. ROYAL AGRICULTURAL SOCIETY OF ENGLAND LONG SERVICE MEDAL (I)

Date: —
Ribbon: Plain royal blue.
Metal: Bronze.
Size: 38mm.
Description: (Obverse) the monarch's bust with the legend ROYAL AGRICULTURAL SOCIETY OF ENGLAND . PATRON . around (Reverse) An agricultural labourer wearing breeches and wielding a scythe with the words LONG SERVICE above.
Comments: *This medal is awarded to employees of Members of the Royal Agricultural Society of England for approved service of not less than 40 years with the same employer or on the same holding. Members can apply for no more than three such awards in any three year period—further awards must be purchased. An additional clasp can be awarded for 50 years service.*

VALUE: £100–150

379A. ROYAL AGRICULTURAL SOCIETY OF ENGLAND LONG SERVICE MEDAL (II)

Date: —
Ribbon: Plain crimson.
Metal: Bronze.
Size: 38mm.
Description: (Obverse) The cypher of the Society with the words ROYAL AGRICULTURAL SOCIETY OF ENGLAND around; (Reverse) a cluster of acorns and oak leaves, with the words FOR LONG SERVICE around.
Comments: *We believe that this medal is a later version of the above and awarded with the same criteria. The example we have seen is from the 1960s. It is possible that the change of design had something to do with the necessity to remove the monarch's head from the obverse. If any reader can tell us more please get in touch..*

VALUE: £75–100

380. CASUALTIES UNION EXEMPLARY SERVICE MEDAL

Date: 2012.
Ribbon: Central stripe of red (blood) flanked by broad stripes of white (training), edged with narrow stripes of blue (origin in Civil Defence), black (blackout and total war) and green (voluntary service).
Metal: Silver-coloured base metal.
Size: 36mm.
Description: (Obverse) Casualties Union Monogram; (reverse) the words FOR EXEMPLARY SERVICE within a laurel wreath with the date of the charity's formation.
Comments: *The Casualties Union was set up in 1942 in Reigate as part of the Civil Defence Training School but became a charity after the war to continue the work of making training more realistic. The medal is usually awarded for 15 years service. Clasps are awarded for 25 years and 50 years of service. When the ribbon bar alone is worn a silver rose represents the 25 year clasp and two silver roses the 50 year clasp. The award of an Exemplary service medal for less than 15 years is represented by a gilt rose on the medal bar and the medal ribbon. The recipient's name, unit and year of award are engraved on the edge.*

Obverse.

VALUE: —

381. CASUALTIES UNION MERITORIOUS SERVICE MEDAL

Date: 2012.
Ribbon: As above but the red and white stripes surmounted by thin stripes of gold (merit).
Metal: Gold-coloured base metal.
Size: 36mm.
Description: (Obverse) As above. Casualties Union Monogram; (reverse) the words FOR MERITORIOUS SERVICE within a laurel wreath with the date of the charity's formation.
Comments: *Awarded for meritorious service above the requirements for the Exemplary Service medal. Clasps are awarded for Life Member and For Merit. When the ribbon bar alone is worn a gilt rose represents the award of a Life Member or For Merit clasp. Two gilt roses represent the award of Life Member and For Merit clasps. No more than two gilt roses may be worn and multiple awards of the For Merit clasp are represented by a single gilt rose. The recipient's name, unit and year of award are engraved on the edge.*

Reverse.

VALUE: —

382. PRIMROSE LEAGUE MEDALS

The Primrose League was an organisation set up in 1883 by admirers of the late lamented Benjamin Disraeli, to promote the idea of Conservative principles in Great Britain. It was extremely popular for many years until its demise in the 1990s. During its existence it awarded a large number of badges, medals and pseudo orders to its members, many of which are avidly collected today. Most are very attractive and well made although regretfully there are far too many to list in this Yearbook, but information is widely available. Its insignia can easily be recognised by the appearance of the League's conjoined PL logo, as can be seen at the centre of the award illustrated here.

VALUE: Various according to age and level of award.

383. BOROUGH OF HARTLEPOOL SPECIAL CONSTABLES' MEDAL FOR SERVICE

Date: 1918.
Branch of Service: Special Constabulary.
Ribbon: Dark blue.
Metal: Silver.
Size: 35mm.
Description: (Obverse) Medieval coat of arms of the city: the legend S'COMMUNITATIS: DE: HARTLEPOL around with stag in centre, with hunting dog on its back. (Reverse) the words in reducing circles: BOROUGH OF HARTLEPOOL SPECIAL CONSTABLE / BOMBARDMENT 1914, AIR RAIDS 1915-18 / ZEPPELIN DESTROYED / 1916 in centre.
Comments: *Awarded to those special constables who served during the bombardment of the town from the sea and by Zeppelin 1914–18. Approximately 120 were issued.*

Value: £250–300

384. ARMY TEMPERANCE ASSOCIATION AWARD OF MERIT MEDAL

Instituted: 1867.

Branch of Service: Army, members of the Army Temperance Association and Royal Army Temperance Association.

Ribbon: Maroon. Suspended from a brooch fastening with palm leaves inscribed PALMAM QUI MERUIT FERAT (Let he who has deserved it bear the palm).

Metal: Silver.

Size: 50 x 29mm.

Description: (Obverse) ATA or RATA (after 1905) monogram, in centre of a beaded oval bearing the words AWARD OF MERIT and WATCH & BE SOBER, surmounted by a five pointed star. (Reverse) officially named to recipient, with rank, unit and date in 2mm block capitals.

Comments: *The Army Temperance Association was a very active organisation dedicated to the abstinence of alcohol throughout the army and, during the Victorian era especially, it issued a large number of medals as various rewards for its members. Most of these are beyond the scope of this book but information can be found in a number of publications dedicated to the subject. However, the medal illustrated here is included as it is sometimes found among veterans' groups. The design was changed from ATA to RATA in 1905. The total number awarded was 631 (257 ATA, 374 RATA) including 4 to women. None were awarded from 1915 to 1920, and only 14 from 1921 until awards ceased in 1927. A few ATA medals have been seen inscribed as REWARD OF MERIT.*

VALUE: £65–85

Above: the medal with RATA cypher. Right: the original ATA medal.

385. CATHEDRAL CONSTABLES' ASSOCIATION MEDAL

Instituted: 2011.

Ribbon: Green and blue diagonal stripes.

Metal: Gold plated base metal.

Size: 32mm.

Description: (Obverse) the association's crest consisting of an eight pointed star bearing a window with a cross surmounted by a crown, with the words "Cathedral Constables' Association" above, all surrounded by a laurel wreath with the Royal cypher at top; (Reverse) A laurel wreath enclosing the words, "For Faithful Service", surmounted by a dove carrying a laurel sprig.

Comments: *The association's medal is issued to officers who have served their respective Cathedral faithfully for 10 years. A bar is awarded for subsequent periods of 10 years. The medal is awarded jointly by the association and an officer's Cathedral trustees.*

VALUE: —

386. BRITISH RED CROSS SOCIETY MEDALS

Instituted: 1911.
Branch of Service: British Red Cross.
Ribbon: White with thin red stripes in various configurations.
Metal: Enamelled base metal.
Size: 38mm.
Description: A red enamelled cross surmounted by a red cross on a white shield surrounded by a white circle bearing the Society's title in gold lettering.
Comments: *The British Red Cross Society has issued various "medals" known as badges over the years. That illustrated is the proficiency badge with a clasp/suspender awarded for proficiency in first aid. Other clasps include Nursing, Hygiene & Sanitation, Cookery, Administration & Organisation, Tuberculosis Course and Infant & Child Welfare. The Society also has its own Gallantry Cross which is a simple red cross bearing the words "For Distinguished Services". See also MYB 165A, 171A, 266 and 355. More information on the numerous awards is available on the Society's website www.redcross.org.uk.*

VALUE: From £10 upwards.

387. ROYAL LIFE SAVING SOCIETY LONG SERVICE AWARD (see also L49A)

Instituted: 2002.
Ribbon: Dark blue with a narrow pale blue centre stripe suspended from a top bar enamelled with RLSS.
Metal: Enamelled base metal.
Size: 29mm.
Description: (Obverse) the emblem of the Society: crossed boathook/oar and lifebelt surmounted by the royal crown, with the words LONG SERVICE suspended below; (reverse) plain, engraved with the recipient's name and year of issue.
Comments: *Awarded by the Society for a minimum of 50 years' service.*

VALUE: £20–30

388. MEDAL FOR THE RECONSTRUCTION OF FRANCE

Instituted: 1921.

Ribbon: French Army Blue (horizon bleu) with white side stripes.

Metal: Silver.

Size: 30mm

Description: (Obverse) A shield-shaped coat of arms surmounted by a vertical sword, over an eagle with the motto "Do Right" (above) and "Fear no Man" (below). (Reverse) A left-facing wyvern with adjacent dates "1916" and "1921" and the legend "Comite Americain pour les Regions Devestees de la France".

Comments: *Issued unnamed, this silver medal was awarded to nursing and welfare staff of the "Comite Americain pour les Regions Devestees de la France" (CARD). This organisation was set up by Anne Morgan in the USA, who had previously worked in New York with the American Fund for French Wounded. She had the support of General Petain to set up an organisation to address the plight of the thousands of French families, refugees and returning forces whose homes and livelihoods had been shattered by the First World War. The headquarters of CARD was at Chateau de Blerancourt, about 75 miles north of Paris. CARD personnel operated for about two years after the Armistice. The medal was issued to all CARD members, some of whom were British, and took its design from the Blerancourt coat of arms, which showed a wyvern .*

VALUE: £100–150

389. SOLDIERS AND SAILORS FAMILIES ASSOCIATION CAPE BADGE

Instituted: 1894.

Ribbon: None.

Metal: Bronze or silver.

Size: 48 x 36mm

Description: Oval with a scroll border. The bronze medal was worn around the neck, the silver medal on the cape with suspension from a plain metal pinback bar and two rings. (Obverse) Left-facing head and shoulder effigy of Princess Alexandra. (Reverse) Inscribed "The Soldiers and Sailors Families Association MDCCCLXXXV" (1885, the date of foundation).

Comments: *The Association was founded by Colonel James Gildea in 1885 to serve Wives and families of army and navy personnel in garrison towns and seaports. Its patron was HRH Princess (later Queen) Alexandra; the nurses of the Association were known as "Alexandra Nurses". The badge in bronze was worn by nurses with up to three years service and were surrendered if the nurse left or continued to serve beyond that time, and thus are very rare. The silver version was worn by nursing staff with more than three years service and could be retained by the recipient after five years service. Male nurses of the RAMC with appropriate qualifications were entitled to wear a version of this badge, but in bronze. Due to the small number of male nurses, the badges are comparatively rare and as such attract a premium. The badge ceased to be issued upon the formation of the RAF in 1918 when the title changed to "The Soldiers, Sailors and Airmen Families Association" (SSAFA) which continues to the present day.*

VALUE:

Bronze	£250–300
Silver	£125–175

390. SCOTTISH WOMEN'S HOSPITALS MEDAL 1914

Date: 1914–19.
Ribbon: Black, green and yellow "Tartan".
Metal: Bronze.
Size: 35mm diameter, 50mm with suspender.
Description: (Obverse) A kneeling woman draws towards her a wounded man and shields him from the grim figure of death, intent on dealing a fatal blow. (Reverse) an embossed wreath around the outer edge; at the top are the letters N.U.W.S.S and at the bottom "1914". In the centre the legend SCOTTISH WOMEN'S HOSPITALS. The medal is suspended from a dark bronze suspension bar, voided, with either side a fleur de lis.
Clasps: None.
Comments: *Much has been documented about the Scottish Women's Hospitals, which were initially funded by the National Union of Women's Suffrage Societies (NUWSS) and the American Red Cross. The units served with distinction in several theatres of war including France an the Balkans. This medal was designed by Miss Hazel Armour and was intended to represent the work of the Scottish Women's Hospitals. The medal, made by John Pinches and in a purple case, was issued unnamed, but with a small card bearing the name of the recipient, which states: "Medal conferred by the Committee of the Scottish Women's Hospitals on . . . in recognition of her valuable service". Most of those who received the medal served abroad, but a few served at home in administrative and fund-raising capacities.*

VALUE:	Un-attributable	£250–300
	Attributable	£350–450

391. FIRST AID NURSING YEOMANRY MEDAL 1914–1919

Date: 1914–1919.
Ribbon: White with scarlet edges.
Metal: Bronze.
Size: 32mm.
Description: (Obverse) Head of a female Greek warrior in helmet facing right with wreath around. Top centre the date 1914; bottom centre the date 1918. (Reverse) Shield with cross moline to centre, around which the words "First Aid Nursing Yeomanry".
Clasps: None
Comments: *The First Aid Nursing Yeomanry Corps was founded in 1907 by Edward Charles Baker who recruited "respectable young women" for training in First Aid and Home Nursing, and who had to qualify in Horsemanship, Veterinary Work, Signalling and Camp Cookery. They had to provide their own uniform and first aid outfit, and pay enrolment and fees. During WWI the FANYC provided ambulance drivers and other staff, earning 95 decorations, including 11 mentions, 19 MMs and 27 Croix de Guerre. A service medal for FANYC was produced after the demobilisation of their active service units in 1920, for those who had served either abroad or at home. A bronze pinback badge was also produced for the same period (scarce). The medals were issued unnamed.*

VALUE:	Un-attributable:	£120–150
	Attributable:	£250–350

392. WOMEN'S HOSPITAL CORPS MEDAL 1914–1919

Date: 1914–1919.
Ribbon: Not known .
Metal: Bronze and enamel.
Size: 35mm diameter, 50mm high with suspender.
Description: Suspended by a ring from an oak leaf spray. (Obverse) "1914, Liberte, Egalite, Fraternite" around a central laurel wreath. (Reverse) "Women's Hospital Corps". Both sides green enamel on a white enamel background.
Clasps: None.
Comments: *The Women's Hospital Corps was formed in 1914 and 21 staff (including 2 men) proceeded to France, and subsequently qualified for the 1914 star for their work in Paris and Wimereux. The medal was awarded by former militant suffragists Louisa Garrett Anderson and Flora Murray to staff of the WHC for service in France during the early months of WWI.*

VALUE: Extremely rare (only example known to date)

393. MEDAL FOR SERVICE TO THE SERBIAN RED CROSS IN LONDON

Date: 1914–1919.
Ribbon: Central cream/white broad stripe, with narrower dark blue each side and red stripes to the edges.
Metal: Silver.
Size: 32mm.
Description: (Obverse) Left-facing pair of male heads in wreath with crown above, beneath the wreath the legend "Service to Serbia During War". (Reverse) Crowned double-headed Serbian eagle surmounted on a Geneva Cross with the legend around: "Serbian Red Cross Society London".
Clasps: None.
Comments: *Issued unnamed, the medal was awarded by the Council of the Serbian Red Cross Society in Great Britain in 1923 for services rendered to Serbia, and the member's name was inscribed upon the Roll of Honourable Service to Serbia. A certificate accompanied the medal. Many of those who received the medal served abroad, but most served at home in administrative and fund-raising capacities allied to the British Red Cross. It is not known how many were awarded, but the medals are very scarce, inferring only a small number were produced.*

VALUE: Unattributable: £250–300
　　　　　Attributable: £350–400

394. NATAL EXEMPTION MEDAL

Date: 1891.
Ribbon: Unknown but example seen with gold with broad and narrow blue stripes towards each edge, the same as MYB127.
Metal: Silver or bronze.
Size: 32mm.
Description: (Obverse) A patterned circle enclosing the words "EXEMPTED FROM NATIVE LAW", usually with the recipient's name engraved thereon. (Reverse) Plain.
Comments: *In 1865 a Letter of Exemption could be given to native people of important rank or lineage or in a position of authority, recommended by prominent colonists. The holder was subject to the laws of the colonists rather than native customs. After 1890 a medal, which could be purchased by recommended individuals, was struck to accompany the letter. That illustrated is also dated with the date of the recipient's original Letter of Exemption.*

VALUE: Silver £3000–4000　　　　Bronze —,

395. EBOLA MEDAL FOR SERVICE IN WEST AFRICA (formally 291BB)

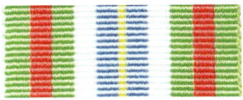

Date: 2015.

Ribbon: Equal stripes of bright green, red, bright green, white, light blue each side of a central thin yellow stripe (the colours of the flags of the West African Nations affected).

Metal: Nickel silver.

Size: 36mm.

Description: (Obverse) The Rank-Broadley effigy of HM Queen Elizabeth II; (reverse) the eternal flame, representing the light of hope surrounded by abstract lines representing the Ebola virus. With the inscription •FOR SERVICE• WEST AFRICA EBOLA EPIDEMIC

Comments: *Awarded to an estimated 3,000 (as of July 2015) military and civilian personnel who volunteered to combat the outbreak of Ebola in Sierra Leone, Liberia, Guinea and their territorial waters. Qualification for the medal is 21 days continuous service from March 23, 2014 (the date which the World Health organisation first publicly recognised the Ebola Outbreak in West Africa) or 30 days accumulated service on working visits within the operational area provided these visits are for a minimum of 48 hours each. If qualifying service is reduced or terminated through death, serious illness, evacuation, wounding or other disability due to service in the operational area and the individual might have been expected otherwise to complete the full qualifying period then the medal will be awarded. The situation in West Africa is to be reviewed on a regular basis to determine whether the medal is still warranted.*

VALUE: —   *Miniature*   £15–20

396. NUCLEAR TEST MEDAL

Date: 2023.

Ribbon: Central white stripe, flanked by two yellow stripes, then two thinner black stripes, then equal stripes of red and blue. These represent, as follows: white and yellow for the flash of the explosion; black for the particle fallout; Red for the fireball; Blue for the sky and the Pacific Ocean where the majority of testing took place.

Metal: Nickel plated nickel-silver

Size: 36mm

Description: (Obverse) The right-facing crowned portrait of His Majesty King Charles III by Jack McDermott. (Reverse) The nuclear "atom" symbol above a laurel wreath and the words NUCLEAR TEST MEDAL.

Comments: *After a long running campaign by veterans of the nuclear tests, Prime Minister Rishi Sunak announced, in November 2022, that a medal would be awarded to UK Service and civilian personnel, and those from other nations, who served at the locations where the UK atmospheric nuclear tests were conducted, including the preparatory and clear-up phases, between 1952 and 1967 inclusive. It will also be awarded to UK personnel who served at locations where American atmospheric nuclear tests took place in 1962 under Operation DOMINIC. Qualifying service for the medal is defined as service of any length.*

VALUE: —   *Miniature*   £10–12

397. THE HUMANITARIAN SERVICE MEDAL

Date: 2023.

Ribbon: Central white stripe flanked by equal stripes of red, light blue, dark blue and purple. The colours represent: white for the civilian population; red for the first responders e.g. Red Cross, Red Crescent; pale blue of the NHS for doctors and nurses who may deploy (as in Ebola); dark blue for the blue light services (Police, Fire, Paramedics etc); purple – tri-service colour of the military as a response and protection force.

Metal: Nickel plated nickel-silver

Size: 36mm

Description: (Obverse) The right-facing crowned portrait of His Majesty King Charles III by Jack McDermott. (Reverse) A laurel wreath with an intertwined scroll bearing the words FOR HUMANITARIAN SERVICE.

Comments: *Announced in July 2023 the medal is to be awarded for serious (level 2) and catastrophic (level 3) emergencies to those in public service and members of organisations that contribute on behalf of the government, such as charities, which respond in support of human welfare during or in the aftermath of a crisis. Examples are given that include combating a life-threatening crisis or providing disaster relief or aid provision, it will be awarded for service both in the UK and internationally.*

VALUE: —   *Miniature*   £10–12

MEDAL RIBBONS

In this section we feature the majority of the ribbons for the medals included in the main sections of the book. Where the same ribbon is used for more than one medal, only one is illustrated here.
(Not all shown to scale, see reference number for actual sizes)

ORDERS OF KNIGHTHOOD MEDAL RIBBONS

(Not all shown to scale, see reference number for actual sizes)

1. The Most Noble Order of the Garter

2. The Most Ancient and Most Noble Order of the Thistle

3. The Most Illustrious Order of St Patrick

4. The Most Honourable Order of the Bath

5. The Royal Guelphic Order

6. The Most Distinguished Order of St Michael & St George

7. The Most Exalted Order of the Star of India

8. The Most Eminent Order (George V)

9. The Royal Family Order (George IV)

9. The Royal Family Order (Edward VII)

9. The Royal Family Order (George V)

9. The Royal Family Order (George VI)

9. The Royal Family Order (Elizabeth II)

11. The Imperial Order of the Crown of India

12. The Royal Victorian Order

13. The Royal Victorian Medal

13. The Royal Victorian Medal (foreign Associates)

15. Order of Merit

16. The Most Excellent Order of the British Empire (Civil 1st type)

16. The Most Excellent Order of the British Empire (Civil 2nd type)

16. The Most Excellent Order of the British Empire (Military 1st type)

16. The Most Excellent Order of the British Empire (Military 2nd type)

17. Medal of the Order of the British Empire (Civil)

17. Medal of the Order of the British Empire (Military)

18. Empire Gallantry Medal (Civil 1922)

18. Empire Gallantry Medal (Military 1922)

18. Empire Gallantry Medal (Civil 1937)

(with smaller miniature emblem when ribbon worn alone)

(with smaller miniature emblem when ribbon worn alone)

18. Empire Gallantry Medal (Military 1937)

19. British Empire Medal (Civil 1922)

19. British Empire Medal (Military 1922)

19. British Empire Medal (Civil 1937)

19. British Empire Medal (Military 1937)

20. The Order of the Companions of Honour

21. The Baronet's Badge (Nova Scotia)

21. The Baronet's Badge (other Baronets)

22. The Knight Bachelor's Badge

23. Order of St John with miniature emblem when worn alone

DECORATIONS
MEDAL RIBBONS
(Not all shown to scale, see reference number for actual sizes)

24. Victoria Cross (Pre-1918)

24. Victoria Cross (Modern)

25. New Zealand Cross with miniature emblem when worn alone

26. George Cross

27. Distinguished Service Order

28/29. Imperial Service Order/Medal

30. Indian Order of Merit (Military)

30. Indian Order of Merit (Civil)

30A. Conspicuous Gallantry Cross

31. Royal Red Cross

32. Distinguished Service Cross

33. Military Cross

34. Distinguished Flying Cross pre-1919

34. Distinguished Flying Cross post-1919

35. Air Force Cross pre-1919

35. Air Force Cross post-1919

36. Order of British India (Original)

36. Order of British India (1st Class, ii)

36. Order of British India (2nd Class, ii)

36. Order of British India (1st Class, post-1939)

36. Order of British India (2nd class, post-1939)

37. Order of Burma

38. Kaisar-i-Hind

39. Albert Medal, original (1866) and 2nd Class, Sea, 1867-1904

39. Albert Medal, 1st Class, Sea, 1867-1949

39. Albert Medal, 2nd Class, Sea, 1904-71

39. Albert Medal, 1st Class, Land, 1877-1949

39. Albert Medal, 2nd Class, Land, 1877-1904

39. Albert Medal, 2nd Class, Land, 1904-71

40. SA Queen's Medal for Bravery

41. Distinguished Conduct Medal

42. Distinguished Conduct Medal (Dominion & Colonial)

43. DCM (KAR and WAFF)

44. Conspicuous Gallantry, 1st ribbon

44. Conspicuous Gallantry

44. Conspicuous Gallantry, (Flying)

45. George Medal

46. King's Police Medal 1916

46. King's Police Medal (Gallantry)

47. Queen's/King's Police Medal

47. Queen's/King's Police Medal Gallantry

48. Queen's/King's Fire Service Medal

48. Queen's/King's Fire Service Medal (Gallantry)

48A. Queen's/King's Volunteer Reserves Medal

48B. Queen's/King's Ambulance Service Medal for Distinguished Service

49. King's Police Medal (South Africa)

50/51. Edward Medal

52. Indian Distinguished Service Medal

53. Burma Gallantry Medal

54. Distinguished Service Medal

55. Military Medal

56. Distinguished Flying Medal pre-1919

56. Distinguished Flying Medal post-1919

57. Air Force Medal pre-1919

57. Air Force Medal post-1919

58. Constabulary Medal Ireland 1842

58. Constabulary Medal Ireland 1872

59. Indian Police Medal (Meritorious Service)

59. Indian Police Medal (From 1942)

60. Burma Police Medal

61. Colonial Police Medal (Gallantry)
62. Colonial Fire Brigade Medal (Gallantry)

61. Colonial Police Medal (Meritorious Service)
62. Colonial Fire Brigade (Meritorious Service)

63. Queen's/King's Gallantry Medal

64. Allied Subjects Medal

65. King's Medal for Courage in the Cause of Freedom

66. King's Medal for Service in the Cause of Freedom

67/68. Sea Gallantry Medal

68. Sea Gallantry Medal till 1922

69. British North Borneo Company's Bravery Cross

70. Native Chief's Medal (i)

70. Native Chief's Medal (ii)

CAMPAIGN MEDAL RIBBONS
(Not all shown to scale, see reference number for actual sizes)

71. Louisburg Medal

79. Seringapatam

82. Sultan's Medal for Egypt

87. Bagur and Palamos Medal

91. Burma Medal

93. Naval Gold Medal

94. Naval General Service Medal

95. Army Gold Cross/96. Maida Gold
97. Army Gold Medal

98. Military General Service Medal

99. Waterloo Medal

100. Brunswick Medal for Waterloo

101. Hanoverian Medal for Waterloo

102. Nassau Medal for Waterloo

103. Saxe-Gotha-Altenburg Medal

104. Army of India Medal

105. Ghuznee Medal (original type)

105. Ghuznee Medal

105A. British Legion Medal

106. St Jean D'Acre Medal

107. Candahar, Ghuznee, Cabul
Medal/109. Kelat-I-Ghilzie

108. Jellalabad

110. China War Medal

111. Scinde Medal

112. Gwalior Star

113. Sutlej Medal

114. Punjab Medal

115. South Africa Medal

116. Sir Harry Smith's Medal

117. India General Service 1854–95

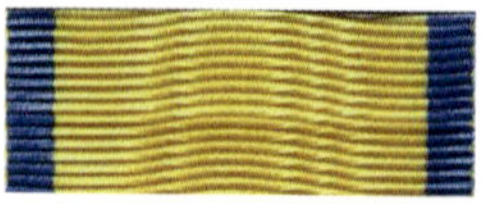

118. Baltic Medal

119. Crimea Medal

120. Turkish Crimea Medal

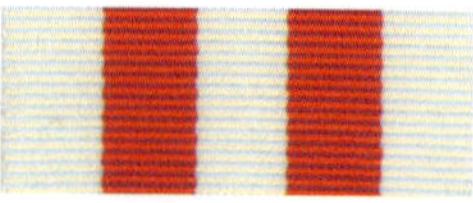

121. Indian Mutiny Medal

122. Second China War (original type)

122. Second China War (second type)

123. New Zealand Medals

124. Abyssinia 1867–68

125. Canada General Service

126. Ashantee/ 137. E&W Africa

127. South Africa Medal

128. Afghanistan 1878–80

129. Kabul to Kandahar Star

130. Cape of Good Hope GSM

131. Egypt Medal

132. Khedive's Star
133. Gordon's Khartoum Star

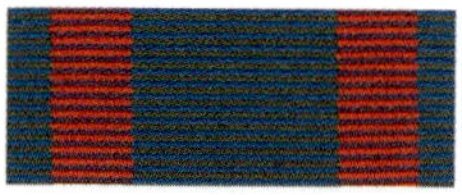

134. North West Canada Medal

135. Royal Niger Company's Medal

136. Imperial BEA Co.s Medal

137. East and West Africa Medal

138. BSA Co.s Medal

139. Hunza Nagar badge

140. Central Africa Medal

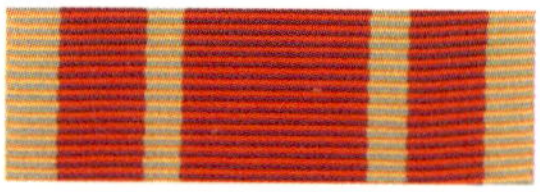

141. Hong Kong Plague Medal

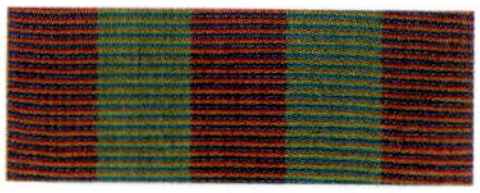

142. India Medal 1895–1902

143. Jummoo and Kashmir

144. Ashanti Star

145. Queen's Sudan Medal

146. Khedive's Sudan Medal 1896–1908

147. East and Central Africa Medal

148. BNB Co's Medal (i)

148. BNB Co's Medal (ii)

148A. BNB Co's Medal (iii)

149. Sultan of Zanzibar's Medal

150. Queen's South Africa Medal
151. Queen's Mediterranean Medal

152. King's South Africa Medal

152A. St Andrew's Ambulance
Association Medal For South Africa

153. St John's Ambulance Brigade
Medal for South Africa

154/155. Kimberley Star/Medal

156. Yorkshire Imperial Yeomanry

157. Medal for the Defence of Ookiep

158. China War Medal

159. Transport Medal

160. Ashanti Medal

161. Africa General Service 1902–56

162. Tibet Medal

163. Natal Medal

163A. Messina Earthquake

164. India General Service 1908–35

165. Khedive's Sudan 1910

166/167. 1914/1914–15 Star

168. British War Medal 1914–20

169. Mercantile Marine

170. Victory Medal

171. Territorial Force War Medal

171A. British Red Cross Society Medal
for War Service

173. Naval General Service 1915–62

174. General Service 1918–62

174A. Iraq Active Service Medal

175. India General Service 1936–39

176. North Borneo GSM

176. North Borneo GSM (Bravery)

176A. Sudan Defence Force GSM

177. 1939–1945 Star

178. Atlantic Star

178A. Arctic Star

179. Air Crew Europe Star

180. Africa Star

181. Pacific Star

182. Burma Star

183. Italy Star

184. France and Germany Star

185. Defence Medal

186. War Medal 1939–45

187. India Service Medal

188. Canadian Volunteer Service Medal

188A/191A. Canadian & NZ Memorial Cross

189. Africa Service Medal

190. Australia Service Medal

191. New Zealand War Service Medal

192. South African Medal for War Service

193. Southern Rhodesia Service Medal

194. Newfoundland Volunteer War Service Medal

195. Korea Medal

196. South African Medal for Korea

197. United Nations Korea Medal

198. General Service Medal 1962

198A. Operational Service Medal (Sierra Leone)

198A. Operational Service Medal (Congo)

198A. Operational Service Medal (Afghanistan)

198A. Operational Service Medal (Iraq & Syria)

198B. Accumulated Campaign Service

198C. Accumulated Campaign Service Medal 2011

198D. General Service Medal 2008

199. UN Emergency Force Medal

200. Vietnam Medal

200A. Vietnam Logistic and Support Medal

201. South Vietnam Campaign Medal

202. Rhodesia Medal

203. South Atlantic Medal

203A. Soviet 40th Anniversary Medal

203B. Pingat Jasa Malaysia Medal

203C. King Hussein Medal

204. Gulf Medal

204A. Brunei General Service Medal

204AA. Sierra Leone General Service Medal

204B. Iraq Medal

204C. IRAQ Reconstruction Service Medal

204D. The Civilian Service Medal (Afghanistan)

205. Saudi Medal for Liberation of Kuwait

205A. Multinational Force and Observers Medal

205A. Multinational Force and Observers Medal (Civilian)

206. Kuwait Liberation Medals

206A. NATO Former Yugoslavia

206A. NATO Kosovo

206A. NATO Macedonia

206A. NATO Service Medal Eagle Assist

206A. NATO Service Medal Active Endeavour

206A. NATO (i) Non Article 5	206A. NATO Non Article 5 (revised) (Iraq)	206B. European Community Monitoring Mission Medal
206C. Western European Union Mission Service Medal	206D. European Security and Defence Policy Service Medal	207. United Nations Medal UNTSO, UNOGIL & UNGOMAP
207. United Nations Medal ONUC	207. United Nations Medal UNTEA & UNSF	207. United Nations Medal UNMOGIP & UNIPOM
207. United Nations Medal UNYOM	207. United Nations Medal UNFICYP	207. United Nations Medal UNEF II
207. United Nations Medal UNDOF	207. United Nations Medal UNIFIL	207. United Nations Medal UNIIMOG
207. United Nations Medal UNAVEM I, II, III & MONUA	207. United Nations Medal ONUCA	207. United Nations Medal UNTAG
207. United Nations Medal ONUSAL	207. United Nations Medal UNIKOM	207. United Nations Medal MINURSO
207. United Nations Medal UNAMIC	207. United Nations Medal UNTAC	207. United Nations Medal UNOSOM I & UNOSOM II
207. United Nations Medal UNMIH, UNSMIH, MIPONUH & MICAH	207. United Nations Medal UNIMOZ & ONUMOZ	207. United Nations Medal UNPROFOR & UNCRO
207. United Nations Medal UNOMIL	207. United Nations Medal UNOMUR	207. United Nations Medal UNOMIG

UN Ribbons change for each operation—see MYB 207 for the full list.

207. United Nations Medal
UNAMIR

207. United Nations Medal
UNHQ

207. United Nations Medal
UNPREDEP

207. United Nations Medal
UNMOP

207. United Nations Medal
UNTAES

207. United Nations Medal
UNMOT

207. United Nations Medal
UNMIBH

207. United Nations Medal
UNMIT

207. United Nations Medal
UNGCI

207. United Nations Medal
UNMISS

207. United Nations Medal
UNISFA

207. United Nations Medal
UNMOGUA & MINUGUA

207. United Nations Medal
UN Special Service

207. United Nations Medal
UNOMSIL

207. United Nations Medal
UNPSG

207. United Nations Medal
MINURCA

207. United Nations Medal
UNMIK

207. United Nations Medal
UNAMET, UNMISET & UNTAET

207. United Nations Medal
MONUC & MONUSCO

207. United Nations Medal
UNMEE

207. United Nations Medal
UNMINUCI

207. United Nations Medal
UNMIL

207. United Nations Medal
UNIOCI

207. United Nations Medal
ONUB

207. United Nations Medal
MINUSTAH

207. United Nations Medal
UNMIS

207. United Nations Medal
UNMINURCAT

207. United Nations Medal
UNAMID

207. United Nations Medal
UNAMID (alternative)

207. United Nations Medal
UNSMIS

207. United Nations Medal
MINUSMA

207. United Nations Medal
MINUSCA

207. United Nations Medal
MINUJUSTH

207A. International Conference
on the Former Yugoslavia

207B. Interfet Medal

207C. Unitas Medal

LONG AND MERITORIOUS SERVICE MEDAL RIBBONS
(Not all shown to scale, see reference number for actual sizes)

208/214. Meritorious Service
Medals/212. Colonial MSM (Canada)

209. Royal Marines Meritorious Service
Medal (first type)

209. Royal Marines Meritorious
Service Medal (second type)

210. Army Meritorious Service Medal
(first type)

210. Army Meritorious Service Medal
(second type)

210. Army Meritorious Service Medal
(third type)

211. RAF Meritorious Service
Medal (original)

212. Colonial MSM
(Cape of Good Hope)

212. Colonial MSM
(Natal)

212. Colonial MSM
(Commonwealth of Australia)

212. Colonial MSM
(New South Wales)

212. Colonial MSM
(Queensland)

212. Colonial MSM
(South Australia)

212. Colonial MSM
(Tasmania)

212. Colonial MSM
(New Zealand)

213/214. Indian Army MSM 1848/88

215. African Police Medal
for Meritorious Service

216. Union of South Africa MSM

217. Royal Household FS QV

217. Royal Household FS GVIR

217. Royal Household FS EIIR

217. Royal Household FS CIII

218. RN LS & GC (i)

218. RN LS & GC (ii)

219. RNR Decoration

220. RNR LS & GC (i)

220. RNR LS & GC (ii)

221. RNVR Decoration 1919

222. RNVR LS & GC

223. RFR LS & GC

224. RNASBR LS & GC Medal (i)

224. RNASBR LS & GC Medal (ii)

225. RNVWAR LS & GC Medal

226. RN Auxiliary Service Medal

227. Coastguard Auxiliary Service LS Medal (ii)

229. Army LS & GC Medal (i)

229. Army LS & GC Medal (ii)

230. Ulster Defence Regiment Medal for LS & GC

231. Volunteer Officer's Decoration/232 Volunteer Force LS & GC (HAC) (first type).

232/231/233/234/242A Volunteer Force LS & GC (HAC)

233. Territorial Decoration
236. Efficiency Decoration (i) UNMOGUA

234. Territorial Force Efficiency Medal

235. Territorial Efficiency Medal
237. Efficiency Medal (i)

236. Efficiency Decoration T&AVR (ii)

237. Efficiency Medal T&AVR (ii)

237. Efficiency Medal (HAC)

238. Army Emergency Reserve Decoration

239. Army Emergency Reserve Efficiency Medal

240. Imperial Yeomanry LS & GC Medal

241. Militia LS & GC Medal

242. Special Reserve LS & GC Medal

242A. Volunteer Reserves Service Medal

242B. Royal Military Asylum Good Conduct Medal

242J. Merchant Navy Medal

242K. Queen's / King's Merchant Navy Medal For Meritorious Service

243. Indian Army LS & GC (Europeans)

244. Indian Army LS & GC (Indians)

245. Indian Volunteer Forces Officers Decoration

246/247. Colonial Auxiliary Forces Officer's Decoration/LS Medal

248. Colonial Long Service and Good Conduct Medal

248. Colonial Long Service and Good Conduct Medal, New Guinea

248. Colonial Long Service and Good Conduct Medal, Sarawak

249. Permanent Forces LS & GC

250. RWAFF LS & GC

251. KAR LS & GC Medal

252. Trans-Jordan FF LS & GC Medal

253. SA PF LS & GC Medal

254. Efficiency Medal (SA)

254A. Royal HKR Disbandment Medal

255. Canadian Forces Decoration

256. Victoria Vol. Long & Efficient Service Medal

257. New Zealand Long & Efficient Service Medal

258. NZ Volunteer Service Medal

259. NZ Territorial Service Medal (i)

259. NZ Territorial Service Medal (ii)

261/261A. Ulster Defence Regiment

261B. Northern Ireland Home Service Medal

262. Cadet Forces Medal

263. Royal Observer Corps medal

264. Civil Defence LS

264A. Ambulance Service (Emergency Duties) LS & GC Medal

264B. Assoc. of Chief Ambulance Officer's Service Medal

264C. Royal Fleet Auxiliary Service Medal

265. WVS Long Service Medal

266. Voluntary Medical Service Medal

267. Service Medal of the Order of St John of Jerusalem

267. Service Medal in gold of the Order of St John of Jerusalem

268/269. RAF LS & GC Medal

270. Air Efficiency Award

271. Police LS & GC

272. Special Constabulary LS

273. RUC Service Medal (original type)

273. RUC Service Medal (post-2001)

273A. Police Service of Northern Ireland (PSNI) Medal

274. Colonial Police LS

275. Colonial Special Constabulary LS

276. Ceylon Police LS & GC Medal (I)

277. Ceylon Police LS & GC Medal (II)

278. Ceylon Police Medal for Merit

278a. Ceylon Police Medal for Gallantry

279. Cyprus MP LS & GC Medal

279A. Royal Falklands Islands Police Jubilee Medal

280. HK Police Medal for Merit (1st Class)

280. HK Police Medal for Merit (2nd Class)

280. HK Police Medal for Merit (3rd Class)

280. HK Police Medal for Merit (4th Class)

280B. Royal Hong Kong Police

280C. Royal HK Aux. Police Commemoration Medal & 280D. HK Military Service Corps Medal

281. HK Royal Naval Dockyard Police Long Service Medal

281A. HK Disciplined Service Medal

281B. Tientsin British Emergency Corps Medal

282. Malta Police LS & GC Medal

282A. Mauritius Police LS & GC

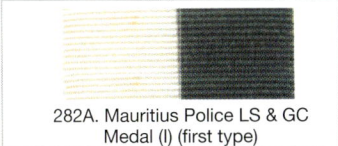

282A. Mauritius Police LS & GC Medal (I) (first type)

282B. Mauritius Police LS & GC Medal (II)

283. NZ Police LS & GC Medal (Second type)

283A. Seychelles Police LS & GC Medal Medal

284. SA Police Good Service Medal

285. SA Railways & Harbour Police LS&GC Medal (&290)

286. Fire Brigade LS Medal

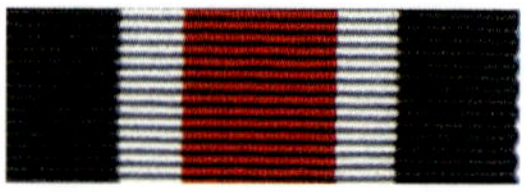

286A. Assoc. of Professional Fire Brigade Officers LS Medal

286AA. National Fire Bridges Association Long Service Medal

286AB. National Fire Brigades Union Medal

286B. British Fire Services Assoc. Medal (20 year)

286B. British Fire Services Assoc. Medal (10 year)

286C. British Fire Service Assoc. Meritorious Service Medal

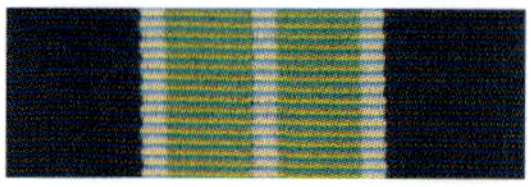

287. Colonial Fire Brigade LS Medal

288. Ceylon Fire Brigade LS & GC Medal

288A. Northern Ireland Prison Service Medal (i)

288A. Northern Ireland Prison Service Medal (ii)

288B. Prison Service Medal

289. Colonial Prison Service LS Medal

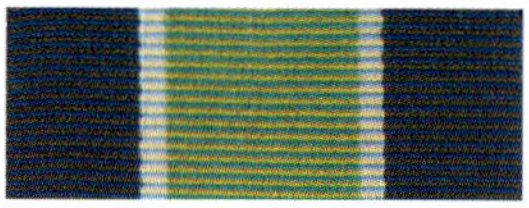

290. South African Prison Service Faithful Service Medal

291. SA Prisons Dept Faithful Service Medal

291AA. NATO Meritorious Service Medal

CORONATION, JUBILEE AND OTHER ROYAL MEDAL RIBBONS
(Not all shown to scale, see reference number for actual sizes)

292. Empress of India Medal

293/295. Jubilee (VR) 1887/1897

294. Jubilee (Police) 1887

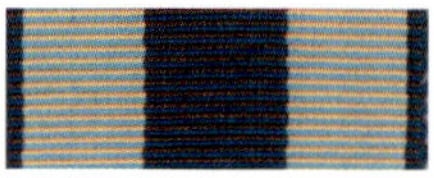

295. Jubilee Medal 1897

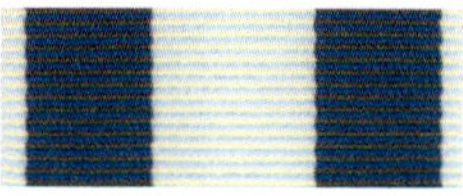

296. Jubilee 1897 (Mayors & Provosts)

297. Jubilee (Police) 1897

298. Ceylon Diamond Jubilee 1897

299. HK Diamond Jubilee Medal

299A. Lagos Diamond Jubilee Medal

299B. India Diamond Jubilee Medal

300. Visit to Ireland 1900

301. Coronation 1902

302. Coronation 1902 (Mayors & Provosts)

303. Coronation 1902 (Police)

304. Ceylon Coronation 1902

305. HK Coronation 1902

306. Delhi Durbar 1903

307. Visit to Scotland 1903

308. Visit to Ireland 1903

308A. Visit of the Prince and Princess of Wales to India

308B. George Prince of Wales Medal

309. Coronation 1911
312. Delhi Durbar 1911

309A. Guildhall Coronation Medal 1911

310. Coronation 1911 (Police)

311. Visit to Ireland 1911

312AB. Queen Alex. Children's Banquet Medal 1914

312D. Visit Of The Prince Of Wales To Bombay Medal 1921

313. Jubilee 1935

313A. Isle of Man Silver Jubilee 1935

314. Coronation 1937

315. Coronation 1953

315A. Royal Visit to New Zealand Medal 1953–54

316. Jubilee 1977

318. Golden Jubilee 2002

318A. Diamond Jubilee

318B. Diamond Jubilee 2012 — Caribbean Realms

318C. Platinum Jubilee Service medal

318D. Coronation 2023

347

MISCELLANEOUS MEDAL RIBBONS
(Not all shown to scale, see reference number for actual sizes)

319. King's and Queen's Messenger Badge	320. Arctic Medal (1857)	321. Arctic Medal (1876)
322. Polar Medal	323. EVII Medal for Science, Art & Music	324. Order of the League of Mercy
325. Queen Alex. Imperial Military Nursing Service Cape Badge	325A. Queen Alex. Imperial Military Nursing Service Reserve Cape Badge	326. Territorial Force Nursing Service Cape Badge
326A. Queen Alex. Military Families Nursing Service Cape Badge	326B. Territorial Army Nursing Service Cape Badge	326C. Queen Alex. Royal Army Nursing Corps Cape Badge
327. Indian Title Badge (1st Class)	327. Indian Title Badge (2nd Class)	327. Indian Title Badge (3rd Class)
328. Badge of the Cert. of Honour	329. Badge of Honour (non-African countries)	329A. The Governor Generals' Medal of Honour
330. Naval Engineers GC Medal	331. Indian Recruiting Badge (GV)	332. Indian Recruiting Badge (GVI)
333. Naval Good Shooting	334. Army Best Shot Medal	335. Queen's Medal for Champion Shot (RN/RM)
336. Queen's Medal for Champion Shot (RAF)	337. Queen's Medal for Champion Shot NZ Naval Force	338. Union of South Africa Commemoration Medal

339. Loyal Service Decoration (SA)

340. Anglo-Boer War Medal

The various Commonwealth Independence Medals are all included as MYB 341

341. India Independence Medal

341. Pakistan Independence Medal

341. Nigeria Independence Medal

341. Sierra Leone Independence Medal

341. Jamaica Independence Medal

341. Uganda Independence Medal

341. Malawi Independence Medal

341. Guyana Independence Medal

341. Fiji Independence Medal

341. Papua Independence Medal

341. Solomon Islands Independence Medal

341. Gilbert Islands Independence Medal

341. Ellice Islands Independence Medal

341. Zimbabwe Independence Medal

341. Vanuatu Independence Medal

341. Swaziland Independence Medal

341. St. Christopher Independence Medal

341. Ghana Independence Medal

341. Kenya Independence Medal

342. Malta GC Anniversary Commemorative Medal

344. Shanghai Jubilee Medal

346. Shanghai Volunteer Fire Brigade Long Service Medal

347. Shanghai Volunteer Corps Long Service Medal

349. Shanghai Municipal Police LS Medal

351. Shanghai Municipal Council Emergency Medal

352. Automobile Association Service Cross

353. Automobile Association Service Medal

354. Suffragette Medal

355. Florence Nightingale Medal

362. Corps Of Commissionaires Medal

364. Royal Warrant Holders Association Medal

365. Royal National Lifeboat Institution Decoration

366. Maidstone Typhoid Medal

367. Boys' Life Brigade Medal

367A. Boys' Life Squad Medal

368. Girls' Life Brigade Medal

368A. RSPCA Queen Victoria Medal/ 368B. RSPCA Meritorious Service To Animals

368c. RSPCA Long Service Medal

369. Marine Society Reward of Merit

372. Securicor Medal for Long Service

373. Securicor Medal for Bravery

373A. Securicor Medal for Merit

374. St. Andrew's Association Medal

375. Salvation Army Service Medal

376. Royal Norfolk Veterans Association Medal

379. Royal Agricultural Society of England Long Service Medal

379A. Royal Agricultural Society of England Long Service Medal (II)

380. Casualties Union Exemplary Service Medal

381. Casualties Union Meritorious Service Medal

382. Primrose League Medals

383. Borough of Hartlepool Special Constables Medal For Service

384. Army Temperance Association Award of Merit Medal

385. Cathedral Constables Association Medal

386. Royal Life Saving Society Long Service Award

391. First Aid Nursing Yeomanry Medal 1914–1919

393. Medal for Service to the Serbian Red Cross in London

395. Ebola Medal for Service in West Africa (Formally 291BB)

396. Nuclear Test Medal

397. The Humanitarian Service Medal

Index Of Medals

Please note: the number indicated is the MEDAL number not the PAGE number.

The following medals are to be found in the deluxe version of the Medal Yearbook.

IRELAND

AUSTRALIA

AUSTRALIA *continued*

CANADA

NEW ZEALAND

SOUTH AFRICA